£2

LIVING AT THE EDGE

LIVING
AT THE
Edge

Recollections and Reflections of a Lifetime

DAVID PYTCHES

Amazed by the Ways of God
Abandoned to the Strengths of Others

Arcadia

Bath, England

Typeset by Arcadia Publishing Services Ltd
Printed by Creative Print & Design
ISBN No: 1-904404-00-6

This book is dedicated to my grandchildren –

Timothy, Ashley, Samuel, Sebastian and Matthew
Zachary and Jordan
Philip, Andrew, Grace and Daniel
and Nina

Trust in the Lord with all your heart
and lean not on your own understanding;
in all your ways acknowledge him,
and he will make your paths straight
(PROVERBS 3:5–6, NIV)

Many thanks to:
Mary Pytches, Charlotte Cocksworth, Debby Wright, Becky
Pytches, Tasha Shaw, Estelle Morris, Dick Pytches, Peter
Pytches, Richard Pytches,
Alan Tweedie, John Dewes, Nigel Scotland

who have all kindly read parts or most of the MS and have
shared their encouragements, suggestions and criticisms so
helpfully and constructively

also to:
Sheila Jacobs my editor and David Wavre, my publisher who
so gently carved away so many of my happy memories to make
this book readable

and also to:
Mike Pilavachi for so kindly writing the Foreword to these
Memoirs in the middle of his hectic programme

Publications and Contributions by the same author:

The Churchman (Contrib.) Vol 81 No 2, 1967
*The Influence of Foreigners & the Struggle for Religious Liberty
    in 19th C. Chile* 1974
Bishop's Move (Contrib) 1977
Come Holy Spirit 1985
Riding the Third Wave (Contrib) 1987
Does God Speak Today? 1989
Some Said It Thundered 1990
New Wineskins (jointly) 1991
Prophecy in the Local Church 1993
Recovering the Ground (Contrib) 1995
Meeting John Wimber (Contrib) 1996
John Wimber. His Life and Legacy (Contrib and Editor) 1998
Leadership for New Life 1998
Burying the Bishop 1999
Out of the Mouths of Babes 1999
Four Funerals and a Wedding 1999
Family Matters 2002
Church Matters 2002

CONTENTS

FOREWORD

It is a joy and an honour to write the Foreword to David's book. I have worked alongside him for over fifteen years now, first as his yough worker at St Andrew's Chorleywood, then as part of his team in the leadership of New Wine and latterly he and Mary have been part of the congregation I pastor at Soul Survivor, Watford. Actually, David is a trustee of the church and also of the Soul Survivor ministries. It would be true to say that I learned more from David than anyone else in the ministry. There may be better evangelists than David, better teachers, even better pastors. I have yet to come across anyone who is a better leader. At a time when the major problem of the church at large is lack of leadership, David's *Memoirs* should be a model to us of what godly, anointed leadership is about. Having been on the receiving end I attempt a brief summary of what I observed:

1. David has always been a brave leader. I cannot overestimate how vital this misunderstood leadership gift is. Leadership is about taking risks of faith and sometimes paying the emotional, mental and social cost that goes with it. In all the time I have known him he never ceased to amaze me in the way that, once convinced, he has gone with whatever he sensed the Lord was telling him to do, even if it has not been greeted with universal approval. Recently I met Carol Wimber in California, and when I gave her David's greetings her first words to me were: 'Ah what a brave man!' This bravery came at a personal cost. Sometimes he would be misunderstood, occasionally ridiculed but he never tried to justify himself. He just got on with the job. Someone has said that choosing to be a leader is like choosing to be ugly. Where so many of us in our longing to be popular and not to cause offence, shirk from the tough decisions, David never did that. I will always admire him for it.
2. David has always been a team man. Sometimes brave leaders

9

can be isolated people, aloof and remote. Not David. Having been brought up in a large and, by all accounts, lively family, he liked nothing better than gathering the whole staff team regularly for feedback, discussion of issues and formulating policy. He relished the debate and interaction and we were all made to feel that our contributions were welcome, interesting and worthy of serious consideration. David did not mind when people in the team disagreed with him and loved it when others on the team excelled. At St Andrew's we all felt valued. While many 'strong' leaders give the impression to those around them that they are dispensable, we all felt that David really needed us. Indeed I spent most of my time working for David convinced that I was utterly indispensable!

3. 'Without vision the people perish' goes the proverb, and David was ever a visionary. We always understood the purpose of what we were trying to do. The unique thing about David, however, was that he never suffered from the 'not invented here' syndrome. He always had a capacity to absorb and implement insights and visions that might come from somewhere or someone else. This requires a high level of humility. I remember going to see him one day with my vision to start Soul Survivor festivals. He listened intently as I enthused away and then with a glint in his eye said: 'Well it sounds ridiculous to me, but it also sounds as if it might be God. Let's have a go.' Life was never dull either at St Andrew's or New Wine when he was in the lead, and yet in a funny way it always felt safe. David knew how to implement vision. He was never in a hurry. Often we kill new initiatives by rushing into them without laying the ground work. Sometimes, in my impatience I wished we could get there sooner but when we arrived at our destination the overwhelming majority of passengers came with us. David knew how to build things to last.

4. David was an encouraging leader. He was always quick to praise. He built up a large team of very strong characters and we happily stayed together for a long time because we were encouraged and affirmed. I remember occasions when our colleague Barry Kissell was preaching how he tried to keep an

eye on David's face to see how he was responding. David invariably loved it. Afterwards he would say with delight 'Barry was on form tonight!'

5. David has always had a sense of humour. Tact and diplomacy forbid me to comment on whether it is a good or terrible sense of humour but I can at least confirm that he has one. He never took himself too seriously and never allowed us to take ourselves too seriously either! Working with him was nothing if it wasn't fun. Sometimes we laughed till we cried. Occasionally when the pressure was on and the stakes were high it was our salvation. A sense of humour makes everything very human and prevents us from an earnest spirituality that soon loses touch with reality. I occasionally have a tendency to pomposity. Whenever I began to believe my own publicity David would sidle up and gently prick the inflated ego. I will always be grateful to him for that.

Leadership is the missing ingredient in the mix of many churches today. We do well to study the lives of those whom God has used in this way. Though this is not a book specifically about leadership these are the *Memoirs* of a leader's life and I believe it will inspire, encourage and inform us so that we may be better equipped to lead the people of God today. It is with pleasure that I commend this book to you.

Mike Pilavachi
Easter 2002

PREFACE

In a great nation, the work of an individual is of so little importance; his pleadings and excuses are so uninteresting; his way of life such a nothing; that a preface seems a sort of impertinent bow to strangers who care nothing about it.

(A PREFACE KEATS WROTE AND LATER
DISCARDED FOR HIS 'ENDYMION')

Almost all our faults are more pardonable than the methods we devise to conceal them. We confess our little faults to persuade people that we have no big ones

(FRANCOIS, DUC DE LA ROCHEFOUCAULD)

Too many start this kind of book cherishing imaginary notions about themselves, and only rarely succeed in breaking through the crust of self-deception. Occasional words of self-criticism are usually outweighed by several pages of self-praise. I trust my own sense of the ridiculous will enable me to escape such illusions. Besides my family know me only too well.

The truly great of this world are in a league of their own – their achievements seem inaccessible for the ordinary soul. Their lives rightly inspire us but they also inhibit us by their accomplishments so impossible and reputations so impeccable. They may even leave us depressed by our failures, our misfortunes and those many opportunities that time and again we allowed to slip our grasp. And there can be a certain censoring of the record in the write-up of such great achievers but success stories can often be a cover for serious character flaws. So perhaps these pages may encourage ordinary mortals, who, like myself, are neither remarkably clever nor highly gifted, to simply press forward through the exciting and challenging struggles of life, to pursue what one believes to be the will of God.

Unless it is feigned or outrageous conceit, self-importance

hardly commends any writing except when perhaps it is spelt out as a deliberate provocation. In a book about his public life Henry Kissinger writes: 'I tell of my first mistake on page 850'! Intriguing conceit that makes you want to read it. Alan Clark writes his 'unput-downable' diaries with naive candour. Scandalous revelations that compel a readership!

Michael Saward, a contemporary acquaintance wrote a most readable autobiography he entitled: *A Faint Streak of Humility*. It evoked a playful rejoinder from Anne Atkins – who had known him for years, and who liked him immensely, but who admitted that she had never detected the faintest streak of humility in him! Still, I think his provocation worked.

However, most people find any hint of real pretension a turn off! But personal achievement can still be spelt out in a way that does not seem to imply arrogance as can be seen by the late Harry Secombe, famous singer and TV star, who summed up his achievements for a newspaper in two dozen unpretentious words: 'Records, books, telly, hymns, peritonitis, diabetes, knighthood, *Songs of Praise*, six grandchildren, devoted wife, prostate cancer, stroke, malaria expected soon – winds light to variable'.[1] A brilliant summary of a brilliant life! Who could do better than that?

I write believing that every life, even the most run-of-the-mill, must have a book-full of interesting experiences, observations and insights. But whoever dares to eventually put pen to paper must have enough self-worth to believe that there is someone out there who might be interested enough to read it. There also has to be enough earthly humanity to keep it real and enough novelty to get under the reader's skin. It's vain to make ourselves look good when we know our own hearts only too well – yet in spite of all care, we might still be doing just that – even subliminally. A reviewer commented recently about an authoress that 'she can't help conveying an impregnable sense of her own superiority'. Alan Paton, in *Cry My Beloved Country* described a much admired priest working for reconciliation who was addressed as 'a good man'. 'No!' said the priest, 'I'm not good. It's just that the hand of the Lord was upon me'. If anyone thinks he may have done something worthwhile he can avoid pretension and be humbled by the absolute truth of that statement.

Some years ago my father gave me a thick but hardly used ledger. He thought I might find the blank paper useful in those days when money was scarce and good paper expensive. The first twenty pages were unfinished jottings leading up to his call into the full time ministry of the church. I carefully excised these, made a few notes, but then carelessly mislaid them. Later, I wished, not only that I could find them again, but that he had filled the journal with even more of his story. What I remembered fascinated me. A great uncle, Bishop J.E.C. Welldon, wrote a biography some sixty-five years ago that he entitled, *Forty Years On*, based on the Harrow School hymn where for a time he was headmaster. His book bored me stiff as a youth but as an adult I casually picked it up again and found myself fascinated. He claimed that his biography had 'been practically drawn from me [him] by kindly compulsion.' Alas! – I can make no such claim. But I hope that the readership (including my own offspring) will find my book interesting – and worth perusing.

I have never kept a journal, but I still have my old diaries to remind me of engagements outside the regular routine, with times, subjects and directional notes. Such specific reminders of the past have evoked some powerful flashbacks providing useful material for many of the episodes referred to in this book. Being more dependent on recollections than records is a good reason why I have preferred to describe this as a memoir rather than an autobiography.

I have already written of some of my perceptions and experiences in my book *Leadership for New Life* and in a chapter of *Recovering the Ground* by Dr Nigel Scotland. Varying aspects of personal testimony at different periods have appeared in *Bishop's Move* by Michael Harper, *Meeting John Wimber* by Canon John Gunstone, and *Riding the Third Wave* by Kevin Springer. And then there is also a book I edited called: *John Wimber – His Legacy*. The story of St Andrew's Church, Chorleywood has already been chronicled by Alex Twells in his thoroughly researched and detailed local history entitled *Standing on His Promises*.[2]

I am not intending to go over all that old ground again. This offering is just a selection of events, of impressions, reflections and influences that build up the story of a personal spiritual pilgrimage. I hope there is nothing in the book that would be seen as a recrimination of others personally.

If I appear hard on the ecclesiastical system in places, it's because I see how hard it is for the system to adapt or reform itself from the centre. I did not strive to find an episcopal role when I returned to England; I needed the comparative freedoms at the edge of it in seeking to further the kingdom of God. If many good things have happened to me, this has been mainly because many good people were around me to make them happen. To quote Max De Pree, I found myself 'abandoned to the strengths of others'.[3] And, of course, the source of all the blessing had to be God Himself.

Chapter 1

INTO THE FRYING PAN

Worship carries us from where we are to where we ought to be
(DAVID STANCLIFFE)

Charismatic worship is wired and inspired – plugged into the sound system, plugged into the contemporary culture, and plugged into the Holy Spirit
(PETER WAGNER)

From afar one easily associates California with the fantasy world of Disneyland and Hollywood. But we were there in the world of reality while encountering many unusual things. We were staying for a week with our always generous hosts – John and Carol Wimber. It was Sunday morning and far too hot to walk anywhere so we were glad to be driven to church. On arrival we found the place already three-quarters full. The youngish congregation, a good balance of the sexes, was dressed (surprisingly for church it seemed) in casual shorts and sloganed T-shirts. Some were clutching cups of Coca Cola, or paper hankies as they mopped their dribbling brows – certainly not the usual church scene! The location was a high school auditorium. Once settled, we surveyed the impressive crowd and the unimpressive architecture. All very plain! There was no pulpit, communion table, lectern or pipe organ to be seen. Just a simple platform at one end.

WORSHIP WAS 'HAPPENING'!
The service appeared to move casually into worship without introduction. The lead guitar at the front emerged unobtrusively and began to silence us with spiritual songs – beautiful, gentle songs that we had never heard before – wooing us into the presence of God and

somehow holding us there. The songs continued without interruption – no coming down with bumps in the middle, no stops and starts for blessed thoughts, no unctuous introductions to the next song – they simply flowed along. This was neither entertainment nor self-advertisement. They were not ministering God to us but enabling us to minister to God. This was worship. Somehow people were just lifted up into the adoration of God Almighty. Sense of time and place was lost as we praised and blessed the Lord. The lyrics were everyday language, slightly ungrammatical to my ears – but the meaning and focus unmistakable, and easy to sing. I noticed one of the guitarists on our side of the platform with tears streaming down his cheeks – sobbing as he played; the real thing, I thought! Worship without pretending! Some had their hands raised high in the air or their bodies laid low on the floor; 'lost in wonder, love and praise'. I soon found myself among them. No one suggested it. It seemed as compelling and natural for me as it was for St John the Divine to fall at the feet of the Glorified Christ.[1]

OUR HOST APPEARED

Then the music ended and our host popped up from the rear of the platform where he had been accompanying the singing on his synthesiser. He gave us all a welcome, drew attention to a few of the notices on the printed sheets handed to us as we had entered the place – and then began to teach from the Bible, taking a chapter from one of Paul's letters. He spoke in an easy, very unchurchy and often humorous style, to some 2,000–3,000 people – who seemed to be hanging on his every word. There was simply no 'hype' at all. Then John quietly announced that after the service prayer ministry would be offered for people in the gymnasium behind us. Crowds were soon making their way over there – as did we, soon after. We had already learnt something of our host and preacher. John Wimber, an ex-pop musician, had visited St Andrew's, Chorleywood, nearly a year previously with a large team. Many wonderful things happened for us on the weekend of that visit – the likes of which we had never seen or experienced before in a local church setting.

INVITATION ALMOST IGNORED

It was then that John had invited us back to California. I told Mary that Americans always said nice things like that, and that we really should not presume to take their invitation literally – it was just their way of being polite. But then, when John was over in England again a few months later he expressed disappointment that we had not taken his invitation seriously. He had really meant it. Of course, we would love to go over, and their hospitality would solve a big problem for us. We eventually scraped enough cash together for airfares, and rang the Wimbers to say we were on our way. We set off for Heathrow, and got on the first plane with seats available, believing mistakenly that stand-by seats bought at the last minute were cheaper! They were not. Our intention was to ring our host on landing but the flight arrived at nearly midnight. Not wanting to disturb them at such an hour we enquired about cheap accommodation. An advertisement announced that a passing bus at the main exit would take us to a moderately priced hostel for nothing. The rooms there were certainly modest and just about clean. Too tired for further inspection we slept through the rest of the night. Our hosts were both shocked and amused when they came to collect us the next day. Our location was the kind of place a man would take a girl from off the street for the night. A rather embarrassing start to our stay, but my conscience was clear – my girl was my wife!

We spent our first day with a crowd of musicians in a sound studio where they were making a recording. Quite an education! But there was still a lot more to learn – as we began to find out that first Sunday.

WATCHING THE TEAMS IN OPERATION

John had suggested that we might like to see how the teams operated after the service if we wanted to learn about their prayer ministry. He advised us not to get personally involved at first, but just to be watching and praying beside others that he had trained. This ministry to the sick and needy was offered after each main service. There were two services in the assembly hall in the morning and one at night. We could not wait to see how they exercised the ministry. We asked one couple if it would be OK for us to join them. They welcomed us warmly. Actually, I had been surprised to see that particular lady in church since the previous day John had taken me to a local hospital to visit her. She looked pretty sick to me – which was the reason John had been called to her bedside. John had laid hands on her and offered brief prayer. She had apparently felt better almost at once, and got herself discharged. Now here she was the very next day with her husband ready to pray for others. Fascinating!

THE LADY WITH THE ZIMMER

We were standing with this couple when up came a large middle-aged lady supporting herself on a Zimmer. Every little step was marked by an obvious twinge of agony, which was reflected on her face. She was puffing and panting as though she had serious breathing problems and looked very bound with what seemed like arthritis. Her husband, who had escorted her, appeared quite desperate. He waited quietly to one side as our friends greeted the 'Zimmer lady' warmly, asking what the problem was – as if it was not pretty obvious, I thought! But then Jesus had asked people what they wanted too, when they came to him.

In the mean time, lots of others were getting 'ministry' all over the gymnasium. Our friends began praying for the 'Zimmer lady' in a relaxed kind of way. After a while they very simply invited God, the Holy Spirit, to come upon her in Jesus' name – just as Wimber's team had done at St Andrew's when they came to us. Our friends now appeared to be simply waiting – and waiting – and waiting – standing beside her as they prayed silently. There seemed no urgency with them, and no pressurising. They were obviously waiting on God and were simply blessing whatever they sensed he was doing. But this was clearly a major 'operation' and since I could not grasp exactly what was going on, I began to feel a little impatient. I am too much of an 'instant coffee' man myself and have always liked to keep things moving. After all, we were only going to be there a week and we had flown thousands of miles (at the cost of two airfares we could ill afford) to see someone ministering a 'healing', first hand!

WE MISSED IT!

Then I happened to notice another couple nearby, whom I also recognised, praying for a man with a whiplash neck. I gently nudged Mary and we sneaked over quietly to join them. We had only been there two or three minutes when suddenly a most wonderful cry went up from behind us. I turned to see the 'Zimmer lady' wreathed in smiles. She was picking up her feet without effort and putting them down with a joyful 'Bless you Jesus' – another step, 'Bless you Jesus!' – and another step, 'Bless you Jesus. Glory! Glory!' It was a very moving sight. Quite obviously something remarkable had happened. And now she was just making a beeline for the exit as though she had a bus to catch. Her husband was still standing where they had been praying, his mouth wide open in utter disbelief. Suddenly he picked up the 'Zimmer' and rushed after her. It was all over! 'Blow it!' I thought, 'We missed it!' We had come all this way to see a miracle, and here we were, stuck with this jolly old neck that looked as though it was never going to get healed! It was all part of our American learning curve. Some folk were appearing to get healed and others not – we couldn't understand why. But then, it was the same with doctors and nurses in our National Health Service back home! They too were God's healing agents, as I knew only too well from frequent beneficial treatment at their hands – but sadly, some of their patients feel a little better for their treatment and some even die. But the doctors and nurses do not give up medicine even when they don't have an answer to the 'why'? Our American friends were doing it because they truly believed God wanted them to do it. They taught that it was a biblical mandate for the church.

TEACHING SESSION ON HEALING

I had been talking to Blaine Cook, who had been in the original team that came to St Andrew's in 1981. He told me that the next day he was going to an Assemblies of God Church to train a team to minister healing there. Just the kind of thing I needed! 'That's something I would really like to attend,' I thought. I asked if we could join him.

'Yes! You're most welcome to help!' he said.

'Help?' I questioned. 'I would not know what to do!'

'Well', he explained simply, 'It amounts to this really – all you have to do is to bless whatever you sense God is doing – bless anything that moves!' It was the same advice I had been given when I became a bishop – but the problem was – I had never seen a lot moving in the Church of England!

We set off for the AOG meeting place. There was quite a crowd with us. I was careful not to wear anything that would identify me with the C of E; one never knew what might happen or who might be there! For a while we listened to Blaine's teaching on the link between healing and Jesus' preaching on the kingdom of God. He explained that Jesus did not heal everyone. He only did what he saw the Father doing, and said what he heard the Father saying (John 5:19). And that healings, when they occurred, were simply signs of the kingdom of God that was here now but yet to come in its fullness and glory. I soon saw that there was a large gap between my approach and Blaine's. He had obviously trained himself to try to listen to God. Hitherto I had only really tried to hear what God was saying through the Bible. Blaine was teaching that God also spoke spontaneously by his Spirit through the Bible and apart from the Bible, but never in contradiction to the Bible.

Then he began to share what he sensed God was saying to him, and to my great surprise people were standing up all over the place in response to particular sicknesses or needs that Blaine was being somehow given or shown – and then describing to us. These people came out to the front and we began to pray for them as we had seen our friends do in the gymnasium the previous Sunday. And we stood beside them, simply blessing what we sensed God was doing.

THE TALL LADY

I found myself praying for a very tall lady who turned out to be a nurse. As I prayed, this lady suddenly began to collapse to the floor. I caught her as best I could, and stayed to pray with her for a while as she lay there. But with so many now coming to the front I felt some pressure to leave and pray for them, too, which I eventually did. I left my nurse friend still trembling gently on the carpet. I had no idea what was happening to her, not realising then that this could all be part of a divine encounter or a healing process. So much was a mystery to me. Then Blaine gave out a 'word' about a woman who had a lump under the left armpit and on the left breast and he asked her to come forward. Nobody moved this time. He must have got it wrong! But then he'd already hit a number of bullseyes and he could surely be forgiven for a small mistake like that! He had yet further words to give out. But then he was on again about the woman with the lump on the breast. Again, nobody moved. I was embarrassed for him and thought, 'Oh Blaine – it's OK to make a mistake but then just accept it and relax. You don't have to prove you are right every time!' I noticed my large nurse friend was still on the floor and still shaking. Feeling a little bit responsible for her and following the new principle of blessing everything that moved under what seemed the power of the Spirit, I casually bent down to bless whatever God might still to be doing with her. Suddenly this rather large frame began bouncing up and down along the entire length of her horizontal body – something quite impossible to do normally. I quickly sidled off hoping that no one had seen me! 'Thank goodness this is not an Anglican Church and nobody knows me here!' I thought.

FEELING THE PAIN!

Blaine was giving out some more words and his whole team was soon fully occupied praying for those who were responding. Then, to my great embarrassment, I suddenly heard Blaine harping back about the woman with the lump on the left breast and under the left armpit. 'Lady,' he said, 'Wherever you are would you please come out – this pain is becoming excruciating. I can hardly bear it any longer!' 'Oh no!' I thought, 'He's actually feeling it!' I had no idea that God might ever speak to anyone like that – but now I was learning that some people can know what God is saying in this ministry by feeling the pain of someone else. And clearly this was so, because the next minute out came the woman with the lumps just as Blaine had described! This was amazing. I was learning fast. Someone in the team soon became involved in praying for her.

I went back to the nurse on the floor. All I said was 'Lord, I bless what you are doing here!' and laid my hand lightly on the uppermost part of her shoulder. I had hardly finished when she suddenly burst out into peels of laughter and began rolling about in her prostrate condition! I took my hand away quickly. 'Help! People might think I was tickling her!' Whatever was I meant to do now? Finally I took the coward's way out and retreated like a good Anglican – just to 'observe'. Several people claimed to have experienced healings that afternoon. I make no claims because, although I believe some were quite obviously healed, it's best to give things time to be checked out by a medic before claiming anything. I ought to mention that we are happy reading about healings in the Gospels even though there is actually no record there of anyone checking their healings with their physicians (except possibly in the case of the leprous men that Jesus sent to the priests).

At last, things were coming to a close and Blaine went to the main door waiting for the rest of his team. I did not want to miss my lift back so I soon joined him there. The large nurse came by and smiled at me: 'Boiy!' she said, 'Yew hed 10,000 volts acomin' out of yor hend – you shur did!' She then made off through the door and was gone. I furtively glanced at my hand. Very strange! It did not look or feel 'charged up' to me!

DON'T START FROM HERE!

Something significant was happening here. It was an Irishman who, when asked for a direction, was supposed to have replied: 'If I were going there I wouldn't be starting from here!' My question now was rather the reverse: 'How did I ever get here starting from there – where I had formerly been all my life?' Some new possibilities for the ministry of the whole church were beginning to make sense. We had talked for years about 'the priesthood of all believers' and 'equipping the saints for the work of the ministry'. This could be a vital part of the answer. We had never actually taught our people how to exercise a simple healing ministry! We had taught about 'the gifts of the Spirit' but few of us knew practically how to avail ourselves of these, nor how to pray for others to be equipped with them – nor how to use them! I had been brought up believing that such gifts had been withdrawn once the church had decided on the canon of the New Testament – when the church had firmed up on which Scriptures should be included and which left out. This made some sort of sense as the gifts had not been operating very evidently in the church. But now I was discovering a whole new dimension of ministry.

Chapter 2

EARLY DAYS

God made the country – man made the towns
(ANON)

*Mystical experience without moral
commitment is a false religion*
(JOHN STOTT)

When I was born in 1931, the country was in turmoil. An all-party coalition was being cobbled together about that time to save the country in the aftermath of the 1928 Wall Street crash. Britain had some 2.7 million unemployed, the pound had just been devalued by 30% and all public pay was being cut which led to riots in London and a brief mutiny in the Navy.

I was the ninth child in the family, though one brother had died as a baby before my arrival. A younger brother, Peter, the tenth and last child, was born three days short of a year later. My father was over fifty. This accounts for his nickname whispered round the family – 'The Old Man' – endearing to us but to others it might have sounded disrespectful!

Every day, after breakfast, the servants were summoned, the chairs were pushed back from the table, and we had family prayers. Father would read a passage of Scripture and then we would all kneel for prayer, remembering family needs, the menacing threat of war etc, and folk in the village who were sick or in trouble. He ended with the Collect for the day, the Lord's Prayer and 'the Grace' – not too long and no ad lib comments.

On one occasion, I left the breakfast table early because a hen was cackling at the far end of our large front garden where it should not have been. A new hen's nest was worth a penny in our family and, still searching, I ignored the shouts of my brothers when the time came for family prayers. Nothing more was ever said about it but my conscience troubled me for the rest of the day. Had I sold my soul for a chicken's nest?

HEARING IT AND READING IT!

Apart from that lapse, I think I have either heard the Bible read or read the Bible myself every day of my life. I learned about the main Bible characters very early on and their impact has affected me positively, building up my faith and giving me plenty to reflect upon.

My position so near the end of a large family gave me a special affinity with Joseph, the son of the Patriarch Jacob. He was also born the penultimate, in his case of twelve, and felt a particular responsibility for his youngest brother Benjamin – just as I did for Peter – not that Peter either wanted or needed any co-dependency from me. My position in the family led me to assume naturally that I must have my father's special favour also. Was that not part of 'the Joseph package'? But alas! Father never gave me any multi-coloured robe to prove it.

The name of 'David' added to my sense of being special. I was not destined to be a king but there could be some kind of a calling from God on my life. After all David was a 'ruddy' (red haired) country boy, like me! Apart from Bathsheba-gate, King David had been generally good news. After hearing my father reading about him in 'prayers' I used to study the story of his battle with Goliath[1] over and over again. The odds without God were tremendous. But with only his sling and five smooth stones David boldly challenged the Philistine giant: 'I come to you in the name of the Lord of hosts, the God of the armies of Israel whom you have defied. This day the Lord will deliver you into my hand, and I will strike you down, and cut off your head . . . the battle is the Lord's, and he will give you into our hand'.[2] Clearly there was a special place in the purposes of God for David, a country boy like me if only I had the faith and the guts. David served his own generation – certainly I should be thinking about how I was going to serve mine. In our garden we had smooth stones a-plenty and I practised with a sling – we had a real one in the house. Apart from smashing a window I managed to cosh myself with a stone. I felt for Goliath! But the idea of a call from God was always in the background. Then I had two other names – George and Edward. Three kings' names in all! Wow! Some current dramas in the highest circles – the accession and then abdication of Edward VIII followed by the accession of George VI – was concentrating the mind around royalty. I had yet to learn that our high calling from God is not usually the road of comfort in a chariot, but rather a rough and lowly path with a breaking heart and blistered feet.

MEET THE ANCESTORS[3]

My father when still a bachelor, had moved back from London to Ipswich, Suffolk in 1914. This was coming 'home' for father – the land of his forebears – and he stayed there for the rest of his life. Harping on about one's 'family tree' is a bit of a bore for others, but the influence of one's antecedents is part of one's make-up. In his book *Roots*, Alex Haley reminds us of how Kunte Kinte found his identity by tracing his roots through slavery in America back to freedom in Africa.

Father often referred to his family tree. The wall spaces of our vast rectory home were crowded with sepia-faced forebears – old ladies in frilly lace bonnets and grim looking patriarchs with grey pointed beards all peered down upon us unsmilingly. They had run their race but left us with some unconscious obligation to live up to our heritage and to do our duty to God and man.

SETTLERS IN SUFFOLK

It takes a long time to become part of rural England. I could get by as a native of Suffolk although the family has been traced back further afield to Halfdan 'The Old' – a Norwegian nobleman of the eighth century – whose great grandson Rognavald 'The Mighty' had settled in Denmark and had later (by 874) gained title to the Earldom of Orkney & Shetland. A descendant of his came over to England with William the Conqueror (1066) and from that time the 'Pecch's' held lands in Essex, Suffolk and Norfolk. Two 'Pecche's' had become bishops along the way – Robert, Bishop of Coventry and Ely (1121) was chaplain to Henry I, and Richard, the Bishop's son was Archdeacon of Chester and Lampas, later to be consecrated Bishop of Chester and

Coventry (in 1161). Celibacy for the clergy was apparently still not a universal rule in the Catholic church!

Suffolk had been home for ten generations of Pytches – spanning some 500 years. One (John Pytches) had raised troops for the Royalists under Charles II. Another (Thomas Pytches) was a major in the East Suffolk Militia, while my great, great uncle John Pytches had been an MP, during the second term of Prime Minister William Pitt the Younger. Other forebears on the Pytches side had been Majors of Ipswich and Justices of the Peace and a couple had been Deputy Lieutenants of the County of Suffolk.

My father (1879–1953), born at Melton, Woodbridge, had some artistic talent, like his own father, but was rather directionless as a young man. He trained as a maltster (brewer). At the same time he also served as a lieutenant, with the 1st 'Volunteer Brigade', Suffolk Regiment, Ipswich (from 1900–1904) becoming an instructor in musketry and the use of the new maxim (machine) gun. He had no settled religious convictions but he was obviously thinking seriously about life. He commented, in his journal, on one of the sermons he had heard at his military camp. 'The parson preached the best sermon I have ever heard to Volunteers. Must look up the lesson for Sunday!'

Still feeling aimless and unfulfilled he wrote: 'My greatest trouble in life now (24th June 1904) is that I have no occupation but I cannot think I was sent into this life to do nothing – and it is not wholly my fault.' Searching for a job as a maltster had meant travelling far and wide. He also spent some time in Ipswich at the School of Art, learning painting and attempting to compose poetry. He took up studying science and comparative religions. He had become 'a seeker' after the truth.

Apparently he was struggling with a drink problem too – something that had troubled him over a long period of time. He became bothered about the matter of possessions. Social issues were beginning to concern him and he was asking himself questions about what he should do concerning the economically poor. If he sold up and gave everything to them, he puzzled over whether they would use the money wisely? He was receiving a small allowance of between £25 and £50 per year but he anticipated a considerable inheritance still to come from his aunts (which in fact never materialised) whose interests he was looking after in Yorkshire.

Father went to hear a Christian 'missioner'. Sensing further stirrings after God in his heart he wrote in his journal: 'I must do all I can. The time is short. My old home – the beautiful house, the garden, the pictures, the river. All must go and I gladly leave them all to follow Christ, feeling that I am but giving back to God what is his own and that I am an unprofitable servant'. He even spoke to the missioner about the possibility of ordination and was told it was the best thing he could ever do and that he should see his local vicar about it. This father did straightaway.

COULD IT BE GOD'S CALL?

When he explained about his possible 'call' the vicar of St John's, Woodbridge, simply leant back in his chair and roared with laughter. Such was my father's local reputation apparently! Father was nonplussed: 'Why?' he replied, 'The missioner said it was the very best thing I could ever do.'

'That man!' snorted the vicar. 'He should never have been ordained. He went to some footling college on the Isle of Man where they train anyone!'

Urged on by his mother, father wrote to a number of theological colleges without much encouragement. Finally he tried that 'footling college where they train anyone' and wrote to the Bishop Wilson College[4] on the Isle of Man.

Father was accepted 'on probation' in 1907 and once there the matter of probation was never raised again. After his two years' training, he served his first title on the Isle of Man at Kirk German (1909–11), and a second curacy at St Saviour's, Brixton Hill (1911–13). In May 1913 he was visiting a Mrs Fraser, an old family friend in London, who was dying. He wrote: 'I saw her many times. I prayed with her and read the Bible. I think she was looking to God in Christ to save her in the time when obviously there is no one else who can do so.' I stress this here as Father talks about a personal 'conversion' experience later. I question his terminology on that point. He must have already had some life-changing encounter with God before he ever went to Bishop

Wilson College, since the total change of direction, the new language, and the new commitment indicate that he was certainly 'born again'.

It was for his last curacy that he eventually came back to Suffolk – to St Helen's, Ipswich, in 1914. He combined this with a prison chaplaincy. In later years he would sometimes refer to his experiences there from the pulpit. 'When I was in Ipswich prison!' he would say, forgetting to explain that his place there was that of chaplain not a criminal! Eyebrows would be raised: 'Fancy! Our vicar's done time inside!' He related once how he had been talking to a prisoner about 'The Light of the World'. He was hardly off the prison premises when he was called back urgently and was appalled to find the prisoner bleeding profusely all over his cell. The poor man had ripped his fist to shreds, punching through plate glass to smash the light behind it. He hated the Light.

When still at St Helen's, Ipswich, Father had become the secretary of the Ipswich Clerical Society (of which he had been a joint founder). Another founder member of the ICS, was Charles Edward Welldon. Through this connection Father met and fell in love with the eldest of his two daughters, Eirene Welldon. They married in 1916 at St Mary's, Cotton, Suffolk, and honeymooned on the Isle of Wight. Grandfather Welldon, was the rector of Cotton in Suffolk from 1909–24. My mother had been born (1896) at Faringdon, Berks, where grandfather had previously been the rector for eighteen years (1891–1909).

After a further year as an army chaplain father moved in 1919 to an incumbency at Pettaugh, Suffolk: a tiny village with a population of about two hundred and a salary of about £200 pa. Father was there for five years.

From Pettaugh, father moved to Gislingham in 1926, staying there for eighteen years. I was born there. Finally father moved to Holbrook, near Ipswich in 1945. Sadly my mother died at the rectory in 1947 not long after we moved there. Father eventually retired to Westerfield Road, Ipswich, and he died convalescing at Felixstowe in 1953, following a second stroke. Both parents were buried at All Saints, Holbrook, in the graveyard behind the church, near the clergy vestry door.

TO THE RECTORY BORN

I was baptised in St Mary's Church, Gislingham – a little Suffolk village of some four hundred souls with a High Street, a Back Street, and a Mill Street. The High Street, as I remember it, had a number of plaster and wattle cottages. Their upper windows had blackening cowls of weatherworn thatch, badly 'pocked' through years of nesting sparrows. It was fascinating to watch the thatchers at work repairing them.

Country children are often in contact with deep things that we tend to close off as we get older – but one can never really lose an internalised rural landscape with all its wild life nor can one ever write off unsought for encounters with the eternal. Arrogantly – and of course erroneously – we imagined that townies who didn't know the difference between a blackbird and a starling must be witless wimps.

We were doubly blessed in our huge country rectory with a great outdoors and a great indoors as well. We always loved the outdoors. Suffolk provided impeccable rural credentials and I have never stopped romanticising over our countrified roots. With friends I refer to Suffolk as the 'Holy Land' – for so it was in a way for me. I met God there frequently both indoors and out.

My 'first fine careless rapture'[5] came when standing on tiptoe to peer into a thrush's nest – frail twigs, dry grasses and soft mosses, woven into the crotch of a bush. And then I saw that clutch of sky blue eggs inside it, shells slashed-marked in coal black, neatly arranged in the smooth mud cup that lined the nest. As a small boy, I would never have understood that such minor raptures were all to do with the 'numinous' of God.

Ecstasy and rapture have certainly been integral to my own experiences of life – just as I am sure they have been common to the spiritual pilgrimages of so many. Such encounters are not simply for the 'stained glass saints' but for quite ordinary sinners of no particular religion; many of whom have still not decided in which direction they want their pilgrimage to follow. Man has been experiencing these happenings, of one kind or another, since the beginning of time.

It's difficult to know always whether ecstasies are natural or supernatural? Are the episodes emotional or religious? Are they in

31

the body or out of it? We are so wonderfully compounded that we seem able to sense the spiritual through the natural and the natural through the spiritual. C.S. Lewis could evaluate these 'numinous' encounters better than most: 'They are not the thing itself; they are only the scent of the flower we have not found, the echo of a tune we have not yet heard, news from a far country we have never visited'. Ecstasies are no proof of right doctrine – any more than dreams are. They are, like miracles, proofs of nothing but pointers to something – enough to make us wonder: 'Oh God, is that you?' Too much focus on such experiences could become unhealthy. We can neither live on raptures nor can we rely on them. No one in his right mind builds castles in the air – though the kind of 'eureka' joy they often inspire is undeniably a mystical part of our inheritance in the kingdom of God. St Paul had his own mountain-top experiences. But he set greater store on his 'thorn in the flesh' than a thoroughly mystical rapture up to the third heaven (2 Corinthians 12). He also gives us warning against mistaking elation for grace.

BECKONING FROM GOD

For my part I can now see clearly how such early experiences were a beckoning from God – an awareness of him at a deeper level of consciousness. It would be quite wrong to assume that we must all have similar experiences, either as part of daily living, or as being fundamental to our inheritance in the wider Christian family. I had to come to terms with this when I met other zealous Christians during my National Service. Many had had remarkable spontaneous conversions – from the guttermost to the uttermost. That had not been my experience. Theirs was the blinding light on the Damascus Road. Mine was a creeping dawn first seen in my parents. I had somehow become aware that Jesus Christ was my Lord and Saviour from a very early age. But my Army friends were cautious since I had not had their experience – and they tended to dismiss mine as mere churchy religion. I learned from this to beware of ever insisting that others must experience the same kind of ecstasies. A mystical touch is just a 'bonus' in life. Others may get very different graces, gifts and blessings. No one is necessarily a better person for having an ecstatic experience. God's love is such 'a many-splendoured thing' and we are all so unique and variously endowed by him in just the way he wills it.

There was little to do, in any organised way, as a 'catechism-and-bread-and-butter' boy growing up in a village rectory before and during the war. Though I must often have complained about being bored as a child, I never felt eaten up by it.

DREAMS OF HEROISM

I recall my parents warning me not to speak to strange men on my ramblings out and about. Since strange men of any kind were a rarity round our home I missed their point entirely. I thought they were worried about German aircrew whose planes were being shot down in the war.

In my dreams, once the war was declared I was going to be the village hero who captured a German, and made him a prisoner. I needed a rifle to arrest him. I thought my homemade wooden gun painted black looked as good as any fake could ever be made to look. My plan was to creep up behind him, put on a deep voice, and order him to raise his hands, disarm him and then march him down to the local police station – as simple as that! After all, my name was 'David' – born to cope with giants. It was no good sharing such fantasies with grown-ups. They would never understand that this really would be no problem for me. According to the Bible, God's purposes were often accomplished through the lower ranks in the family. My older brother Dick was fighting for our lives in the Army somewhere in Europe, and Jack was defending us in the Home Guard. Maurice was in Simonstown revictualling our Navy passing by South Africa, Roy was about to join the RAF while I, nearly the youngest in our tribe, was going to save the Suffolk village of Gislingham by an act of amazing heroism: I was going to catch that German Goliath while the rest of the village were still in their homes cowering back in panic. But I had to find him first and sadly he never seemed to show up in Gislingham.

NATURE AND SCRIPTURE

Growing up, I was fortunate to have Peter to come with me as we ventured into the 'great outdoors'. I assume now that Peter, like me, was making the same 'numinous' connections and somehow computing the little mysteries of life around us – all of nature speaks of God, though I don't think we ever discussed it in anything like religious terms. We took it all for granted as we tramped the fields watching nature grazing, chasing, fighting, mating – and dying. Death was not reserved for the animal world either. We knew the whole community and we knew people who died there. My father was usually one of the first to know. Certainly our village gravedigger seemed busy enough; 'In the midst of life we are in death',[6] but we children could come to terms with that – it was happening all the time. We had a symbiotic relationship with nature. Death was as normal as life in our world, and could, like the kestrel in the sky, be down on you before you knew it: 'your life? It is even a vapour, that appeareth for a little time, and then vanisheth away'.[7] This did not make us feel depressed or morbid – it simply taught us about the cycle of nature – that earthly life had its limits. It was from the Bible that we learned of its real solemnity: 'It is appointed unto men once to die, but after this the judgment'.[8]

I think that nature and Scripture mingle well in the soul of a child. Nature showed us that life could be orderly yet messy, peaceful yet aggressive, ominously mysterious yet overpoweringly beautiful, chaotic yet purposeful. Understand created things if you want to know the Creator.

MUSEUMS AND MANSIONS

Father sometimes took us out to broaden our taste for culture. There was a small museum in Bury St Edmunds which displayed a gruesome ducking chair used to drown witches in the seventeenth century. Four of them had been hanged in Lavenham during the 1640s. He also took us to displays of art – ancient and modern, at Christ Church Mansions in Ipswich – especially to see the East Anglian artists like the portrait painter Gainsborough and the master landscaper Constable. Constable taught us to see the shades and intensity of nature in a new light. These paintings were a contrast to the rather drab old 'oils' – heirlooms that covered our spacious rectory walls. To offset the carved oak chairs that ringed our dining table were paintings of beagles, wiry pointers and chestnut steeds – the latter characterised by their hogged manes and decked tails – thickset stallions once owned by hunting forebears. Visitors would politely enquire if they were by George Stubbs or John F. Herring? No doubt they were wondering what other purpose could there be for tolerating such dismal pictures? Sadly they would have been too early and too ugly for Sir Alfred Munnings, also renowned for his equine paintings – and incidentally an esteemed Old Boy of Framlington College – a place I was one day destined to attend. His name there would be 'dropped' approvingly by the head on speech days.

All this served to intensify our childhood awareness of nature – it was everywhere – on our walls, out of our windows, on our walks – it filled our little world entirely!

WALLIS'S FARM

Only a hedge and a deep ditch separated Wallis's farmland from the rectory grounds. They were our nearest neighbours. We took turns at fetching milk and butter from their farm – a daily chore that earned us extra ha'pennies. All the farms around us rotated their crops. Cartloads of stinking manure were stacked in the corner of fields, each shrouded in a haze of frantic flies. 'Cum nex' moock-spreadin" this stench of compost would be strewn across the land and then ploughed in. Most of the 'moock' came from the horses kept for farmwork such as ploughing. Those were usually chestnut Suffolk Punches, the smallest of the shires, but immensely strong for cultivating the land. Leguminous crops and clover took their turn with the grain crops. Sugar beet and turnips made a regular appearance in the fields. Now and again, a fallow year would follow when cattle and sheep gave the field the 'golden hoof'. I'm not sure whether it was their droppings or their grazing that the farmer prized for his field. The old system of organic farming had many ecological spinoffs – wild flowers, butterflies, bees and singing birds to gladden the countryman's heart – so different from the soulless intensive farming of today.

But now the ponderous shires plod no more and the art of farming has been turned into the measured science of agriculture. Of course, so many of these nostalgic perceptions were those of a child. There was another side to it – the conditions were hard and most of those bandy-legged labourers were poor and seemed very old at 50. But modern advances have removed man from his intimacy with the soil – and with his sheep and cattle, each one known individually by name are now mostly ear-tagged with an impersonal numbered disk. And most of the workers from the land have gone. Farms that once employed a dozen may now employ only two and no one seems to care.

NATURE LOVING CLERGY

Nature loving clergy were the men that shepherded our rural churches. They represented a long tradition. A study of the records of hundreds of the local museums, naturalist societies, and field clubs across Britain, reveal just how many parochial clergy took a prominent role in their organisations throughout the nineteenth century. They were the collectors, the recorders, the classifiers and educators – they wrote myriads of articles on their areas of expertise, inspired by their habitual observation of their rural environment.

A story that fascinated me as a child was that of the parson who found his headaches invariably got better when sitting under a willow tree reading in his garden. This led to the taking of aspirin which can be extracted from willows for headaches. Marvellous!

My boyhood environment had made me feel so very secure, and now I realize, so privileged – with father, mother and God always where one felt they ought to be. There seemed such a 'rightness' to that closed little world. For all its possible limitations one was thankful for it. But life moves on like a river. One can never dip into the same flow twice yet the nostalgic memory remains. I remember the vibrant happiness of home as I remember our life in the village.

REVIVAL COMES TO SUFFOLK

About five years prior to his move to Gislingham (within the same diocese) in 1926, father had another significant spiritual experience that changed his life. This was during the Lowestoft revival in Suffolk.[9] Father often referred to it as his 'conversion'. Today we probably would call it a 'renewal' experience of the Holy

Spirit. Most revivals seem to take the church by surprise – there is no adequate language to describe them and the manifestations and effects long term may vary from one revival to the next. And there's no way of knowing, at the time, all that is actually happening in so many different people's lives, during these movements of God's Spirit. It usually takes a while to see how God, and the local church, are helping those so touched to process the new work of God in their lives and to begin to see the true fruit.

Whatever one may choose to call it, my father's experience at Lowestoft had put new a fire and compassion into his soul, and he began to be involved in evangelistic missions, working with a leading Suffolk layman and lifelong friend named Kenneth Cutting, of Abbot's Hall, Pettaugh.[10]

GOD OF MAMMON

My father's later move to Gislingham (population 420) was a great help financially because 'the living' was up to £628 (net) a year.[11]

With the income so small it might be wondered how incumbents could ever afford servants, and my parents actually employed two maids and a gardener. The maids (a kitchenmaid and a-maid-of-all-work) usually lived locally and came into 'service' at the age of fourteen or fifteen, being paid the grand total of five shillings a week. This would be gradually augmented to ten shillings a week by the time they had reached eighteen. At that point they were usually sent off with a reference from my mother to help them obtain a similar, more permanent position, in a big country or town house.

We rarely discussed money in the family because we knew there was not much about – but there were some honourable ways for augmenting one's tiny income such as fetching the milk from the farm, finding a chicken's or a wasp's nest. When we believed money was owed to us we would knock on my father's study door and ask him for it – usually urgently – and often catch him on his knees praying.

Another source of income for me was 'blowing' the organ in church. I always claim that I have been in the paid ministry of the Church of England since I was seven or eight!

The congregation at Gislingham seemed to be about forty to fifty on a Sunday morning and some twenty plus in the evenings. Most people made their way to church on foot in those days, as we did, dressed in our best Sunday-go-to-meetin' suits with short trousers. We had long socks kept up by itchy elastic garters. Some who cycled left their bicycles propped against the church hedge. They never thought of locking them. Such was the pecking order in the feudal psyche, and such their respect for the parson of rural churches, that even Peter and I would be deferentially greeted by 'Good morning Master David!' and 'Good morning Master Peter!' If we grew up with exalted delusions about our 'station in life' it was not entirely our fault! How was I to know that such deference had grown out of the civility poorer folk had adopted towards the people who employed them, since they were utterly dependent upon them for food, shelter and other favours?

My father would usually preach on Sundays. I grew up hearing sermons before I could understand them and so developed a habit of 'switching off' when my father was giving a sermon. When, at a later date, someone asked me what his preaching was like I had to admit that I did not really know. But people who remembered were complimentary. He could be quite fiery at times. And his voice tended to go up at the end of a sentence, which made him easy to hear in those days, long before electrical amplifiers were available – and he did not have to develop a 'parson's voice' to make himself audible. Acoustics could be a serious problem in some churches.

CRASH COURSE IN PRAYER

Every year one of the highlights was the visit of Mr Gardner from the Caravan Mission to Village Children. He was a gifted children's worker and spoke our language. His visits were landmarks in my own spiritual pilgrimage.

Prayer had never been easy, but I knew it was the right thing to do. I often observed my parents praying when they thought they were alone. I used to kneel nightly at my bedside and pray the prayer my mother had taught me:

'Jesus, tender Shepherd hear me.
Bless thy little lamb tonight.
Through the darkness be thou near me.
Keep me safe till morning light.
All this day thy hand hast led me
and I thank thee for thy care.
Thou hast clothed me, warmed and fed me.
Listen to my evening prayer.'[12]

We would recite the Lord's Prayer and then ask God to bless everything from grandparents to guineapigs! These prayers served me well until the day when my parents were out and Gypsies came selling wooden clothes pegs at the back door – also offering to tell our fortunes or heal any warts for money. The maids panicked and said the Gypsies would curse us if we didn't give them something! Catching their fear I rushed up to my bedside to ask the Lord to send the Gypsies away. I discovered my usual bedside liturgy did not quite stretch to such emergencies. It was my first effort at extempore prayer. I wasn't very impressed with it.

I was not to be tested again in quite the same way until about seven years later, when I found my father alone sobbing over the diagnosis of my mother's cancer. I suggested prayer but father who normally prayed so readily couldn't rise to it: he was too choked up. He signalled me to pray. Once again I found myself extemporising in supplicatory prayer, but this time embarrassed at not seeming to have the appropriate language for it. I found it frustrating not to be able to say what I really wanted to say. I came to realise later that often no prayer was called for other than a simple 'Oh God! Oh God! Please help!' And he knows what the heart is really crying out for.

My Garden of Eden

By the time I was seven I was making a little progress in my spiritual life and then I sinned – blatantly and deliberately. The many trees in the garden were fair game but there was one tree, the fruit of which we were not allowed to eat – that was the pink blossomed apricot against the redbrick wall at the back of the kitchen garden. Of that tree my father had said quite plainly 'Thou shalt not eat of it'. Though it was an apricot tree it bore very little fruit in our most unsuitable climate.

One day, just walking round the garden I decided to give those apricots a closer look. Something within me told me this could be unwise. Even more foolishly I stayed to study the fruit more closely. The apricots were all lovingly wrapped, by father, in transparent paper (no plastic in those days) – to protect them from ants and wasps etc. I observed that one of them, less visible from an adult angle, was ripening quite well. It was nearly ready to eat. I pressed the apricot with my little fingers just to check if it was really doing as well as it looked. It was quite soft, and I thought perhaps nearly ready to fall, so just to double check I gave it a little tug. I was right. It fell off in my hands. Just like that! Peter was looking on and I suggested he might like a bite! The wretch, always full of integrity, would not be tempted. Every effort at implicating him failed. Didn't he know the story? Adam and Eve both ate of the forbidden fruit? I knew exactly what I was doing. It looked good to eat. I ate it. It did not taste good – quite bitter in fact. And I wished I had not taken it. It was the fall of man all over again! Soon I heard the voice of my father walking in the garden! He approached the back wall slowly and examined the apricots closely, as I had done. There was one empty wrapping still attached to the twig. (Oh foolish boy – you should have removed the evidence completely.) That empty wrapping was incriminating indeed. I knew the script. I would blame Peter. He 'gave me of the tree and I did eat,' I lied, compounding my sin. Of course Peter flatly denied it. My father said no more. He knew. Peter knew. God knew and I knew. I was naked and I could not imagine how any fig leaves could cover my shame; no lie could clear my conscience. Plain guilty, I deserved to be cast out of the garden. Worse still I stubbornly refused to admit my guilt. I wanted time to think up some face saving alibi. I needed to confess and seek forgiveness but I was blinded by pride. I struggled with the bitter taste for weeks and months. I am ashamed to confess that I never owned up to my father – and he never mentioned the 'apricot affair' again. But that little episode loomed large in my mind for some time to come. Shakespeare depicts Lady Macbeth constantly washing her hands to get rid of that 'damned spot' after the murder of Duncan. 'All the perfumes of Arabia will not sweeten this little hand,' she sighed. I only had apricot juice on my hands but I understood where she was coming from all right.

PRIDE ASSERTS ITSELF EARLY

Obviously younger brothers who got 'uppity' needed some lessons in humility and when we were cheeky to them, older brothers often took us in hand. I remember how Jack, after due warnings, would swiftly wrestle us to the floor and twist our limbs up in excruciating knots while ordering us to beg for mercy. The moment I begged for mercy I knew Jack would release me. 'Just beg for mercy my boy!' he would insist! But pride was asserting itself. Not likely! Not to a mere brother! Mercy was the last thing I was going to beg from him! Did he think he was God? I certainly deserved the treatment Jack was meeting out to me, but now he was expecting me to beg him for mercy. I would protest loudly pretending injustice and feign the most frightful pain. I would plead pitifully to any other brothers nearby that I was being bullied (sisters were useless in this area), or better still beg a parent to intervene. Sometimes these tactics worked, but if they didn't then all other ploys exhausted, I would have to humble myself and beg for mercy. Once free, of course, one could always sneer that not a word of it had been meant! Unchristian little sibling!

RICHMAL CROMPTON MUST HAVE KNOWN THEM

William and Ginger would have been just right in our village crowd. Every story that Richmal Crompton ever wrote recaptured our village youngsters to a 'T' – their individuality, their philosophy and their language. And that spoilt brat 'Violet Elizabeth Bott' who haunted their lives so sorely was our Rosemary Driver (without the lisp) – our local farmer's only daughter who never threatened us with 'thcweaming'. She was much more underhand – she 'told' on us! We were only playing doctors and nurses, after all. There were serious questions of anatomy needing answers. How could little girls possibly be little girls with nothing to show for it? Our game of doctors and nurses never got far. Whatever she told her mother I don't know, but she was stopped from coming to play with us after that. Little girls could be so sneaky! However, we still shared the same governess.

I have only pleasant memories of Mrs Garner and enjoyed our daily lessons at her house. We left the rectory on foot, going out the back way through the kissing gate to make a short cut across the fields for the main road. We then went along the High Street to Mr Dawkin's grocery store, joining up with his son Ashley, who came with us to school down the lane opposite his father's shop. I don't remember much that we did at Mrs Garner's except that we read the *Rupert* serial each day, and cut it out from the *Daily Express* to paste the serial story in a book. She also sent us out to collect every kind of tree leaf which we then had to draw and identify – something I have never forgotten. Mrs Garner's face had an interesting feature which small boys like us could never get over – a yellowing incisor protruded slightly from the top left gum giving the impression (which may have become magnified over the years) of a small tusk on a wild boar. But then many country people had teeth like derelict graveyards in those days. Mrs Garner succeeded in keeping us all fully interested and occupied and never got cross with us, though she caused me endless worry about keeping the seat dry in her end-of-the-garden long-drop privvy. How could we help it? The aperture crafted in the wooden seat was cut about four inches from the edge and the anatomical proportions for little boys could never adequately correspond – no way! So we never succeeded in pleasing her on that one, sad to say, and always felt guilty about it. Among her many skills was music. And she was not alone. Her husband Jimmy had a fascinating set of drums paraded in their shining glory in her front room – out of bounds for us.

'THE RHYTHM SWINGERS'

The Garners were childless but had a secret nightlife that they never mentioned. 'The Rhythm Swingers' was a local dance band organised by none other than my very enterprising oldest brother Jack. He played the ukulele, the trombone, the saxaphone and trumpet while Dick played the double bass. Jimmy Garner was on the drums. Mrs G. played the piano. Maybe one or two others were involved as well – I don't think I ever knew.

The 'Rhythm Swingers' looked the part all togged up in their red shirts with gold cuffs and epaulettes, white cricket trousers, and patent black shoes. Mrs G., the only female in the group, had a red blouse and white skirt. Jack had made the bandstands on which their music rested and these were coloured to match the bandsmen's shirts – red with a diagonal gold 'dash' across the front sporting a big 'R' (for 'Rhythm') at the top and a big 'S' (for 'Swingers') below. They produced their own publicity. Jack even had his own printing kit. He had learnt this skill from Cowell's, the printing business in Ipswich (first made famous by advertising Bovril with the face of a bull on the side of the bottles), where Jack had had his first job through the family connection with the firm. His advertising efforts seemed very professional. For this home printing they used tiny lead slugs – each word laboriously put together with tweezers – one letter at a time and reading backwards. Jack was helped by his taller, but younger brother Dick – shortened from the family name Dickinson. Except for his wartime service (commissioned in the Army) Dick worked all his life at Fison's – another bigger family concern. The 'Rhythm Swingers' soon got invited to more 'gigs' than they could cope with. They were out frequently.

THE 'FLAPPER' AND JAZZ GENERATION

My father would wait up for them nightly 'to sanctify them in prayer' when they came in, in case like Job's sons they had 'sinned and cursed God'.[13] But not being in the mood for sanctification Jack and Dick preferred to wait outside in the dark till they saw Father's lamp go wearily up the stairs to bed. With beer-bated breath, they would then creep in through a rear window and beat it up the back stairs to bed. Jack and Dick had grown up through the 'Flapper' and Jazz generation of the 'Roaring Twenties'. Like most teenagers Jack would frequently challenge my father on various points – politics, religion, class and there were disagreements over noise. Jack liked jazz and practised full-blast with his saxaphone at the back of the house. I had yet to appreciate that this is the way life is, and found such filial disagreements disconcerting. Dick doubtless thought just as Jack did – but kept his opinions more to himself!

It seemed to my priggish little mind that my older brothers, following the example of the sons of Eli, were walking in the ways of wickedness. I could claim no personal revelation, like little Samuel in the Bible,[14] but I decided I should broach the subject of my older brothers' spiritual welfare openly one day at Sunday lunch. The true state of their souls needed to be determined. I felt it was for their own good! If something ought to be said then someone ought to say it. If no one else would, then I would respond to the call of duty!

WILL THEY GO TO HEAVEN DADDY?

Our place for lunch was usually the smaller side table where the 'little ones' were relegated on Sundays when the full family complement was gathered. There was not enough room for every one round the big table. Choosing an appropriate lull in the conversations I raised my eight-year-old treble voice and enquired earnestly: 'Daddy will Jack and Dick go to heaven when they die?' After all I was concerned about their spiritual welfare! It had been a worrying thought that my father (though he was by no means 98 and his eyes weren't dim like old Eli) had perhaps neglected his paternal duties in failing to correct his older sons. Father might be grateful for a little help from me, I felt! A slight stir caused by the sudden intake of breath round the table made it difficult for me to catch father's response. And I really didn't think my well-intentioned query deserved quite the scowls of dis-approval from brother Jack when I was simply doing this for his good! Obviously even death at the bottom of a dry well would not have been good enough for me. Poor Joseph![15] How well I understood his problems with those older brothers of his, but obviously I still had so much to learn about the Christian life!

THE WILL OF GOD

I must have picked up from my parents that it is was essential for a Christian to find out what the will of God is for one's life. This was reinforced by our daily use of the Lord's Prayer – 'Thy will be done on earth, as it is in heaven'. Obviously one had to try to discern God's will and then keep in the centre of it as faithfully as one could. I was not trying too hard as I didn't like one direction I feared it might lead me.

With my varied family connections (for example, my father's distant cousin, the Rev John Ascough Rickards who had served two chaplaincies in Argentina under the aegis of the South American Missionary Society, and my great uncle, a one-time bishop in Calcutta and Metropolitan of all India) and the added influence of visiting missionaries to preach, perhaps it was inevitable that I should be thinking that this might lead me eventually overseas. I felt no passion at all for work in a foreign land. I could not stand hot climates and was hopeless at languages but I still knew I must try to keep open. I describe this confusion since 'according to all the books' the call of God for many seems to have been a very straightforward process! But there were major hurdles to jump before ideas of the mission field turned into pushing doors. It was all still a long way ahead – and I wanted to keep it that way.

THE CALL

It was about this time that I first heard of the American evangelist Dwight L. Moody who had listened to a preacher saying: 'The world has yet to see what God can do through one man totally committed to his will'. When the young Moody heard those words he said, 'Lord let me be that man!' and I thought: 'Yes – and me too, Lord!' It was a consecration of myself to God (another one of a succession) and a clarification of my call. This was confirmed soon after.

Mother would come into our bedroom to kiss us all good night after we had washed and said our prayers. We would count those kisses jealously and if any one got more than the other we could persuade her to come back and give us another round, pressing her poor cold nose once again to our warm little cheeks. One night mother mentioned that she had been praying that at least one of her sons would be called into the ordained ministry of the Church of England. It seemed just so obviously right to me that she should be given a son who was 'ordained', and I resolved to take up that challenge.

John G. Paton, a missionary to the New Hebrides, once wrote:

'Nothing so clears the vision and lifts the heart as the decision to move forward in what you know to be the will of God.' I felt my heart being lifted as I made it my decision to move forward in what I was fairly certain now must be the will of God for my life.

This decision soon became public once I told my parents when they began to seriously discuss our future careers with us. I thought it would please my father and mother very much – and I learned later from others who knew my father that it did – but the parents knew only too well that it had to be a real call from God and not just a gesture to please them. They wisely cautioned me about being sure that it was God's will for me. I remember being slightly miffed when a grown-up friend asked me later what I was going to do in life and I said I hoped to be ordained. He replied, quite naturally, 'Oh! Following in your father's footsteps, eh?' Of course, I had to say 'Yes' because in fact it was true. But it was not all the truth! I was feeling called of God but no longer simply because my father was a parson or my parents wanted it.

Seven generations, looking back, have each produced at least one ordained minister for the Church of England in our family. Soon after my own ordination, Peter,[16] Jack[17] and then John (my sister Estelle's husband) also followed by being ordained – all this after my parents had both died. More ordinations have since followed by marriage for two more generations.

MY SISTER MARY

I think the older members of the family found my sister Mary, who had Down's syndrome, rather an embarrassment. All the rectory guests who stayed over the weekend were expected to attend one church service with the family. The different hymnals, or prayer books, laid out along the narrow pew shelf could be daunting for the unchurched. But Mary, ever helpful, would hurriedly grab her copy of *Hymns Ancient and Modern* and locate the hymns for the service. Then, with a flourish for the whole congregation behind her to see, she would lean across the rest of us and thrust the book triumphantly into the hands of our mortified guest! On occasions Mary would even slip out to take up the collection if she thought the sidesmen were not moving into action quite smartly enough. We younger ones among us accepted

Mary as a normal given in life – she had smiled down upon us ever since we were in our cradles. It was extraordinary the amount of happiness she brought with her wherever she went – always smiling and on the lookout to please. Indeed her loyalty and help was usually a positive bonus. Approached the right way she could be persuaded to do all sorts of little favours. After my father passed away Mary spent her last years well looked after in an old peoples' home in Ipswich – they loved her for her happy disposition and ever-readiness to help. She eventually developed Alzheimer's disease and sadly didn't recognize us in the final years before she died (aged fifty-nine) in 1983, and her ashes were interred at All Saints, Holbrook – with my parents.

Chapter 3

EDUCATION

*Will the boy who borrowed the ladder from the caretaker last month
please return it otherwise further steps will be taken*
(SCHOOL NOTICE BOARD)

*My problems all started with my early education. I went to a school for
mentally disturbed teachers*
(WOODY ALLEN)

In 1940 Peter and I went away to a preparatory school at Old
Buckenham Hall[1] near Attleborough, in Norfolk, some seventeen
miles to the north of Gislingham. One of OBH's few claims to
fame was the 'old boy' musician and composer Sir Benjamin
Britten.

After our initial homesickness, boarding school days proved
happy ones indeed (1940–43). Once a term, mother would cycle
over to be with us for an afternoon, bringing welcome homemade
goodies for our tuck boxes.

Our headmaster, T.J.E. Sewell, taught us Maths and Latin.
He was invariably late for the class, but he had a rule that from
the moment the class assembled we were all to begin in a loud
voice reciting Latin grammar straight from the book. The
usefulness of Latin only dawned on us as time went by. Of course
it helped greatly later, both in grasping English grammar, the
etymology of many English words, and as a foundation later for
learning Spanish!

We had Cubs and Scouts at OBH run by the Second Master,
Mr Hall. Scouting, a great preparation for both the Army, good
citizenship and the mission field, was fun – games, paper trails,
camping out and cooking – all the little skills and the country lore
that one picked up working for those coveted badges intrigued

me. I looked forward enthusiastically to our gatherings – especially when I became a patrol leader.

It was while I was attending OBH that I discovered books; I also heard the clarinet for the first time – played by a young master called John Davison, who was temping from Jesus College, Cambridge. John would bring down some of his fellow undergrads from Cambridge for a classical music evening in the school each term. Pure ecstasy!

On another occasion, a choir from the US Airforce (stationed locally) visited us – about twenty black men singing *a capella* – chanting profoundly emotional 'spirituals'. Such unheard of harmonies uttered by so many huge men! I picture them still – those strong black faces streaming with tears as they sang and hummed about the Lord and the sufferings of his people. 'There are only two things that pierce the human heart. One is beauty. The other is suffering,' said Simone Wiel. I was experiencing both right then with an intensity never dreamed of before. Other such musical 'serendipities' for me were attending a performance of the Vienna boys choir years after and later still hearing a Zulu choir in South Africa. Music – one of God's great gifts to humanity! And again in a completely different way I later encountered the powerfully simple worship from the 'Vineyard' in California.

Peter and I were in the same class all the way through our time at OBH. He usually came second and I came third – highly mortifying since he was the younger. I gained no distinction at OBH, other than in the last year when I was presented with a little cup for being the most helpful boy in the school. This secretly pleased me but it was such a goody-goody kind of thing one could hardly boast about it! In any case I felt it was possibly given me as some kind of compensation. I'd never complained about Peter being ahead of me – how could I? I loved him dearly.

INTRODUCTION TO THEOLOGY

The 'temping' master, Mr Davison, the son of a Luton rector, was going on to train for the ordained ministry of the Church of England. He felt my father was too conservative and gave me a book called *The Synoptic Gospels* as a corrective. Not wanting to appear narrow minded I read it dutifully. That was my first introduction to theology. I found it pretty boring at that stage.

At least I learned that the word synoptic meant that the writers of the first three Gospels wrote from a common point of view – much as newspaper reporters did when recounting the same incident. More cynically I learned that theologians can't resist inventing a new word to make what they mean more obscure. I have spent my life trying to keep things as simple as possible so that everyone could get a foot in the door.

MY FIRST REAL BOOK

I read my first real book, *Gone With The Wind* when I was thirteen. This was supposed to be rather naughty. The book dealt with a fascinating chunk of American history. The horrors of civil war, and questions of civil rights (slavery) were as seriously challenging as the romance was intriguing. Soon after this I read my first 'spiritual' book – apart from the Bible and portions of *Pilgrim's Progress*. It was called *Behold He Cometh with the Clouds* by J. Oswald Smith. My parents had been seriously discussing the book. There was talk of the political revival of the Old Roman Empire with a leader who would unite the world but who turned out to be the Antichrist. He would have the mark of the beast – the number 666. Scary stuff indeed! Was this a coded reference to Hitler? He seemed to be a world power doing terribly evil things. But then again what about Stalin? Just as bad! I still had a lot to learn about eschatology – the end times! What suddenly struck me at that time was that all I had heard or read in the Bible, and repeated in the Apostles' Creed was leading up to a world crisis that culminated in the Second Coming of Christ. He is really coming one day and it could be much sooner than we think. Like the Old Testament prophet Daniel when he received divine revelation, I was stunned. The Lord's sovereign purposes already revealed to us in the Bible made me tremble with an awesome godly fear.

END OF THE WORLD

Whilst God himself had his overruling master plan with the bringing in of his kingdom in fullness and glory, the world was caught up in the destructive intrigues of an 'Enemy' who like a master terrorist was out to destroy as much as he could before his own eventual doom. Seeing that I had to decide which side I wanted to be on, it confirmed my commitment to serve the Lord. I knew that there could be a high cost to it. As for working out the end time details, I soon realised it could be a sad and frustrating exercise. Too many Christians had become so unchristian in their divisions over the precise minutiae of 'the last days' scenario while neglecting their basic obligation and responsibilities in this world – doing God's will and serving Christ in loving our neighbours. The whole range of Christian teaching was becoming a serious challenge to me and the call to lifelong commitment was being clarified. There seemed no time to lose. A day was certainly coming when we were all going to have to give an account of our stewardship. That was the main thing to keep in mind.

I started to study my Bible more intently and looked up all the references from Oswald Smith's book. I learned that we could even hasten his Coming by missionary work. Once all the nations had heard the good news – then Christ would come again. Was this a missionary call I wanted to hear? Did I really want to hasten Christ's coming? These were the questions I kept asking myself and, if not, why not? The whole subject was also a wholesome challenge for a teenager trying to come to terms with hot hormones – a challenge to commit to a holy lifestyle. As St John pointed out, 'Everyone who has this hope in him purifies himself, just as he is pure'.[2]

WHAT WE MISS

In 1947 my mother died an early death through cancer. She was fifty-three. We all miss something unique in the personality and gifting of our loved ones; the parting is so final and the pain is universal. I always felt that mother bequeathed to us her happy and optimistic spirit, her love of fun and sense of the ridiculous; something that has sustained us for the rest of life – and it certainly sustained me through the silent family grief at that painful time.

Mother was one of those remarkable women who seemed to lighten every room she entered. A totally unselfish soul with such a gift for making others seem loved and special – a superb encourager.

The next day Peter and I went back to school. We were fifteen and sixteen years old and had already moved to Framlingham College.

FRAMLINGHAM

The school had been founded in the 1860s in memory of Prince Albert. His bronze monument still gazes over the front lawns across a reedy mere, where rest the proud remains of Framlingham Castle – an ideal setting for our Shakespeare plays each year. With regard to the fees at 'Fram' there was a reduction for sons of clergy, another for brothers, and yet another for those who came from Suffolk. We got in on about a third of the stated fees and this third was generously paid for out of a bequest left by Maurice Welldon, a deceased great uncle who had no family of his own.

Roy, my older brother, had been our John the Baptist at Framlingham College. Roy had moved there from Seaford College when war broke out in 1939 and made a name for himself at 'Fram' on the sports field. Because of this we immediately gained some recognition amongst the senior boys in our house who still remembered him. Roy rarely opened his mouth when he laughed because he had a very bad front tooth and sought to avoid attracting attention to it in case he was made to see the dentist. His unusual laugh just rumbled inwards with a 'mo-ho-ho' earning him the nickname 'Mo'. I was now to be 'Mo 1' and Peter was 'Mo 2'! Such harmless nicknames from the head of house were clearly an unexpected asset to we two new boys and helped greatly towards our settling in happily. I enjoyed my time at 'Fram', though most of the younger teaching staff had gone off to the war. The remaining ones appeared to be the shell-shocked survivors of World War I – elderly and kindly but a bit past it. I think I forgot more Latin than I learned while I was there.

Both of us were to become successively heads of Kerrison House (Blue) and Peter, who stayed on after me for another two years was to become the deputy Head Prefect of the school – making us all very proud.

One of the highlights for us at 'Fram' was when the six Pytches brothers took on the school at tennis – and won!

TRAINING UP OTHERS

I played a lot of squash, but, unlike my predecessor as head of house, I was never going to be a champion. I decided I would serve the house better if I used my privileged position with ready access to the courts, to train up some of the promising younger members in the house, hoping that they might bring some glory to the house as they came to the top after I had left.

I was more than surprised to be awarded the Hamilton Penny Cup for the best all rounder in my house during my last year there. To keep me from getting big-headed however, the school games master, who selected and coached the hockey team and put me in the school first eleven, gave me an appalling write up in the magazine for my pathetic role as goalie. This was especially mortifying since, during the whole year, he had never ever given me a word of constructive criticism about my goal keeping – in fact he had never said anything at all. Why, I puzzled, had he not replaced me. There was always plenty of competition to get into the School First. Since I was leaving at the close of the summer term, there was no way I could possibly redeem myself either! Very humiliating! One just had to put it down to training for life – indeed extremely useful preparation for the many future occasions when one might have felt oneself unjustly criticised or misrepresented by the media.

HOUSEMASTER SACKED

One day, as head of my house at 'Fram', a younger boy in another house reported to me that he was being abused by his housemaster. I was aware that boys had passions on younger boys but I imagined it was all fairly innocent. Although it seemed inappropriate to question this boy too closely, I did ask if there was anyone else involved. He said there were others. I thought I really ought to report this. To my surprise my housemaster refused to hear a word of it and told me I must go straight to the school chaplain. I did, and he went straight to the headmaster. The offending master was out of the school by noon the next day.

I heard later that many of the staff had been worried about what was going on for some time, but were powerless to do anything without willing witnesses. Apparently father received a warm letter of commendation for services rendered to the school, from the chaplain, but father never mentioned it to me. That kind of thing was never referred to at home. Father no doubt assumed we would pick up all we needed to know about sex from nature. Possibly we learn too much and too soon about sex today. I look back feeling grateful for that extended period of comparative innocence.

I was beginning to feel I needed to make some purposeful moves towards ordination if I was really going to take God's call on my life seriously. So I left 'Fram' and, aged seventeen, moved on. At father's suggestion, I had applied to the Bible Church-man's Missionary and Theological College in Bristol.

Father was one of the original supporters of the Bible Churchman's Missionary Society (BCMS)[3] which was started under the Rev Dr Daniel Bartlett in 1922 – a breakaway from the Church Missionary Society on a question of biblical authority. The BCM&T College was in Pembroke Road, Clifton, very near the Bristol zoo, and the suspension bridge.

BRIEFING BEFORE THE INTERVIEW

My father had briefed me before the interview and explained that I needed to be very clear about the meaning of the cross, and about personal forgiveness for one's sins. He asked me to spell out how I knew whether mine were forgiven or not. I was not very good at quoting the Bible, or finding the references for verses when I wanted them but I knew Mrs Alexander's hymn – *There is a Green Hill Far Away* and could quote the line that ran: 'He died that we might be forgiven, he died to make us good, that we might go at last to heaven, saved by his precious blood.' And I followed on with the later verse: 'There was none other good enough to pay the price of sin; he only could unlock the gate of heaven, and let us in.' Father nodded his approval. So did the Principal later at the interview.

POCKET MONEY

I was given two small grants for my first year at Bristol, one by the Rev 'Pa' Salmon of Woldingham in Surrey, from his Ordination Candidates Fund, and a similar grant from Suffolk County

Council. The combined total covered the fees for tuition, and full board and residence. I was left with a half-a-crown a week as pocket money for travel and pay for books, hair cuts, shoe repairs, soap, toothpaste and razor blades, stamps, extra eats and church offerings. I accepted this impoverished state of affairs as something to be grateful for, and do not remember feeling at all sorry for myself. I just knew I had to be very careful with money to survive. But then I had never had much money in my pocket anyhow. Many of the other students were in the same predicament.

First impressions!

Arriving at the college, I was greatly impressed to be addressed as 'Mr Pytches' by the Principal, the Rev William Dodgson Sykes.[4] The Principal, whom I later discovered to have been a brilliant Cambridge prizeman, actually showed me to my room that first day. He also insisted on carrying my bag. I remarked on this to a fellow student: 'What amazing humility! I could never have imagined my headmaster ever doing a thing like that.' Straight-faced my new friend responded quickly: 'Didn't you notice his hand outstretched and waiting for a tip!' Such delightful drollery! I'm really going to enjoy it here, I thought.

Sometimes students used to get invited for a meal over at the 'Prinnery' as we students dubbed the Principal's house. I respected him greatly. He was a godly man – kindness itself! Always thinking of practical ways to help get us through the exams and considering our futures.

It was a surprise blessing over fifty years later to find myself leading a training day at Witney (Oxon), in a school belonging to the Community Church, and to discover that its gifted leader was Roger Cole, whose mother Joan was the daughter of my old college Principal.

Giants in those days

That year at the BCM&T College taught me much – not least to have a Quiet Time every morning with Bible reading, meditation and prayer. I also worked through the Bible Diploma course that proved a great help for the future. I tried to regain the ground I had lost at 'Fram' by studying Latin again as I worked for the London matriculation – this being a standard requirement for university entry in those days. I still struggled with Latin grammar.

Principal Sykes suggested I apply to Bristol University ready for the coming Michaelmas term. But I was beginning to think I ought to do my National Service first. The experience of rubbing shoulders with older men who had proved Christ in the armed forces left me feeling that my own Christian life had been untested. I learned how these men had been put on the line for their faith: 'There were giants in the earth in those days'.[5] Also, missionaries on leave[6] were invited regularly to the college to speak on their work abroad and to encourage us in our praying for them. I felt God was continuing to keep me focused on the unwelcome challenge of work overseas.

REVIVAL HOUR

On Thursday nights, some of us used to gather together in Charlie Reade's room to listen to *Revival Hour* from Long Beach, California, coming through by radio (we still called it a 'wireless'). This programme was broadcast by David Fuller (an enterprising and inspired American pastor), who had just founded a seminary under his own name. Fuller Seminary today is one of the most highly respected across the world, and has had many beneficial influences on my own life, not just through those broadcasts but through the seminary staff and its publications. (I never actually got to visit the place till the early 1970s where I met Dr Geoffrey Bromily again, whom I had first known when he was the Vice Principal under Dodgson Sykes at Bristol, in 1948.)

We students loved the *Revival Hour* though we mocked the accents and mimicked the religious terminology. That programme was well communicated and very refreshing. I had never heard people talking about the Lord in such an unstuffy way. He even called his wife in to help: 'Honey! Won't you read the letters for us now please?' 'Honey' would then read letters from people across the world who had been inspired by the programme. I have always loved hearing how people are uniquely blessed by God. Personal testimony appeals to most people and it certainly enhanced my own faith. The pianist was amazing too – his fingers simply skimming the 'ivories'. I never forgot the impact of those services on the air.

Every day, after lunch, the students prayed together fervently for the regular Saturday night open-air meeting in the heart of the city. The variety of needy people who turned up and the bluntness of some of their penetrating questions helped us to keep our theological feet well and truly planted on the ground. If we were not speaking publicly our job was to get alongside these folk, listen to their woes, and find ways of helping them. Great training!

When mother died my father took over writing to us weekly at school and continued for the rest of his life. Later, when I was at Bristol, I think I must have been experiencing some spiritual 'highs' as I discovered more and more of the grace of God for myself, and he warned me to keep my letters low-key and not go over the top – he must have sensed I was getting too intense in my new zeal!

MATRICULATION

The time came to sit for my matriculation. It was out of term time. We gathered in a lecture hall for the examinations. I was still nervous about the Latin grammar since at Framlingham I seemed to have forgotten more than I had ever learned. When it came to that Latin paper, I prayed as I turned it over, and began writing out all the answers as quickly as possible. When candidates finished they were required to tie their answer papers together with the piece of string provided. This was meant to be threaded through the hole punched in the top left hand corner of each page. In my nervousness I dropped my string, then, leaning forward to pick it up, I caught a glimpse of the answers spread open on the desk in front of me. It was devastating! I had quite clearly got my declensions all wrong. Oh what a fool I was! In my confusion I prayed desperately: 'Lord! Are you showing me the right answers before it's too late?' I was sweating! But would God really show me in that way? In the end I prayed that if he really wanted me to change my answers he would show me some other way . . . but the heavens were as brass. Nothing! No sign! Reluctantly, I tied my papers together and handed them in, praying that, at least, I might have had some right answers to the rest of the questions. I left the lecture hall very depressed. Returning to my room I immediately double-checked with my grammar book. Amazing! I had put down the right answers after all. Thank you Lord! At the end of August I heard with relief that I passed my matriculation.

Chapter 4

ONWARD CHRISTIAN SOLDIER

My salad days – when I was green in judgement
(WILLIAM SHAKESPEARE)

therefore whosoever shall confess me before men, him will I confess also before my Father which is in heaven. But whosoever shall deny me before men, him will I also deny before my Father which is in heaven
(MATTHEW 10:32,33 KJV)

Wanting to get my National Service behind me, and needing to prove the power of Christ to keep me in a tougher environment than I had hitherto experienced, I joined the Army.

Our initial training camp with the Rifle Brigade (The Green Jackets) was just outside Winchester. Half the new conscripts seemed to have previously met in Wormwood Scrubs! Other recruits were from Eton; the rest, like me, from less notable backgrounds.

Being kitted out in our uniforms we discovered that the quartermaster only had two sizes – too large or too small! The Army barber left me as bald as a coot with only my ears and eyebrows surviving the onslaught. We visited the medical centre and came out full of injections and vaccinations that produced painful swellings and fevers.

But although I enjoyed my time in the Army, I will never forget how appalled I was at the bombardment of filthy curses and blasphemous language that flew endlessly across the barrack room. This continued echoing round and round my mind even in my sleep during those first early weeks. Many of my fellow 'rookies' seemed to have a vocabulary almost limited to such language for whatever subject they were addressing. Apart from its offensiveness it was so utterly boring and lacking in any trace of creative imagination.

At boarding school, there had been a bell to signal fifteen minutes silence in the dormitory at bedtime for saying our private prayers. One could hardly expect such encouragement in the Army! National Service would be a testing time of my convictions, my commitment and my call. I prayed hard that I would have the courage to kneel and pray by my bedside that first night in the barrack room – it would be much harder to start later in front of a room full of raw recruits if I failed to do it the first night. I managed to get a bed in the corner, which made me a little less conspicuous though I did not escape the usual mockery from the others, who soon dubbed me the 'Sky pilot'. But strangely they would often ask me, privately, to pray about their problems – some personal crisis, usually over girlfriends they had left at home, who, feeling bored or abandoned, had taken up with other men. One night, on my knees, with my hands over my ears, I was trying to pray and fell asleep – not surprising, considering the heavy training programme. I suddenly awoke to hear the barrack room NCO standing beside my bed swearing at me profusely and calling me some kind of a pervert! I got up quietly and jumped into bed. He did not seem to expect any response so I did not explain that I had simply nodded off. He obviously thought I took prayer far too seriously! Of course, it must have been very embarrassing to have me kneeling by my bedside, reading my Bible and silently praying every night in a public barrack room. I would not have been surprised had the odd boot been flung at my back. I liked a verse in Ezekiel: 'yet will I be to [him] as a little sanctuary'.[1] I was surprised to find such a sanctuary in a barrack room but strangely it proved to be so.

PROUD OF OUR BRIGADE

Parades were terrifying. Sergeants were ogres. They would call out 'Putches', 'Piecheese', 'Patches' or even 'Pictures'. I could easily guess it was my name they were struggling with (it's correctly pronounced like pitches for football). But we soon grew very proud of our particular military tradition going back to the Brigade's formation. The Green Jackets had faithfully defended the interests of the British Empire against the local rebels during the American War of Independence. They had the fastest pace for marching (180 steps to the minute), and carried their rifles upside-down across the shoulder – to stop the rain coursing through their barrels. It made sense and it also made us feel a rather special kind of soldier marching with our rifles the wrong way up! As we did so we sang ditties left over from World War Two, crudely mocking the reproductive capacities of our nation's former enemies (though, of course, with no factual knowledge on the subject). I just about managed to stretch my conscience and sing them along with the rest. When we first started rifle drill, we were ordered to shout out a swear word for each drill movement. As we all shouted together, I managed to muster something like 'blow', 'drat', 'darn' and 'dash' – almost the full range of expletives my parents and my conscience had ever permitted except for a favourite outburst: 'My Giddy Aunt'!

THE ROYAL ARMY EDUCATION CORPS
A friend advised me not to apply for a commission and reckoned that the Education Corps would be the ideal preparation for the ordained ministry.

The personnel officer checked the records of my role in the Junior Training Corps – Army Cadets – at school, where I had been a sergeant, and urged me to reconsider. I was not tempted until I saw the officers in their Number One uniforms. But then I discovered I would need a private income to enjoy such a role, and not having a penny to my name it was out of the question as far as the Rifle Brigade was concerned.

Those going into the Education Corps were posted from Winchester for further training at Bodmin, Cornwall.

CONSIDERED A PIONEER!
War had recently broken out between North and South in Korea, and we thought when we had completed our training we would be sent out there but I found myself being posted to Bovington in Dorset as a sergeant instructor. My new boss in Bovington had read my CV and decided I was a missionary pioneer. He 'posted' me out to Lulworth Cove, some five miles away on the coast, to

start an educational centre at the Gunnery School. I duly reported to the adjutant for duty and was, soon after, ushered into the commandant's office. The colonel explained that he had a team of non-commissioned firing instructors on camp who were all highly skilled in gunnery, and were essential to him for training the many young tank corps officers being sent to his Gunnery School. These experienced and older NCOs did not have the basic education certificates that, from now on, would be required for them to maintain their present ranks. Part of my new job was to see they all got their certificates in education. It certainly was a challenge. Another part of my job was to teach some illiterate soldiers on camp their three 'R's among other things.

The freedom of Lulworth for an education sergeant was refreshing – no guard duties and my own sleeping quarters. It became much easier to read the Bible and pray in private. I ate my meals in the sergeants' mess. Again I needed to make it clear where I stood and I always made a point of bowing my head as I silently asked God to bless my food before meals. This attracted the attention of George Parker, the mess cook, who, sadly, was a backslider. He had been brought up in a church but had fallen away. He told me how he had once been a strong swimmer but had found himself being dragged out to sea by a powerful current off Parkstone. In desperation he cried out to God who miraculously saved him. In spite of a vow that he would turn back to God, he didn't. Soon after, he found himself in a similar predicament, and again cried out to God, who again miraculously saved him from drowning. And once more he broke his vow. His life since had been a miserable one and he asked me to help him. I tried to do so but there could be no real answer without repentance and amendment of life. He wanted any kind of help but that.

One day, after silently giving thanks to God for my food, two others sitting with me suddenly lurched at me and tried to drag me to the window to throw me out. The cook quickly alerted others who came to my rescue. Had it simply been my silent blessing of the meal that had provoked them? A couple of weeks later these sergeants were demoted and posted elsewhere for committing adultery with the wives of other sergeants temporarily posted overseas to Korea. Possibly, innocent of their misdoings, my presence at their table as a Christian had disturbed their consciences.

FIRST MOTORBIKE

I enjoyed my educational work and would have gladly done it simply for my board and lodging. I had never earned so much money in all my life before. I bought a motorbike – an Enfield 350 cc. This gave me new freedom from the restrictions of camp. But even so I felt I should start saving for the future, and so I was being careful about how much I spent on petrol. And then there were other unforeseen expenses. I lent my machine to a fellow sergeant who got a puncture late at night and rode it all the way back to camp on a flat tyre. He arrived back with the tyre in shreds – completely ruined, and calmly left it parked without explanation or apology outside my office. He later claimed he had no money to buy me a new tyre! As a Christian I had not anticipated such a situation and was unsure how to respond to such blatant abuse. 'Turning the other cheek' could be quite painful when it came to it! If I simply repaired it there was a possibility that others would then want to borrow it too and, thinking I was a soft touch, leave me to pay the bills again. So I began keeping it out of sight and travelled locally as much as possible on my bicycle.

Besides the chapel on camp, I found another group of Christians at Bovington a few miles up the road. Bovington was the HQ of the Royal Armoured Corps (Tanks). I had located this group thanks to Captain May, the General Secretary of the Soldiers' and Airmen's Scripture Readers Association.

DISCOVERING CAPTAIN HAGUE

Their local rep was Captain Ted Hague MM (promoted from the ranks following an act of bravery on the battlefield – hence the Military Medal and not the Military Cross). Ted Hague had had an awful past. Apparently abducted by Gypsies as a baby he spent his childhood selling clothespegs and matches from door to door, always fearful of beatings if he had not sold enough. Finally he was adopted by a Christian couple he had frequently called on during his sales round and Ted later followed his new parents in the faith. He became a gifted evangelist amongst soldiers and to watch him leading people to Christ was a delight. He lived very sacrificially on the periphery of Bovington in a converted railway carriage. He and his wife were unstintingly hospitable to soldiers like us and we spent long hours studying the Bible in their home along with several other National Servicemen. We loved it. On first introducing myself to him, he had greeted me warmly, and then asked me what denomination I belonged to? I replied, 'Church of England'. There was a moment's disconcerting silence until he sighed: 'Oh well – never mind!' I don't think I ever let him forget it. Our friendship was going to be an education both for him and for me.

Ted Hague, a Plymouth Brother, always demanded a 'Thus saith the Lord' for any opinions expressed in his group. This forced me to search my Bible thoroughly, as I found I did not always agree with him, especially on things like infant baptism and liturgical worship. He believed that liturgy was vain repetition – something he insisted Jesus had condemned. I did not think that Jesus was condemning repetition per se, meaning that any form of repetition was wrong, but that it was vain to keep repeating the same words without thinking what they meant. Ted and his wife Margery were lovely people, their hospitality was great, and their conversation was refreshingly pure and challenging – such a contrast to what I was hearing all day long!

But there seemed a slight lack of reality and a strain of legalism about some of the folk I met with regularly in their home. I was discovering there were different sorts of evangelical spirituality (though I don't think we ever used that phrase in those days). My friends were absolute on what was permissible whereas I felt my inherited spirituality was much more moderate. Father did not smoke but there were cigarettes in the drawing room for visitors – or were meant to be (they tended to disappear quite fast with so many boys in the house). Father did not drink but he would provide beer for others who visited. Father rarely went to the cinema but he did come with us to see Charlie Chaplin's silent film *Modern Times*, and then the new Walt Disney sound film *Snow White and the Seven Dwarfs* (I was terrified by that witch). We saw

The Wizard of Oz, and loved the Laurel and Hardy films – and any film with my hero Will Hay.

Such things as cinema were rather frowned upon by my new friends whilst I felt my Anglican background gave me a healthier freedom. Their narrowmindedness did however begin to influence me. I have since regretted never seeing *Cry My Beloved Country* – partly because I would have benefited from the enlightenment on the political state of affairs and the moral issues involved at that time, and partly because later I actually went to South Africa for some renewal conferences and visited another Soweto on the edge of Port Elizabeth.

BREATH OF FRESH AIR

Our camp Medical Officer was a Dr Tom Bryan. He was a civilian with a practice in Wool nearby. He told me that he earned enough to educate two of his sons at Monkton Combe School by this extra surgery work before his breakfast at the Gunnery School. Tom and Faith Bryan's home soon became another spiritual oasis for me. They had a regular Sunday afternoon children's gathering at Wool (between Bovington and Lulworth). A few of us (soldiers) used to help at this and then, with little need of persuasion, to stay on for a huge tea afterwards. I did not feel quite so much on the defensive there as I did with the Hagues as the Bryans were C of E! They had once been medical missionaries with the CMS in Rwanda where Tom had incidentally acquired enough research material for an Oxford doctorate in medicine on his return. Tom's cousin was currently the Master at St Peter's College (then St Peter's Hall) and Tom kindly wrote to him about my going there when I left the Army. The Master encouraged me to apply but I felt really too indebted to the BCM&T College at Bristol, and thought it would be disloyal to change course now. I was also a little suspicious that a possible prestige motive in my case might not be quite Christian.

A SOLDIER'S CONVERSION!

One of the major landmarks during this time was the privilege of being a kind of spiritual midwife in the conversion of another soldier. I shall never forget the night Ron Gould told me he wanted to become a Christian. We had been to a missionary meeting at the Bryans, and were on our way home. We just dropped our bikes and knelt by the roadside where he committed his life to the Lord in the moonlight. It was a truly blissful moment for me. I sensed something of that joy that Jesus talked about when he said: 'There will be more joy in heaven over one sinner who repents than over ninety-nine righteous persons'.[2] To compound our excitement, Ron's girlfriend became a Christian during his next home leave to Stoke on Trent. She got linked in with a good church there. Sadly, Ron was tragically killed in a motorcycle accident soon after his demobilisation, leaving a wife and baby.

RIBBING AND RAFFLE TICKETS

My fellow sergeants simply could not believe that I spent so many evenings out at Bible studies and circulated wild rumours around the mess that I had regular dates with a woman. But I had decided it was no use having a girlfriend at that stage in my life. And I would not want to form a special friendship with any girl unless I felt that God intended marriage to be the outcome of it. I really did not want to lead a girl up the garden path and give her any false hopes about a long-term relationship. It would still be years before I could ever afford to marry and have a family.

One underwent a good deal of ribbing on account of one's Christian faith, but generally it was light hearted. I would often overhear (as they intended) the loud parodies of supposed 'church' life when the troopers were queuing for classes outside my education centre.

There was one particularly difficult day when all the sergeants in the mess were summoned by the Regimental Sergeant Major. We were told that we each had to sell two books of twenty-five lottery tickets – the proceeds to go to the sergeants' mess. I was not opposed to supporting the mess – it was a kind of club for us – but in all good conscience I was not happy about selling lottery tickets, and none of my friends would be likely to buy one either. But to ensure that everyone complied with his wishes we each had to file past the RSM, with the Provost Sergeant at attention beside him, and sign against our names for every book of tickets we took from him. There seemed no way out. I was praying fervently about what I should do, as the queue before me was diminishing. But once I was face to face with him, I looked him straight in the eyes, and said quietly: 'Sir, I'm very sorry, but my conscience has never allowed me to buy or sell lottery tickets on principle.' I waited for the usual noisy string of abuse, and could hardly believe my ears when he ducked my gaze, and replied quietly, 'That's all right, sergeant,' and nodded at me to move on quickly! Prayer was answered. The RSM obviously wished to avoid a public discussion with me on the subject of ethics before the rest of the sergeants' mess.

THE BIG TEST

Eventually the time came for the exams and all my men, most of whom had not found the work very easy, had to sit them. Following this I was summoned to Bovington to be on the marking board. In all honesty I could not 'pass' some of them, much as I desperately wanted to. It weighed heavily that the camp commandant at Lulworth wanted them all to get through. I handed in my pile of their marked papers with a heavy heart. I remarked to the major in charge of the examining board that the bad results were very serious because the colonel at the Gunnery School had almost 'ordered' me to ensure they all passed! I suggested to the major that he might like to double check to see whether I had been too hard in my marking? How was I ever going to look the CO in the eye again I wondered? It was therefore with an uptight feeling that I received a summons from the adjutant, pretty soon after my return, to report to the colonel. I duly marched in and saluted nervously, but could hardly believe my ears when he started congratulating me for getting all his men through with such high grades! I could not imagine how the major in charge had fixed it! The colonel went on to assure me that I was destined for great things in life! All this, naturally, I took with a very big pinch of salt.

THE CO's TESTIMONIAL

My time was almost up in the Army. The CO wrote out a kind testimonial for my discharge and I had to sign that I had read it before taking it away with me. It was so exaggerated that one would think I must have bribed him. It ran:

> Sgt Pytches is a young man of high integrity and keen intelligence. He has carried out the heavy duty of educational training for this School for the past year in an exemplary manner without supervision. If he has one fault it is that he is somewhat inexperienced in administration. This fault is completely outweighed by his capacity for work, intelligence, education and sincerity. I cannot recommend him too highly for any task that demands those qualities that I have already enumerated. He has a pleasant cheerful disposition and is popular with everyone. I am very sorry to lose him.

I could not recognise the man so described, but it was signed by the Colonel Commandant, the Gunnery School, RAC Centre, Lulworth. Supposing it might, some day, be useful I kept it, but since I was hoping to train for the ordained ministry of the Church of England I did not imagine it would ever help me much. Little did I know! He may have exaggerated most of it but he had certainly not exaggerated my great weakness for administration – something that has bugged me all my life.

GOD INTERVENES OVER MY MONEY

I was packing for my approaching demobilisation when I came across the little stack of money I had been hiding away for the future. I lay back on my bunk to think about how rich I was! I had saved about £275 – a lot of money in those days. I was thinking, 'All this money – and it's all mine. I've never been so rich in my life before!' Suddenly I sensed a voice within me saying: 'That money is not yours but mine!'

Surely that could not possibly be the Lord! Was that really you, God? I was startled to conclude that quite possibly it was! I immediately began rationalising very self-righteously: 'Well yes, the money is yours all right Lord, but I am saving it to help pay the fees for my training in your service! It's all I've got for the next three years. I think I have really been very sensible! I know it's not nearly enough to cover all my costs for university but it would irresponsible to give any of it away!' Then God seemed to be telling me: 'Give every penny of it to Captain Ted Hague, to help pay off the pressing debt still outstanding on his railway carriage home! Trust me!' Such a preposterous idea staggered me but I could not shake off the conviction that God had spoken. However much I argued I still had no peace. Ted Hague was startled too when he got the envelope with the money in it. He seemed very reluctant to accept it. Maybe it helped him at last to believe that perhaps an Anglican could be a Christian too!

When I arrived home in mid-September, 1951, funding really did become an urgent priority in my prayers. During all my time in the Army I had been comforted by the thought that somehow God would provide for me financially. I had not worried about it at all. Now I was wondering about how I was possibly going to get enough to keep me for three years and to pay my university fees etc? My faith seemed to have evaporated! 'Pa' Salmon had generously encouraged me to come back to him after my National Service, but I was not sure that I would get much from that source – I thought it would be a drop in the bucket compared to the total sum I would need.

Suffolk County Council had also told me that when I got a place at university I should come back to them, but having only a matriculation entry level, I did not expect much from that quarter either. They had not given me much before. But every little bit would count – so I applied. They sent me a long form to fill in which I completed, and returned together with my CO's testimonial for good measure.

AN EXTRAORDINARY INTERVIEW

I was finally called for an interview. It was nearly time for the start of the university term if I was ever going to get there. By that stage, I could not see how it could really happen. During the interview they asked me what I had done since they had helped me before. I told them about my teaching work in the Army. For some reason they seemed most impressed. Had they read the camp commandant's report about me, I wondered? And they seemed especially interested in the fact that I had, amongst other things, been teaching illiterates. They quizzed me thoroughly about how I had tried to tackle this. Finally someone suggested that, since my need for funds was rather urgent they should discuss my case there and then! Apparently, they were only interviewing and not intending to allocate or adjust any grants immediately, but in my case they were making an exception! I was duly sent out and after about twenty minutes of fervent prayer on my part and twenty minutes of urgent appraisal on theirs, I was finally recalled to hear their verdict. 'We have decided to grant you a major award – this will cover everything for the next three years subject to good reports from your tutors!' they said. I was dumbstruck. I did not even know that such large grants were ever available for anyone, let alone me. I thanked them profusely and left silently thanking God – the whole interview seemed to have been taken out of human hands.

A year later, my brother Peter, who had three higher-school certificates to his credit, applied for a grant from the same board and they turned him down flat. They said he did not qualify. Peter was naturally very disappointed and mystified. He asked them, 'How could this be so when my older brother who only had school matriculation, was given a full grant award . . . just the previous year?' 'Ah yes,' they said, 'We never talk about that around here! No one has ever been able to fathom out how we came to award it – he certainly did not qualify!' This admission of anomaly now gave Peter a chance to appeal, which he did, and this time they awarded him a full grant also. In any case he was far more deserving than I was.

Chapter 5

TESTING MY VOCATION

The need is never the call. The need is the opportunity.
The call is the call of God
(OSWALD CHAMBERS)

Our lives are our own to spend but we spend them only once
(OSWALD CHAMBERS)

The Church Selection Board I attended soon after was supposed to be modelled on the War Office Selection Board set up by the Armed Forces for sorting out potential officers. The church selectors task was to advise the bishops regarding a candidate's call and suitability for the ordained ministry in the Church of England.

All the candidates were summoned to the bishop's palace in Surrey. One man thought he would nip out for a quick visit into Guildford to do some shopping. He was, unfortunately, met near the gate by the Bishop of Guildford himself who was not actually one of the selectors, but who gently enquired of the young man what he thought he was up to. The candidate, perhaps thinking that the situation called for a rather religious answer, replied that he was feeling led by the Holy Spirit to go down the town. 'What a pity,' replied the bishop, 'that the Holy Spirit did not tell you that today is early closing! Perhaps you had better go back to where you were meant to be!'

Things seemed to go well until my final interview. The secretary, a large cleric, had the disconcerting habit of viewing one as a side dish that hadn't been ordered. He suddenly asked me what I would do if I were turned down? Ominous! I mentally raced through the options: 'If I say I'll simply try something else like teaching he will think I am not really called. If I say it will knock the bottom out of my life if I am failed, he will think I am unstable and can't cope with setbacks.' So I looked straight at him and replied that I really did not think for one moment that I would be. Even as I said it, I realised this might come across as arrogance, but hopefully it rang with the inner conviction that I felt.

'Oh,' he replied, 'What makes you say that?'

'Er – well! I have felt called for a long time. I have tested this in the Army. I have prayed about it many times – and have also considered lots of other alternatives that I would really like to have taken up, but it always came back to what was God's will for my life.' I added that I felt I already knew quite a lot about what the call entailed, having been brought up in a rectory: I had had encouragement from two theological college principals and many other friends about going into the ministry. I was already accepted into a university (at no cost to the church) to read theology – all this seemed to indicate that I was 'on course'. It was a relief to learn soon after that I was being recommended. I envied the overseas ordination candidate who, when asked if he would be disappointed if the church did not ordain him that year, replied: 'Oh not at all! God has already ordained me. He's just waiting for you guys to get the paper work done!'

BACK TO BRISTOL

I went back to Bristol in 1951. I liked the city, loved the Clifton Downs. Bristol had been John Wesley's and George Whitefield's first preaching base that led to the great eighteenth-century revival and had therefore strong historical links with the rise of Methodism. Winston Churchhill was the current Chancellor of its university. It had recently opened a Department of Theology and a few years later established its own chair for this.

In pursuance of my theological studies at the university, I had returned to the old Bible Churchman's Missionary and Theological College, which now had a new name – Tyndale Hall.[1] This name seemed very appropriate because the English Reformer and early Bible translator William Tyndale (1494–1536) had been born in the West of England. However, this new name did not mean that the college was severing its links with the Bible Churchman's Missionary Society. It was still identified with the original rift from the Church Missionary Society in 1922 over the issue of biblical authority and remained as a rallying point for 'true Scriptural evangelicalism at home and abroad'.

Its new Principal John Stafford Wright (known to us as 'Staffy'), a recognised Old Testament scholar, had just been appointed. Always very approachable, surprisingly broadminded and a convinced evangelical, he was a well-read man, with wide interests that included speleology and psychic phenomena!

It was a great privilege to sit under the staff at Trinity most of whom were university lecturers also. They developed in me a true love of wholesome biblical theology and the place of prayer. But what I did not realise at the time, was that their model for our future ministry was that of the academic teacher. Though I loved Tyndale, I left with this unrealistic, even unconscious mental picture of the kind of men and women God wanted in the parishes. My ideal rector was an outstanding academic like John Stott at All Souls, Langham Place, London. My model for evangelism was Billy Graham, who made thousands into new converts to Christ – but his methods were far removed from anything the ordinary members of the church could in any way replicate. But there had to be other models for parish ministry and evangelism if the church was going to survive – but what were they?

Furthermore, I don't think we were given sufficient awareness and teaching on the significance of the kingdom of heaven – God's great master plan and ultimate reality for life. We still understood little of the implications of cultural barriers in communicating the good news, and we left with no models for alternative ways of 'doing church'.

We still had limited understanding of local church infrastructures, church growth, church planting, or any ideas about alternative ecclesiologies. Nor was there practical guidance on how to 'equip the saints for the work of the ministry' beyond giving the lay folk Bible studies to lead. We had no clear concepts of whatever those ministries might be. We knew how to involve them in dusting pews, handing out hymn books and serving tea!

We have insufficient teaching on the dynamic invasive presence of the Holy Spirit in the local church today, of the place of apostleship (in the sense of anointed leadership), or of prophecy (in the sense of hearing what the Spirit might be saying to individuals and the churches). Lack of training in all these areas became acutely relevant to me later in my ministry. I finished my years at Bristol with an almost blind loyalty to the Church of England, and it never occurred to me to question the training I had received or the Church in which I received it but in reality, there was something seriously wrong. Not only has the church in the UK not grown over the last fifty years, but attendance at most churches has been rapidly declining. Only 2% of the population attend the Church of England today.

SERIOUS GIRLFRIEND

Whilst reading theology at university I joined the Christian Union, where I got to know my first real girlfriend. Life could never be the same again. She was a very pretty medic and I found myself making excuses to be 'accidentally' wherever she might be. But there was an underlying problem. Her training could take seven years. Then she failed her first year (probably my fault?), and the year had to be repeated. One day she told me of a dream she had about us. Was it prophetic or wishful thinking? We were on the mission field in the heart of Africa and in her dream she was operating on a patient in a primitive mud-hut. I was standing beside her holding the lamp! A noble romantic picture of humble service to humanity and I should have been pleased, but I felt uneasy with this perception of my role. It was the first serious hint that our friendship was heading for trouble – a warning I could not shake off, but which I painfully refused to take seriously simply because I did not want to give her up. But she was a gift I could not keep. Separations of that sort are always heartbreaking. I loved her but I could not have her! I believed at the time that one could never fall in love like that again.

NO ROOM AT THE INN

The end of that beautiful friendship coincided with my father's death in 1953. For the last three years or so, father had lived in Ipswich.

Actually I had to prompt him into his retirement. I cringe today to think of my cheek!

Father's going was the end of a family home for Peter and myself. There could be problems over vacations. With no real home base, deciding where to go for Christmas could be difficult. Different family members invited me but I was usually pretty penniless, and could hardly afford presents all round, let alone any significant contribution to the usual good fare. Besides one felt slightly intrusive. One year (1954) I had spotted a special deal offering a £50 cheap rate student trip to Israel for two weeks. Being over the Christmas period, this was ideal for me. With £10 in my pocket, I set off by train, ferry, and train again to Paris and Marseilles. Then picking up the boat to cross the Mediterranean we finally arrived at Haifa. We had a great party of Argentinian Israelis on board and they entertained us en route with some typical Israeli music and dancing. Entering Haifa was a great experience as I watched the young Jews catching their first glimpse of Eretz Israel – the Land of Israel – their future homeland. On arrival we found the country unbelievably barren with the wrecks of armoured cars everywhere. The Israelis had established kibbutzim (communities with everything in common) where we stayed as we moved from place to place. They had exciting programmes for developing the land and had already planted over 6,000,000 trees – one for each victim of the World War Two holocaust.

THEY THOUGHT THAT HITLER WAS A CHRISTIAN?

It was there that I first met widespread resentment against Christians. My new Jewish friends believed that Hitler had once been a Catholic and the Pope had not done nearly enough to help the Jews in the war! One certainly finds out how other people are thinking (rightly or wrongly) when one goes abroad! I was surprised by the country's size when I got there; no bigger than Wales. I thought the experience of Chrismas Eve in Bethlehem, on the Palestinian side, would be like a dream come true, but the church built over the cave, and the cave itself, rather shocked my pious fantasies. The city of Jerusalem was still divided into two, which made moving around complicated. It was worrying seeing

75

opposing forces, armed to the teeth, facing each other across the streets in the capital. I have been back several times since and it is quite wonderful to see how the whole country has been transformed. The fir trees, first seen as skimpy ferns, have grown up into forests on the mountain sides and this has even changed the climate. Swamps have been successfully dried out by the planting of eucalyptus trees. A visit to the Holy Land is as good as reading for a university degree – a totally revolutionary experience.

GETTING TO KNOW SAMS

At Tyndale I became involved in leading the college prayer meeting once a term, when the topic was South America. This came about in a rather surprising way; it was something I would never have normally undertaken. We once had a Quiet Day at Tyndale directed by Arthur Goodwin Hudson – a one-time chaplain of St Andrew's Church, Santiago, in Chile, South America, who was currently the General Secretary of the South American Missionary Society. Bemused by his pronunciation of particular words I used to mimic him in front of my friends. One little admonition I remembered – which I grossly exaggerated in its repeating – was addressed to any who thought when they left college that 'they would don seven league boots and make it all the way to Canterbury'. Since there was probably not a single student who had ever imagined such a thing, it seemed good to make a joke out of the idea. Any thought of a career structure in the Church of England was a concept completely foreign to the kind of servant ministry we felt we were being called to. In any case 'evangelicals' were distinctly out of favour amongst the church hierarchy and to date no one from Tyndale had ever been consecrated a bishop anywhere in the world. (Strangely, Goodwin Hudson himself was probably one of the first when he was called to be an adjutant to the Archbishop in Sydney, Australia!)

To my great surprise, the Senior Student, David Woods, asked me to take on responsibility for the South American prayer meeting at college due to my great 'interest' in Goodwin Hudson, the General Secretary of SAMS! This in no way committed me to sign up for actual missionary service abroad, but I found out all I could about the prayer needs of SAMS. After some general patter I began to grapple with a list of specific prayer requests gathered from some of the missionaries on the field. I was surprised by how nervous I felt – but then there were so many gaps in my real knowledge of what was going on out there.

First of all, there was a new missionary in Chile, Muriel Parrott, who was having difficulty with the language. The students all seemed to think that was a huge joke! The next request for prayer was for the Rev Mr Leake having problems with some baptisms in the Argentine Chaco. This was a fairly normal sort of request I thought, but now the room was convulsed. I like a good laugh but I did not think this was quite the right time and place for so much hilarity. Having quietened them down a bit I trotted out the next request: Mr Train needed prayer as he was moving to a new station! Well, by this time the place simply exploded. How could I say all this whilst keeping such a straight face, they wondered? But I was not trying to be funny. In fact I had never tried so hard to be serious. My friends were rolling on the floor. I was looking out over a scene of absolute disaster! I left the meeting utterly depressed. I'd give it just one final go and then pack it in.

When my turn came round again to lead a prayer meeting for SAMS, it was unbelievable – the place was packed out and every chair was taken. People were sitting on the floor – even up on the window sills. Soon after this I was approached by the missionary secretary of the University Christian Union and asked to take on their South America prayer meeting also. I don't know how effective I was in getting South America across to the pray-ers but a lot of South America was getting across to me personally. God has strange ways of working.

GOOD FRIENDS
My roommate next door was Hector H. Huxham; a very caring person who was to spend the major part of his life's ministry as a hospital chaplain. He had a delightfully droll sense of humour.

Michael Saward, another fellow student, was a real character; he actually came to college wearing a bowler hat. Unusual and outrageous people have always intrigued me – especially when they were gifted as well. Another friend was Roger Beckwith, an Oxford graduate (since then earning a Lambeth DD). His bed was usually so covered with the books he was studying that he often chose to sleep on the floor rather than disturb them! Yet another friend was Roy Rimmer who was to be the best man at our wedding. He had been a paratrooper in the Army and after training at Cambridge and Tyndale had a spell in Norway with the Navigators. Following that he served very effectively in London and East Anglian parishes.

There were many other unforgettable characters, which of course is one of the great benefits of college life. Two or three medical doctors were also in training with us, destined for various parts of the mission field. Patients in college needing medical attention had the rare satisfaction of doctors lining up for the privilege of attending to them!

During my third year at Tyndale Hall, my brother Peter suddenly appeared, disillusioned with his studies in engineering at University College, London and now thinking about a call to the ordained ministry. He had recently had rather a sudden and dramatic spiritual experience that caused him to turn back to Christ. I had given him a little pocket New Testament before he went into the Army. When he was in London later he came across the words in it, where Jesus had said: 'Whosoever therefore shall confess me before men, him will I confess also before my Father which is in heaven. But whosoever shall deny me before men, him will I also deny before my Father which is in heaven'.[2] He had served eighteen months in the Army and realised that he had never publicly owned the Christ he had known about from infancy.

After prayer, following ordination, I felt led to challenge my eldest brother Jack to consider ordination too. A year later Jack joined the student body at Tyndale where Peter, his youngest brother by fifteen years, was soon to become the Senior Student. Father would have been so pleased.

Chapter 6

I TURNED MY COLLAR ROUND

*'The sheep look up and are no longer fed' is not so. Today 'the sheep are
fed up and are no longer looking'*
(WITH APOLOGIES TO BISHOP MICHAEL MARSHALL)

*All the holy men seem to have gone off and died. There's no
one left but us sinners to carry on the ministry*
(JAMIE BUCKINGHAM)

Years before theological colleges were invented, one took a degree
at university and was expected to learn about the 'cure of souls' as
a curate. Getting the first curacy[1] right was considered very
important. The ideal was to go to a good vicar for one's first title
and to the parish that offered the most experience for the second.
Some men served three curacies. Now they often serve only one.
I had been impressed by the Rev Basil Gough when he had
directed a Quiet Day at Tyndale earlier. Michael Farrer, a friend
from Tyndale, went off to serve his first title under him at St
Ebbe's, Oxford.[2]

The parish covered the most run-down area of Oxford – but
the church was packed out Sunday by Sunday with
undergraduates. It also had an eclectic gathering from across the
city. Basil Gough needed a second curate to help at St Ebbe's.
Michael Farrer was to be the 'gown' curate to attend to the
undergraduates, and the new curate would be the 'town' curate to
care for the parish.

CITY OF TOWERS AND SPIRES
I felt very honoured to go to St Ebbe's Church. Basil, the rector,
and Stella his wife[3] were very considerate people to work with.
Basil loved his ministry to the young undergraduates. He wanted

these undergrads to know enough about the gospel to let it radically change their lives and the lives of others through them. He used to say 'If a man has no convictions at twenty he will have nothing at forty!' He believed that while he would ever be ineffective in trying to do the work of ten men (the kind of reputation previous St Ebbe's rectors had had) he could aim to train ten men to do their work effectively. I think he achieved his goal.

Oxford University, being founded in the early thirteenth century, the city of 'towers and spires' certainly had its major attractions for me – not to mention its fascinating history associated with the fourteenth-century philosopher and reformer John Wycliffe, the Bible translator William Tyndale, the martyrs Bishops Hugh Latimer, Nicolas Ridley and Archbishop Thomas Cranmer.[4] Then there was John Wesley, the dedicated and disciplined revivalist[5] and his hymn-writing brother Charles, who had been educated at Christ Church at the same time as that wonderful preacher George Whitefield was at Pembroke College (across the road from Christ Church). They started the Methodist Club whilst there – a movement that eventually gave its name to the Methodist Church.

I was also intrigued by John Henry Newman – the evangelical turned Catholic, who had been the rector of St Mary the Virgin[6] where, with his unusually attractive voice, he had delivered some of his most famous sermons. He also authored hymns like *Lead Kindly Light* – expressing a prayer which in his case led him to Rome. And C.S. Lewis was at Magdalene College in our time. There was no end to men of past and present distinction who have shaped our culture and church history.

The final personal interest in Oxford for me was the fact that my grandfather, Charles E. Welldon, had graduated from Keble College and had captained the University tennis team against Cambridge University – the latter being captained by his twin brother.[7]

THE NERVOUS BISHOP!

Having been offered a title at St Ebbe's, my next priority was to meet Harry Carpenter, the new Bishop of Oxford. I was the first to see him about ordination. He had recently been Warden of Keble College and was an Anglo-Catholic in the tradition of Kenneth Kirk but not nearly so extreme![8] I was not sure who was the most nervous at our meeting – myself or Bishop Harry.

The stole was a liturgical vestment consisting of a long narrow strip of woven silk. Stoles had always been worn for ordinations during Kirk's time and an exception in my case would be a break with tradition at Christ Church Cathedral and it seemed nothing less than folly to attempt breaking with tradition at a place like Oxford. Without wishing to make a big fuss I really did not want to wear one on being made a deacon – especially as one was not legally obliged to do so. I understood that the stole was still the one thing a Roman Catholic bishop stripped from a priest if he were ever defrocked. I certainly did not view the ordained 'priesthood' according to the more prevalent views held by the greater part of the Church of England – especially in Catholic quarters. So being excused the wearing of the stole was asking for something rather difficult of my bishop. Dr Carpenter was obviously anxious, fearing I might be stirring up some kind of trouble for him if he exempted me. He wanted to know if I had been put up to this in any way by my college, my Principal or by Basil Gough. I assured him it was entirely my own initiative.

He eventually resolved the issue by sending me down to Bishopscourt, in Rochester, to be made deacon by a doughty old evangelical stalwart, Dr Christopher Chavasse. Chavasse had been a former rector of St Aldate's, Oxford.

The next year Bishop Carpenter graciously agreed to ordain me 'priest' in the cathedral without a stole – this was apparently a first after many a long year. During the service I heard some desperate whisperings going on behind me, ending in the words '. . . no stole' followed by further hushed mumblings terminating with the name St Ebbe's. St Ebbe's was regarded as 'low church' – the lowest of the low in Oxford – and mention of it seemed to explain my eccentricities!

PONCING ABOUT IN FANCY DRESS

Ritual certainly has its genuine place but I myself have always been wary of too much of it. I like things done 'decently and in order' but so often rituals can degenerate into fussy 'power dressing' making the Christian's personal walk with God seem artificial. Also ritual can so easily become theatre, magical, unreal or just an act preoccupied over the outward form of things. Prime Minister David Lloyd George, certainly not renowned for spirituality himself, disliked the ritualists of his day and called their religion 'salvation by haberdashery'![9]

Archbishop Robert Runcie is said to have told a reporter that his wife refused to follow him round the diocese of St Albans with the children, when he was bishop there, because, as she said: 'It's not good for them to see their father poncing about in fancy vestments and being worshipped by the locals, so I shall take them off to the Abbey instead!'

One bishop travelling on a train 'in mufti' recently, was asked by a woman with whom he was chatting what his work was? He pointed to the episcopal ring on his right hand: 'Does this give you a clue?' he asked. 'Oh!' she said, 'You must be gay!'

I rather shunned the idea of an 'enthronement' when later I became a diocesan bishop – it seemed so far removed from the language and example of the Gospels.

PRIVILEGE WITH LIMITATIONS

In a way, once I settled in, St Ebbe's was a much more limiting place than I had imagined. Basil's example, care and training were excellent. He always insisted that his staff were in church a half-hour before every service, giving plenty of time to deal with last minute emergencies – and ready to lead the worship in a unhurried quiet spirit – something I have never forgotten. He also insisted that his staff spent as many mornings as possible in the study – reading, preparing talks and praying. My job was to visit the sick and the lonely (as directed by Basil) and to help with the Church Youth Fellowship. This was run by a small committee under the creative leadership of an Oxford graduate, Dr John Webb,[10] a young atomic scientist then working at Harwell nearby. He was also an accomplished musician who later played the organ at our wedding.

The other part of my job was to work among the remaining inhabitants of an area centred round Paradise Square. These people felt very unsettled as their homes were in the processes of slum clearance. I have to confess that I felt very inadequate and utterly devoid of imagination as to how to tackle such a depressing challenge. It was also humbling to realise that I had absolutely no idea of how to communicate with such streetwise kids. The excuse for never coming near the church of 'the blessed St Ebba' was that it had been taken over by those 'snooty' university people. They were not in fact snooty and without them the church would have been declared obsolete some twenty years previously. But our locals considered the ethos there totally irrelevant for them. I recognise now, of course, that it really was so, but then I was still blinded by my loyalty to our ancient traditions.

MY CONTRIBUTION

I learned many useful lessons while at St Ebbe's. I arrived rather intoxicated with the discovery of theology, and, rather fixed in that academic mode, I had lost something of the heart of the faith – the pure adoration of God. I was brought up with a jolt by a neighbouring curate from St Clement's, Pat Ryley, giving a talk to our young people. He took the words King David had heard from God – 'When thou saidst, Seek ye my face; my heart said unto thee, Thy face, Lord, will I seek'.[11] It helped me to understand a little better what Archbishop William Temple meant when he said he never began to pray without first picturing Jesus standing before him.

Possibly my only useful contribution at St Ebbe's was to pioneer their church bookstall. It was Basil's idea. I remember going to a local Christian bookshop in St Clement's parish, and suggesting that they let me select a number of books from their shelves to take back with me to St Ebbe's (without paying for them). I asssured them they would be displayed at the back of the church and any purchasers could deposit the cash for it in a clearly marked wallsafe by the door. Each time I returned to St Clement's bookshop I would pay for any books sold and collect some more. The manager was initially aghast at the idea but later he saw the possibilities. The plan went well. If this wasn't the very first experiment in actually selling books in an Anglican Church, supplied that way from a local bookshop, it was certainly one of the earliest. It was 1955. Later sales became so good that eventually they set up a whole new Christian bookshop beside St Ebbe's church.

THE UNDERLYING PROBLEM

The unspoken question was, how on earth would anyone ever reach the local folk in the parish let alone persuade them to come into our church for worship? Loyalty to my denomination, my college and my rector meant that I still could not begin to question our traditional ways of 'doing church'. It was a problem I was going to face again and again during the early years of my ordained ministry. Our failure to impact the remaining unchurched in the parish was more than outweighed by the incredible buzz of eclectic life among the undergrads at St Ebbe's. This was the result of the very successful ministry there by Basil and Stella Gough with Mike and Annette Farrer. But I also sensed that probably neither Basil Gough nor Michael Farrer had many real answers for my side of the work.

Our local residents seemed much less concerned about their spiritual welfare that they were about the abolition of their community. The powers-that-be had decided they must all be rehoused in menacing high rise buildings on the edge of Oxford. They were obviously finding it difficult to evaluate the promise of better constructions (internal plumbing and electricity) against the prospect of losing their much valued neighbourhood network. I seemed powerless to help them over this major issue though I felt inwardly outraged on their behalf. The very idea of anyone having to live in those high rise buildings depressed me.

TOWN NOT GOWN

If anyone asked what was being done about the parish side of the work it could always be said that the Church had a 'town' curate for this – me!

There had been a question, before I came, about whether someone with a 'red-brick' university degree (like mine from Bristol) would be really suitable in an Oxford church? Actually someone doing my job would have probably been better equipped if he had been older and had no degree at all, and simply knew how to get alongside those still left in that doomed and decimating parish. Such a man would probably have had more ideas than many a university graduate!

St Ebbe's was the favoured church for the OICCU[12] and also for the 'Bash' campers. 'Bash' was the nickname for the Rev E.J. Nash, who was a Scripture Union staff member with a vision for Christian camps etc for boys from the top public schools in Britain. St Ebbe's was also a strategic centre for evangelicals. I remember how the first meeting for evangelical leaders ministering in university cities was held at St Ebbe's Rectory in 1956. This elite group came together under the brilliant chairmanship of John Stott. It was also the local planning centre for the Oxford Evangelical Research Trust, to be called 'Latimer House', and to be based at 131 Banbury Road, near Wycliffe Hall.

Once a term, Basil used to organise teas at the Rectory for potential ordinands, and these were followed by endless interviews with these young men about preparing for their future in the ministry of the church. Basil was in great demand for godly counsel. Many undergraduates from St Ebbe's were later ordained, and have become significant church leaders, parish clergy, college principals, deans and bishops etc both at home and abroad. One of those undergrads who later joined the staff at St Ebbe's was Pat Harris. He became a bishop in the Argentine Chaco and then for nearly ten years was the Bishop of Southwell back in the UK. Two other bishops were Colin Bazley who has been my successor as Bishop of Chile for the last twenty years or so, and also Colin Buchanan, who used to pack a second-hand hearse with undergrads and bring them to St Ebbe's on Sunday mornings.

Colin tried to persuade me to go to his home church for my second curacy. I was flattered but did not feel called. He was later to become, for many years, the Principal of St John's College, Nottingham, and later still, a bishop in both the dioceses of Birmingham and Southwark.

While at St Ebbe's I fell in love again with a really beautiful girl, the daughter of former missionaries who had served in Egypt. She worshipped regularly at St Ebbe's in the term time. Basil did not like his curates to be seen going out with girls unless the relationship was serious. With these good intentions I made the mistake of becoming engaged to be married, before we had really got to know each other sufficiently well. After a while I began to realise it was not going to work, and the engagement had to be broken off. There is no way this sort of thing could be done painlessly. I have worried about her for the rest of my life. How often one would like to start one's days all over again and do things properly – without ever hurting others in the process!

During my third year, my old Tyndale friend Peter Dawes who was finishing his first curacy in London, was invited to replace Michael as the 'gown' curate. I like to think I was able to persuade Basil a little in favour of appointing him. Peter was another friend who eventually became a bishop.

At Oxford, we were blessed with many gifted preachers in the pulpit and I noticed some of them seemed to enhance their presentation with very delightful smiles. A young curate is always trying to improve his technique in the pulpit and I thought perhaps I should pratise preaching with a smile too, so I tried it. But only once! Someone kindly came up afterwards and asked me if I was ill! I decided it was safer to revert to my usual grim pulpit look.

STILL RESISTING THE IDEA

Basil Gough wanted God's very best for all his curates. He had always felt bad that he had never made it to the mission field himself (it would never have been his true calling anyhow), but he frequently challenged others to be praying about it for themselves. He would keep asking me what I thought my next step should be? Rectors have to be thinking ahead about their curate's replacement! But I was still keeping my options open about the mission field at that stage.

I really did not want to go to work in another language in another culture wherever that might be. With my fair skin I could not cope with a lot of hot sun and there did not seem to be many places for missionaries where the sun did not shine fiercely. And I had struggled with several languages – Latin, French, Hebrew and Greek – and knew I would never be a linguist. I so identified with the young man P.G. Wodehouse described in Cannes 'into whose face had crept a look of furtive shame, the shifty hangdog look which announces that an Englishman is about to talk French'.

But I was sensing increasingly that if I was open to seeking God's will (as I had promised the Lord that I was), then if the first class folk would not step forward, the third class guys must be ready and willing to fill the gap – just in case!

Two events occurred in 1956 that had a wide impact on the English scene. One was the attack on Egypt when her President, Nasser suddenly nationalised the Suez Canal.[13] This attack was ordered by Prime Minister Anthony Eden.[14] Then, with the public outcry from the rest of the world and the lack of any support (indeed opposition) from America the British had to climb down, and Anthony Eden resigned. Suddenly one felt a little less secure about one's place in the world. The Empire had lost its grip.

Then we had a publication by John Osborne that everyone seemed to be raving about, called *Look Back in Anger*. It was all part of a significant turning point in our English culture, but I felt no enthusiasm to read it. Personally I felt no anger at all about the past – indeed I was very proud of England's 'good old days'.

INTRODUCING MARY

The secretary of the Young People's Fellowship at St Ebbe's when I arrived was a very friendly girl named Mary Trevisick who came from North Devon. She had been educated at West Bank, a school for young ladies in nearby Bideford, but the headmistress had finally decided it was time for Mary to leave (aged sixteen) after, amongst other things, being caught streaking round the college for a dare! Mary had come up to Oxford to train at a rather snobbish secretarial college known as 'Miss Sprooles' and had lodged, at first, with her sister Ruby, whose husband had a job with the University Chest. Once qualified, Mary found work in Oxford, and a friend took her along to St Ebbe's where she soon became a committed Christian. She then became the secretary for the YPF. She had a great gift for getting alongside newcomers and making them feel welcome – something many other young people seemed to find quite difficult, but something that is really important for making a fellowship friendly. Although

Mary was very easy to talk to I had no thoughts of making a serious date with her as she seemed far too argumentative! She actually questioned things that were done in church, which to her, as a comparative newcomer, seemed very strange, quite off-putting and unnecessary. To me they were sacrosanct traditions beyond question! How could she be so presumptuous?

It was nearly two years later that I began to realise that Mary was someone I was just naturally choosing to be with – and I began to think that we could easily become more than 'just good friends'. Having made one serious mistake at St Ebbe's, I had not consciously given Mary any hint about how I was beginning to feel. I really did not want to mislead her, and was determined to prevent any growing sentiments I might have, to keep me from God's will – if perhaps he had someone else in mind for me. I had once asked Mary what she thought about going to the mission field and was secretly relieved when she said that she would go, if God called her, but she rather hoped God wouldn't – an honest expression of feelings which corresponded exactly with my own. I always believed missionary work was very important but when ever I heard a hint of a call, my response was the typical one 'Lord, here am I – send my sister!'

A SLIGHTLY UNUSUAL PROPOSAL

I moved from my 'digs' near Folly Bridge to a flat – the top floor of Holy Trinity House (the former Rectory of Holy Trinity Church) and very conveniently about 100 yards from St Ebbe's. It was springtime – the time 'when a young man's fancy lightly turns to thoughts of love'.[15]

I was more and more attracted to Mary but nervous about how to broach the subject of marriage – bearing in mind my previous premature engagement. With no premeditated plan of action I asked her if she would like to help me choose some saucepans for my new home. She agreed. On entering an ironmongers, we were approached by a polite salesman who enquired if he could help us in any way. I said simply: 'Yes – have you any saucepans please?' He led us to some samples.

'How do I decide which I should buy?' I asked him.

'Well!' he replied, 'How many are there in the family, sir?'

In a flash I simply turned to Mary and said: 'How many would you like?'

Slightly shaken Mary smiled: 'Oh, I should think a dozen would be all right!'

'OK,' I replied, and we bought the largest set!

As I said it, I knew that I really meant what could have been implied by the question. It had obviously been inconsiderate of me to veil a proposal in that way – and she has never let me forget it. But before I could ask for her father's permission to marry I had to have some idea about how she might be feeling herself and the 'saucepan affair' gave me a good clue! With his permission, I proposed to her properly soon after in a leafy lane running beside Codden Hill above her home in Bishopstawton, Barnstaple, followed by a prayer for God's blessing on our future life together.

Mary decided she should spend the next six months at Dalton House, Bristol – the Bible Churchman's Missionary College for women. She paid for this out of her limited savings. Two terms could just be fitted in before we were to be married in January the following year. It would give her the opportunity to get some good Bible teaching, and just in case – learn some tips about life and work on the mission field.

I was twenty-seven and Mary twenty-two when we married. Our wedding day, on 8th January 1958, turned out to be a freezing cold one. After the wedding, we enjoyed a luxurious honeymoon in the Royal Bath Hotel, Bournemouth, paid for by my ever-generous mother-in-law.

MARY'S ORDINATION!

Back in Oxford, at a reception party put on by the young people, Basil solemnly announced that our marriage was Mary's ordination to the ministry of the church. This sent cold shivers down her spine – just as well he had never mentioned it before she had married me! But, in fact, it turned out to be true! Basil was still urging us to be prayerfully considering the mission field and we finally knocked on the door of BCMS. They said that if we felt it right to proceed further, Mary would be required to go back to college and complete the course which, they presumed, she had rashly abandoned for the sake of our marriage. When that was done we could re-apply. But with no clear sign we sensed we had come to the end of the road about missionary work.[16] Wilfred Stott, a veteran missionary who had interviewed us kindly wrote us a personal note hoping we would not be put off by this setback as he was sure we were destined for the overseas mission field somewhere! We appreciated the encouraging spirit in which it was written but regretted that it still left the question of the mission field open just when we had hoped the door was really closing.

WHAT ABOUT SAMS?

Soon after the BCMS interviews we were encourged by Basil Gough to attend a SAMS conference in London. An elderly clergyman there named Anderson gave some simple but inspired Bible readings each day from the Psalms. I sensed the Lord speaking to me as I underlined a verse highlighted by the talk: 'Ask of me, and I shall give thee the heathen for thine inheritance, and the uttermost parts of the earth for thy possession.[17] Rather reluctantly, I did, and we applied to SAMS. They wanted us to go out immediately to the Argentine Chaco to minister the sacraments to three tribes that had no priest. Almost subliminally I registered my first query about Anglican Church missionary practice. Something must be artificial about a system where national Christians could still not break bread together regularly under their own leadership. I realised that though I had a high view of the sacrament, I had long had a lesser view of the priesthood. I believed the sacrament was something for Christian believers to celebrate frequently as a God-given means of grace. Why had the Chaco not got their own priests after all those years of missionary work?

If the elders were not well enough educated, or in good enough standing for ordination, perhaps we were looking for the wrong kind of priests or even superimposing the wrong kind of church structure and order? I did not realise then that I was touching the nerve of what, for me, was a fundamental problem about the relevance of some of our inflexible Anglican traditions and attitudes for missionary situations. We had been tending to export this problem all over the world for years and yet continued to maintain such an anomalous position. We were supposed to be a church that highly valued the Holy Communion but our organisation seemed to inhibit its members from having the bread and wine.

Twenty years later Professor Andrew Walls from Edinburgh University,[18] made the same observation from his wider research in Africa: 'Mission Churches, Catholic and Protestant have insisted on the practice of their countries of origin, that only a priest or minister is permitted to officiate at the sacrament – and they never have enough of these to make sacramental worship more than a periodic experience for most African Christians'.[19]

SUPPRESSING THE UNTHINKABLE

I suppressed my ideas as unthinkable; their implications were far too radical. Our traditions must be sacrosanct. After all, they enshrined the good, the wise and the orthodox. I needed them as a cradle for my spiritual security; a framework for my ecclesiastical identity – and our traditional doctrinal orthodoxy was my litmus test for heresy. To criticise something so fundamental would seem like shooting myself, not in the foot, but in my soul. I had not appreciated that tradition, like the curate's egg, is only good in parts. I had yet to read Cyprian, a third-century theologian, who had once said 'Ancient tradition can just be an old mistake'! It would have been helpful to have known that.

So I simply said to SAMS that I did not think that being a mass-priest was quite my style. I added rather reluctantly that I was still open to anything else that might come up – hoping of course that nothing would. I'd done my duty. I had applied to two missionary societies. We relaxed and looked forward to settling into parish work in the UK.

We had two tempting offers for second curacies. One was from Llewellyn Roberts[20] who wanted me to take over a daughter church in the parish of New Malden where he was then rector. He explained that the daughter church had not seen enough of their rector and, if we went, I would be needed to preach in the parish church and he would seek to put that right and come to the daughter church fairly regularly: 'We would ring the changes!' I was intrigued by all that 'ringing the changes' might involve. But I felt I was really about ready to take charge of something myself.

Such an offer came from Canon Frank Colquhoun, at Holy Trinity, Wallington, not far from New Malden in the same diocese of Southwark. We both liked him and I certainly felt I would have a lot to learn from him. He offered us more than double the pay that we had been receiving at St Ebbe's,[21] plus a few other useful perks. We were to take charge of the daughter church of St Patrick's. He said he hoped we would be willing to stay for several years because a church like St Patrick's needed that to give it stability. We felt very privileged to be invited and hoped we would not disappoint his trust in us.

OH NO! SO SOON!

However I did made it clear in my acceptance, that, though humanly speaking, we would love to come, and we would also love to give the longer commitment, we had an even higher level of commitment to the Lord. We had assured SAMS that if ever a call came to do something in South America that we felt could be 'us', we would do all we could to make ourselves available. In spite of all that, Frank still said 'Yes – come!' and we settled in very happily for the long haul.

There was a very striking old lady at St Patrick's called Mrs Kimpton, a most respected member of our congregation. She used to hold sewing parties for an annual sale for SAMS in her house, and she was delighted by our interest in the South American Missionary Society. Her younger son, Colonel Tony Kimpton, was the SAMS' treasurer.

We had been at Wallington only about three months when the phone rang. It was Tony Kimpton who told us that there was now a place in Chile and asked us if we would consider going out there? I admit my heart sank but I explained that we were still open to considering it. However there would have to be a little delay as Mary was expecting our first baby. And as far as our obligations to the parish were concerned – I suggested he should try and sort it out with his old friend Frank Colquhoun, our rector.

We went to see the SAMS General Secretary, Arthur

Goodwin Hudson. He greeted us warmly and eulogised about Chile, where he had once been a chaplain, and told us of all the wonderful mountain scenery and lovely fruit there – peaches, grapes and melons! Strangely I found it quite turned me off. If we were going to make a sacrifice let it be a proper one! I'd forgotten that God had also promised the children of Israel 'milk and honey'!

They wanted me to go and teach in their Bible Institute in Quepe, so it was agreed that we would go to Chile after the baby had arrived. But in the end we never went to head up the Bible Institute at Quepe at all – situations change fast on the mission field. We were engaged to pioneer church planting in the urban environment of Valparaíso, Chile.

Basil Gough was delighted to know we were going at last to the mission field.

PREMATURE BABY
Our first baby came early on the 24th of December 1958. I was present at the birth. She was put in the premature unit for a month or so. It is a most unnatural feeling – being unable to embrace one's baby because she is stuffed with tubes and encased in a perspex bubble. Next morning in church, I proudly announced that my first Christmas present had arrived early, weighing four and a half pounds, and already unwrapped when I got it! Mary also had to stay in hospital to bring her hypertension down. I longed to get them both home. People rallied round, gave us presents that were greatly appreciated and readily offered any meals if I needed them. During the next ten days I had twelve Christmas dinners at twelve different tables! I've never really enjoyed turkey since then!

It's amazing to discover how much one loves one's children. I found I loved all four of mine so much and would often tell each one privately that she was very special to us. This clearly delighted them enormously, but I told them not to tell the others which of course they did. I am sure that God thinks each of his children is special.

UNFINISHED HISTORY
A golden jubilee publication of St Patrick's even included a brief

reference to our very short time there, recording touchingly that:

> David Pytches accepted the appointment at St Patrick's on
> the understanding that he had offered his services with the
> South American Missionary Society, and would be released
> when the way opened up for him to go out. In the event the
> call came much earlier than anyone expected; and David
> with his wife Mary and their daughter Charlotte (the first
> of four) left in the summer of 1959 after a bare year at St
> Patrick's – but not before they had made a host of friends
> and stamped their personalities on St Patrick's as clearly as
> they were to do in so many churches in South America.[22]

We have been very proud to be associated with such a wonderful
church that gave us tremendous support over so many years
whilst we were serving overseas.

Chapter 7

RELUCTANT MISSIONARIES

A true missionary is God's man in God's place, doing
God's work in God's way for God's glory
(ANON)

I knew immediately when I had reached the North Pole,
because in one step the north wind became a south wind
(ROBERT PEARY)

Come on Tuesday night at 7.30 and hear Bertha Belch
all the way from Africa
(ANNOUNCEMENT IN CHURCH)

Thoughts of the mission field still filled me with awe. How would I ever get over home sickness when missionary work meant so many years between leave? Tear-jerking pictures of the young John G. Paton came to mind, setting off for the New Hebrides in the mid eighteenth century – a gripping saga of self sacrifice and life-long service to God.[1]

Through Gates of Splendour,[2] just then published was the account of five North American missionaries trying to reach a remnant of some 600 Aucas in the forests of Ecuador, one of the world's fiercest tribes still unevangelised. These missionaries had spent months befriending a small group spotted fishing in the river. They 'prepared' them with presents of combs, fishhooks and other hunting equipment that they had lowered to them from the air. Finally they landed their plane on the same beach[3] where they had previously dropped the gifts – only to be brutally massacred. Whatever one might think of their strategy I was greatly challenged by their bravery. Some people obviously still took God seriously! Their story was never far out of my mind. One of the martyrs, Jim Elliot, had written: 'He is no fool who gives what he cannot keep to gain what he cannot lose'. Of course, I could not really compare the steaming jungle of Ecuador full of awesome Aucas with the pacified Araucanians in Chile, where SAMS missionaries had been working for years. But would I ever be courageous enough in any way to put my own life or Mary's, or Charlotte's in jeopardy as those men had done to reach the Aucas?

But courage is resistance to fear – not the absence of it. Lack of courage should not excuse one from the call of God. However, when the call actually came I had fought it – feeling I would not really have the nerve to make what might possibly be a life-long break with England.

We left for Chile in the autumn of 1959. It was goodbye to family and friends – and for how long? Would it be forever? Harold Macmillan, consummate actor and cunning politician that he was, was still holding the reigns of Government, and boasting that we'd never had it so good in Britain. Prospects in Latin America, a land renowned for revolutions, did not seem nearly so good. I had pictures of the Russian revolution, but it was not till we arrived that we discovered most revolutions were usually less dramatic than that.

Unbeknown to us, a major revolution was in fact lurking beneath the surface in Chile, as we would one day discover – but not till thirteen years later.

GREAT SUPPORTERS

Wallington had given us a tremendous send off. We probably did more good by leaving St Patrick's than we could ever have done by staying. The church folk became great supporters of mission. At the time they had only one overseas missionary – an elderly lady working with CMS Rwanda and soon due for retirement. Our departure seemed to trigger off quite a chain of new missionaries setting off later from Wallington for different parts of the world. We take no credit for that – it was the Lord's doing.

Whenever we returned on leave, Wallington always found us a house to live in, so it was just great to feel we belonged there still. When our eldest teenage girls came back to the UK for educational reasons, Vernon and Jean Hedderly[4] readily undertook to be their guardians for us, and we could not have had better. The girls went to Mary's parents in Devon for parts of those holidays except when they were due to fly back to Chile – which was planned for once a year.

DID I LOVE THE CHILEANS?

People asked us, as we left, if we had a love for the Chileans. We had to admit that we had not. To my knowledge I had never met a single Chilean in my life. How can one 'feel' love for people one doesn't know? It was not our love for Chileans but our love and commitment to God that compelled us. We were going to Chile to work with an old college friend, Tony Barratt. Inwardly, I still had very little faith that we could ever be much use working in another language when I had found languages so difficult. Going to Chile just seemed as though God was calling us to 'get lost' and 'die'. Not a new idea of course! Jesus said '. . . whoever loses his life for my sake will find it'.[5] And again: 'unless a grain of wheat falls to the ground and dies, it remains only a single seed. But if it dies, it produces many seeds'.[6] I had no idea at that stage of how true those words might prove to be. It's probably nearly always the way with those who set out to follow Christ – however weak and useless they know they really are.

FAREWELLS ARE AWFUL

My own parents were not around when the time came for us to leave, having themselves long since done their own departing. And until we had children of our own I never appreciated how difficult it must have been for Mary's parents to see us off, seemingly to the ends of the earth! Mary's mother and father came to Barnstaple station to bid us goodbye. We could all sense the tension. I was taking their youngest daughter away on a long sea journey to the uttermost parts of the earth. They were getting older, and though they never said it, we had to face the fact that we might easily not see them again. What was more we were taking their granddaughter with us. The whole venture was far more costly for them than for us. It was our choice – they had no say. But we had to follow what the gospel demanded. Father and mother must always be honoured but nevertheless it had to be

God first: 'He that loveth father or mother more than me is not worthy of me'.[7] We also believed the gospel promises: 'Everyone who has left houses or brothers or sisters or father or mother or children or fields for my sake will receive a hundred times as much and will inherit eternal life'.[8] Prior to World War One, Mary's father had emigrated to Canada and knowing what long absences meant he simply asked us to write home regularly – for Mary's mother's sake. It was the least we could do.

ABOARD THE *REINA*

We sailed in mid-October 1959, aboard the SS *Reina del Mar* (Queen of the Sea). Our journey led us to some fascinating places as we unloaded and loaded cargoes in various West Indian islands, and then on along the coast of South America. Never in my wildest dreams had I imagined myself in such surroundings. I had thought our calling was the urge of the missionary not the itch of the tourist – but I had failed to appreciate that the Lord could provide perks in the path of duty. I really did not mind how long the journey took. I was certainly in no hurry to reach our ultimate destination of Valparaíso in Chile.

We were blessed to be travelling with Ros and Douglas Milmine. Ros claimed to have a little private income of her own and most generously invited us to join them on their visits inland from most ports of call; we appreciated their kindness greatly – we could never have afforded it ourselves. Of course they were experienced missionaries and we hung on their every word as they told us what living in Chile was like. But they had no idea how they really scared us with some of the stories so casually recounted! The tale of the missionary who had been scratched by a cat and died of rabies was received with outer calm but inner panic. An off-hand humorous comment about the Mapuche house-warmings in *el campo* (rural out-back) when the chief guest would be presented with raw lamb's lungs as an honour, was no less disconcerting! Visiting missionaries were often treated as chief guests apparently! I made a mental resolution: 'Henceforth eschew all honours and never agree to any invitation to a housewarming in *el campo*.' Raw lungs indeed! How revolting! Whatever next? Well at least there weren't any cannibals.

No turning back

As Valparaíso, our port of disembarkation, drew ever closer we lowered our focus from those amazing mountains behind the port to the serried ranks of cheering people welcoming home their friends and loved ones once again. Suddenly England seemed a long way away, and five years before our first leave home seemed an eternity! Here I was, bringing my lovely wife and baby to a completely unknown world; a thousand unknown faces speaking in unknown tongues, all from strange places with unpronounceable names. People, it seemed, would be there for everyone else but not for us. I needed to be strong for Mary though I did not feel it. But there could be no turning back now.

We were soon into the port that I was later to get to know very well. Tugs hauled the hawsers from our ship to loop them ashore round massive iron bollards on the wharf.

We not only had to go through the processes of disembarkation but we had to get through the customs as well.

Slowly we watched as the creaking gangway was craned down. Once in place, a mad rush of garlic-smelling porters pushed and shoved their way up and along the decks to cart off the luggage – each porter identified by a metal tag. Doug Milmine was on the lookout for Number 23, a good trustworthy Pentecostal, who had always helped our SAMS missionaries apparently. It had been arranged for him to be there for us now but he was nowhere to be seen. Eventually Doug asked another porter if he had any idea where Number 23 might be? The obliging porter stopped, doffed his cap with great reverence, and in a low tearful whisper, he murmured: 'Murio, senor!' (He died, sir!) The porter then agreed to manage our luggage for us.

This was no sooner settled than suddenly Numero 23 appeared, huffing and puffing up the gangway, apologising profusely. A most sudden resurrection indeed! Those porters did not miss a trick. We soon had things sorted out with No 23 and he served us faithfully, not just then, but for many years to come.

Once on land, we were pleasantly surprised to meet Michael Hemans (local schoolmaster), who was later to become a great friend. Next morning we were helped through customs by Peter Hardy who ran an import/export agency in town.

But we spent our first night in Chile at the cheapest hotel, very near, or possibly within, the 'red light' area. We had no idea of its reputation then. Years later I had to visit a couple who were actually in a brothel in that region. To avoid misunderstandings I donned a black suit and clerical collar, and tucked the biggest Bible I could find under my arm indicating the pastoral nature of my visit, in case onlookers should come to other conclusions.

Mary's great dread was fleas – more on behalf of the baby I think. She had never actually seen one herself so I dutifully stripped down the bed for her. After thorough investigation I assured her there were no fleas there, and she could go to sleep in peace. In the process of stripping back the bedclothes, however, I had had the impression that I was handling a kind of secular Turin Shroud – there was the distinct impression of a body on the bottom sheet. It could have been there before, but I refrained from mentioning it to Mary. She had enough worries as it was.

But fleas turned out to be about the worst of the animal hazard league in Chile. No tigers! No snakes! Just the occasional puma in *el campo* and, once in a very blue moon, a nasty harvest spider. For years, in my anti-flea fervour, I powdered my bed regularly with DDT. We thought it was perfectly harmless in those days. Goodness knows how much of the stuff I must have inhaled at night! Mary did not quite get through that first night ashore in peace. There were strange click-click-clicking sounds on the stone floor. Creatures the size of mice seemed to be scuttling around in search of biscuit crumbs. No one had warned us that cockroaches tend to come up through the bathroom drains after dark!

A COUNTRY WITH A VIOLENT HISTORY

We soon discovered that Chile was indeed a wonderful country with colourful and hospitable people. The land had originally belonged to the Amerindians divided of many tribes, perhaps the most famous being the Araucanos (now an ethnic minority) who had fiercely resisted the Spanish 'Conquistadores' to the South of Santiago. Actually they called themselves Mapuche – 'the Land (*Mapu*) People (*che*)'.

History records how two cruel and illiterate Spanish Captains, Francisco Pizarro and Diego de Almagro, first captured the Inca capital of Cuzco (Peru) in 1532 and smashed the Inca empire. Before the Spanish ever appeared, the Incas believed their doom was already written in the stars. Doubtless any nation that ritually sacrifices its own children senses the judgement of God upon them. The Incas had certainly seen the Spanish as the direful instruments of that pending doom.

Pedro de Valdivia, one of Pizarro's captains, led a fresh force south in 1539, founding Santiago (St James) in 1541. By then, the Spanish were too well entrenched ever to be driven out of Chile.

There followed nearly a hunded years of cruel warfare between the invaders and the invaded until a treaty was eventually signed at Quillan in 1641, providing an Araucanian reserve around central Chile. Their northern *frontera* (frontier) was to be the Bio Bio river that separated them from the Spanish. However this was not the end of trouble for the Araucanians. Armed Spanish soldiers frequently raided the reserve and stole their women. The successive Spanish military commanders were answerable to the King of Spain via his Viceroy in Lima, Peru and their Captain Generals in Chile. The King was getting bad reports of the soldiers' misbehaviour from the Jesuit missionaries active in the area.

The long coastline also made the Conquistadores vulnerable from alien attack. English pirates joined those who preyed on the Spanish, hoping to relieve them of some of their hoardes of gold. Francis Drake had been dispatched from England with his plundering fleet of corsairs to loot the ships and ransack the coasts of Spain's colonies including the furthest kingdom of Chile. For generations to come, 'Aqui viene Drak!' ('Here comes Drake!') was an effective bogeyman scare word for Chilean children when they misbehaved.

The best and fairest commander the King of Spain ever had on the Chilean *frontera* was a man named Ambrosio O'Higgins, a native of Sligo, Ireland. Irish Catholics were highly favoured by the Spanish for their hatred of Protestants but O'Higgins was also greatly respected by the Araucanians for his fairness. From the *frontera* he rose rapidly in royal favour, was promoted to being Captain General of Concepcion, Chile (1788) and from there, soon after to Lima in Peru to take over the Vice Regency itself. On his way up the political ladder, O'Higgins had sired an illegitimate son named Bernardo who was later to become one of the foremost revolutionary leaders in the Chilean Independence movement. Bernardo O'Higgins was nominated Supreme Director General of Chile from 1818–23. Once in power, he encouraged foreigners (especially the English) to help develop the country's rich potential and populate its vast coastline so vulnerable to enemy invasion.

INFLUX OF FOREIGNERS

One of the first whom Bernardo O'Higgins persuaded to join him was Admiral Thomas Cochrane (later Earl Dundonald), a demi-god of the British Navy. Cochrane modelled the new Chilean Fleet on the British Navy. His feats at sea bordered on the miraculous. For sheer fighting prowess, audacity and ingenuity, Cochrane has seldom, if ever, been surpassed in the annals of war. Lord Cochrane later became an admiral of both the Brazilian and the Greek Navies.

Among the many other foreigners who arrived to help Bernardo O'Higgins' development programme were merchants, bankers, doctors, educators, farmers, miners, engineers, road and railway builders – people who were welcomed for their skills and their access to foreign resources. Over some twenty years I made a study devoted to the influence of foreigners in nineteenth-century Chile and their struggle for religious liberty. I started this as an exercise in learning about Chile's culture and ended by submitting it for a higher degree. A fascinating thesis but of limited interest. These foreigners made a significant impact upon the new republic and proved O'Higgins' imaginative foresight to have been well worthwhile. It also explains why the Chileans, traditionally are anglophiles.

Chile is a long thin country stretching 2,600 miles in length. It is never more than two hundred miles at its widest. On the map it somewhat resembles a stocking in tatters from the knee downwards with so many islets and inlets. There are the towering snowcapped Andes on the east and the wide-open Pacific on the west. Chile is enclosed still further by the Atacama desert in the north and its archipelago merging into Cape Horn in the south. Its population was around two million in O'Higgins time and had risen to about twelve million in our days there and now amounts to two million more.

DARWIN AND THE MISSIONARIES

Captain Fitzroy had been commissioned by the British Admiralty to do some hydrographical studies of the Southern Ocean and had invited Charles Darwin as company on the voyage.

Darwin recorded the abject poverty of the Indians he observed as he was sailing by Tierra del Fuego.[9] Darwin was shocked by the savage race he observed and commented on their speech 'accompanied by almost unintelligible gutteral, jerky and clicking sounds. They had been described as stunted, ill-shapen figures with filthy greasy skins, long tangled hair, hideous bedaubed faces. They were notable for both their violent gestures and pilfering habits. They plundered and massacred shipwrecked crews, and were regarded by sailors as about the most repulsive specimens of humanity.' Darwin believed they were completely incapable of being Christianised, and rated them below even some of the animal creation – 'miserable lords of a miserable land'. Their language, it was believed, had no term for expressing the existence of any Supreme Being.

Yet it was to this degraded race that Captain Allen Gardiner (the founder of the Patagonian Missionary Society, later SAMS) was eventually drawn to share the gospel. Although he never lived to see it, being martyred by the very 'wretches' he longed to reach, later missionaries achieved great success there. The indigenous people eventually became so pacified that the Argentinians later built a garrison in Ushuaia, the first settlement founded by SAMS missionaries. Tragically the soldiers in their turn brought diseases that wiped out the original inhabitants. But no one expressed more surprise at the early success of the SAMS' Christian enterprise than Darwin himself, who gave a regular subscription to its funds until the end of his life – 'about as emphatic an answer to the detractors of missions as can well be imagined'.[10]

Chapter 8

THOSE WHO PAVED THE WAY

Before you can move the world you must first move yourself
(DAG HAMMARSKJOLD)

The most influential leaders in history, the social reformers and pioneers have been men and women of action because they have been the men and women of thought and passion
(JOHN STOTT)

The South American Missionary Society had been at work in Chile for about a century by the time we arrived. We were being called to water in a tiny way what others had effectively planted well at tremendous cost. Our hero and mission founder, Captain Allen Gardiner, was a Naval lieutenant and desperate 'seeker' after spiritual truth when his Naval duties brought him to Chile (for the second time) in 1822.

He left Chile very depressed at the state of the Catholic Church he found there. Until her independence from Spain in 1818, Protestants had kept themselves pretty much undercover, wary of the dreaded Inquisition which regarded Martin Luther, Henry VIII and Francis Drake all as incarnations of the same devil. But even after independence there remained strong opposition towards Protestants – even with regard to them having a place of their own to bury their dead – and they were not allowed interment in Catholic cemeteries. Protestants were also forbidden to have any identifiable church buildings, nor were their children regarded as legitimate for inheritance purposes unless they had been baptised in the Catholic Church. In spite of that, some chaplaincy churches were eventually erected to accommodate the many prosperous and powerful foreign settlers. (Such antagonism finally changed following Vatican II nearly 150 years later though today sadly the Vatican II rapprochement is less apparent in Chile than it was nearly forty years ago.) Gardiner was given a Bible which led to a powerful spiritual experience in 1822 that changed his life. From then on he wanted only to devote himself to missionary work.

After two attempts at starting work in South Africa, he made four further attempts at establishing a base in Chile before he finally starved to death in 1852, a fugitive from the very inhabitants he hoped to reach in Tierra del Fuego. Over the years, he had produced a book of strategy about mission work in South America, gathered a committee, and laid the foundations for the Patagonian Missionary Society – soon to become the South American Missionary Society that was now sponsoring us.

Following part of his father's plan, his son, the Rev Allen Weare Gardiner, opened up an English chaplaincy in the new coal-mining centre at Lota, near Concepcion in 1860. Coal mining had become a major enterprise since the introduction of steamships and railways by foreigners. There were a good number of English and Welsh colliers settling there by then with spiritual needs.

The latest plan for us when we left the UK had been to pioneer urban work in Valparaíso. I begged our field superintendent to let us experience something of the work in the south first, partly to see how missionaries had tackled the work and partly to learn the language – something I never did very well. (I'd been there ten years when a Chilean friend told me that I spoke Spanish like a native – of England!) Experience in the south would also demonstrate to us that the gospel could be truly relevant in another culture. I had a sneaking feeling that Jesus was probably English. He always looked English to me and spoke English and enjoyed our English hymns of praise! But I soon found, of course, that Latin Americans regarded Jesus as a Latin American. They even got quite touchy about a modernised version of the Bible put out in 1962 by the Bible Society. 'What was good enough for St Paul,' they said, 'is good enough for us' – waving their old versions defiantly in the air.

So Mary and I went down to Temuco and out to Chol Chol to work under Reg and Thelma Bartle, who soon became our good friends. They kindly shared their home with us until they left for furlough in 1960 and we stayed on. We found we had entered into an enormous spiritual heritage. Previous missionaries had laboured long and hard in evangelising, educating and caring through their churches, schools and hospitals – not to mention industrial and agricultural programmes. Two of the former missionaries had received the 'O'Higgins Orden del Merito', the highest civil award the nation had to offer for services to the people of Chile.

THE NEW MISSIONARY'S RECEPTION

A reception was arranged for me by the Mapuche Church leaders on my arrival. They would normally gather once a month for a meal for sharing any problems they had in their churches, and to pray for each other. They loved to hear about what was going on in the wider church around the world. It was not all that easy to make things culturally relevant. One of them once asked me casually how far we were from England? But how could I convey the idea of such distances to him! Seeing my dilemma, he 'simplified' his question: 'Well, how many days would it take by ox-cart?' I had a hard job working that one out!

Another reason why these church pastors valued these regular gatherings was to enable them to learn new hymns and songs to take home and share with their congregations way out in *el campo*. Visitors to their churches later might be very surprised (sometimes painfully so) by the extraordinary variations they would hear on the original tune. The pastors also heard a Bible-based talk, and returned home with the duplicated outline to use themselves later in their own *reducciones* (rural hamlets). I met an evangelist among these men named Segundo Nahuelpi. He was one who shared the good news around the *reducciones* in his area singing his own gospel songs in his native Mapudungu (as their language was called). In his quaint nasal chant, he used the music of traditional Mapuche folk songs that his people easily recognised. They listened to him captivated. He had proved a very effective evangelist and I counted it a privilege to have known him.

There was a quite a crowd of leaders to welcome us that day as the new missionaries. Mary however could not make it as the baby was unwell. This was a blessing for her since she would have been even more horrified than I was at what I found in my place at the seat of honour – a raw pig's tail! The Bible held out promises about treading upon serpents, and being protected from scorpions in the service of the Lord, but I certainly had no faith about eating raw pork. And I would never expect the Lord to protect me against such an avoidable folly!

'Whatever do I do?' I wondered. No one had warned us that the Mapuches honoured their guests in this way and I did not want to offend my hosts on our very first meeting. A sudden brainwave! I picked up the tail and, thanking them for this choice honour, stuffed it into the top handkerchief pocket of my jacket. 'This is how we always treat such honours in England,' I said, smiling nervously. Fortunately, they all laughed with me. Of course Reg Bartle was behind it. The Mapuches, who loved the joke, would never have treated a guest they did not know in that way. Chileans have a wonderful sense of humour.

EARTHQUAKE!

During my early months I was plagued by a series of huge mouth ulcers and an ongoing fever – which I learned was a form of foot and mouth disease – very painful. This spread down the throat and would not clear up. We used to travel into Temuco, where the Milmines lived, to have tests to find out which antibiotic might do the trick – but they all seemed ineffectual. Did this all, I wondered, constitute a pre-run of the first chapter of Job? Although I did not realize it at the time, I recognised later that the eventual cut-off point of this painful ordeal followed a prayer for my healing by a Chilean pastor, who laid his hands on me in the name of Jesus! I was still an unbeliever when it came to healing! But my mouth suddenly cleared up and I never again had ulcers with such fevers.

Just before we were due to return to Chol Chol, following another visit to Temuco about those ulcers, we were struck early one morning[1] by a devastating earthquake. We were still in bed. A table by our window shot across the floor and hit the opposite wall with a thump! Outside, the noise sounded like an ammunition dump being blown up! A frightening sensation – one hardly knew what to do – the whole world seemed to be teetering on its axis. Nobody had ever mentioned earthquakes to us either when we talked about going to Chile! Fortunately, in our case, the building we were in was of a wooden construction and though many things broke, the house itself did not suffer much real damage. Neither was there a high mortality rate round the Temuco area, but many, many people living in *adobe* (mud brick) houses lost their homes.

The quake was grade eight plus on the Richter scale. I had never bothered to think about what it would be like to suffer an earthquake. It is the most awesome thing to experience the earth heaving unpredictably for such a long period beneath one's feet, and to hear the crashing and crying across the nearby plaza. We later learned that three hundred miles of rural coastland had sunk six foot below sea level under the impact. This was followed by a tidal wave which swept inland doing further damage. Many one-time hills were left as islands. Reg Bartle was over on the coast at Nehuentue that weekend. He had to flee to the hills for safety as he saw this *maremoto*[2] rolling towards the shore towering over the lesser waves ahead of it. Reg found himself stranded for two days on a hillside which was now an island. He could hear people crying out through the night for help, clinging to tree tops and telegraph poles. He could only watch helplessly as cattle and homesteads floated out to sea. We did not know what had happened to him and we were very concerned for his wife, Thelma, in Chol Chol waiting anxiously for his return. Numerous after-shocks followed. The land was beginning to feel like jelly. One never quite knew if the latest shake was a prelude to a bigger one or an aftermath of the previous one. Reg eventually arrived home safe and sound. A scary time! During the whole period Mary said she was clenching her teeth so hard for so long that they ached for weeks after – and she was still coping with hypertension following the birth of Charlotte. Such was our initiation into the life of Chile!

REPORTED MISSING

Our main problem was that we simply could not get news back to the UK. We knew from the BBC that they would have heard all about the earthquake but we could not let them know that we were all safe. The local newspaper in Barnstaple, where Mary's family were well known business people, had picked up that we were out there and a reporter was ringing Mary's parents every day for the latest news about us. After nearly ten days, with still no news, we were eventually reported as 'feared missing'. This was picked up by one of the London evening papers that then reported us again by name as 'missing'.[3] This was then picked up by my family in England.

My brother-in-law, John Morris, phoned London to verify this item of information. They suggested a call to Reuters, the international news agency, who offered to help, and who eventually got through to a local radio station in Temuco which managed to contact the Milmines there. Their report that we were all safe was headlined in *The Sunday Telegraph* the next morning – the first accurate news about us in the UK. Mary's poor mother had been worried stiff.

A whole book could be written about that earthquake – a first for us but certainly not our last. Another major one occurred in 1971, when we were in Viña del Mar, and living in a house on a hill at the top of seventy-five steps. It struck at night whilst Mary was in the bath. She called to the children to clear out of the house quickly as she jumped out of the bath, her flannel still in her hand. Stark naked, fleeing our hillside home, it was an interesting question as to where she should apply her small flannel when she finally reached the level of the road below. Fortunately I had managed to grab some extra clothes on the way out that saved her from the cold and further embarrassment.

CHOL CHOL

Chol Chol, a one-horse trading centre for the Mapuche indians, was situated a little to the north of Temuco. Nowadays it has good roads for transport passing through, but it was still pretty cut off forty years ago. The place had been a focal point for SAMS pioneer work since 1895. We had a mixed school there with separate boarding apartments for boys and girls. We also had a hospital being run by an English nurse – none other than the Muriel Parrott who, doubtlessly in answer to those college prayers of long ago, was now speaking the language fluently! Besides there being a church in Chol Chol, it was the focus for a whole network of rural churches. Many students, formerly trained in our school had gone back to their *reducciones* and opened up their own little schools. These often served as meeting places for churches also. About thirty of these churches fanned out into the coutryside – some of them way up in the foothills of the Andes.

Strange are the things that impact the visitor to Araucania! Nightly in the distance one could hear the *machis* (witch doctors) pounding away on their drums and chanting out their spells. One can soon get as used to this as a city dweller does to traffic! Then there were the endless high-pitched croakings that went on and on and on – all through the first part of the night. Natterjacks by the dozen exchanging their 'wolf-whistles' among the willows at the river's edge, their shrill nocturnal cries drilling into our dreams! Then sunrise again – silencing the natterjacks – and signalling to a host of crowing roosters from surrounding homesteads to shake us from our slumbers for another day.

Another disturbing sound at night was even nearer home – bump, bump, bump – rats acrobatting inside the wooden walls of our house. And nothing we could do seemed to deter them from their relentless gnawing, even in the wall right behind my pillow.

The mission only had one vehicle, a Unimog, shared between its three centres. This was a war-like truck of German make. We had just had the earthquake in Temuco. As the Chol Chol schools needed a fresh supply of rations I took these with our luggage, plus Mary and the baby and set off on our return. Just before the track entered Chol Chol itself there was a very long, high wooden bridge. Ours was probably the first vehicle to cross over after the earthquake. I was rather nervous about whether it would take the weight of the truck following such a shake-up. What sort of test could one make to check it out in that kind of situation? I was praying fervently!

To ensure Mary's safety I suggested that she should carry the baby over first. It would certainly take their weight. But if it was going to collapse under the rumblings of the truck, it would be better that she was already safely on the Chol Chol side of the river with Charlotte. Once she was across I drove over very slowly in the Unimog, with the door open, so that I could jump clear into the water if anything nasty happened. It didn't! The mission field, I soon found, never lacked excitement. We seemed to pass from one crisis to another. When we arrived in Chol Chol we found the headmaster, Ian Morrison, extremely worried about his responsibilities for some of the younger boarders in the school. He wanted to evacuate them immediately. I drove off with Ian in the cab and the children in the open truck behind us. Having already crossed the bridge once that day I was now more confident about driving it over a second time. Beyond it was a rather boggy plain. The track was topped with loose wet stones. After 400 yards the Unimog suddenly skidded and made a frightening sharp turn down into the plain with the truck nearly overturning onto the children in the process. Several were thrown out but unharmed. We thanked God together for our escape from a terrible accident.

ON HORSEBACK – JUST!

At Chol Chol we used horses to carry us the long distances that separated our base from the rural churches in *el campo*. Mary was a skilled horsewoman, who had won many cups in gymkhanas as a child back in Devon. She found it hard to understand why I did not take to riding as easily as she had and urged me to start galloping as soon as possible! I arranged to take lessons from a local Chilean.

On our first Christmas in Chile (a time prone to bring on homesickness), Mary had a mysterious present for me wrapped up in a shoebox tied with romantic pink ribbon. 'Not because you have earned them yet, but I think you need them' she wrote on the card. Inside were beautiful silver spurs, just like the ones the local cowboys (*huasos*) wore. My horse, 'Bomba Atomica', always seemed so lethargic on her outward journeys. And she would stoop to nibble a juicy tuft of grass whenever she felt like it. It is difficult to appreciate just how humiliating it was when that wretched animal refused to budge. I should have plunged in those spurs to get the animal moving properly but how far could one go before the animal might suddenly go off pop?

Bomba Atomica certainly took her time on the outward trail

but the return was a race like the Derby! I simply had to hang on grimly – my black *manta* billowing wildly in the wind and my *sombrero* trailing behind me on a cord.

I recall one terribly wet and windy day riding across the plain outside Chol Chol – Bomba Atomica was sloshing and slipping everywhere in the mud. The cold wind blew cruelly while rain sliced into my face and numbed it. Bomba Atomica, like me, was hating it. Between the gusts of wind I could hear the curses of drunk Mapuches, laid out in their open *carretas* which were being dragged unsteadily by oxen who knew their way home only too well. I felt sorry for those oxen. I felt sorry for my horse and I felt very sorry for myself and was suddenly overcome by a sense of cosmic aloneness. Almost before I knew it I was shouting out bitterly: 'Lord, why ever did you lead me to such a wretched place as this – it is just too unbearable! I'm only here, Lord, because I wanted to be in the centre of your will. I thought that would be a place of peace and usefulness and instead it's sheer hell and utter futility. And I can't even ride this pitiable animal properly!' No sooner had I prayed that desperate prayer than I sensed an unbelievable calm; that peace which passes all understanding; a peace which the world cannot give, which was invading my innermost being while outwardly the wind still continued lashing the rain furiously into my face. Just one more of those mystical raptures!

LEARNING THE ROPES

Reg Bartle, who was in charge of the work in the Chol Chol region, taught me the ropes as best he could. I remember a long journey out in *el campo* to call on a Mapuche church leader he needed to see. Reg told me always to greet with a loud 'Alloa' from a distance, to let the owner know that a visitor was approaching his *ruca* (a reed-thatched one-roomed abode). Hopefully he would then rein in his dogs before we actually got to the door. It could be dangerous to dismount until they were all settled. In any case, if only the wife was at home, one should never dismount. Reg advised me when out riding to wear Wellington boots, just in case any dog was still tempted to take a piece out of one's leg. I was grateful for this advice. Reg had had to learn these things the hard way. I preferred learning from his wisdom.

Having discussed the matters we had come about our host invited us to stay for a bite.

Often after eating the family would chat and drink *maté*. The *maté* put into a gourd had boiled water poured on top of it. 'Mine host' would then add sugar and begin sucking it up through a silvered metal tube (*bombilla*). After a few more sips he would pass the 'bombilla' with the gourd to the guest on his right to enjoy. That was me! I was feeling pretty tense since I had noticed that 'mine host' had been spitting blood before the social round began! 'Lord! How have you brought me here to this TB riddled family?' I cried inwardly. Reg never seemed to worry about such minor details. The perfect missionary!

The work done by a long line of missionary predecessors in Araucania had been amazing. The Mapuches were basically animistic but their joy as they came out of darkness into the light of Christ was something to behold. People say we should leave folk in other cultures well alone – and not upset them when they are supposed to be so happy in their animism. In our experience most of them were not. It was a religion of extreme fear.

TURBULENT PRIEST – NOT ME!

I was still a very loyal churchman priding myself on doing things properly. Reg had gone on leave by now and I was left in charge of the region. Those rural churches, which fanned out from Chol Chol across the region, needed communion, and for this a regular visitation was necessary in churches where they still had no ordained leader. I was quickly becoming the mass priest I always wanted to avoid being, but I was learning slowly. On arrival the local leader would strike the church bell (a bit of iron hanging from a branch) to summon the people. They would begin drifting in to the meeting place – usually the local schoolroom, with its small windows open, but plenty of added daylight filtering in between the rough pine planking of the walls.

After my first visit I vainly imagined that I could do a bit better than my predecessors. The frustrated builder in me had dreams of constructing a 'proper' little church on a hill, with a tower. We could use all that clear white quartz strewn across the countryside. Of course I later realised that the congregations should be left to build any more permanent churches as and when they wanted or needed them.

Arriving at our outback churches, founded by others before I ever appeared in Chile, I would tether Bomba Atomica securely, take my surplice from my small saddlebags, shake out the creases and disappear discreetly behind a mimosa (wattle tree) to robe up. From there I would emerge Persil white as if from another planet. I blush today to think of what I was doing. We had very few Mapuche clergy but they too were equipped with convocation robes – black scarves and yellowing surplices. I suspected that they never wore any of this except when missionaries were about!

I stood myself deliberately at the north end of the wobbly little table on which I had placed the bread and wine on a white cloth, just as the rubric of the *1662 Book of Common Prayer* instructed. It was not so easy to keep good order however. Once, a couple of dogs dozing peacefully all through the absolution suddenly leapt up during the *Credo de Nicea* (Nicene Creed) to start a pitched battle.

It was about this time that I realised I had unconsciously developed a 'parsonical voice'! I had picked up some vocal inflections from one of my Anglican heroes in England assuming it would enhance my preaching in some way. But such inflections did not transfer easily into Spanish. I had to ditch the 'voice' altogether and start speaking naturally. Listening to some of my contemporaries preaching back in England, even today, I can still detect from whom some of them acquired their mannerisms and inflections.

ONLY A CATTLE SHED

Once I rode out some twenty miles on horseback and found that we were locked out of our usual meeting place in a schoolroom. The local Catholic priest had bribed our schoolmaster with a new portable radio not to let us in. This was prior to the Second Vatican Council (1962), after which we were regarded more charitably as 'separated brethren' by the Catholic Church, and made much more welcome in South America for a few years. But on that particular occasion we had no place for our gathering to 'break bread'. It was too wet to meet in the open air. Finally one man went off and cleaned out his stable for us. We gratefully accepted his offer though the environment was none too savoury. The significance was not lost however as we reminded each other of the place where the Christ Child had been born.

Over the years I have had the privilege of celebrating the Lord's Supper in cathedrals, in churches, in chapels, in lounges, round dining room tables, in kitchens, in ships' cabins, in community rooms, in hotel rooms, in motel rooms, at hospital bedsides, in bedrooms, in gardens and in wide open fields the world over but the little celebration of the Lord's Supper in that stable with those humble Mapuches was about the most unforgettable of them all.

STRUGGLING WITH CRITICISMS

Our doorbell in Chol Chol was ringing constantly – people from *el campo* would arrive at any hour to ask if there were letters for them; others came with something to sell; others to check when they might expect the next visit to their church. Then there were folk from afar taking advantage of a brief visit to our little town to get married in the nearest 'civil' office, and coming to us for a quick nuptual blessing after it! They had come a long way for all this and one needed to be ready for such surprises. Next there was someone wanting to borrow the mission bier for a funeral. They used this to wheel the coffin in style to the local cemetery. Then they wanted *creosota*! Whatever was that, I wondered? It turned out, obviously, to be creosote. This was urgently needed to do the funeral properly – no matter the smell of it, the coffin had to be painted black! 'Whatever next?' I inwardly groaned; how had the mission got itself into this nanny role to the community?

Chol Chol was in many ways a SAMS show piece for years of sacrificial missionary work. But the new recruit (me) arrogantly presumed to criticise the way missionaries had ever allowed such traditions to develop; to question how we could ever be expected to manage all this today, and to suggest how better things could, or should be done in the future. And how could we begin to straighten things out now without upsetting too many church folk or townsfolk?

Before we had left the UK we had both read a very challenging little booklet for missionaries called *Have We No Rights?* from which it seemed quite clear that the Lord's servants could plead no real rights for themselves – only for others. But this pampering of nationals did not seem good to me. Was I being wise or foolish? Was I becoming a cynic? Did I really appreciate the amazing sacrifices and successes of earlier missionaries? If so, how could I dare to criticise!

I was visiting a church in Brazil a year or so later and stayed with the chaplain – a very sad and bitter man. He told me how, as a young man, he had read a book by a missionary pioneer in Brazil that had enthralled him. Eventually he went out to join forces with his hero, the book's author. When he got there he fell in love with his pretty daughter and they married. As time went on he met up with some of the characters in the book that his father-in-law had described and he became totally disillusioned. They appeared so poor and ignorant, and some had been through times of serious backsliding.

He had never fully appreciated the original pitiable state of so many of those people that his father-in-law had been called to work amongst. Had he stayed longer and tried a bit of pioneer work himself he would have done, but its takes a long time to learn Portuguese and then the local language. The older man could see how far these Amer-indians had come since they had first seen the light of Christ – both in their understanding and their changed characters. He could still get excited about the power of the gospel. My new friend had been seeing them (as we all did) through the eyes of his English culture. In his view, the men whom his father-in-law loved and trusted were nothing at all to write home about.

If I had ever attempted to analyse my own soul at the time I would probably have assumed that SAMS was rather lucky to have us! But after a few months on the field, so much scum began to surface that I was soon wondering how SAMS had ever come to accept us in the first place.

THE SUBJECT OF HEALING

People would often arrive with an urgent request for us to visit someone who was very sick – they wanted a prayer for healing. When they were into animism the witch doctor would always go through a ritual for healing for a fee – a sheep or a chicken perhaps! But I found myself fighting shy of going out to actually pray for healing. I had had no training in that. In any case we had two mission hospitals with dedicated nurses to cope with the sick – and I felt we were doing a really good job in that area. Besides we had a lovely service in the *Book of Common Prayer* to help the sick find peace in the face of approaching death, but there was little in the service suggesting that bodily healing should or could be expected. Healing was more than my faith could stretch to at that stage: even though I recognised that Jesus had healed the sick to great effect. What aggravated my problem, embarrassing to relate, was that the Pentecostalists were into healing in a big way – and really seeing people healed to the glory of God. The kingdom of God was amazingly good news for these people. Without wanting to admit it I found this rather annoying – and very threatening! Those wretched Pentecostals did not seem to realise that the gifts of the Spirit had been withdrawn once the church had fixed the canon of Scripture: a misleading theory which I had been taught and believed.

REG AND THELMA RETURN TO CHOL CHOL

I had learned many lessons in Chol Chol but I like to blame Bomba Atomica for our eventual retreat to the north. When the time came to go up to Valparaíso I could not wait to get there. I have always been so grateful to St Paul who spelt out one very practical but rather surprising aspect of divine guidance – 'when we could stand it no longer'.[4]

Mary was ready too. She had just had our second baby – Debby. Strangely, looking back later, I came to regard the Chol Chol experiences as beyond price and not to be exchanged for anything. Seeing the reality of Jesus in a completely different culture was reward enough. It had been a good preparation for the next phase in our lives.

Chapter 9

VALPARAÍSO – HERE WE COME!

The only thing that keeps our mission house from falling down is that the termites are holding hands
(ANON)

Healthy things grow. Growing things change.
Changing things challenge.
Challenging things make us look to God
(JOHN WRIGHT)

Every place has its compensations. Although the accommodation and the windy location of Valparaíso (literally vale of paradise) had its challenges, nothing could beat the atmosphere of its cosmopolitan past, its cobbled streets and rickety funiculars[1] *ascensores*. Added to this were the extraordinary sunsets played out across the Pacific! These were glorious enough in themselves, but with their refractions of salmon pink rising and falling across the Andes behind us, they gave such beauty a mystical dimension. To crown the wonder was the towering Aconcagua[2] whose snowcapped cowl glistened regally with the same roseate hues. Valparaíso was still the biggest port on the West Coast of Latin America – and a harbour with a history. It was the focus of the foreign settlers in the early eighteenth century, where the Anglican Church in Chile first began. Nearly a century later the city also birthed the original Pentecostal Church that has divided, subdivided and spread across the whole continent today.

THE *ANGLICANA*
We felt so right about getting stuck in at Valparaíso. Ever since I had started thinking about missionary strategy I had felt that one should, like St Paul, build up work in the city and train up

nationals to go out to evangelise their own countryside or hinterland. We had taken over the old English church of St Paul's on Concepcion hill, from another missionary who had initiated Spanish work there a few months earlier. It had all started with a flourish but then he found he did not have sufficient Spanish to sustain it. By the time we actually arrived up in Valparaíso to take over, there was only a very small congregation left, but when starting something new every person counts, so we were very thankful for what we had.

The whole project under my predecessor – including rent and children's education – was costing SAMS much more than they had bargained for, although it would have seemed very cheap to people in the secular world. Part of our mandate was to reduce expenses in every way possible. Having always lived on a shoestring we were not too daunted by that. Our answer was to convert the *Anglicana*, a slightly dilapidated clubroom behind St Paul's, into a suitable place for living in as a family.

I particularly enjoyed the practical challenge of levelling off the stage at one end and putting up dividing walls with the cheapest wood available – thin pine strips from dismantled tomato boxes. This kind of work did not depend upon my poor Spanish fortunately! I also put in a second loo, a wash basin and a shower.

Since a place was being dismantled a few blocks away on the hill, I went down and bought some old doors and heavy pine beams rather full of used nails. The Chileans were shocked to see this *gringo* (foreigner) carrying the doors up to the church on his back. Middle class Chileans would never do that. To appear to be involved in manual work was considered demeaning – 'Well!' I thought, 'Jesus was a carpenter!'

In Valparaíso we would buy sufficient bread for the family every day from our local bakery round the corner. And daily I would descend on the funicular to the shops below to collect our mail from the post office where we had a key to our own *casilla* (post box).

Outside public places like the post office (and especially outside churches) one was confronted with innumerable beggars – often people terribly deformed or handicapped through birth or accident.

119

BAD NEWS FROM THE UK

I had not been in Valparaíso long when I had news that my oldest brother Jack was seriously ill in the UK. He had been taken to St Thomas's Hospital in London with failing kidneys. A recurring problem which had kept him out of the Army during the war. I asked our little congregation to pray for him, which they did, faithfully. When finally I told them the tragic news that Jack had died, to my great embarrassment they all began to weep copiously for me – while I remained standing before them grieving but dry-eyed! It must have seemed strange to them that I did not go home for the funeral but I simply could not have afforded it. Chileans get quite mystified by English responses. I learned later that some of the young people would deliberately invent bad news to tell me and study my reaction with curiosity. There are many crises where Chileans would either burst into tears or explode with anger when our more English approach would be to blink, count to ten and explore all possible solutions – saving our emotions for private expression later – if at all.

MISSIONARY METHODS

Our superintendent from the south, Tony Barratt, came up to see us. He seemed delighted at the way we were setting about things. 'This is wonderful, David! You are conquering the concrete jungle of the city!' he said, looking at our attempted conversion of the *Anglicana*. I don't suppose Tony could ever fully appreciate what that simple humorous encouragement meant for us at that moment of time. 'Wow!' I thought, 'I had not imagined that anyone could ever think we had done enough here yet for anyone to get enthusiastic about it!' The power of his words was just wonderful. I was feeling the distance between ourselves and the rest of the team down south. Coming to terms with the fact that our work would initially be very slow going I made a resolve to try and speak encouraging words to those that might find themselves under my charge at any future time. I wish I could say I have always succeeded. I think it is so important.

Our mandate was to plant urban churches. Simple to say but much harder to do, as my disappointed predecessor had already found out!

I picked up a couple of books by Roland Allen on *Missionary Methods – St Paul's or Ours?* and *The Spontaneous Expansion of the Church*. Having glanced through them, I dropped them like hot bricks. However could I follow his counsel? Roland Allen had once been a High Church lay missionary in China, but his analysis of St Paul's missionary methods contrasted seriously with most of the things that had or were being done by the Anglican Church overseas. And I could not imagine St Paul starting his work as I was starting mine in a large old church building! I began to fish around desperately for help from others – but whoever could I hope would come up with better principles than those of St Paul? He should obviously have been our model for missionary work among the Gentiles! He had been a diligent and most effective church planter. Thinking through the relevance and long term potential, the cultural credibility and the ethos for an Anglican Church in Chile, and how to plant such churches, was a serious problem that bugged me for the rest of my time there.

HOW TO CHURCH PLANT
But we had to expand the work somehow and somewhere. I consulted a successful Assemblies Of God missionary from North America on the subject of church planting.

'Yeah, it's a cinch,' he replied, 'All you have to do is to rent a storefront on a main road going into town, get a guitar and advertise a healing meeting.'

'Ugh! A healing meeting?' I caught my breath in horror, but tried not to show it. Inwardly I dismissed the idea as vulgar! Besides how could I ever afford to rent a shop when I didn't even have enough to rent a flat for our family. How could I hope to do anything on £300 a year and a minimum allowance for working expenses? And I couldn't play a guitar even if I had had one, which I had not. Of course I realise now there was a lot more sense to what he was saying than I had realised at the time, though I am not sure that Paul would have tackled it that way either! Rent a shop! Guitars! Healing meetings!

'Very dubious,' I thought. Better stick to our traditional approach. After all, our mandate was to plant urban churches to provide a decent *via media* between Roman Catholicism on the one hand and Pentecostalism on the other.

One method we tried to increase our membership, was to distribute tracts in the streets of the shopping centre below our hill – something we both disliked doing intensely – but in our desperation to break new ground we had to try everything. Mary would take one side of the street and I the other. It did actually open up some fruitful conversations with a few interested people. Then I remember seeing a large foreign-looking man walking towards me and wondering whether to give him a tract or not. In the end I did so because one never knew what the end result might be if one did not try. The man took it, studied it carefully and finally asked me whether it was any good. It turned out he was a North American living in Temuco – who actually published the tracts! We became firm friends.

Very soon missionaries from the south decided they must come up and take advantage of our vast accommodation. We enjoyed their friendship greatly and appreciated being able to catch up with all their news. After levelling off the stage of the old Church Hall we had built light partitions – not quite reaching to the very high ceiling – to create spare bedrooms. Then the Blaxlands from Australia joined us for six months before going to Santiago – to take over the new centre from the Milmines who were leaving for furlough. Tony Barratt was obviously happy about our progress because the next thing we knew was that he was sending us a Chilean couple to train. 'Train!' I had no idea how I was going to develop things myself – let alone train someone else. I had not realised, at that stage, that one learns a lot working alongside someone else who is still learning how to tackle problems himself. Tony had not told us how he expected us to finance these Chileans either. Antonio and Ines Valencia duly arrived with their family. They lived on the stage end of the hall and we developed the other end. I introduced them to our little congregation and tried to encourage everyone to help with their financial support – explaining in Spanish that I did not know how we were going to '*soportar los*' (meaning 'support them financially')! However, what I was actually saying in Spanish was: 'I don't know how we are going to put up with them!' Rather an unfortunate start for our future working life together!

WEEKLY RADIO PROGRAMME

We soon developed a very good relationship with Michael and Janet Hemans – two local school teachers. Michael was the grandson of the founder of the SAMS work in the Temuco, Chol Chol, and Quepe area – a remarkable pioneer. Michael's mother, Berith Hemans, had married a one-time chaplain of St Paul's, Valparaíso, who had died suddenly of a heart attack some twenty years previously. To make ends meet she had started an English primary school that she called St Paul's. Michael and Janet were teaching there when we arrived.

Michael Hemans had learned to play the organ at St Paul's whilst his father had been the chaplain there, and had actually become very proficient. Janet, his wife, was a North American redhead who sang beautifully. She and Michael both had music degrees from Wheaton College in the US – where they had first met.

Broadcasting seemed a very good way of publicising the Spanish work at St Paul's (now given its name in Spanish – *San Pablo*) and we set about exploiting this excellent talent by starting a regular Spanish service on the air. I could not forget those *Revival Hours* broadcast from Fuller those many years ago! We used a recorded peal of bells (the Gloucestershire Tripples) from an English country church as a twenty-second signature tune and then faded it into the background as I introduced the service: '*Esta – es – La Hora – Anglicana!*' ('This – is – the – Anglican –Hour'). It was actually for only half an hour but '*Media Hora!*' sounded too clumsy for a Spanish introduction so we said '*Hora!*': I still had not grasped that the word 'Anglican' was pretty meaningless to Chileans in general.

Every item had to be brief on the air. We used one canticle, the *Nunc Dimittis* (to keep the Anglican flavour!), the beautiful words of the aged Simeon on taking the Christ Child in his arms, when he had said, 'Lord, now lettest thou thy servant depart in peace ... for mine eyes have seen thy salvation . . .'[3] One listener was actually converted through hearing those words! She became a church member soon after. We would include a creed, a prayer and the Lord's Prayer in the service, a brief Scripture reading by Antonio Valencia, who would also sing a solo, or a duet with Janet. Each week Antonio would translate a gospel sermonette by

Frank Colquhoun, short and succinct, which he then included in the recorded radio broadcast.

Altogether we had a beautiful and balanced service to broadcast which modelled measured liturgy and biblical teaching – it certainly helped build up the congregation in San Pablo. Many also listened who did not come, and a Catholic priest told me that he had always believed that the services were actually broadcast live each week directly from the church. I took that to be a compliment. But what kind of Anglicanism were we trying to reproduce in Chile? To be good Anglicans we needed the liturgy, the Church calendar, clergy dress etc and Church architecture! All costly. Again I was concerned about the hymns we were singing – all translations of the English favourites. They were very different from the kind of music that Chileans would choose to sing themselves but we had no other at that time.

DISCONCERTING QUESTIONS

I was uncomfortable and uncertain about what I was actually trying to reproduce in Chile. Other questions looming in the back of my mind concerned the model of the ministry in our St Paul's Church. And how would we ever staff and finance another church like it, let alone build one like it – with its long carved oak screen and amazing organ? The latter was built with money raised as a memorial to Queen Victoria in 1901 and is still considered the finest pipe organ on the West Coast of Latin America. And I, their pastor, was also financed from the UK. How would we ever finance our national clergy once we had them trained? A total sum would be needed to sustain such an organisation that would far exceed anything our Chilean friends could or would ever be able to keep going financially themselves in the future.

THE CHURCH OF THE FOURTEEN SEATS

Having fourteen seats built into the wall on one side of the street St Paul's had become well known in the area as *La Iglesia de la Catorce Asientos* (The Church of the Fourteen Seats)!

We started growing a very happy little church, all the time bearing in mind that we needed to be thinking of planting other churches, without really having a clue how or where to start these either. These were days long before those invaluable courses on church planting were being offered at Fuller Seminary in California by people like Prof Peter Wagner and John Wimber. (Indeed Wagner was still currently serving as a missionary with the North American Christian Mission in Bolivia (until 1972), studying the rapid growth of Pentecostalism there which was fast becoming a serious challenge to the Catholic Church in Latin America.)

UNUSUAL VISITORS
In 1962 Prince Philip was making a visit to Valparaíso and Viña del Mar, and would be attending a short church service in English on the Sunday morning. St Peter's Church in Viña would not be nearly big enough for this. The English chaplain from Viña (who had prior claim on St Paul's Church building for major services in English, and who had initially objected to my coming into his 'parish' to develop Spanish work) advised me that he would require the use of St Paul's Church for this occasion and graciously invited me to lead the intercessions for it, which I did. Afterwards we had been invited by the British Consul to a reception at the 'Hotel O'Higgins' in Viña del Mar.

Suddenly we heard our names being called out. The Prince had asked for the young clergyman who had led the prayers in church? So I went forward with Mary beside me, and shook the hand of His Royal Highness. The Duke fired several questions at us including one about how we got the job. It was an unexpected interlude. Two years later we went through a similar routine with Lord Mountbatten and a couple of years after that we had a visit from HRH Queen Elizabeth II herself.

ST PAUL'S SCHOOL
Charlotte had started at the nearby German School, but moved to St Paul's School when Mrs Hemans, the founder of the school, died, and we took over the running of it from Michael (who eventually became the organist at St Andrew's Cathedral in Sydney, Australia, in the face of considerable international competition).

Michael came to see me with a plan about the future of the

school. His friend, Keith Evans, an accountant, would buy it if SAMS would like to run it. We agreed and put in three teachers – to be financed by the school. The Rev Peter Woods, who had just arrived, ran it to begin with. Then, Margaret Lutley took over as the school's new *Directora*. Another teacher was Daphne Richardson who later married the owner Keith Evans. The arrangement with SAMS worked well until the earthquake in 1965, when the school was very badly damaged. Evans then sold it to the diocese that managed to raise money overseas for its re-building. I felt it was good to exploit the school to give us another bridge across to the kind of Chileans who were the most likely to be attracted to *La Iglesia Anglicana* (the Anglican Church). But I was never keen on the diocese buying the school. Margaret and her team certainly did a great job among both the children and their parents, many of whom were delighted to form part of the new Spanish Church of San Pedro being started up by Peter Woods in Viña del Mar. So far so good!

Chapter 10

SPONTANEOUS CHURCH

*We cannot control the direction of the wind but we can set our sails to
catch it when it comes our way*
(ANON)

*A man has made at least a start on discovering the meaning of
human life when he plants shady trees under which he knows full
well he will never sit*
(D. ELTON TRUEBOLD)

A Chilean married couple was moving off from our Valparaíso
church to the other side of Viña del Mar, to a new housing estate
called Gomez Carreño. I knew of the place because Tony Valencia
and I had already visited there before a single house had been
built. Pacing round that empty site we had prayed that God would
raise up a church there for his glory. Little did I imagine how this
might ever happen – nor that the answer might come so soon –
and in such a simple way over a cup of tea!

The couple from our San Pablo congregation had asked us to
dedicate their new house in Gomez Carreño. We were delighted,
and went up there to bless it. We then stayed for some
refreshments. The cake was nice but the tea was awful! Such is
our national reputation that the Chileans think we can't live
without it – so, when they entertain English folk, they are bound
to make tea for them. Sadly, some of the Chileans don't make tea
very well! On this occasion, the tea in my cup had been stewed
and then served as a less than warm thick black syrup enriched
with once boiled milk leaving a surface – like the duckweed on a
millpond – of floating skin. I eventually got it down, and was still
trying to disguise my tears of distaste under the pretext of blowing
my nose, when I suddenly heard my hostess saying: 'Wouldn't it

be good if we could have a church up here?' Still blinking away the remaining tears I nodded, and trying to be positive, I responded with a very practical question: 'Where could we have it?' My next question would have been 'And how could we afford it?' But she had already solved all that in her mind. 'Have it here,' she said, 'in our living room (lounge).' I took a fresh look round the little room: ten foot by twelve. My first thought was 'where could we put the organ?' I mention this to show how, though I knew we had to try new ways, my ecclesiastical mindset was still very traditional. But Fresia was pressing on with her case: 'There are 40,000 people up here on this estate and not a single church. We must do something.' I said: 'Yes – I'll certainly think and pray about it.' She was right. Reading the Bible without traditional Anglican spectacles on it all seemed pretty obvious – the church did not have to be in a special building: 'Greet also the church that meets at their house'[1] – the house of Priscilla and Aquila.[2]

Helped by Margaret Lutley and Daphne Richardson from our school, and some of the young people from our church, we visited from house to house and gathered people into that little room to worship God Sunday by Sunday. We found a very simple Bible correspondence course which they could do at home along with a Gospel of John. Those who opted for the course had to read a set passage and then answer the questions that were staring at them from the text. Most people were delighted to get their answers 100% correct. We would then invite them back to Fresia's house to be awarded their certificates. These we enhanced with a red wax seal with a crown impressed into it from a silver teaspoon given to us as passengers on the *SS Reina del Mar* by the Pacific Steam Navigation Company – a memento from our voyage when we first went out to Chile in 1959.

LOS PICAFLORES

We had an extra kickstart for the work in Gomez Carreño with a visit from Tony Barratt's musically talented family who came over to Chile for a holiday from Paraguay, where Tony was by then heading up the mission work. They had formed a music group called *Los Picaflores*.[3] They wore typical Paraguayan dress and used harps and guitars to accompany their singing. We opened up the church to an evening with them at Valparaíso. This went down so well that we hurriedly built an open-air platform for them in Gomez Carreño for a further presentation the next night. With no previous advertisement it drew huge crowds. They had never had anything like it up there before – and it served to launch our work in the area. (*Los Picaflores* later completed a world tour and appeared on TV in the UK several times.)

Daphne Richardson, inspired by the performance, started putting psalms and other passages of Scripture to music – music with a *latino* flavour. She taught a number of Chilean young people to play and sing them. The music was cyclostyled and made into a booklet – a major step towards the 'Chileanising' of our worship.

Once we had a sufficient regular attendance in Gomez Carreño, the congregation moved onto another site with a bigger hut to meet in.

CHAPLAINCIES AND MISSIONARIES

Bishop Ivor Evans – who usually visited us once a year from Buenos Aires, – had a tragic accident travelling from Temuco to Santiago on the coach one night in 1962. He had an urgent call of nature on the journey and the driver kindly stopped the coach. Seeking privacy he stepped out of the headlight beams. When he did not return they searched for him and found him dead at the bottom of a dark gully just off the roadside. His tragic unexpected death marked a turning point for the work.

Up until this time the major development in Chile had been a mission in Araucania, the reserve of the Mapuche Indians (whom the Spanish had called Araucanos). This mission had become well known and respected as *La Misión Araucana*. As a mission it assumed a certain amount of flexibility about how church was 'done'. This freedom was the cause of some criticism from the chaplaincies. There was also a difference of theology and degrees of misunderstanding and mistrust on both sides. Neither had Bishop Ivor Evans' visits always been happy ones.[4] We lived too far apart geographically and met too infrequently (he in Buenos Aires on the other side of the continent) to communicate adequately.

Evans' sudden demise raised the question of the future

oversight of the work in Chile. When Archdeacon Townsend from far off Río de Janiero (and never once seen in Chile), proceeded to appoint the British chaplain in Santiago (400 miles north) as the vicar general over our much larger work, with no prior consultation, it seemed a highhanded move on his part. (Over the 'diocese versus mission' issue, chaplains tended to represent diocese though by constitution chaplaincies were independent and 'congregational' in operation, except for their episcopal licences.)

OFF TO BRAZIL

Our SAMS superintendent (Tony Barratt) thought it was time, whatever the cost, to go over to see Townsend. There were a total of three chaplains in the whole of Chile, and one of those was a SAMS missionary with whom we had very close links. All the rest of the work came under SAMS. We wanted to tell the Archdeacon on the other side of that vast continent, that we were actually in the process of approaching Canterbury (still the Metropolitan) about a separate diocese for Chile. If this called for some kind of election we could muster plenty of clergy votes! Tony Barratt asked me to go with him to Brazil. He wanted to put forward Douglas Milmine for the job of diocesan bishop in Chile, and Doug would certainly have been a popular choice, though he himself did not want the job. It was my first flight ever and I was awed at the thought of joining the international jet-set – our missionaries never went anywhere by air in those days! Neither did I relish the thought of flying nor leaving Mary alone with the two small children for so long.

Archdeacon Townsend was the senior man left in the diocese of The Falkland Islands and South America and had obvious ambitions for ending up as Ivor Evans' successor. Our response had taken him by surprise and he became only too willing to accommodate in any way he could regarding the west side of the Andes, so long as we would leave him to work things out on the east. About eighteen months later we had our first bishop of Chile, with responsibility for oversight in Bolivia and Peru. The new bishop was a former SAMS missionary, Canon Ken Howell, from London. The original diocese had been divided off, and Cyrel

Tucker from Cambridge was appointed to the Argentine, Paraguay and Uruguay.

During that visit to Brazil we met up with Mac and Peggy Farmborough – Mac, an old college friend, being then chaplain at Niteroi. We also called in on Bill Flagg in Asunción, Paraguay.

WHEN THE PRESIDENT CAME TO CHURCH
A member of our church in Valparaíso was an ardent Christian Democrat – a great supporter of President Frei: she must have told him about St Paul's. One evening when I was preaching, I spotted two strange men appearing simultaneously in each doorway at the rear of the church. They seemed to be looking around for someone. As it turned out they were just checking the place out for security reasons. A second or two later I recognised President Frei,[5] who slipped in and sat at the back for about ten minutes – and then, just as suddenly, left. This was the first of a couple of unannounced visits from the President of the Republic. (Incidentally, Frei's wife was the sister of the Cardinal Archbishop of Valparaíso.)

Chileans are incredibly sophisticated politically. They love politics and talk it all day – even children in Chile have decided political views. It was often said that when two or three Chileans met together there was a political party – and when they separated, there were two more! The question arose in St Paul's Church, after Frei's visit, as to which party we, the church, supported. It seemed strange to some of our members that we did not support any party as a church. It was a good teaching point that had not previously arisen. In the first place different members might want to support different parties. In the second place the church must always be free to oppose any Government. In the third place we taught members to obey the laws and pay taxes, and in the fourth place, we consistently prayed for whichever Government and President was in power. This we did for Allessandri, then Frei, after that Allende, and then Pinochet.

BECOME 'GRANDPARENTS' IN IGNORANCE
Margaret Lutley came to live with us in the *Anglicana* at Valparaíso once Antonio and Inés Valencia had moved out to

Gomez Carreño. A couple of years later Tony and Inés invited us to a *manifestacion* at Gomez Carreño. Mary asked me whatever that could be about and I had to admit I didn't quite know.

When we arrived we found it to be quite a long 'do', with lots of speeches, and even some poetry. Then, finally, one of the Chileans turned to Mary and myself, and said solemnly: 'Don David and Señora Maria, we have invited you here today because we want to tell you the good news. You are about to become grandparents!'

I looked at Mary and she looked at me, wondering whatever was coming next. We didn't think Charlotte quite ready to be having children yet – being only seven years old.

The speaker continued. 'You see, just as we are your daughter church, planted by your young people, so we are now sending out our young people and planting a new church on a new estate – just like you did for us – and that will be your granddaughter church!' I was amazed and delighted. That had to be the Lord's doing. We had never given a single teaching on church planting. In any case I would not have known how to start such a course. It had just 'happened'. But clearly we were teaching so much more effectively by what we did than by what we said. They saw what we had done, and quite simply how we had done it. Now they had just gone ahead themselves and done the same when they had their own opportunity. We were really getting into church planting by then – though half the new plants were still being staffed by foreign missionaries.

INDECISIVE BOSS

Besides the original plant at St Paul's, in Valparaíso, Paul and Esme Russell had started a church in Villa Dulce. Helped by his wife Evelyn, Peter Woods, by then the chaplain to the St Peter's English congregation, also had a parallel Spanish work (San Pedro) in Viña del Mar, whilst Eddie and Renie Gibbs had a new plant going in Quilpué (soon to be taken over by Brian and Gill Skinner). Other new plants were also beginning to spring up spontaneously. But to keep things going we were taking a lot of risks. We were putting leaders into some churches who had had very little training. Our bishop, who was really a very good man, could never seem to make up his mind and did not seem to understand the need to take risks; he could hardly be called encouraging towards what we were doing. It was frustrating to have one's leader saying there must be some other way – but offering no practical suggestions, when something urgent clearly needed to be done. And in our rapidly growing work we were being confronted by even more challenges. There would never be enough money to send all the potential Chilean clergy we needed overseas for training, even if we had ever felt it wise or desirable to do so. And how would we ever pay their salaries when they returned? A healthy church cannot be dependent upon outside funding. Chileans would have to learn to build 'Anglican' Churches their own way in Chile as they went along. We would need to have a local on-going training scheme so that most of the up and coming leaders could continue running their own churches. But we did not have anyone available to run this until eventually John Cobb joined the team and was willing to start working out a training programme for them.

FURLOUGH BACK IN THE UK

After three years in Valparaíso (and five years in Chile) we looked forward to our first leave back home in the UK. We flew by Lufthansa.

During this time in the UK, SAMS asked me to go on their behalf to Sydney, Australia, for a month. The prospect of my visit to Australia in March 1966 was very tough for Mary being left with the already unsettled children back in the UK. We had had a third daughter in 1963, Becky (who had been born at the German Hospital in Valparaíso, as her sister Debby had been). And Tasha was newly born in England. I enjoyed deputation work down under, including preaching in St Andrew's Cathedral for SAMS, but hated leaving Mary and the girls. (I preached in the cathedral again at the invitation of Canon Jim Glennon for a renewal service years later – this time with Mary present. We prayed for a lot of people there and things got pretty charismatic and I heard after that our visit had been rather frowned upon!) Then it was back to the UK and soon after we were returning aboard the French SS *Pasteur* bound for Buenos Aires – from there across the Andes once more by air, to Chile.

We were back for another four years this tour and the time passed quickly. We worked hard and loved most of it. Wallington Missionary Mart had generously sent us back with a Land Rover. The vehicle was a tremendous asset in the work and a great blessing for us personally as a family. We could also get away on our days off and explore.

FRUSTRATION BUILDING UP

By the time our second leave came round it was ten years since we had first landed. I was feeling frustrated about the slow progress that our diocese was making toward a programme for gradually handing over the leadership to nationals and allowing the church to become truly Chilean. We had talked a lot about how we might initiate the process but nothing happened. For every year that *gringos* like myself remained in the leading roles, I felt the church was actually being handicapped for the future. We needed to make moves that would clearly set the diocese free for Chileans to take over. We were being almost compelled to grow an Anglican Church, which understood itself as a traditional foreign entity enshrining a fundamental English ethos. Nevertheless it seemed vital to foment the dynamic of spontaneous expansion however much this seemed to constitute a threat to all our traditional ways of 'doing church'. 'What kind of a church would it finally be in Chile?' we asked ourselves. We could not really say! Our tradition seemed unthinkingly to predetermine the ecclesiology of a new wineskin before the new wineskin could come into existence. The early church seemed to have developed much of its own ecclesiology as it went along. Couldn't we trust the Chilean Church to do the same? A first step forward might be to have local bishops who were actually involved in a church planting programme where the local leadership team under the bishop could begin working out a flexible and temporary kind of structure to hold the growing work together. We wanted to implement this pretty early in the southern part of our work, as it was long overdue. Our bishop did not appear to welcome the idea for Chile. However, he may have liked it more than he let on. We discovered he had circulated our document called 'Regional

Episcopacy' among other bishops at Lambeth 1968 – possibly to get their reactions. The vision for this study had emerged from our Field Advisory Council (FAC) while the details had been developed and written up by Douglas Milmine and Eddie Gibbs.[6]

Even so, our bishop still did not appear to be either positive or encouraging about a process for down-grading the role and image of a traditional bishop and limit his field of operations to facilitate transitions from one culture to another – faster.

DISTANCES AND DIFFERENCES

Mary and I, living some distance from Bishop Ken Howell in Santiago, found it very discouraging not knowing how we were expected the work to develop in our area. We were confronting major missiological problems. How could we develop a spontaneous indigenous Chilean Church and still keep a semblance of Anglicanism about it? We needed to be flexible about our traditional ecclesiology for new Chilean wineskins. It was Jesus himself, the founder of the Church, who said we could not put new wine into old wineskins. If we did that we could lose both.

For me personally there seemed little point in continuing if we could not see some progress in this direction. If what we were doing was OK we wanted the bishop to bless it. If we were wrong we wanted the bishop to correct it or direct it into something better. We could then judge for ourselves if we thought we were capable of leading the Chilean Church forward along such a path or leave it for others to manage who saw their way more clearly. Time was going by fast. All the while we worked very hard as a missionary team, and were seeing exciting Church growth.

WAS THIS GOODBYE FOREVER?

So in 1969 we left for our second furlough with our four beautiful daughters and, though we didn't say so, we felt this was probably 'goodbye' to Chile. Antonio Valencia had moved down to St Paul's, Valparaíso, and we brought in a new man, Omar Ortíz, who had been converted and trained under Douglas Milmine, to take over at Gomez Carreño. We felt we were, at least, leaving the area looking reasonably orderly with someone nicely in charge in each place.

The return journey to the UK was a wonderful trip and a needful relaxation. But I was still troubled about what to do when I got home to England. I just could not cope with these feelings of disloyalty towards my bishop. Mary, I knew, would have been quite glad to pull out after some difficult times health-wise in Chile with the small children. All common enough crises with little children, I suppose, but it was extra hard coping in a foreign culture – without the normal family support network to help out in emergencies.

When we reached home we talked it over with SAMS, and told them we were thinking of staying home and some of the reasons why. We did not want to make a fuss or have to give public explanations. But we soon came under a lot of pressure to return.

IT JUST HAD TO BE GOD

I told Mary we could never go back simply out of response to human pressures, when it involved so much for all of us. I could not go back to build something when I had no clue what the building was meant to be. But we promised we would just keep praying for God's will, most dearly hoping it would be a parish in the UK. I had not appreciated just how much I loved England till we were home again. If we were going back it would clearly have to be God calling us.

And then the shock! God did just that! He called both of us surprisingly, unmistakingly and separately – in different places completely and at the same time – me, out preaching, and Mary, home praying! We committed ourselves to go back, not because we wanted to, but simply out of obedience to what we believed to be God's will. I wish we could say that we felt very blessed by this fresh commitment – we didn't. In fact we felt bad.

A few weeks later, at Southampton, climbing the gangway of the SS *Pasteur*, with the four girls in tow, Mary cried out in her heart, 'Oh, God, I can't get off this boat as I am getting on. You will have to do something!' It was to be the beginning of a whole new series of chapters – no! Much more than that – a whole new life and ministry together.

Chapter 11

RETURNING

In returning and rest shall ye be saved
(ISAIAH 30:15, KJV)

The will of God is always a bigger thing than we bargain for
(JIM ELLIOTT – MARTYR)

We were crossing the Bay of Biscay again, heading for the East Coast of Latin America. Tasha was the only one of us still on her feet. The sea was so rough. But then suddenly the sea calmed and so did our stomachs, as we headed across the Atlantic for Río de Janeiro in Brazil and then Buenos Aires in Argentina – where we would disembark before flying over to Chile.

Amongst the other passengers on board was a new missionary, Jenny Thornton, returning with us to Chile as a nurse. She was going to work in our hospital at Maquehue Pelal, near Temuco, in the south. We already knew her actually, because, whilst working as a secretary in Buenos Aires some two or three years previously, she had visited the SAMS work in Chile whilst on a holiday. During that visit she felt called to take up her nursing again, for which she was well qualified. She was returning now after a year of missionary training in the UK.

WHATEVER HAD HAPPENED TO JENNY?

Quite clearly something had happened to Jenny since we had previously known her. Mary was determined to find out what it was. But she became rather worried when Jenny admitted to having had some kind of 'Holy Spirit' experience. We had already come across Pentecostalism in Chile – admittedly not at very close quarters because we had heard too much about them. We had not been at all impressed with what we had heard and, of course, we always heard the worst because that was what we wanted to hear. But Mary could not let the subject drop with Jenny. She argued with her every inch of the way. Jenny remained quite relaxed not trying to push her 'experience' at all – no hard sell. At last Mary asked her: 'Jenny, tell me, what difference has this experience made to your life?'

Jenny thought for a moment. 'Well!' she said, 'It was like falling in love with Jesus all over again.'

MARY HAD TO HAVE 'IT'

That did it. Mary had to have 'it'.

How could she get 'it'? She must pray for 'it.' She spent hours alone in the stern of the ship crying out to God against the roar of that mass of water heaving over and over in the wash behind us – a restless vortex mirroring Mary's innermost turmoil. She was also reading through her Bible frantically – day after day – down in the cabin – and up on deck and then back in the stern. She was constantly coming back to those words of Jesus: 'Which of you fathers, if your son asks for a fish, will give him a snake instead? Or if he asks for an egg, will give him a scorpion? If you then, though you are evil, know how to give good gifts to your children, how much more will your Father in heaven give the Holy Spirit to those who ask him!'.[1] So Mary simply asked.

Nothing!

She asked again.

Nothing!

Thinking perhaps she was not in the right state to ask, she used her time in the stern of the deck to do even more heart-searching and repentance. She must have 'it'.

She asked again.

Nothing!

Increasingly desperate she continued crying out to God. One night before she went to bed she read the words 'weeping may remain for a night, but rejoicing comes in the morning'.[2] She thought: 'God is telling me he is going to do something tomorrow!'

Tomorrow came, and as soon as she could find the time on her own, she opened her Bible again at those simple words in St Luke's Gospel. Suddenly she saw something she had not seen before: 'Ask and it will be given to you'.[3] Suddenly she understood.

That was it! She had asked – she must have received. Why had she ever doubted? She began to praise God: 'Thank you Lord – you have heard my prayer. You have given me your Holy Spirit. Thank you Lord!' Of course, she knew she must already have had the Holy Spirit – she could not be a believer without him – but she also knew that the Holy Spirit seemed to have been burning very low in her life for the last few years.

FILLED TO BURSTING

She rushed to find Jenny to tell her that she had just been filled with the Holy Spirit. As she said it she felt herself being filled to bursting – an anointing so powerful – she had to keep walking round and round the ship till she sensed her feet again firmly back on the deck. She never recounted her experience to anyone else for a long time, thinking they would want a replica of her experience, and not the Holy Spirit of Jesus, who is always available to touch different people in different ways at different times for different purposes.

It's quite a shock to suddenly wake up in bed with a charismatic! Now it was my turn to be really worried. In one of her prayer times she even received the gift of tongues! My Giddy Aunt, I thought – whatever is going to happen next? I had been so opposed to all this for so long, and a loyal Bible-loving, card-carrying evangelical all my life.

But whatever had happened to Mary was obviously good. It also blessed our marriage in so many ways – and released Mary most surprisingly and energetically into a whole new ministry back in Chile. After a few months I asked her to lay hands on me and pray for me in tongues, so that I too might receive the same releasing gift she had. And she did just that, but there was no 'cloud nine' experience for me. Indeed I felt worse. I had not realised then what a lot of sorting out the Lord had for me to do before he could release me into something so good. I was not getting this grace on the cheap it seemed. But I certainly needed it. We had returned to take on the work started in Quilpué – taking over temporarily from Eddie Gibbs until Brian Skinner arrived back – now ordained with a family of five. He had previously worked as a farmer in the south and had been very successful there, but felt running such a big farm was counterproductive to our missionary work in Araucania where all his Mapuche neighbours had only small-holdings. He now took over the beginnings of the church at Quilpué. This move fitted in well all round.

OH DEAR! THE SAME OLD PROBLEMS

Once we were back into the work we found ourselves confronted with the same old problems again – and they all seemed to trace back to our bishop. How confusing! And he really was such a dear man! I had extracted a secret promise from Vernon Hedderly – before I left England – that if things got really difficult again the Wallington Missionary Mart would underwrite our return to the UK. Without that, one felt completely trapped with a large family to get home, the distance being so far and the cost of travel so high. One day Ken Howell said to me: 'David, I would really like you to come up to visit me in Santiago! I think there are a few things we need to sort out.'

I readily agreed – thinking arrogantly to myself: 'You bet there are!'

We fixed the date and I prayed furiously. Was this going to be the opportunity I had waited for – for so long – to put the bishop straight? As the day drew nearer, several other missionary friends told me how hopeful they were of a positive outcome, and their belief that these 'missionary-versus-diocesan' problems would soon get sorted out. They seemed to be depending on me for so much. 'Help Lord!'

Finally the day came and I caught the train to Santiago. From there I took a *lievre* – a rattly little twelve-seater that raced across the city. Sitting near the back, I started praying again for help. So much depended upon this meeting. I began making a list of all the things I thought the bishop was doing wrong. It was crucial for the future of our work that I painted the canvas fully. I did not want to fudge it or forget anything at this interview. Folding the finished list, I tucked it into the little New Testament that I had in my pocket, and then turned to a familiar passage which I thought would be helpful to read – I Corinthians chapter 13 – as a preparation. I thought for a while on those inspired words by St Paul about love – truly beautiful! Suddenly I started to re-read three or four verses again: Love is patient, love is kind. It does not envy, it does not boast, it is not proud. It is not rude, it is not self-seeking, it is not easily angered, it keeps no record of wrongs. Love does not delight itself evil but rejoices with the truth.[4]

'HAVE I GOT AN "ATTITUDE"?'

'Wait a minute,' I thought, 'Where did those words suddenly appear from?' I started to re-examine the verses and then my attitude to the bishop in their light. *Love is patient* – I had no patience with him. *Love is kind* – I had no kind thought for him. *Love is not rude* – in my mind I could not think of anything rude enough to say to him. *Love is not easily angered* – I had been seething with anger for the past five years. *Love keeps no record of wrongs* – I had just completed my list and had it there in my New Testament as my bookmarker!

'Lord,' I thought, 'Whatever am I meant to do about all this – I am more confused now than ever!'

'Repent!'

'OK, Lord, I will, but what should I do just now as I meet the bishop? I really can't get into repenting at this meeting!'

'Just tell him how sorry you are about your attitude and ask him to forgive you.'

'But Lord, if I start that now, I'll get side-tracked from all the important matters everyone in our area wants us to see sorted out!'

'Repent! Tell him how wrong you have been!'

'Lord, you know, this really is THE most inconvenient moment to bring all this up!'

'Do what I say!'

'OK, Lord! But I'm almost at the bishop's door, and I shall need your help!'

AT THE DOOR OF THE BISHOP'S HOUSE

I got off the bus and walked along the pavement to Ken Howell's door. It felt like going to the dentist to have a molar out. Ken himself opened it. I knew his office was at the back of the house, and I thought I had better get it over and done with before taking one more step inside, otherwise I might never do it. He had hardly closed the door before I blurted out: 'Bishop, before we go any further I want to apologise for not loving you as my brother – to tell you I am so sorry and ask you please to fogive me?'

I can't remember his reply but he soon had his arms round me; we both sank to the floor sobbing. He was even gracious enough to ask me to forgive him! When I eventually got up I knew that this just had to be the Lord's doing. Scales had just fallen from my eyes. God had also worked a paradigm shift in my mind – not the last one by any means! – and this was the beginning of a new thing God was doing in my heart. I found a miraculous love released in me for Ken Howell that just amazed me. There was a whole new desire to worship God that was bursting to come out of me with praise. I found the barriers between myself, and the bishop, the Roman Catholics, and the Pentecostals, had simply vanished. A proud spirit of Phariseeism had been cast out. There were more personal blessings to follow almost impossible to describe, and I believe others even perceived a little change in me after that also. Because I believe such divine anointings can be so significant in both Christian ministers and in their ministries I have written in general about this in my book *Leadership for New Life*[5] under the chapter heading 'Apostolic Leadership'.

THIS WAS NOTHING NEW!

I had not forgotten that my father had had a similar experience well after his ordination, that greatly affected his own life and ministry. I knew of John Wesley's similar experience at Fetter Lane long after his conversion at Aldersgate Street when he had felt his heart 'strangely warmed' on the 24th May 1838. Wesley was used by God over a period of more than fifty years to lead a revival of such significance that it probably saved England from the kind of bloody revolution going on simultaneously in France. Incidentally this movement eventually impacted Chile – since Methodism arrived there in the 1870s and the Pentecostal revival movement that had broken out in Valparaíso in 1907 came out of the small Methodist Church in Chile. That movement had come about as a rejection of liberal theology brought down by North American missionaries and a desire for both the gifts of the Holy

Spirit and for indigenous leadership. This movement gathered momentum throughout the century and spread right across the country – indeed the continent of Latin America. These mysterious out-pourings of spiritual life, whether in churches or individuals, have always fascinated me because they give an answer as to how the fire is generated or, once quenched, can come to life again. They show how the church gets re-focused and fresh motivation. They give us a testimony. How much we desperately need this new fire today! So I felt I was in excellent company. And I was privileged to be living in the region of Valparaíso where the fire had once fallen before in Chile! At that time I had had no direct contact with the Charismatic Renewal except for one of our missionaries in the south – whom I had hitherto been quite keen to avoid on that account.

FIRE

I was later interested to read of the experience of Blaise Pascal (1623–62), the remarkable French mathematician, physicist and religious thinker – and the father of the modern computer. On the evening of Monday, 23rd November 1654, when Pascal was thirty-one years old, he had a close brush with death in an accident – and this was followed by a profound encounter with God that changed the course of his life. Lasting from 10.30 pm until 12.30 am, the experience 'strained and exhausted language', and Pascal could find only one word to describe it: 'Fire'. But the experience was so vital and pivotal to his life that he wrote down a record of it that he kept sewn into the lining of his doublet, and for the rest of his life he took the trouble to sew it into every new doublet he had made.

This experience is sometimes called Pascal's 'second conversion', following the first when he was twenty-four, but clearly it was this anointing that set him ablaze for God – a divine fire that consumed him for the last short years of his life. Whilst encouraging all Christians to seek such fresh touches of God I would never call it a 'second conversion' myself. It was just one of the numerous experiences of the living God waiting throughout life for those who thirst and cry out after him. Maybe it could be actually a 'second blessing' but it must never be considered the last. Someone asked Mary once: 'When do I get the "second blessing"?' Her classic reply was: 'Between the first and the third!' Whatever people may like to call it, I found my experience had brought me into a whole new level of expectancy from God that certainly fired me up!

During the rest of my interview with the bishop there ensued a very positive discussion about our work and its future.

PUBLIC GESTURE CALLED FOR

I felt I needed to make some public gesture to indicate my change of heart and we invited Kath Clark (the missionary I had formerly wanted to avoid!) to come up from the south to talk about renewal in the Holy Spirit. I knew she would understand. Kath had been teaching in a little rural Bible School. Some two years previously, her students had been studying the first Epistle of Paul to the Corinthians. They came to the list of spiritual gifts in chapter twelve, and quite naturally asked Kath, how they could have these gifts today? She had simply called them out to the front and prayed for them. Many of them had had a powerful experience of the Holy Spirit right there as she prayed. When news of this reached us in the north soon after some of us were quite horrified. Here we were trying to train Anglicans and she was turning them all into 'Pentecostalists'! She was asked to stop and she regretfully did so. But the day of her vindication had now come in Valparaíso at least. She was now free to pray openly for as many people as she liked as we were being blessed in our region with the beginnings of a glorious visitation of the Holy Spirit. It proved remarkably fruitful in the growth of the work under our charge.

THE JESUS PEOPLE

Reports were coming in of a similar movement of the Holy Spirit followed with the so-called 'Jesus People' in the USA – a movement on a far greater scale. I was later able to meet many of their leaders at John Wimber's conferences in Anaheim, LA. This movement had attracted many of the 'sex 'n' drugs 'n' rock 'n' roll', anti-Vietnam flower-power people crowding the sun-swept beaches of southern California. They were being drawn in their droves to the Christian faith. Who would not have been excited by the incredulous reports about it in *Look*, *Time* and *Life* magazines, that we had been reading in far-away Chile? During a two-year period in the mid-1970s, well over 8,000 baptisms took place at New Port Beach in California, and there had been over 20,000 conversions to Christ. It was one of the most remarkable moves of the Holy Spirit that had ever occurred in American history with offshoot plants spreading the world.

One of the prime movers used by God in that revival was a hippie named Lonnie Frisbee who was later also to visit us in John Wimber's team in 1981.

NEW CHALLENGES

By the end of that first year back in Chile, I had been consecrated a bishop for the region of Valparaíso. I was thirty-nine. One nice little touch was that the day of my consecration (authorised by the 101st Archbishop of Canterbury) happened to be on St Thomas's day (1970), the 101st anniversary of the consecration of Bishop W.H. Stirling (1869), the first Bishop of the Falklands and South America. My consecration took place in St Paul's Church, Valparaíso.

Being a bishop brought a whole range of new challenges for me. The first problem was a personal one about whether it was diplomatic for me to remain so closely identified with things charismatic! I had a little discussion with the Lord about it at the time. 'Lord, I think I need to hold back a bit in this area as a bishop because I am concerned about your reputation!' I felt he did not seem much impressed, and sensed him saying, 'Don't worry about my reputation, David, you just keep open and obedient to my Holy Spirit!' Perhaps the Lord had not quite understood me – 'But Lord, I am concerned about the reputation of the Anglican Church!' This still did not let me off the hook either. The Lord had been concerned about the Anglican Church for a long time! Still is!

Finally I owned up: 'Well, Lord, I think the truth is, now that I am a bishop, I am concerned about my own reputation!' I had no sooner clarified the issue when I sensed the Lord saying: 'But David, who cares about your reputation? My Son made himself of no reputation.'

'Ah! Yes, Lord!'. There was no way out. I must simply press on along whatever unpredictable road the Lord might have in store for me.

DOMESTIC PROBLEMS

My next problem was a domestic one. There was no bishop's house. Where were we to live? Peter Hardy, Union Church treasurer, who had seen us through the customs nearly ten years earlier[6] generously offered us the free use of their manse.[7] We had just to pay for gas, water and electricity etc. The manse was rather up-market for us, on Cerro Castillo (Castle Hill) and was almost opposite the summer residence of the President. This was an amazing change of environment after all those years in the *Anglicana*. After being 'abased' we were now learning like St Paul 'how to abound' (until their chaplain felt he would like to live there himself once more). We began searching again and ended up renting a house only accessed by a climb of some seventy plus steps. It had one advantage – someone had kicked in the water meter half way up so we, the occupants, were charged a minimum standard rate for any water we used.

The church was growing in Gomez Carreño and I was helping one day in extending the wooden building for their meeting place. I was just unloading the Land Rover when I collided with a piece of wood on the roof rack. As I jumped up onto the bonnet in my usual haste, I had not noticed one plank projecting further than the rest. The result was quite a deep wound that just missed my right eye. However the skin was cut away a little below it and the gash was bleeding furiously. I was by then alone on the site. There was no time to lose. Pressing my blood soaked handerchief to the wound I drove one-eyed down to Viña del Mar and straight to a hospital. They found a doctor who was with me in next to no time. He took me into the operating theatre where he looked carefully at the damage.

He gave me ten stitches in all and would not take a peso for it! I left the hospital feeling very grateful and very brave! He had made an excellent job of it and it all healed up neatly. But painful surprises of a very different sort were soon to strike.

Chapter 12

CHILE'S MARXIST PRESIDENT

Communism is the opiate of the intellectuals
(CLARE BOOTH LUCE)

*Communism is like 'Prohibition' – it's a good
idea but it won't work*
(WILL ROGERS)

Modern society is hypnotised by socialism
(ALEXANDER SOLZHENITSYN)

*In a Capitalist society man exploits man – in a
Communist society it's the reverse*
(ANON)

We came through the turmoil of Chile's civil war, with some basic ethical problems still unsatisfactorily resolved about lawlessness, violence, and terrorism. It was not difficult to see it all coming but when it did finally come one felt totally unprepared for the terrible problems involved and the fundamental questions it raised. The rise and fall of Salvador Allende's regime is a fact of history that for a while was the focus of the world's attention. The arrest of Augusto Pinochet in the UK nearly thirty years later, once again revived international interest in the general leading the coup that toppled Allende in 1973.

The Allende affair impacted my life in so many ways – without my fully appreciating all the ramifications of its happening at the time. It also became a major factor in the sending of our eldest daughter Charlotte back to the UK in 1972 to finish her education as a teenager. This had an indirect bearing on the course of our future ministry. Of course such personal matters fade into the background against the unfolding drama of Allende's election in 1970 – an event that influenced the lives of a nation with twelve million inhabitants and the minds of millions more worldwide.

WHAT ARE THE FACTS?

Many reports about Allende's accession to power, and the military intervention that followed three years later, have been endlessly circulated. Included among all these reports and rumours are the real facts, the interpretation of those facts, the subjective selection of the facts, the later reinterpretation, the deliberate distortions of those facts, and the possible discovery of facts still coming to light.

A book called *Chile: An Accusation and a Warning*[1] convinces me that – in spite of some grave over-reactions by Chile's Armed Forces – too many of the actual events that provoked the coup have been simply air-brushed out of the historical record for purposes of political propaganda. One of the fairest accounts giving a different perspective from my own may be found in *A Vision of Hope* by Trevor Beeson and Jenny Pearce.[2]

The rapid collapse of the Union of Soviet Socialist Russia (USSR), and the slower processes of dismantling the Marxist regime still continuing in China, has since revealed to the world that Marxism could never do what it claimed to do. Yet for the record it must be said that many of the social evils those Marxist idealists were elected to heal still remain unhealed in Chile today. Capitalist alternatives, when they are inspired by self-interest, as indeed so much even in that tragic Marxist 'experiment' also turned out to be, may too easily and too often overlook the exploitations and sufferings of the oppressed – instead of finding constructive ways for correcting and healing them.

DIFFERING VIEWS OF THE SAME EVENTS

In discussing the election of Allende and the intervention of the Armed Forces there will be many who see things from quite different perspectives. A political animal I am not; just a 'conservative' with a small 'c' by tradition. I had not really thought out my political views up to that time. I had simply picked up my father's world-view. He taught me to have respect for authority, law and order, to behave decently and fairly, and to employ

common sense and pragmatism to solve social problems. I
expected a just taxation system so that the State could run our
health and educational services adequately, police and protect us
from our enemies effectively and reach out to the poor and
oppressed constructively. I held to Reinhold Neibuhr's view: 'The
sad duty of politics is the establishment of justice in a sinful world.'
The question is always about the best way of achieving this end in
a world where all are so capable of sin and so prone to selfishness.
That was, more or less, where I was coming from.

The awful tragedy and trauma of those who suffered or lost
loved ones in Chile's civil war during the early 1970s cannot be
belittled or ignored. Such internal conflicts bring incalculable pain
and too often involve innocent men, women and children as in
Afghanistan today. I can only witness to what I saw and heard in
Chile and accept that other people's perspectives will vary greatly.
Some may totally disagree with me. But we can still try to respect
each other's points of view.

DEMOCRATIC ELECTION

Although in 1970 Chile had the biggest 'middle class' of any
republic in Latin America, most of the land surface was still
owned by a small minority – however unreachable for civilisation
or unsuitable for cultivation much of that mountainous land
surface might be. But the State had already moved considerably
towards a more equitable redistribution of wealth. Under the
Christian Democrats (1964–70) led by President Eduardo Frei,
Chile had become one of the most Socialist countries in Latin
America (with the exception of Cuba) in terms of the ownership
of industry, with 50% already under State control.

Allende was elected President of Chile on the 4th September
1970. He was the first Marxist ever to be chosen democratically –
though there were queries about some improprieties along the
way. As he received less than 50% of the votes,[3] Allende's election
was subject to ratification by Congress. An extreme right wing
group *Patria y Libertad*[4] tried to prevent this by an attempted
abduction of Chile's military Commander in Chief, General
Schneider. Their futile motive was to create the climate for a
'State of Emergency' – hoping in some way to frustrate the needed

ratification of Allende's election by Congress. The tragic
assassination that followed was unintentional. General Schneider
drew his revolver when they were trying to kidnap him, so his
panicky abductors shot him. He died in hospital three days later.
The whole ploy had been destined to failure.

USA's INVOLVEMENT

So was the attempt at intervention by the ITT[5] emanating from
the USA, offering to finance other blocking operations. The early
exposure of this was quickly exploited by Allende for propaganda
purposes. He immediately ordered the confiscation of all the ITT's
assets in Chile (at that time valued at 92 million dollars).
Whatever sums found their way to Chile from the USA during
this time hardly compared with the sums that came to the
Government from Russia for the advancement of the 'Marxist
revolution'. In spite of boasting that Chile would no longer be
dependent on foreign aid if his party were elected, once in power
Allende was soon approaching the USSR to provide the
equivalent of 400 million dollars in project aid and tied import
credits covering the period until the end of 1972. And when that
time came Allende actually went to Moscow himself to beg for
more. But further help this time was limited to 50 million dollars
in similar credits. Russia by then was negotiating for a much
needed grain deal with the West and did not want to risk
upsetting President Richard Nixon at that point in time.

STATUTE OF GUARANTEES

But before Allende's election was finally ratified, the Christian
Democrats, who were handing over the Government, drew up a
'Statute of Guarantees' to provide some fundamental safeguards
for a society which, it was feared, was about to lose certain
freedoms under the incoming Socialist/Marxist Government.
These guarantees were designed to preserve the accepted
democratic norms for the press, the trade unions and the
universities, along with the preservation of the traditional
distinctions between the legislature, the executive and the
judiciary. This Statute was approved, by the Chamber of Deputies
on 15th October and by the Senate four days later after 'the

longest fifty days'. Allende confirmed his agreement, and Congress, thus reassured, finally ratified his election. Of course we were all greatly relieved to learn of those guarantees and felt we could relax.

ALLENDE'S PRIVATE ADMISSION

But Allende soon shrugged off the 'Statute of Guarantees'. He admitted that his public promise to affirm and respect these 'guarantees' as 'a moral law before our conscience and before history' was given as 'a tactical necessity'.[6] He needed his election to be ratified by Congress. He told Regis Debray that he gave the assurances because 'The important thing was to take control of the Government'.[7] But once in the seat of power it would be a different story.

In spite of this treacherous admission, Allende had initially come across as a good man, who wanted to do the best he could for Chile.[8] He proved himself a brilliant political manipulator – a master of the art of divide and rule. He had once claimed that whoever drew up the agenda of a meeting could determine its outcome. It was the divisions in his Government that brought about his eventual downfall. There was considerable rivalry from the outset between the six separate parties in the *Unidad Popular*[9] Government (UP) that he had been elected to lead, though in the early stages their machinations were not aired so overtly and some of their highly publicised policies appeared highly commendable.

The parties included, amongst others, the Communists, the Socialists[10] and the Radicals – along with three other much smaller left of centre parties. From the start each of the larger parties was out to gain the ascendancy over the other, and each continually undermined the other.

HOW COULD WE CHRISTIANS CO-OPERATE?

Many of the churches felt that if this new Government was truly going to help the poor and bring more justice to the oppressed then we must do all we could to support it. The Anglican Church has a worthy history of educational, medical and agricultural projects designed to help the underprivileged in Chile, but we knew we were only scratching the surface in that area and if there was more we could do we should do it.

Our representatives went to local meetings of the UP to see how we could co-operate practically with them. There was much talk about using our church buildings for community meetings and educational projects, and it was suggested that we could combine in tackling some of the social problems like poverty and drunkenness that blighted the community. With the plight of the poor brought into new focus, some of our Christian students in the university were encouraged to mobilise groups and move into areas of extreme poverty to help improve the conditions there. But they soon discovered, to their surprise, that the other political groups did not welcome their help there at all.

BEGINNING THE MARXIST EXPERIMENT

Once in power, Allende's Government moved rapidly into confiscating private properties, with the apparent hope that by undermining Chile's traditional economic structures he could destroy the financial base of the opposition and the free press.

There was also an extreme left wing group of younger people called the MIR[11] (Leftist Revolutionary Movement). One of its leaders was Pascal Allende, the President's nephew. Since this movement became one of the most sinister elements empowered by Allende, a few of its many objectives and activities need spelling out.

It was originally founded in 1965 by a group of 'Socialist Party' dissidents living in Santiago and Concepción. They were young middle class Chilean intellectuals (many still students) who were becoming 'impatient and contemptuous of parliamentary democracy', and the 'possibility of changing the system from within' – they were not unique – they had their philosophical counterparts in North America and Europe. These people had no doubt been inspired by Frantz Fanum's book *The Wretched of the Earth*. They rationalised the use of violence and believed it was inevitable as the only way to ultimate success. The MIR was also committed to anarchy but it had gone to ground in 1969 after their murder of Frei's vice president. As soon as Allende came to power in 1970 he declared an amnesty for all 'political prisoners' and a number of leading MIR-istas were released back into society – and immediate revolutionary activity once again.

ROLE OF THE MIR

The MIR quite openly maintained that if Allende's Government was really bent on radical change, sooner or later it would have to 'break the legal fetters upon it' by sweeping aside the Congress and the whole judicial system. This would provoke a violent reaction from the opposition and spark off a civil conflict in which the MIR, and other paramilitary groups, would come into their own. The MIR had no time for any reform programmes to be effected with the help of other sections of Chile's burgeoning middle class. They were pledged to sabotage all overtures towards compromise between the Government and the opposition.

There were attempts at making converts from inside the Navy[12] and the Army – notably amongst the elite 'black berets' – the Chilean 'special-forces' group. They were partially successful, and, at the end of 1970, the Army High Command was compelled to expel a number of NCOs from that unit because of their sympathies with the MIR. This did not inhibit the MIR from pressing on with its wedge-driving between the conscripts and the professional officers in the Armed Forces.

The MIR also produced its own training manuals covering the employment of weapons used by the Chilean Army; it acquired detailed charts showing the organisation and deployment of most of their regiments; it also had notes and tactics of the Chilean Navy in coastal operations. The MIR had safe houses for permanent hideouts, temporary shelters, houses used for making explosives, and supply depots. They provided expert training on guerrilla tactics in which Cuban immigrants also played a vital role. They had no problem acquiring arms, both from a flourishing black market in Argentina and importing others via Cuba.

The MIR was soon organised in building up popular support from the depressed 'slum-dwellers' in Chile's growing 'shanty' towns that skirted her major cities. Almost overnight, walled encampments suddenly appeared in a number of city suburbs.

In mid 1972, around Las Condes – an affluent commuter suburb of Santiago – a MIR-ista assault squad arrived one night in municipal trucks loaned by the Communist district prefect, carrying prefabricated timber walls and rolls of barbed wire. By the next morning the new settlement was erected, shielded by

153

barbed wire fences, complete with flags, posters and a sign bearing the designation – *'Campamento Fidel Ernesto'*.

Another such camp, the *'Ché Guevara'* settlement, in the San Pablo suburb of Santiago, was built on land illegally seized by MIR-ista commando squads. The *'Ché Guevara'* settlement originally housed more than 2,000 families. Discipline inside was rigid and the place was run with revolutionary austerity. Some 800 families were later weeded out from *'Ché Guevara'* for lack of discipline[13] or political obtuseness. The settlement was ringed with defensive walls and watchtowers. This was yet another of a number of training camps preparing for the coming armed struggle that the MIR intended to mount.

FACTORY WORKERS AND FARM LABOURERS

Similar militias and vigilante groups were being trained amongst the workers in the factories and the labourers on the farms. Whilst Allende was in power the MIR-istas were allowed a fairly free hand to entrench themselves in the difficult hinterland of the Andean foothills.

For more than one year, the area around Lake Panguipulli in the south was run as a kind of private 'fiefdom' by the infamous 'Comandante Pepe'. Such *campamentos*, extended from Punta Arenas in the south to the capital, Santiago. They were in frequent conflict with the Army that persisted in its search for illegal caches of arms.

One of our SAMS missionary doctors, who had built up a medical practice in the town of Carahue serving both the town and the surrounding area, was asked by the Chilean National Health Service to move his surgery temporarily to another location in nearby Galvarino. He could not understand why until he discovered that the neighbouring coastal town of Nehuentue had suddenly been transformed into a huge camp for training locals for guerrilla warfare. They wanted Dr Bill Maxwell, a foreigner – highly respected locally – to be well out of the way while this was being set up.

A line of hospitals stretching across Chile from Temuco, Nueva Imperial, Carahue and Puerto Saavedra were filled with leftist doctors involved in the importation and storage of arms while innocent looking hospital ambulances were used for their transportation.

All this kind of activity was being widely reported to an increasingly outraged populace, but Allende would neither agree to close down the guerrilla bases, nor outlaw the MIR. His plan was obviously to have a paramilitary force to counter the possibility of military intervention – an inevitable response if his government ever acted unconstitutionally. Allende had openly promised that weapons would be available for the masses when they were needed. The ordinary citizen of Chile sat helplessly by waiting for the time bomb to explode.

UNBELIEVABLE TENSION

Sensing the interminable tick-tick-tick, I was tempted to get out with my family while the going was still good. The mounting tension was unbelievable, but duty prevailed. I wondered whether my being a foreigner might be an embarrassment for the Chilean Church.

Meanwhile, the MIR kept up a continual harassment of the middle classes, and gunned down both civilians and police with apparent impunity when it suited them. So much for Allende's 'peaceful road to socialism' which so impressed the West.

Some of the MIR had ominously formed a personal bodyguard for the President. Captain Araya, Allende's Naval *aide de camp* was mysteriously murdered in August 1973. Even though one of the MIR-istas was charged with this crime they continued to be a law unto themselves. What with sporadic bombs, street battles, strikes, shortage of food and lack of medicines, we were increasingly concerned about the sense of pending revolution in the air. Something dire seemed about to happen at any moment – a storm was about to break!

Allende had made a statement in his victory speech the night of his election on 4th September 1970: 'We have won the presidency, now we must win the power'. But by now he realised that he was going to need more time than his expected first term in office (six years) to gain enough votes for winning a second popular election; indeed it was becoming increasingly unlikely that he could ever be re-elected. Winning 'the power' was now seen to mean the taking of absolute power to himself as a dictator. Again, after a further (and final) conversation in 1973, Regis Debray summed up Allende's views as follows: 'We all knew that it was merely a tactical matter of winning time to organize, to arm, to co-ordinate the military formations of the parties that made up the Popular Unity Government. It was a race against the clock.'

MOST SOCIALIST STATE

The take-over programme for the State-ownership of industry was progressing steadily, with some 80% of industrial production now under State control. Chile was rapidly being turned into one of the most Socialist countries in the world outside the Communist bloc. Whatever the doctrinaire benefits of this might have been the effects on production were catastrophic. Some 4,900 Chilean farms had been commandeered by 1972 – those taken were mainly picked for their strategic positions over crossroads, bridges etc. By the end of Allende's first two years an estimated 75% of the agricultural land had been brought within the so-called 'reformed area' with a very diminished level of productivity – yet another strategy designed to erode the economic power of the opposition parties and to bankrupt the independent media.

Many factories were also taken over and manufactured production in Chile was also slowing down in a major way. Workers had to dedicate so many hours a day to political instruction (later discovered to include military training with modern arms). Simultaneously, the State was taking over complete ownership of the American copper mines in the north in spite of the fact that the State was already receiving 84% of the profits from copper mining in Chile.

ROLE OF COMMUNISTS

Not all the parties in the *Unidad Popular* were Socialist. One of them was the Communist party[14] and they were taking orders directly from Moscow. Allende had put them in control of the economy for the first two years, until he found them becoming too powerful to manage. With far too much money chasing too few goods inflation was rampant – soon to be calculated at nearly 1,000% pa,[15] though figures vary on this. Allende had inherited foreign reserves worth 400 million dollars when he came to power at the end of 1970, and already by June 1972 the country was 28 million dollars in the red.

SCARCE GOODS

Allende's programme for nationalising and the resultant fall in productivity was followed by a scandalous rampant black market.

The scarcity of goods for sale had two counter-productive effects. Firstly, was the practice of *acaparando* (hoarding) – people began buying up many things they did not even want as a frantic investment for their money that was devaluing so rapidly. Secondly, this hoarding sorely deprived others of products they desperately needed and created an increasing scarcity of goods on the open market.

Then there were the *colas* (queues). Scarcity created such desperation that people tended to join any queue they could see in the hope of buying something in very short supply. Long queues full of frustrated womenfolk, who rightly felt they were wasting their time, gave them a sympathetic forum for the public sharing of their grievances and circulating anti-Government propaganda.

Perhaps one of the most extraordinary decrees passed by the Allende administration was that of the *pan unico*. The plan was to produce just one kind of bread in the shops for everyone. Soon all the bakeries were producing just this *pan unico* – it looked and tasted grey. This was a relatively small move by the Government but it caused major grassroots grumbles. The idea of a *pan unico* may have been a concession to some doctrinaire principle of equality, but it seemed tactically maladroit for any Government dependent upon the popular suffrage for eventual re-election. Why aggravate even one's own supporters so unnecessarily? Fortunately after some six months the Government realised its mistake.

High inflation and the shortage of foodstuffs provided the Marxists with the pretext for the imposition of rationing that gave neighbourhood committees (dubbed the JAP) scope for supervising the daily lives of ordinary citizens. The form of rationing consisted of a *canasta popular*[16] for each household. This was a fixed price package containing the basic necessities – but to call them 'popular' was a misnomer. Homeowners had to buy the same things at the same time every week regardless of whether they all wanted soap powder (for example) that week or whether they actually had the money to pay for the goods on the day they were made available. They also complained that the system was being used to impose political controls. In some neighbourhoods they also had to produce their electoral registration cards as well as their identity cards. Another reason why they were unpopular was because the process was very time-consuming. Women complained of having to queue for long hours in order to buy a single chicken. What was more both the men and the women were expected to do several hours of guard duty each week to prevent the store being raided!

SOLVING UNEMPLOYMENT

Trains no longer ran to time. The railway between Valparaíso and Santiago had employed thirty men. When Allende came to power they had to take on another seventy although they were not needed and there was no work for them. All these employees now had to undergo daily 'political instruction'! By duplicating this process in all the State-run institutions, it was claimed that the number of employed persons in Chile's workforce had been increased by 80%, no matter the fall in production rates. By this means Allende hoped to ensure continued support from the grassroots especially when added to that there were wage increases for the lowest paid that were denied to blue collar workers and professional men who were also struggling with the rapid inflation.

The Government was holding down the legal salaries of both skilled workers and professionals at a time of soaring inflation and holding down the prices in selected industries private firms. In so doing he was weakening the Chilean middle classes considerably and driving them closer and closer to bankruptcy. In this way the State could gradually expropriate all private capital. The final goal was to gather political power into the hands of a narrow ruling group.

SOCIALISM WITH A HUMAN FACE

The UP was beginning to show signs of serious disunity. One

underlying rift was between the old Communists and the New Left, who had differing opinions about the Russian invasion of Czechoslovakia in 1968. Marxism in Chile would be a superior version: 'socialism with a human face', as Allende called it. And the West seemed to love that! But then Stalin actually had a human face too!

If Allende was as high minded as we struggled to think he was, he had major headaches keeping his UP together as each party continued the undermining of the others. Allende also developed a 'gift' for saying different things inside Chile from what was being reported to the outside world.

One of the smaller parties in the UP Government was the Movement for United People's Action (MUPA). This party was becoming divided over the way things were developing and expelled some of their leadership. The less militant half gained control of the *Radio Candelaria* and the party property in Santiago. Passers-by were treated to the spectacle of two groups from the same party within Allende's ruling coalition actually fighting each other in the streets over their own property.

Meanwhile Fidel Castro was 'assisting' Allende by sending down numerous Cuban 'experts'. Indeed he came down to Chile himself and stayed for over a month. The Anglican Church in Cuba had a centenary celebration. We sent up two clergy, Antonio Valencia and Herminio Merino to represent us. In the course of the usual Latin American embrace one of the Cubans whispered: 'You've got Fidel Castro with you in Chile now – you can keep him!'

STRIKES, STRIKES AND MORE STRIKES

The Government then decided that the time had come for all trucks and taxis to be nationalised. Many upwardly mobile Chileans had striven by means of hard sweat to work themselves up from carrying freight on donkeys, then to owning a horse-drawn cart, moving on to a small truck and finally to a bigger one or even a small fleet of them. Overnight a life's work and savings were to be swallowed up by the State. It was the truckers and shopkeepers 27-day protest strike that gave Allende his biggest political crisis in his first two years.

There was a further truckers strike[17] in July 1973. This second strike lasted for over forty days, right up until the eventual military coup. Supporters of Allende have claimed that this was financed by the CIA.

There was increasing violence in the streets, but the lack of goods in the shops prompted the women in Santiago to organise a consumers' protest and arrange what they called 'the march of the unfilled pots' when they walked along the streets banging their empty saucepans together. The courage of these women was amazing. This idea was also taken up by the protesting poor in Valparaíso and Viña del Mar, who used to come out onto the hills at night to bang their saucepans too. But the revolutionary process continued unabated and ultimate victory for the Marxists seemed inevitable.

OPEN LETTER FROM SOME OF ALLENDE'S SUPPORTERS

As if all this was not enough, an open letter to the President of the Republic was published purporting to come from 16 doctors who had voted for Allende in the election of 1970. What they described about the health service was replicated in nearly every other department where the Government had control.

This letter revealed to the general public the sinister processes which had been developing everywhere in the State-controlled areas of Chilean life.

The letter was written in Spanish, of course, and addressed to President Allende. It ran as follows:

Señor Presidente.

Nothing is more frustrating . . . for a human being than to put one's confidence and hope in an ideal, and then to find oneself defrauded when the very man in the position to effect that ideal is destroying it.

We supported your presidential candidature believing that the watchwords and programmes of your Government which attracted so many Chileans who elected you as our leader, would be being formed into a promising reality

Your [own] qualifications as a [medical] doctor . . . made us believe that you would dedicate a considerable part of your efforts in office, to bringing about better medical services within reach of all Chileans.

We believed in a policy of health for the protection of the 'under privileged' children of Chile. After nearly three years of your Government, we have seen with amazement and sorrow how all the flags raised during your electoral campaign have been soiled with ineptitude, sectarianism and deceitfulness, which has sunk this country inexorably into economic chaos, and the gravest social and moral crisis of our history.

Mistaken Economic Policy

We have been witnesses of how the improvisation of a mistaken economic policy has given rise to an uncontrollable inflation that has deeply injured the proletariat. How political differences have provoked a battle without quarter, dividing Chileans in an irreconcilable manner resulting in a tragic number of deaths. How the often proclaimed austerity and purity of 'the new man' has resulted in the plunder of the national treasure by small corrupt groups. . . How discipline has been turned into a total loss of authority. How education for all has been turned into an instrument for narrow and dogmatic indoctrination, not only in the centres of education, but right through all the means of communication.

Chimera of Democratization[18]

The chimera of the democratization of health has ended up in the paralysis of a system that has ceased to function. Every hospital in the country is lacking [essential] supplies. A state of disorganization and political persecution [prevails]; where people unfit for the job, whose only qualification is the possession of a card of a partisan political affiliation, are (being) placed in positions of the greatest responsibility.

We cannot make ourselves accomplices in this deceit being practised on the population . . . It is not possible for us to continue practising honest medicine without medical supplies nor surgical instruments equipped only by our own good will. Furthermore, in spite of this [goodwill] the doctors themselves are being stigmatized as responsible for this [chaos] by means of a vile campaign of calumnies

161

emanating from official sources of diffusion.

It has not been easy for us to take this step, but . . . we have joined forces with the organized movement of the doctors of Chile, adding our voices to the clamour of the majority of citizens, that demands a radical and profound rectification of your Government policy, failing which, we ask for your resignation from the high position in which . . . our votes have placed you.

We believe that this decision of ours . . . will be seen in the future as a disinterested and honest gesture by people who have recognized their mistake in time.

This open document was signed by sixteen medical doctors.[19] Anyone living through those years would have to agree that the doctors' letter reflected what was happening right across the nation of Chile. But however could the country extricate itself from the awful mess it had got itself into now?

THREATS TO THE ARMED FORCES
There was a constant broadcasting of threats to the Armed Forces warning them not to intervene in the revolutionary process taking place. They were told that all their family movements were known and that any attempt by the military to frustrate the left wing forces would result in the liquidation of their loved ones. We were privately warned to be careful of what we said to each other on the telephone as they were probably tapped.

It was a climate of fear and frenzied paranoia. Wondering seriously if we would ever get out of Chile alive, I asked a more senior officer how long the Armed Forces could possibly allow this state of affairs to continue? He assured me that the military would certainly never intervene until it was quite clear that the majority of Chileans had had enough of it. I remember thinking that surely they must have had enough of it already!

FALSE ALARMS
There were one or two false alarms. There had been some kind of attempted coup at 9 am one Thursday (11th June 1973). Colonel Roberto Souper rolled out of barracks in Santiago with his

Second Tank Regiment – a total of 412 men participating. He stationed his tanks outside the presidential palace and the Ministry of Defence in the centre of the capital, without any co-operation apparently from other Army units. Within two hours Colonel Souper and his men had surrendered. Though the true purpose of this fiasco seemed a mystery at the time, it may simply have been a trial run to reveal the extent, readiness and effectiveness of Allende's paramilitary power.

RUMOUR, PANIC AND OUTRAGED PARANOIA

It's almost impossible now to convey the atmosphere of outrage among Chileans from the right and centre parties resulting from the total impact of fear, lawlessness, hopelessness, chaos and disconcerting ignorance – combined with an eerie sense of impending doom. Possibly the most galling thing about it was that the world outside was still thinking it was all a wonderful Marxist experiment – democratically authenticated!

Rumour and panic were rampant. True or not it was believed that a plot was being hatched by the Left to eliminate a large number of outspoken military leaders who were capable and still prepared to stand up to this appalling Socialist 'revolution'. I could not speak for the whole of Chile – some regions of such an extended republic may never have picked up such frightening rumours.

Our family was suddenly confronted with a tricky little domestic problem as things were moving towards some kind of climax. At this time, we were still living opposite the President's summer residence. Charlotte's flaxen hair attracted a lot of admiration from Chilean males, and one of Allende's young guards approached me politely one day and asked permission to begin taking her out. I did not want to offend him. Fortunately I was able to fob him off gently by telling him that plans were actually in hand to send her back to England for her further education. He looked disappointed but accepted my word.

Chapter 13

CIVIL WAR

It is easier to ride a tiger than dismount it
(INDIAN PROVERB)

A Truth not quite Self Evident
(*THE DAILY TELEGRAPH*, 24TH DECEMBER 2001)

There followed a speedy succession of crises. Cabinets were being re-shuffled monthly. Events, it seemed, must be moving to some kind of climax. On 22nd August 1973 the Chamber of Deputies ruled that the Government had gravely violated the Constitution. 'It is a fact,' the resolution ran, 'that, from the beginning, the present Government has attempted to sieze total power, with the evident purpose of subjecting everyone to the most rigorous economic and political controls. And of achieving [this] by the installation of a totalitarian [State] absolutely opposed to the system of representative democracy that the constitution upholds . . .'

As a result the Chamber issued the following declaration: 'The armed forces and the *Carabineros* [police] must be a guarantee to all Chileans, and not just to a section of the country or a political combination. Therefore, they should not participate in the Government of a sectarian minority, but maintain the rule of the Constitution and the law . . . in order to guarantee institutional stability, civil peace, security and development.'

This resolution, which also catalogued a series of illegal acts by Allende's Government, was carried by eighty-one votes to forty-seven. The majority was not quite large enough for initiating the processes for the President's impeachment. Under the Chilean Constitution a two thirds' majority was required and they were two votes short for that.

The significance of this resolution was that it seemed to create a basis for military intervention, so long as it was intended to re-establish the rule of the Constitution and the law. Thus it marked a turning point in the relationship between Congress and the Armed Forces.

A number of church leaders organised an ecumenical day of prayer in Valparaíso round about the 8th September concerning the prevailing state of emergency, and I, for one, was praying secretly for the hasty overthrow of Allende. There seemed no other way out of the crisis the country was in. It was widely believed that a large majority felt the same way at that time: 80% was one figure quoted though, of course, people were careful not to publicly express such thoughts.

CHAOS

To add to the chaos, the main road to Chile's capital was frequently strewn with *miguelitas* – nails manufactured like 'jacks'. Whichever way these fell, they left jagged spikes facing upwards along the road. I set off for Santiago one day and had to turn back having encountered numerous vehicles completely stranded with as many as three punctured tyres on one machine.

The shortage of food we were experiencing in Viña del Mar was countrywide. Then came the announcement by Allende himself that there was only sufficient grain left in Chile to keep the population in bread for three more days. But he offered no plan nor hope for resolving the problem. We still happened to have half a sack of flour. It was full of mice droppings and Mary had been going to throw it out. But in the crisis we simply could not waste it. We came to no harm and shared some of it with others – and it did them no harm either apparently – indeed it kept us going till that particular crisis was past.

I had a strange experience preaching on Moses one Sunday morning in Union Church just before the 'coup' and, without drawing a direct parallel to the current situation in Chile, I pointed out that Moses was chosen by God to deliver the nation of Israel. As I looked out over the congregation I noticed an admiral and suddenly felt – 'He's the man!' Whatever could that mean? I had imagined that any initiative from the Armed Forces would come from the Army, the senior service in Chile, not the Navy.

I did not mention anything to anyone of what I had sensed – it would have sounded like seditious talk! Later I learned that this particular admiral had in fact had a leading role in the planning of Allende's overthrow.

There were increasing threats from the Left about dire retribution for the families of officers and troops who might dare to intervene. But on Tuesday, 11th September 1973 at 4 am, the first Armed Forces tanks started to roll across the streets of Santiago. I was reliably informed later that both the British and the American embassies had been previously forewarned by the military.

Unaware of how far things had actually progressed in Santiago, I had set out early that morning (6 am) from Viña to take Becky to hospital for some medical tests in Valparaíso. It was frustrating to suddenly encounter a military roadblock along the way. A soldier asked me to identify myself and explain where I had come from. He then politely instructed me to return to Viña del Mar. 'But I need to get my daughter to hospital!' I protested and asked to speak to the officer in charge. He was also politely unyielding. I drove away and tried other routes that I knew but every roadway was blocked. Something strange was definitely in the air!

ALLENDE'S SUICIDE
I returned home hastily to put on the radio and managed to ring up a friend just before the phones were cut. The radio was broadcasting the latest news – this must be the long expected military intervention! The broadcast continued with patriotic music and solemn announcements about curfews etc.

Other announcements followed. Three hours later we suddenly found ourselves listening to a dialogue taking place between a General Pinochet, who had very recently been appointed Commander in Chief of the Armed Forces by President Salvador Allende, and the President himself who was still inside the presidential palace in Santiago. The palace had already been struck by a couple of Air Force bombs. Allende was being urged to surrender. Pinochet was offering him a safe air passage *gratis* – for himself, his wife and family – to any country in the world that he chose to name. The military did not want to make a martyr of him. Allende however finally outwitted them.

The decision inside the palace was to surrender but Allende never emerged. His personal doctor, who had been with him until they had all decided to leave, had assumed that Allende was following behind him in the corridor. But he wasn't. He was making a final broadcast on *Radio Magellanes*. 'This is the last time I shall speak to you . . . having an historic choice to make I shall sacrifice my life in loyalty to my people . . .' He ended with the words: 'I have faith in Chile and its destiny . . . to build a new society. Long live Chile! Long live the people! Long live the workers! These are my last words. I am certain that my sacrifice will not be in vain. I am certain it will be a moral lesson which will punish treachery, cowardice and treason.' There seems no doubt that Allende really wanted to create a new society but the way he sought to bring this about, and the way his subordinates became corrupt and struggled between themselves, meant that for the latter half of his presidency he had lost control of his Government. As he finished his broadcast, the party who had been with him were drawing near the main exit of the palace and realised that they needed a white flag to indicate their intentions of surrender.

Remembering his white coat the doctor made his way back to the presidential office to retrieve it. Reaching it he found Allende still in his chair, a machine gun lodged between his legs – he had shot himself dead. Outside the palace, Allende's remaining supporters quickly put it about that the military had murdered him! Similar statements are still being circulated thirty years after the event.

Awaiting investigation, Allende's doctor was arrested and interned since he had been the last man to be with the President alive, and the first man to see him dead. In a filmed interview later shown on British TV he related to Julian Pettifer, a BBC reporter, that he was absolutely certain that Allende had taken his own life. Strangely, this filmed interview was suspiciously lost in the laboratory back in the UK. Pettifer had to make a second trip out to the internment camp on Dawson Island for a repeat interview.

THE TAKE-OVER

The take-over was soon effected. There were Armed Forces everywhere. This was a civil war – a dreadful thing which leaves scars that last for decades – but the sense of law and order being restored was an extraordinary morale booster for those who had lived in that lawless limbo for the last three years. How easy it is to take such basic things as law and order for granted when one has them!

By this time we were living in our house in Pasaje Benedictinos, on the edge of the *estero* in Viña del Mar. The *estero* was a dry riverbed, except for a few days after heavy rains in winter when it became a torrential flood. For the rest of the year it provided a site for a huge Saturday market. Passing beside the centre of the city it was also used for car parking and a football pitch on weekdays.

We had plenty of reminders that the war was not over for some time after the coup when MIR-ista guerrillas, still at large, would climb along the huge drains that emptied into the *estero*. From this vantage point they would machine gun the military doing guard duty on the bridges. Our house actually came into the crossfire from this once or twice. Bullets were not the only reminders of the struggle going on around us. One night Mary was nearly blown out of bed by a bomb which exploded beside the railway line, less that fifty yards from our house.

Once the phones were reconnected, Mary tried to contact home in the UK. Her mother was most relieved. It was the first time they had spoken since the coup though Mary had kept her regularly in the picture by letter. Her first question was: 'Are you quite safe, dear?' 'Oh – absolutely!' said Mary, clapping her hand quickly over the mouthpiece as an unexpected burst of machine gun fire sounded too close to our window for comfort.

MY OWN OBSERVATIONS

As a foreigner, and yet a leader of a Chilean institution with a fairly wide network of contacts, I simply include some of my own observations about what was going on. When the military intervention happened the majority of Chileans believed it was really necessary and not before time. This has to be stressed since there has been so much disinformation concerning the supposedly happy state of Chile under Allende and the wonderful achievements of a regime that was terminated by a cruel military dictator.

At first, because of the run-down state of Chile's economy and the unwillingness of foreign governments to help, there was a considerable tightening of the belts. But its eventual revitalisation under President Pinochet was quite remarkable. And the ultimate restoration of the country to democracy and the civil powers was something few generals who have taken over the national leadership elsewhere have ever managed to achieve voluntarily!

HOT WATER

I was back in the UK a couple of months after the coup and was soon in hot water for one of my public comments. In a Sunday programme for the BBC, I commended the military for their final intervention, but begged the prayers of God's people over Chile's future since there were inherent risks under any military dictatorship.

Privately I thought that the rapid and drastic actions of the military were understandable.

There had been constant threats broadcast over the radio about what would happen to the families of the military if the Armed Forces should ever think of intervening, causing widespread paranoia in many areas over these threats. After the coup the military soon formed hit-squads to eliminate the hidden cells of MIR terrorists to forestall a dreaded counter-attack. These were not imaginary. There were verifiable attempts on the life of Pinochet himself.

The MIR-ista armed opposition remaining within the republic was being greatly encouraged by the almost spontaneous and global opposition to Pinochet. Orders were given that the MIR were not to leave the country without the permission of their party. 'They reckoned to die in action rather than take asylum'.[1] The overseas opposition had arisen from sheer outrage over the coup and ignorance of the real disastrous state of affairs existing under Allende's Marxist misgovernment. Few people abroad gathered that it was due to Allende's loss of control in his own

Government, the violations of Chile's Constitution, increasing civil disorder, the internal attempts at dividing the Armed Forces, and the establishment of an armed independent para-military force within the republic. But such were the factors that finally compelled the military to intervene.

Any charges against Pinochet being circulated, whether true, partly true or totally untrue, have proved very helpful to the supporters of Allende in trying to regain some credibility. Even today the media will tend to focus on the tortures of Pinochet, rather than, say, the terror networks of Fidel Castro.[2] The BBC still speaks of the Cuban Fidel Castro as 'President', but the Chilean General Augusto Pinochet as 'Dictator'. This is in spite of the fact that after seventeen years of rule, President Pinochet voluntarily handed over the republic to a democratically elected Government, something that Castro has not yet done – not even after fifty years of his autonomous rule.

MARXIST PROPAGANDA

It is often very difficult to get to the real truth about anything. We all have our prejudices and our blind spots. Over those years many would have read the regular articles in a respected British daily by its permanent reporter in Chile and believed they were getting a fair view of what was actually going on there. I would read them and ask myself, 'Are we both living in the same country?' One of our more politically 'pink' friends in Chile wrote cancelling her subscription, explaining: 'I am perplexed and confused because, if I cannot trust your reporting of a situation that I can verify for myself, how can I trust it on matters beyond my personal knowledge?'

This reporter asked me for an interview. I agreed, keeping it low-key and polite. I did not expect his write-up to be complimentary but was dismayed to find his published article so unnecessarily and deliberately scurrilous. However, I found I was in good company. The British ambassador received the same treatment. Years later I was not surprised to read that the reporter had finally been sacked by his newspaper after the discovery that for all that time he had been in the pay of the Kremlin! I spoke to the assistant editor of a leading Sunday newspaper later, and he told me that their paper, like so many others, had relied on that same source themselves, not having a reporter of their own in Chile. So the British public were hearing a very slanted view most of the time.

Even the Central Committee of the World Council of Churches, with its own infiltration of Marxists, was pumping out distorted facts and figures, expressing its hostility to the coup. In the end such a Marxist bias seriously tarnished the image of the WCC and led to its decline as a credible voice for Christian integrity. The organisation was clearly selective in its condemnations, as were so many other seemingly respectable news agencies at that time – including the Anglican Communion and the Catholic Church.

CHILE'S XENOPHOBIA?

When I first went back to the UK at the end of 1973, nobody would believe that we had 13,000 Cubans in Chile helping in Allende's 'revolutionary experiment' and illegally training the workers in the use of arms. These were joined by like-minded revolutionaries from all over Latin America – and coming from as far afield as North Korea. When the Junta finally expelled all these extreme left-wing foreigners, they were included in the number of 'refugees' by the external media propagandists! I could not quite grasp why later the editor of *The Guardian*[3] should want to discuss Chile's 'xenophobia' with me?

'Whatever could he mean?' I wondered. Chileans have always been particularly hospitable to foreigners. Why would he call them xenophobic? But I soon realised he was referring to the thousands of foreigners who had streamed into Chile with the one purpose of hijacking a nation into a Marxist revolution that the majority of the nation never wanted. These were immediately expelled from Chile by the military following the coup.

The Cubans among them were soon being posted across to Angola, West Africa, to reinforce the MPLA there. People I met in Britain in 1974 could not accept that we had so many Cubans involved in Allende's revolution.

POLITICAL BIAS

Without denying or justifying any terrible happenings, one would simply ask that Pinochet be judged in the light of practices right across South America at the time. Even today the world is selective about who comes in for condemnation. Pinochet was not treated the way we treat other national leaders – like those of Argentina or Cuba, Russia or China.

The Russians have done many terrible things in Chechnya and the Chinese in Tibet. But testimonies to suppression, brutality and murder are now brushed aside as these leaders are welcomed in the UK and entertained at Buckingham Palace. A recent BBC documentary[4] showed a young Chechen looking terribly starved following his imprisonment and torture by the Russians. All his front teeth had been either knocked out or broken at the roots and he had been threatened with having his nose and ears cut off if he did not reveal the whereabouts of his companions in hiding. We honour the leaders of China or Russia when they visit Britain for trade negotiations but we arrest Pinochet when he comes to England for a back operation.

EXAGGERATIONS IN THE FOREIGN PRESS

When I was in the UK at the end of 1973 I was stunned to read of the number being circulated by the Chile Committee for Human Rights as 15,000 'murdered by the military'! Respectable church newspapers reported 20,000 dead. Other extreme propagandists were talking of 30,000. Knowing it just could not have been anything like such numbers, I rang the offices of the Chile Committee for Human Rights in London, of which my own Archbishop was one of the sponsors, to query the publication of such exaggerated information. I heard what I had expected – it did not matter what the actual figures were, the vital thing was to 'get the ". . ." military out!'

The West continued repeating these exaggerated figures for years. There were only twelve million inhabitants in Chile and such a vast number of deaths would have been reflected in the feedback from local communities who had relatives who networked within the country. News of any death travels fast and we were in touch at the grassroots with families in many urban *poblaciones* and rural *reducciones* along the length and breadth of Chile.

We actually had a BBC reporter in our home in Chile a year or two later who had himself grossly misrepresented the number of dead at the time of the coup. I asked him how he could possibly have come up with such an exaggerated number of deaths. He was apologetic and explained that he had assumed that by counting the combined number of bodies in the mortuaries of Antofagasta, Valparaíso, Santiago and Concepción, and then multiplying the average by the total number of mortuaries across the country, they could calculate the most probable figure. He had not realised that those four cities were the major areas of conflict. Most of the other mortuaries would not have seen anything like that increase, if any at all.

Amnesty International today gives an actual figure of 3,197 dead and 1,202 disappeared – there were another 800 dead amongst the Armed Forces. These figures represent the total number of lives lost. Too many and too tragic, but nowhere near the figures being circulated at the time. The far greater number of missing persons in the Argentine had much less publicity. But Britain had a lot of trade with Argentina and the Government at the time did not apparently see fit to break off relations with Argentina as with Chile. Such is 'realpolitik'.

There were reports of torture before Allende's regime, during Allende's regime, and more reports of it during the military regime that followed, and even since that time. I say this without in any way condoning it. Torture must always be wrong – a violation of human rights. 'No one should be subject to torture, or cruel, inhuman, or degrading treatment or punishment'.[5] Ignorance of the law does not constitute innocence, though I wonder very much whether Chile's Armed Forces had ever heard of the 1948 Universal Declaration of Human Rights, let alone Article 5, prior to the military intervention.[6] It will never be known how many actually suffered from torture at the hands of the Armed Forces after the coup, any more than we can ever know how many were tortured before it.

Whilst torture is to our minds indefensible it has been endemic in Latin America ever since the Spanish Inquisition (and not only in

Latin America). Torture is unChristian, reprehensible, brutal to the victims, brutalising to the torturers, and often counterproductive. Most victims, innocent or guilty can be made to say whatever the torturer wants them to say, whether it is true or false. Without knowing personally of anyone who was tortured in Chile when Pinochet was in office, Bishop Colin Bazley (the regional bishop for the Temuco region) and I publicly deplored such practices. There was no way of verifying the scale of it, though Pinochet inherited a police force that would have already institutionalised it. The Lutheran Bishop Helmut Frenz and the Catholic Bishop Aristia later reported in Helsinki[7] that as founders of the Peace Committee in Chile they went to see Pinochet to protest at torture. According to them he replied: 'You are pastors and priests and you have to think and act in that way. If I were in your position I would undoubtedly be acting as you do. But consider that I am the President of Chile. And in this capacity I must say to you that State security is more important than human rights'.[8] The military, of course, were very fearful of the threatened reprisals broadcast widely before the coup. This had created a sense of urgency to find out where any pockets constituting a threat of such retaliation still remained. The argument of the authorities was that they knew of no other way of extracting vital information from prisoners who refused to reveal the secret of their enemy's whereabouts.

HE KNEW AS MUCH AS HE NEEDED TO KNOW

Manuel Contreras, Chile's Minister of Defence under Pinochet, still serving a prison sentence for a political murder in the USA, said in a telephone conversation recorded by a BBC reporter in Santiago,[9] in response to a question about how much Pinochet knew of what was going on in Chile, replied: 'He knew as much as he needed to know.' In a recent videotaped message marking his eighty-fifth birthday, Augusto Pinochet expressed regret publicly for excesses committed by the Armed Forces under his administration without admitting to any personal responsibility for it himself.

Although we openly opposed torture, we could not hide our suspicions about such a large number of refugees who left Chile under the pretext of being tortured. There have always been Chileans (whatever the Government) who could not wait for any excuse to leave Chile for economic reasons. These would happily invent or exaggerate stories of torture, which could be neither proved nor refuted, for a prize as desirable as a free passage to the West and the added promise of housing, welfare and work in some of those countries (like Sweden) that had offered to take them in. Indeed we knew personally of cases that fitted that category.

A couple of years back I discussed this question of torture with a former official at the British consulate in Valparaíso, who had had the responsibility for processing many of the refugees at the time. She told me that it was difficult indeed to corroborate claims of having been tortured. They had had to take the applicant's word for it and process the visa. One can imagine how the total number of claims from all the consulates of all the different countries must have soared when these figures were factored in. To compound confusion people were being arrested on malicious rumours following personal vendettas or by people who coveted another man's position at work. On their release from interrogation these victims found themselves unemployable and applied for visas on the same pretext.

THE CASSIDY CASE[10]

'Torture' headlines were soon regularly displayed to the outside world – especially following the arrest of the dedicated young doctor Sheila Cassidy, a British Catholic medic from Santiago. In her book *Audacity to Believe* she describes the barbaric treatment she received at the hands of the secret police in Santiago. The book relates a moving account of how she was secretly asked by her Catholic friends to tend a wounded but wanted man – Nelson Gutierrez, a leader in the MIR, involved in a shoot-out with the police. The search for Nelson Gutierrez and his fellow terrorist, Pascal Allende[11] was hot news in Chile. Gutierrez, being badly wounded, had been hidden and cared for at great risk by some Catholic nuns. Learning somehow of her mercy trips, the police arrested Dr Cassidy, and obviously hoped to force her to reveal where Gutierrez might still be in hiding. They did not succeed. Cassidy comes across as exceedingly courageous.

The story of her ordeal at the hand of torturers is utterly sickening and I would not doubt the account of her personal experience in any way, though some of her other statements about Allende's supposed achievements and the overlooking of some of Allende's glaring failures might well be disputed. But she, in turn, might well want to dispute my version of events.

Besides helping a badly wounded man in his hour of great need, her ghastly experience actually resulted in at least two other very positive results. The first was that her willingness to suffer for the Christian principle of love clearly had a profound impact for good on the other atheistic Marxists incarcerated with her. The second was that her ordeal raised the profile of the evils of torture and the need to fight against the continued practice of such an abhorrence worldwide.

PUBLIC THANKSGIVING FOR THE COUP

Soon after the coup, I was asked to represent the Anglican Church and to lead in prayer at a central Celebration in the football stadium, along with the senior Catholic chaplain of the Chilean Navy. I naturally consulted with our Regional Council who confirmed what I had myself believed. Whilst committed to upholding the 'powers-that-be' in our prayers, we needed to be wary of any appearance of aligning the Church politically following reports of prisoners being ill-treated. After my declining to take part, one of our Chilean clergy, Alfredo Cespedes, a non-stipendiary minister, was personally approached to represent the Anglican Church. He came to see me about it and I reminded him of the decision of the Regional Council and warned him not to do so on any account. But he did! And he did it beautifully, blessing each member of the Junta by name and thanking God for the military intervention. He was seen by everyone on the national TV, and applauded by a great many, especially among the British community.

This was something that simply could not be ignored. He had blatantly defied the deliberated decisions and direct authority of his church. There was nothing for it but to inform the Regional Council that his licence would be rescinded. All hell broke loose among many of the English-speaking community in Viña del Mar.

I was a Communist! At last I had revealed my true colours. They had suspected it all along! I was obviously a lapdog of the Archbishop of Canterbury who was known to be 'red'![12] Even the British consul begged me to restore Cespedes' licence, but there was no way I could do that until he had explained himself to the church and sought to put things right, which he never did.

STAFF SERGEANT'S DISMISSAL

One quite prestigious member of our Regional Council was very upset when the decision went against our participation in this Celebration of Thanksgiving for the military intervention. This person even rebuked an active staff sergeant on the Regional Council for lack of patriotism when he had opted for our neutrality as a church. It was probably she who reported him for disloyalty to the Navy! The staff sergeant was straightway hauled up for a peremptory dismissal. He came to see me immediately afterwards and I felt obliged to ask for an interview with the senior serving admiral in Valparaíso. Once in his office I explained our position about the Celebration of Thanksgiving, and how we had come to our decision on the Regional Council. I explained my deep concern that this staff sergeant had lost his job for agreeing with the majority opinion expressed there. I knew he was a greatly respected man with an excellent service record. I left the admiral with a photocopy of a House of Commons report from *Hansard* where I had been cited immediately after the coup as publicly supporting the military intervention.

That night I had a knock at my door and there was our staff sergeant in his uniform, smiling. He told me he had been re-instated – something which to his knowledge had never before been known to happen in the Chilean Navy! We thanked God together with a prayer.

WAS I COMMUNIST OR A FASCIST?

What a twisted world we live in! I found myself regarded as a Communist in Chile and a Fascist in the UK. A well known Aid agency led me to understand that we would not be likely to get any further grants for social projects in the diocese if we did not publically identify the church with the opposition to the Military

Junta! I had approached the agency after an urgent call from a man who ran a large orphanage in Santiago. Previously aid for this had been coming from a Lutheran church organisation in Germany, but suddenly this help had been completely cut off. Lutheran supporters were using this retention of aid as a protest about the military intervention in Chile. I had not, till that point, realised that churches would suddenly cancel support for orphans on such grounds. There are some Governments I could never support but if it had been right for me to support an orphanage in the first place, I don't think I would ever stop supporting it as a protest against the Government.

RELENTLESS HOUNDING

There has been a relentless hounding of Pinochet ever since he was arrested in hospital in the UK. A fresh charge has been levelled against him since his return to Chile. He was accused next of responsibility for the 'Caravan of Death', the destruction of a nest of terrorists in Antofagasta in the north which, until this time, had been attributed – even by the Marxists[13] – to General Sergio Arellano Stark. General Pinochet is very small fry compared to so many others guilty of far worse but the intention seems to be to make a token example of him to the world. Pinochet's mission was to restore his nation to law and order, and lead the people of Chile out of its poverty back to prosperity. He had come to power at the critical time of Chile's own financial collapse following his predecessor's mismanagement, combined with the adverse effects of a world recession after the oil crisis of 1973. He succeeded in his objective and restored the republic into a large measure of stability and prosperity without apparently enriching himself during his seventeen years in office unlike so many of his contemporary world leaders who stashed away their millions into foreign bank accounts. Nor was his character tarnished by affairs with women. Pinochet had come to power through a coup to find himself suddenly thrust into the hot seat. He immediately set about seeking to do his duty.

Chapter 14

IN THE HOT SEAT

If you can't stand the heat get out of the kitchen
(PRESIDENT HARRY TRUMAN)

*Leaders need a paradoxical combination of arrogance
and humility to succeed*
(ANON)

I was about to learn some hard lessons myself. As the head of the Anglican Church in Chile, I suddenly found myself a national leader on an international stage. And wherever I went there was pressure for my opinion or an explanation about the role of the military in Chile. People were obviously waiting for some words of condemnation! To utter any measured word in Pinochet's favour was to invite vituperation. I had yet to find an apt sound-bite that would serve to reconcile the urgent need for security in order to preserve the individual human rights of millions and the protection of human rights for certain individuals where their interests clashed. The paradox seemed irreconcilable. This was an area where I felt vulnerable – where I felt I might be letting people down. Most of my friends abroad kept silent which was painful enough, though some wrote tactfully hinting that one often saw more from the touchlines than the players did midfield. Well, after all, they had the media reports! Commonsense told me that the military intervention in the cause of state security was a top priority for any government while my conscience told me that any abuse of human rights was clearly wrong. But whilst publicly deploring any violation of individual human rights (which I did) I felt very uneasy about all the criticism of Pinochet – a man who sincerely believed he had been doing his duty in resisting men of violence and restoring national security in the only way he knew how and furthermore bringing the country out of bankruptcy into a stable economy.

Michael Ramsey, the Archbishop of Canterbury, and still, at that time, the Metropolitan for the Southern Cone of South America, had appointed me to be the Bishop of the Diocese of Chile, Bolivia and Peru in June, 1973. When Beryl Howell (my predecessor's wife) developed a brain tumour Bishop Ken Howell had to take her back to the UK for further treatment in 1972. Ken Howell appointed me, a recently made bishop over the Valparaíso region, as the Vicar General of the diocese in his absence. I was the nearest bishop geographically to the capital. He had not been home long, however, before he decided to resign due to Beryl's health. The Archbishop of Canterbury requested the diocese to send him the names of clergy who might succeed Ken Howell. Two names were eventually forwarded to the Archbishop: Colin Bazley and myself.

MAJOR TASKS TO TACKLE

It was, of course, an honour to be made the diocesan bishop. I did not ask for the salary of my predecessor. This remained the same as that of the newest missionaries though it was still more than any that the nationals were receiving.

Beside the political issues one of the matters that immediately concerned me was the need for an Anglican Church constitution compatible with Chilean law that was adapted to the flexible needs of a new diocese. It was fortunate that John Cobb, a comparatively new missionary, was willing to give this his attention – something which could take a long time and a lot of hard work. Besides this he was helping to initiate a training programme for our church leaders.

We were entering a most exciting time. The church in the area was still in the throes of spiritual revival. It was also a very difficult time, with criticism from abroad being sometimes quite spiteful. On our return to Chile, by air, after leave in 1974, I went to the Customs to collect some extra luggage sent by sea. I found all our cases ransacked and trashed. Insulting remarks about Pinochet were painted all over them.

I soon felt that it was going to be too much for me to cope with the responsibility of the diocese beyond Chile. We had very little money for travelling the great distances needed to oversee anything satisfactorily in the other two countries. I really needed an associate bishop over Peru and Bolivia. The English chaplain in Lima appeared to be assuming he should take over up there – which our missionary team involved in Spanish work there did not welcome. They wanted a 'missionary' bishop to be working alongside them. Incidentally there was only one English chaplaincy in Peru.

THE ENGLISH HAVE THEIR PRIDE
Eventually I approached Bill Flagg – who was bishop of Northern Argentina and Paraguay and by then the senior bishop in the Southern Cone – to ask him if he would consider moving to Lima and take over as bishop of Peru and Bolivia. From there he would work with us towards its eventual creation into a new diocese separate from Chile. Bill agreed to this after he had set in motion a proposal for the division of his own diocese, which he was leaving. The plan was that Pat Harris would be made a bishop of Northern Argentina and Douglas Milmine of Paraguay.

I went up to Peru to prepare the way for Bill. The chaplain of Lima was naturally feeling very sensitive and was obviously not going to make things easy for me. His concern was understandable. 'Nobody knows Bishop Bill Flagg!' he protested quite reasonably. He asked me to meet a group of influential members of his English-speaking congregation. I arrived to find them all well briefed for our meeting.

They raised many objections that were quite reasonable from their point of view. But a bishop was really needed for overseeing the growing 'Spanish-speaking' work – wherein the future of the church lay – if it had a future. Behind it all was their real, but unarticulated concern, that one day their bishop might actually be a Spanish-speaking Peruvian – the last thing they wanted at that stage. The English had their pride – our fathers had once been part of a British Empire!

The crowning thrust from Lima's council of the Church of the Good Shepherd was to accuse me of extreme discourtesy for not having previously consulted with the British ambassador in Peru about appointing Bill Flagg. Was not the ambassador the representative of Her Majesty the Queen, and Her Majesty the Titular Head of the Anglican Church? Had I lived in Lima I probably would have put him in the picture at an early moment, but in reality this kind of appointment had nothing to do with the British ambassador *per se*. I would not really have wanted to give him the impression that I thought he had any powers to sway the matter one way or the other from outside the church. I had already experienced attempts of that kind from the British consul in Valparaíso, when he had tried to pressurise me over Alfredo Cespedes. With as much grace as I could muster, I reminded them, with due respect to the ambassador, that even though the Queen was indeed the titular head of the Church of England, Her Majesty claimed no jurisdiction whatsoever over the Anglican Communion in general, nor the Anglican Church in South America in particular. And I was quite sure Her Majesty would not want it! Bishop Bill Flagg moved to Lima as soon as he could and did an excellent job there. The frustrated chaplain left soon after for a parish in England.

My far-flung diocese

Another part of my far-flung diocese was Easter Island, one of the most isolated fragments of inhabited land in all the oceans of the world, made up of volcanic rock. The inhabitants of Easter Island are Polynesian. These stranded people worshipped the frigate bird that they undoubtedly envied for its freedom to come and go. Their lonely island lay in the middle of the Eastern Pacific, 2,500 miles from Chile's coastline. The first European to discover it was a Dutchman, Jacob Roggeveen, who arrived there on the evening of Easter Day, 1722 (hence its name). Captain Cook visited it fifty-two years later, on the second of his great voyages around the world. He befriended the people and made the first detailed survey of the island. One thing that puzzled him, however, was how the inhabitants, with only the simplest ideas of engineering technology, could have erected a row of some dozen giant carved rock figures – besides others standing like isolated sentries randomly placed about the island? Some of the carvings were as much as thirty feet tall and weighing sixty tons. They still remain there today to greet their visitors.

Sadly funds did not stretch to an episcopal visitation, though there was a regular six-hour flight by Chilean Airline from Santiago.

SANDY POINT

But I did get down to Sandy Point. Although at the time we still had no Spanish-speaking work in Punta Arenas (Sandy Point), I had to fly down occasionally for the English community before Spanish work was established there. I vividly remember one very rocky flight when the pilot warned us we might have to land wherever we could – and 'wherever we could' was not looking too good as I glanced down rather anxiously over the mountainous terrain below – the graveyard of not a few lost planes in the past! I wrote a little note for Mary telling her how much I loved her and the children – just in case I never saw them again, and folded it into my pocket Bible. I showed it to her after I had returned safely and still have it today.

The small port of Punta Arenas, almost surrounded by sea also had a river. Men were busy panning for gold there – as we had done outside Viña del Mar – but they were getting far better results. The port shivered between the freezing sea and a bleak hinterland. Miles of space sparsely scattered with skeletal trees like witches crouching over broom sticks – their leafless fingers stabbing the face of the biting wind. Low ridges of distant hills hid isolated farms where sheep and *guanaco* (llama type) grazed. Lonely shepherds guarded them from condors by day and pumas (small lions) by night. Freezing snowfalls in winter often drifted up to trap the sheep. But the weather there had a maddening habit of switching suddenly from one season to another – spring showers, blazing summer sunshine, violent autumn gales and downpours, winter sleet and snow, then spring showers and summer sun again – four seasons twice over in one day.

Clearly it was a problem for the English community in Punta Arenas to decide who should have the painful duty of providing hospitality for a religious type. On my first visit there I was parked on a feisty old spinster who regaled me with stories of the gory bull-fights that she had once seen in Spain. She described these so dramatically and with so much gusto and so many guffaws, that I could not quite tell whether she approved or disapproved, and was unsure whether I was meant to laugh or cry.

FIRST AND LAST WHISKY

She had kindly opened a bottle of whisky for me – one of many she explained that she had inherited from her late uncle who had crates of it stored away in his attic when he died which would now be stored away in hers until she died unless someone drank some of it for her! She invited me to help myself, apologising that she had no sodawater to go with it. 'My uncle always reckoned Scotch was much better neat!' she said. 'Quite!' said I, – being almost a teetotaller myself and knowing nothing about the best way to get the stuff down. But since she had gone to the length of opening the bottle on my behalf I felt obliged to sample it for politeness' sake. There were some tumblers beside it and, in my ignorance, I filled one of them nearly to the brim and gingerly took a sip. Uhh! I had no idea anything could taste that bad! My eyes crossed while violent electric currents hoovered my brain. It immediately cured me of a vice even before I became addicted! Fortunately at this point my hostess disappeared to attend the British consul knocking at the door. I searched the room desperately for a way to dispose of the whisky. Spotting a vase of wilting flowers I tipped in the rest of my glass. The flowers perked up wonderfully and, through my choking tears, I got the distinct impression that they were even smiling at me!

ENTER THE CONSUL

After greeting the consul I watched how he poured himself a mere fraction of the whisky I had put in mine. (Oh! So that was what one was meant to do – how naive of me!)

The consul had come to discuss the service I was meant to be leading at the cenotaph the following day.

My hostess waited for a fine spell after lunch and took me down to the cemetery to see the cenotaph where we would be having the service. This was a depressing monument of ebony black that commemorated the heroes of both world wars. As we walked to the site we passed a number of impressive mausoleums wherein were vacant shelves – marble slabs, clearly visible through the glass, and ready for the next *defuncto* in the family. 'Mine hostess' sniffed disapprovingly, nodding in their direction. 'I have left instructions in my will that they are not to put me on one of those things when I die,' she stated in such a loud imperious tone: 'No! I've been a spinster all my life and I don't intend to spend eternity on the shelf!' I nodded comprehendingly – but still wondering whether to smile at her macabre humour or to frown sympathetically.

I noticed little boys scurrying around, gathering up the flowers that had been recently placed on the graves and blessed under the tender prayers of loved ones. As soon as the mourners had gone, the little sharks grabbed them up and rushed to the cemetery gate to re-sell them to the latest grieving visitors. Just how many times could one re-cycle the same flowers in one day I wondered!

NEW ACCOMMODATION NEEDED

The architect who owned the house we had been renting in Viña del Mar gave us notice that he wanted to move back there as soon as he could. So we had to start looking for another place. The diocese had sold Ken Howell's house in Santiago. We had used most of the proceeds to buy an office in the capital but there was still a little cash remaining to buy something for us. But very few premises seemed to be up for sale just then. Property was at a premium. No one wanted to rent their houses since with the rate of inflation rising so fast rent prices became quite meaningless in a very short time.

One day Mary was at the bakery queuing for bread when she heard of a house for sale in an ideal area. We gathered up the family and drove round to the address though we had no idea who might be living there. As we turned the corner to face the house all hearts leapt. It seemed just so right, so warm looking in the glow of nightlights, and so friendly. Our children were getting very excited at the prospect of having this as their new home. But the owners were very surprised to see six complete strangers standing before them looking so eager. We explained why we had come but they said that they had no plans to move. We returned to our car feeling a little foolish and very disappointed. I left my card just in case they should ever hear of a suitable place for us.

On the way home, as the girls were expressing the disappointment we all felt, I remembered a book I had recently read. It had stressed the importance of giving thanks to God in all things. So I suggested that we ought to thank God for what had happened. 'How can we do that, Daddy?' demanded the girls. 'We really wanted that house, and we're shattered!' That's the point, I tried to explain. God knows what he is doing and we can thank him for that. Maybe he knows the place is going to fall down next week in an earthquake! Maybe he even has something better for us, and he just wants to see if we will still trust him! So let's try it. We began thanking God. When we got out of the car everyone was looking quite cheerful again despite the urgency of still needing a new home to live in.

Our family has never forgotten this episode because by the end of the week we had actually moved into that dream house. The owner was an admiral who had suddenly been told to report to Santiago for a new post. He was worried about his empty house being commandeered by squatters in the present climate (it was just before the coup), and he asked us if we could possibly move in quickly so it would not be left vacant. He said that we could use the house for six months and when his future was clearer, if he needed to sell it, he would give us first offer. In fact, we stayed there for six months with no rent to pay, and then he decided to sell. The diocese was able to buy it. Because the rate of inflation was so high at the time, and we were able to pay for it in sterling, our new home cost the diocese a mere £2,500. The owner seemed well pleased and so were we. That house became our home for the rest of our time in Chile.

A MISSIONARY'S DREAM COME TRUE

Of all the churches, the one in Gomez Carreño was the most impacted by the renewing of the Holy Spirit. They were having meetings every night and many new converts were added to the church. I could hardly believe my eyes. This was the stuff every missionary dreamed of.

After a few weeks, Omar Ortíz, who was in charge there, came to see me. He was exhausted and needed a break desperately. He had been up every night until midnight leading people to Christ, and enquirers were knocking on his door again at 6.30 the next morning. I agreed he ought to get away as soon as he could.

'So you will come up and take charge in my absence?' he begged. Knowing that that was practically impossible, I explained that I couldn't.

'Who will take charge then?' he groaned, 'If I can't find someone I'll never be able to get away!'

'Well!' I said, 'The Holy Spirit seems to have started all this and I am sure he will help others to hold the fort for two weeks!' The others in the church managed very well and the great work continued without him there.

He returned refreshed and, soon after, reported that he had at least a hundred candidates ready for baptism. He felt we should do these in the river. By now we had just had the coup and needed permission from the Military as they were nervous about large open air meetings. But they made no problems for us. We all arrived at the river on the appointed day. Some candidates were baptised standing on the shore, and after confessing their new faith, water was poured over them in the Name of the Father, the Son and the Holy Spirit. Others were baptised standing up to their knees in the river, and water was poured over them too after their confession of faith. The rest were baptised by immersion in the river – demonstrating, I thought, the wonderful comprehensiveness of the Anglican Church! I had never immersed a candidate for baptism before, let alone in a swift current of cold running water. We got them to hold their noses whilst we ducked them under backwards – baptising them in the name of the Trinity. Because of the current it was quite a job to keep a steady grip with one's feet on the riverbed, while simultaneously keeping a safe grip with one's hands on the candidates being baptised.[1]

There was a welcome new dynamic clearly operating amongst us. But I still understood so little about the working of the Holy Spirit. And I understood even less about the gifts of the Spirit. One day the young people were having a meeting when a boy spoke in tongues for the first time. A girl present burst out in amazement: 'You are saying this . . . and now you are saying this'. She was interpreting the tongue through a spontaneous gift of the Holy Spirit. It seemed just as it might have happened on the day of Pentecost!

OUT OF MY DEPTH

I could see there was all something really good going on here, but there were major difficulties, especially as it spread to other churches. New leaders, taking over churches where the Holy Spirit was beginning to move, were having problems as they had no experience in leading that kind of church, and could not or did not always sense what the Holy Spirit was doing. The leader himself might be rather lacking in confidence and react by becoming too controlling – and actually end up by quenching the Spirit. I could see this kind of thing happening and felt myself to be personally inadequate to help the leaders who may themselves have felt helpless. I had had no personal experience of running a church where the Holy Spirit was moving in this way.

NEW CHURCH PLANT

Things were still moving on apace. There was now a small group of believers in Achupallas, another impoverished *poblacion*[2] that had sprung up on a hill outside Viña del Mar. We managed to get a piece of land after endless red tape, and put down a cement base on the site. We did not invest a lot of money in building: we didn't have money to invest. But ever since I had had the Land Rover I had been in the habit of picking up cast-off doors and windows, planks of wood and old sheets of zinc and storing them in my garage for some such eventuality.

We all pooled what we had, and managed to erect this little meeting place at Achupallas.[3] The locals made it look really nice inside by nailing up strips of cheap hardboard on the walls and painting them. We then fitted electric light. When it was ready, they asked me if I would go up there and lead an evangelistic week.

HAVE MERCY ON MY BABY!

About the third night of my mission week, I was hurrying up the narrow track from the road, when a woman I had never seen before rushed out of her ramshackle home, and pushed a rather grubby bundle – with a baby in it – right into my arms. '*Padre*,' she pleaded desperately, 'Pray for my baby! She's dying and the hospital says they can do nothing more for her!' I am ashamed to admit that I was initially slightly miffed at being interrupted in my holy reverie as I was rehearsing the talk I was about to deliver. Then I thought that there really was no hope for the baby if the hospital said there was nothing more that they could do! I was confused about what I ought to do! Having no faith to believe her baby could get better I inwardly groaned. Healing was just not my line at all. Suddenly I had a flashback of the story Jesus told about the Good Samaritan. Jewish clerics, being preoccupied with their Temple duties, had passed by a victim of mugging (and I was just about to do something similar). But the Good Samaritan did what he could with the little he had. There was no way out. I'd just have to give it a go! So I stretched out my hand and placed it on the baby's tiny head and prayed simply for God to heal it '*en el nombre del Padre, el Hijo y el Espiritu Santo*'. I then smiled at her weakly and headed on up the hill, conveniently forgetting all about the dying baby.

Two nights later, at the same spot, at the same time, I saw the same woman rushing towards me again, with the same grubby bundle in her arms. 'Help, Lord!' I prayed. 'Whatever am I going to do now? I've prayed everything I know how! How do I get out of this?' Next minute she was hugging me with her one free arm and thanking me profusely. 'My baby is completely well!' she said. That just had to be God! I thanked him with her in the name of Jesus. Then I blessed the baby, and have never seen her again to my knowledge from that day to this. The mother had the faith to believe that God would heal her baby, and God did it. There have been plenty of times when he does not appear to heal, but if we never ask we'll never see. I didn't realise it at the time, but this experience opened the door to a whole new range of possibilities for me.

GREEN VALLEY

There was another shanty-town on a headland the other side of Valparaíso called Valle Verde (Green Valley), a slight misnomer as it was almost on a cliff top. A fairly new convert from our church in Valparaíso – a motor mechanic – had taken it upon himself to visit there regularly on Sundays to talk to people about the Lord. This man, Luis Palominos, had an evangelistic passion that warmed the heart. He was forever requesting leaflets to distribute there and reported back regularly on how things were going. He even had a vision for planting a church there one day. It was tough going, with opposition from local Communists, but he apparently had sufficient encouragement to keep going.

Then he married a lovely Christian school teacher called Alicia and we lost touch with him. Some two years later, he re-emerged. He was living in Quilpué now, miles from Valle Verde. And he had another vision – this time for setting up his own garage to support his wife and family. Admirable – until I found he was hoping I could lend him money to buy the land. English people must have money – they have vehicles! And who else could he turn to anyhow? But I really could not help him in any significant way financially. As he left me I casually asked him what had happened to his vision for Valle Verde? 'You never told me why you gave it up!' I said. He hung his head slightly and mumbled something that left me none the wiser though perhaps a little sadder.

About six weeks later I had a phone call from Luis, asking me if I could possibly visit him in Valle Verde? I was surprised but said that of course I would come. He told me his address and I eventually located him, not in a house, but in a two-roomed hut behind the house he had given as his address. He and Alicia welcomed me and began talking about the usual problems of gathering a church together. I scanned the room casually as they talked. Four sides of thin wall were pasted over with newspaper to keep out the sharp sea winds striking their home, but there was nothing on the floor to stop it blowing up my trouser legs. I shivered. The hut was raised a foot from the ground and I could see daylight through the bare floorboards.

I could not fail to notice two well-worn Bibles by the bed – the only books in the building! They told me that Luis was now seeking to gather a small group together to worship and study the Bible, and how Alicia had been able to get some of the mothers together during the weekday. And Alicia told me to tell the Señora Mery (meaning my Mary) that she was expecting a baby! Then she looked me straight in the face – and asked earnestly: 'Don David, tell us what you really think – do you truly believe it's

God's will for us to be here?' I gulped. Were they having second thoughts about the vision? They must be feeling the strain of living in this shack. I shot up a desperate arrow prayer to God.

A SACRIFICE I COULD NEVER MAKE

It did not take much to imagine the sacrifice they were making. Then I thought about the poor people in that community – those other mothers. Who would be there to help them if this couple could not do it? It had to be through people like them. I looked at Alicia and said: 'Yep! Alicia, I believe it could really be God's will, but how can we help you?'

'Oh no! We're not expecting you to help!' she said. 'It's all right. That's all we needed to hear. If it's God's will we know we can trust him to supply our needs. We can manage.'

I left, after a prayer for them, feeling an awful fraud. They were willing to embrace a sacrifice I just knew I could never make – in a place like that. But how else does the Kingdom of God grow – except through costly sacrifices?

TAKING A BREAK

Getting away from it all with the children was becoming vital for our own survival. We began taking one or other of the missionaries from the school with us on Saturday outings.

Our holidays had to be of the cheapest, but Chile was a good country for camping in the summer. For three or four years we joined up with the Bazley family and the Skinners and Jean Porter, a nurse, going to a small farm on the edge of Lago Colico, a lake in the south of Chile. Its clear blue water came straight down from the mountains still icy cold. The children swam and sunbathed there all day. No shops! We were completely alone except for the bleating sheep and the goats deftly negotiating the rocks behind us.

On a later holiday, we went by ourselves as a family. We drove up the mountains along a turn-off inland about 100 miles south of Santiago, and camped in a beautiful place with a stream and leaping trout. But I was so cold at night and it was so noisy with the stream that we decided to move on. We were told there was a nice place along a deserted track ahead of us and, after travelling for miles, we were almost at the borders between Chile and Argentina when we were surprised by signs of advanced civilisation! Ahead was a tall barbed wire fence with aggressive looking dogs dashing up and down on the other side. We followed this to a high gate, electronically controlled, with a bell and voice feedback built into the pillar supporting it. A brass plaque told us that the place was called *Sociedad Dignidad* (Dignity Society). A wooden looking woman appeared from a kind of sentry box and shouted, 'Go away! Go away!' We weren't welcome there, obviously!

We turned back and finally found a farm, where we persuaded the German owner to let us camp by his gently flowing river. It was one of the most wonderful holidays we ever had. The owner turned out to be a retired head of a Governmental department. We asked our new friend about the *Sociedad Dignidad*.

'They're Germans,' he said, disapprovingly, 'But we don't talk about them. We don't know them and we don't like them, and they play no part in the German community in Chile.' He seemed to be hinting that many of the women there had probably been nurses in German concentration camps during World War Two. The place was rumoured also to be a refuge for wanted SS men. There were also many dysfunctional children up there – some of whom occasionally escaped and created a stir in the press. Helicopters sometimes patrolled the boundaries and now and again a plane was supposed to come into land from over the Argentinian border. There appeared to be a lot of heavy traffic along the track after dusk each night but no one seemed to have any idea what was really going on there. Successive Governments must have authorised their stay over a long period of time. We wondered whether in fact our farmer friend was positioned on this track to keep an eye on things from the outside. Whatever – it all provided a mysterious dimension to our holiday!

I BELIEVE IN MIRACLES

I have nostalgic memories of reading books to the girls on holidays. They were all prodigious readers but enjoyed being read to. One book sent to us later that we all read was Kathryn Kuhlman's *I Believe in Miracles*. I did not know what to make of it then, but I was just hearing of a young medical student, Luis Ruìbal César, a Roman Catholic from Colombia. He had been to one of her meetings, but could not get in. He was reportedly so amazed at the miracles taking place outside the Tabernacle in Pittsburg that he gave up training for the medical profession and became a healing evangelist (and, incidentally later one of the pioneers of the current revival in Colombia). Later I met a doctor in California, one of Kuhlman's team in America, who gave me a photocopy of reports of healings that had all been responsibly double-checked by medical specialists. This I later came to understand, all turned out to be 'preparatoria' for my future.

STRANGE STORIES OF TEETH FILLING

It was just after the military intervention that Gigi Avila, a healing evangelist, came to the football stadium in Valparaíso. The crowds that gathered there nightly were growing very large. Gigi Avila was visiting from Puerto Rico. Mary heard about this visit and decided to go. I was too busy! When she came back she said that I really ought to make the effort to get there – some quite amazing things seemed to be happening; healings, and even teeth being filled!

'Teeth!' I said, 'Are you mad?'

She told me of a woman who had testified that she had had to go to her dentist for an appointment. After probing her teeth her dentist accused her of having visited a colleague! Two or three of her teeth appeared professionally filled and he knew it was not his work. She insisted she had seen no other dentist but him. He accused her of lying. Then she suddenly remembered that she had been to the stadium the night before and she must unwittingly have had her teeth filled there! Her dentist dismissed it all as shamanism! But if it could be done by occultists how much more could it have been done by God? The crowd began praising the Lord. And there were many other reports of such teeth-fillings – some were false and attributed to pious imagination and many were true but disregarded by cynics who believed the crowds were duped! This was in 1973, the first time we had ever come across such miracles. We have read of other cases since. (Francis McNutt opened his book on healing with such a story of teeth being miraculously filled but his publisher thought that he might lose the average reader before he got past the first chapter! So he included it as an epilogue.[4])

FACING UP TO MIRACLES

We had several from our churches who experienced such miracles. Our new organist[5] from St Paul's, Valparaíso, attended one of these meetings where there were testimonies from the platform of teeth being filled etc. As people were speaking of them, she became increasingly aware of an aching tooth that had spasmodically flared up. The pain was becoming increasingly acute that night in the stadium. She pulled her scarf more tightly round her face for protection against the wind and grumbled to herself that while all these people professed to having their teeth filled, she was going through agony! But when she got home, she realised the pain had gone! She looked into a mirror to check it and saw that the tooth had been miraculously filled.

She also had a TB ulcer near her armpit. A friendly nurse (who also attended St Paul's) used to dress this for her every evening. That night she told the nurse about the miracle but since the nurse had not actually seen the state of her tooth before, she remained somewhat sceptical. The nurse completed the dressing and left. Before going to sleep, our organist thought: 'Well, Lord, if you can do this for my tooth, please heal my TB ulcer.' She found herself in a state of semi-consciousness for a couple of hours. During this time she sensed the 'tips of doves' wings' (using her own words) gently air-brushing the wound as she lay on the bed. She knew she must be imagining this, since it was covered with a light dressing. She slept soundly through the rest of the night. When she awakened in the morning she checked the dressing and found the wound covered over with new skin like a baby's, and all the pain had gone. She called her nursing friend, who simply stared at the place she had dressed the night before, and burst into tears!

There were many more fascinating reports. I found it quite easy under the circumstances to alter my diary and make space to get there after Mary had led the way.

Where the warfare is the hottest in the battle fields of life,
You'll find the Christian soldier represented by his wife!

(Anon)

I went the very next night with the whole family. I had never seen anything like it. Crowds were coming up by the coachload from as far away as Santiago. Amazing healings! After each testimony, Gigi Avila would call out *'Quien fue?'*[6] and the crowd would roar back: 'Jesus! Jesus!'

CHANGE OF PROGRAMME

When, under Allende, the curriculum in secondary schools was in the process of being 'reformed' to incorporate Marxist values, we had begun to see writing on the wall for our children's education. Up until that time we had imagined them going through the Chilean State system to university, but with Allende's radical changes we began to think of alternatives for Charlotte as the time came for her to leave St Paul's. We started her on some Wolsey Hall correspondence courses to study at home, and in the evenings she went to the French Academy where she did well. Then, when we were on furlough in the UK she was able to board at King Edward the Sixth's School, Witley, in Surrey – something we could never have done without a grant from Surrey County Council and the kind help of Vernon and Jean Hedderly acting as her guardians. This seemed a good experiment at the time but with our more defined family values today, I cringe to think that we even considered it. Debby was able to follow her the next year. The school staff there were always most helpful both to our children and to us!

This furlough was not entirely agreeable, as so many of the SAMS supporting churches wanted to know about the coup, and seemed naturally hostile to Pinochet, having relied on the British media for their information. One did not know where to begin to explain the situation as we saw it. I was quite clearly still a Fascist in many people's eyes! Furthermore, there was an important gathering in central London, where I was expected to meet a number of significant church leaders, which I missed completely, due to my total ignorance of the meeting – everyone seemed to have been invited to it except me, the speaker! This left a number of significant people quite frustrated and angry, so I was told later. I still have no idea who those people were and imagine they still have no idea why I never turned up. This did nothing to enhance my tattered reputation in the UK! Not that I tried to enhance it.

After my statement on the BBC *Sunday* programme I was invited by the Archbishop of Ireland to speak to his clergy at a diocesan dinner in Dublin and clearly no one who questioned me, or who spoke to me after, had believed a word I had said. People in the West had made up their minds about the situation in Chile. There was clearly no desire to understand the real reasons behind the military intervention.

Chapter 15

CONDEMNATION

Anyone can hold the helm when the sea is calm
(ANON)

The ultimate measure of man is not where he stands in times of comfort and convenience but where he stands at times of challenge and controversy
(ANON)

During that visit to the UK at the end of 1973, I had explained to David Jacobs on the BBC *Sunday* programme that 'without supporting everything the Junta may do after they have come into power yet I support the [military] intervention. It is generally agreed that politics in Chile is a luxury that the country can ill afford in its state of total ruin'. This may have sounded hard to swallow in comfortable Britain where Allende's propaganda had been digested so indiscriminately, but the fact was that Chile had just been through the most terrifying experience of a near total breakdown of the rule of law and order. I felt I had spoken as any observer with common sense would have done after experiencing the awful realities of that Marxist ordeal. And I was by no means alone in Chile at the time in believing in the futility of having another popularly elected Government until the rule of law has been clearly re-established, and the disastrous state of the economy restored. Under Allende, Chile had witnessed the spectacle of parties in a constitutionally elected government undermining even their own ministers whilst in power – careless of the fact that the nation was collapsing around their feet. They demonstrated complete disloyalty to their own leader – how could they expect the rest of the country to remain loyal to their government? The British would never have tolerated any such

197

disastrous management from Westminster, not even for three weeks, let alone three years. However in public pronouncements supporting the military intervention, I continued to stress the need to pray for Chile, since the setting up of any dictatorship was certainly a potential danger.

But such candidness was clearly out of place! Frankness has probably been both my weakness and strength throughout life. In this case it embarrassed my friends and enraged my enemies. And, during all that time of preoccupation with the political struggles and the cultural adaptations necessary for a foreigner to live and work with Chileans, I had become relatively unaware of the huge cultural changes taking place in the Western world.

SLEEPING THROUGH THE CULTURAL REVOLUTION

Washington Irving tells a story of Rip Van Wynkle resting on the Katskill Hills overlooking the Hudson River, and sleeping on right through the American Revolution. I seemed to have slumbered too, and like Rip, was waking up with shocked surprise! I had not noticed how the assassination of John Kennedy in the prime of life and Martin Luther King in his struggle for freedom, combined with the widespread opposition to the Vietnam War, had all begun to break down a traditional mindset. I had been impercipient to what had been happening at home during the 'Swinging Sixties'. I had missed the cultural impact of 'Beatlemania'. Surely that had been simply a passing craze of youth! Who would ever credit that a pop group could so influence the culture of a generation? And then there was the Pill which seemed to have turned sex into a kind of free-for-all, and struck a mortal blow to traditional morality.

> *Sexual intercourse began*
> *In nineteen-sixty three*
> *(Which was rather late for me)*
> *Between the end of the Chatterley ban*
> *And the Beatles' first LP*[1]

The 'baby boomer' generation – the generation born in the aftermath of World War Two[2] – that was emerging in that new cultural explosion, seemed to be embracing a humanistic, hedonistic philosophy of life. They could not seem to relate to the traditional values of their parents; a 'Me' generation who believed they could have and do just about anything they wanted.

The new 'baby boomers' were looking for one of two alternatives – to opt out of the system or to change society. Che Guevara – the Latin American revolutionary in his black beret – was a romantic martyr idolised by this new generation. The 'democratic' Marxist experiments that had been taking place in Chile – supposedly 'socialism with a human face' – inspired them. They lapped up so much of the propaganda about the revolution under Salvador Allende. Not surprisingly the new generation were incensed by the military intervention under General Pinochet. This had smashed their grand illusions of a great democratic experiment, a revolution without rifles, committed to major social changes on behalf of the oppressed living in a capitalistic world.

The swing to the left in England was becoming marked even on the Bench of Bishops. The Oxford theologian John Macquarrie was reportedly 'astonished to find so many of the bishops'[3] being swept along among the fashions and slogans of the popular thought of the 1960s. For my part, I was foolishly assuming that the overthrow of a Marxist regime anywhere would have been readily welcomed by the free world everywhere – but so many in the West, it seemed, now thought otherwise. How mistaken could one be?

And there was yet this other factor to be reckoned with. The decline in moral standards in the West and the constant focus on violence on TV in an increasingly cruel and destructive society, had been accompanied by a decline in the integrity of news reporting in the media. In the race to boost their newspaper sales, journalists seemed no longer objective or deferential to authority. An aggressive, cynical, disrespectful attitude by reporters was soon coming across on the screen and appeared now to be accepted practice for the media. Typical of this was the treatment meted out to Mrs Mary Whitehouse, a middle class mother and school teacher, who fought a long campaign against the portrayal of violence on our TVs. Some considerable media sophistication was becoming necessary when dealing with journalists. Also one knew that what one said would almost certainly be edited, in such a way even that one could hear oneself being made to say something quite opposite to what one was actually trying to say. I realised too late that one really needed a spin-doctor to play the media at their own game. It seemed one could no longer simply be frank and honest with the media and still appear to have any credibility!

It is vital for a nation to have a free press and we must do all we can to protect that right but the media today seems often to be setting the political and moral agenda and in the process has assumed the role of judge, jury and executioner.

MY MOST HORRIBLE YEAR

If there ever can be such a thing as an *annus horribilis* 1973 was such a one for me. For the first time in my life I felt abysmally alone – the nadir of Elijah under the juniper tree – not that I was physically alone; nor was I ever tempted to give up on life. A great Scottish preacher, Alexander Whyte, who, when passing through a difficult phase in his ministry, countered the kindly com-miserations of a friend: 'Yes! But I am happy in my family.' That was always my consolation. And I felt very understood and supported by mine. But what religious leader did I know of within reach who had been through this kind of dilemma, and with whom I might consult over the Pinochet issue in which I had become so immersed because of the nature of my role there? I really needed pastoral help but there seemed nowhere to turn; in any case, we had not heard about such counselling ministries in those days! Trying to process the realities left me as dazed as a punchdrunk boxer. I needed to talk myself through the facts and the issues. But the facts were so variously interpreted and the issues were so complex and confusing!

Had I failed the Lord? Had I failed the Church? What would Christ – so compassionate for the poor, the outcasts and the oppressed – have done? Would he have condoned the military intervention? But then would he have ever condoned the Marxist revolution?

I wondered what saintly advice the Lutheran pastor Dietrich

Bonhoeffer would have offered me? He was hanged in Nazi Germany in 1945 for his involvement in the failed plot to blow up Adolf Hitler.

It seemed to me just a little bit too facile to say – as Archbishop Ramsey said to President Pinochet – 'From the Christian point of view Marxism is an evil thing. But Marxism is not going to be defeated by ruthlessness. It will only be defeated by justice.' Not only did Pinochet have to live through the local realities and lead the country back to peace and prosperity, he also had to establish law in a society where there was a well-armed segment committed to lawlessness. Didn't God anoint all sorts of leaders to bring a violent judgement on Israel's oppressors and even on Israel itself? Didn't Paul defend the authority of the secular ruler when he wrote: 'for he does not bear the sword for nothing. He is God's servant'.[4] But then where does peace-making come in? Jesus had also warned that he who took the sword would perish by the sword. His teaching, often enshrined in such stark paradoxes, leaves a freedom for different applications in varying circumstances. Individuals should be persuaded in their own minds and act with a good conscience towards God.

Again I was expected to join in the worldwide condemnation of Pinochet – and I just could not do that. Should I have adopted a Brer Rabbit policy of 'lyin' low an' sayin' nuffin'?[5] But I fully believed Pinochet had actually saved the country from disaster and so, in the name of justice, I had to say my bit in defence of the need for the coup. And then, however painful, I had to live with the consequences of that – the realisation that the majority of people had an inflexible mindset on the matter, based on selective propaganda that they had heard and read. There seemed no way of ever setting the record straight. Soon there was no one interested in further discussion. The focus for the rest of the world had been re-directed. There were the grisley killing fields of Cambodia to think about now – Pol Pot and a million bleached skulls stacked up as a witness to the horrors of genocide. There was Idi Amin from Uganda too – but strangely no outcry for these to go on trial for the wholesale atrocities they had committed. The kaleidoscope was being shaken – the political maps were being redrawn.

History for everyone else was moving on, while I was still floundering in my own cultural time warp and frustrated with my own inadequacies and confusion.

INVITATION TO THE ARCHBISHOP

If we were ever to have the freedom to develop Anglicanism in Chile in a way that could adapt to the national culture, we had to work towards the Southern Cone dioceses being formed into a separate Province. These originally consisted of Chile, Bolivia and Peru, North Argentina and Paraguay, South Argentina and Uruguay, and Ecuador – though Ecuador eventually opted for the Northern Province – linked in with the Episcopal Church of the USA. We felt it would help if the Archbishop of Canterbury, our Metropolitan, could come out to South America to see things for himself. But such a prospect placed him in rather a predicament.

I made a personal visit to Lambeth to invite the Archbishop to Chile. The staff I met at Lambeth Palace tactfully confirmed that my public approval of the military intervention had not gone down too well in most quarters of the UK Church and Ramsey already had his own assessment that certainly differed from mine! But the Archbishop was nevertheless interested in doing what he could to advance the formation of the Southern Cone Province.

Once his forthcoming visit to Chile became public news, Lambeth was inundated with protests, ranging from the Primate of the Canadian Church to the various Chilean refugee and human rights organisations. They believed such a visit would be seen as an endorsement for the military intervention and perhaps even of me. To counter this, Ramsey published his own protest to the Junta in the name of human rights concerning all Chileans still in detention.

Ramsey was the first Archbishop of Canterbury ever to visit Chile while still in office. He arrived on 20th September 1974, nearly a year after the coup, amidst some political awkwardness. His critical remarks about the Junta had, of course, reached Chile ahead of him, and had stirred up opposition, not only from many Chileans, but from many of the British there as well. The Archbishop came with an entourage that included his chaplain (who later became the Bishop of Sherbourne), and another large friendly man, John Miles, who looked like a personal bodyguard but was actually his press secretary.

Michael Ramsey and his wife Joan were a delight to entertain. Ramsey, with his impressive craggy face, wandered around cassocked in purple, gently humming tunes of well known hymns – chiefly those of the evangelical William Cowper. According to Timothy Ross, in a feature article in *The Observer*,[6] the Archbishop was coming out to take us to task for not adopting more critical views of the Junta. We were interested to hear what he would have to say to us on the subject. In fact he said nothing!

THE VISIT

Everywhere we went with the Archbishop we had armoured escorts and were driven at break-neck speed. I felt he might be in greater danger from our Chilean chauffeurs than from any possible snipers! We took him to visit the Intendente of Valparaíso – the highest civil dignitary in the city. Actually it was acutely embarrassing being present at that meeting. Here was an Archbishop of few words, who had 'inherited the faculty of being silent in several languages'[7] and an Intendente accustomed to the effusive exchange of compliments and congratulations – something far from forthcoming at this meeting. The poor Intendente was clearly deflated and quite uncertain as to how to sustain a conversation with a foreign dignitary – a religious, non-Catholic – who had publicly criticised his Government, and now seemed to have nothing else to say.

Amongst other things[8] the Archbishop was taken to the church in Gomez Carreño, before going back to the capital of Santiago. We thought he would prefer to see some of the new Spanish work, rather than the more traditional chaplaincy churches.

Gomez Carreño gave him a great welcome, and he adapted himself to their culture marvellously. The singing with drums and guitars was 'out of this world'. The next day the BBC reporter present told me that he had replayed a recording of it over and over again throughout the night. He was intrigued by the vocal offering of the congregation being led by those simple musicians. Ramsey matched it all by preaching a superb sermon on the Holy Spirit's fire, and to their delight, spent some time talking to folk afterwards. When we finally got him back into the car, he turned to Joan and murmured, 'I saw you clapping!' Joan simply smiled. 'And I saw you tapping your foot to the music!' she said.

No cameras allowed in *callampas*

The Archbishop's whole visit to Chile was being covered by the BBC. The Archbishop was keen to visit a *callampa* (shanty-town), but the Chilean authorities were hesitant in agreeing to it. Ever since I had first arrived, I had discovered that Chileans were very sensitive about pictures of their poverty being shown across the world and whenever we took photos, even for our SAMS magazine, people would ask why we needed to publish such pictures? They did not like us exposing their shame to advertise our work; it was the 'always dress smartly in public' syndrome – image is very important to them.

Finally a military official advised me that the Archbishop could visit a shanty-town on the way to Santiago the next morning on condition that the TV crew did not know and did not accompany him. Ramsey agreed to those conditions. That evening the TV crew reported to me that they were going ahead of us to the capital for the night, and would meet up with us again the next day in Santiago – unless the Archbishop was going to do anything else before he got there. Was he? 'No!' I said instantly, and they left. I knew that if I had hesitated a second they would have sensed that I might be hiding something. But what appalled me was the ease with which I had just told a flat lie without even flinching! And I called myself a Christian! Remembering this even now brings me into a cold sweat and takes me back to my 'Garden of Eden' experience at Gislingham! How could I have done it? But what else could I have said to that film crew? Of course, I repented, but the blatant loss of integrity was devastating!

When we arrived in Santiago next morning we were invited to dinner at the Embassy. Mrs Seconde, the ambassador's wife, had thoughtfully invited a number of other church leaders also. The British Ambassador (a Roman Catholic) admitted to being surprised when the Archbishop predicted that there could be union with Rome within ten years! So was I. It's more than twenty-five years now since Ramsey prophesied about that re-union. But if 'Homer', usually good, 'nods'[9] for a moment a great man can be forgiven for a minor slip!

INTERVIEW WITH PINOCHET

The Archbishop had a private interview with President Pinochet. During the half-hour together Ramsey again pressed respect for human rights for all detainees. His biographer suggests that Ramsey had a very poor opinion of Pinochet, believing him for some reason to be 'a stupid man and a totally non-political animal'.[10] Future events I think have shown some of those opinions to be as unrealistic as Ramsey's timescale regarding re-union with Rome. Any President who could put a referendum out at the end of seventeen years for opinions as to whether he should continue in office or hand over to the politicians, and still get over 40% of the votes in his favour, would surely have some grounds for concluding that his people must have felt, as Pinochet himself would have done, that he had actually served his country pretty well. The state of Chile's economy had improved annually by 8.5% during the last fifteen years of his time in office. Ramsey never lived to see how, following the wish of the majority, Pinochet handed back the country in a far healthier state to a democratic Government. Incidentally, and sadly, Chile seems to have been sliding slowly back into economic decline ever since Pinochet left office.

VISIT TO PINOCHET YEARS LATER

In 1999 I went to visit the General, who was then eighty-four, with Archdeacon Alfredo Cooper, a friend from Chile. Pinochet was a house prisoner on the Wentworth estate in Surrey – an imprisonment that cost the British Government £4,000,000! He was still recovering from an operation on his spine. We were asked to limit our visit to ten minutes. The former President stood up to greet us and embraced us in true Chilean style. We sat and talked and he never once complained about the inordinate length of time the legal proceedings concerning his arrest were taking. I studied him carefully as he talked to us – head upright like the old soldier that he was, with a passive resignation to the fortunes of life – a man confident that he had acted dutifully for the protection and reconstruction of his country. After chatting about Chile, we prayed for him and presented him with a Bible in Spanish. Then we stood to say goodbye. He proceeded to embrace us again and thanked us for our visit. Walking to the door, hanging on to Alfredo, he stopped for a moment to indicate a Jerusalem Bible lying open on the desk in an alcove. 'You may not believe it,' he said, 'but I read that every day.' Just reading the Bible, of course, does not exonerate anyone from anything, but for me it seemed to have some positive significance. We left him thinking that the world would never understand all that he had done for Chile. Would the truth ever be fairly recorded in the future annals of Chile's history?

CRUDE CARICATURE

Of course Ramsey could not really know what Pinochet was like from a few minutes of halting discussion through an interpreter. According to his biographer, Ramsey had been fed a crude caricature before he ever met Pinochet, that he was 'a wife-dominated, weight-lifting unintellectual with his chic uniform and his whiffs of eau-de-Cologne and superstition'!

Immediately following his interview with Pinochet, Ramsey posed for photos. Back in the UK, he was asked whether he minded being surrounded by so many guns. He replied: 'Guns are the ritual of Latin America . . . I noticed them as little as pipes and cigarettes'. In fact guns were never prolific after the first two weeks following the coup, but they may have been a little more evident when Ramsey visited since they were there for his protection. The Archbishop had expressed a little irritation with the presence of a Chilean, Lieutenant Tovar, who kept as near to him as possible at all times. Then he learned from the Catholic Nuncio, later confirmed by the British Embassy, that there was a threatened attempt upon his life.

HAD I MODERATED MY VIEWS?

According to his later comments to the media (as per press releases supplied by the British Embassy), Archbishop Ramsey said that I had moderated my views concerning the military intervention. We enjoyed having both Joan and Michael Ramsey.

We loved her homeliness and enjoyed his gentle humour, but although he readily discussed areas of charismatic renewal, he had never appeared to want to discuss the politics of Chile once he arrived so I could not imagine how he believed I had moderated my opinions. Perhaps I had moderated the way I expressed them. He had come to Chile with his mind made up. But I am sure that his statement to the press was kindly meant: he was trying to defend me in a nice sort of way.

I wondered what Ramsey thought of Cardinal Silva's approach. He was the Roman Catholic Archbishop of Santiago. Initially he had publicly expressed qualified support for the military intervention; as I had.

But after his original support of the coup, he may have become increasingly worried about it on two counts: one because the Junta was not immediately handing the country back to a democratically elected Government. And two, because some of his own Catholics were being detained or were on the run from the police. Many of his younger priests and nuns (especially the foreigners), who were working among the slums and shanty-towns had become increasingly revolutionary. But even two weeks after the coup, a nun, who said she had seen dead bodies in the Capital's Mapocho river, reported that she had found the Cardinal unsympathetic and unresponsive. Left wing priests were also expressing their criticism about the Cardinal's 'uncombative stand'. But leaders are always a target for criticism.

A RECURRING PROBLEM

With the re-establishment of law and order under the Junta we now had more time to focus on our own goals once again. A recurring problem was surfacing with increasing frequency. When we originally set out for Chile, we had the vision for building up the Anglican Church as a kind of *via media* for those who were no longer attending the Catholic Church but could not take the anti-intellectualism of Chilean Pentecostalism. I justified the role of Anglicanism in those days with the argument that Catholics believed the Bible but then taught believers more than the Bible – while Pentecostalists believed the Bible but with their restricted views on its interpretation and their lack of education actually taught less than the Bible! (In fact many Pentecostal evangelists could hardly read the Bible.) The Anglican Church, on the other hand, with its reformed tradition, lectionaries, liturgies and rituals taught the Bible in a balanced way, we thought! This had its appeal – people were joining us and we were seeing people coming to a living faith in Jesus Christ that was clearly blessing them and their families.

But as time went on, following my encounter with the Holy Spirit which came to a head in the bishop's house in 1970, I began to feel increasingly shabby about this approach. It left me feeling I was preaching a negative critical message to justify our church's growing presence in Chile. A further problem was that in searching after a distinctive identity to justify the Anglican Church it was becoming increasingly clear to me – an Englishman – that so much of Anglicanism was derived from its English ethos. This was very difficult to disentangle from the way we were presenting it. And a healthy church in Chile would need to have a definitely Chilean ethos. It was a tension that was unsettling me, and beginning to dominate my thinking, however hard I tried to suppress it. Leaders need to know where they are going! Would it not be simpler to offer our services to the charismatic stream within the Catholic Church or be more available to help in the biblical formation of Chilean Pentecostal leaders? But any decision about that was being taken out of my hands by a new set of personal circumstances.

Chapter 16

OUT OF ONE HOT SEAT, INTO ANOTHER

He is not leaving under a cloud
(MET OFFICE SPOKESMAN ON THE RESIGNATION
OF A BBC WEATHERMAN)

The Lord blessed the latter part of Job's life more than the first
(JOB 42:12, NIV)

ONLY A CURATE![1]

Oh I am only a curate, so pale and so small,
Newly ordained I'm the humblest of all,
My home is a garret, my stipend's a shame
But deep in my heart burns a bright little flame

I look at the vicar and envy his life.
With his new parish car and his competent wife
As I walk round the parish, so young and alone
I long for the day I'll have one of my own.

I'm a vicar; my hair has turned very grey
I work ten days a week and a twelve-hour day
My home is much larger but draughty and old
And my bones are arthritic from the damp and the cold

My free time is Monday or that's what they say
But the diocese fix all their meetings that day;
I'm tempted to ask when I'm saying my prayers
For the job of archdeacon with no parish cares

Oh I'm an archdeacon, a man of affairs;
I check all the terriers and count all the chairs
My job is to keep down the costs of admin.,
So I've got no time for salvation and sin.

I have to do what the bishop ordains;
I drive the carriage but he holds the reins
This makes my task hard and although I'm no snob
I find myself wishing that I had his job.

I am a bishop so blithe and so bland
I have a crook and a ring on my hand
Resplendent in gaiters and smart purple stock
I have to shepherd this troublesome flock.

My stipend is larger but sometimes I groan
When I look at my diary, my time's not my own;
When faced with the bore of diocesan strife
I long for the calm of an archbishop's life.

Oh I'm an archbishop, the top of the tree.
I'm the front man for the whole C of E.
I live in a palace and wear a gold cope
I chat up the Romans and lunch with the Pope.

But now that I've made it I know it's all vain,
I wish I were back as a curate again;
Amid all this pomp I remember with shame
The wonderful joy of that bright little flame.

And so if you're tempted to moan at your lot
Or envy the grass in the other man's plot
Remember that sweet though the pasture may smell
The field that looks greener has cow-claps as well.

COLIN FAWCETT QC

DEPUTATION WORK IN NORTH AMERICA AND CANADA

Many problems in life remain unresolved but life itself moves on. I had been busy travelling – doing deputation work and helping to create a network for SAMS support across the USA and Canada – a programme full of encouragements and surprises. One particular memory was in Alberta, Canada, where the bishop I was trying to interest took me to meet the Chief of the Cree Indians.

At the end of our conversation the old Chief offered me a duplicate copy of a treaty signed by his great-grandfather and Queen Victoria's then diplomatic representative in Canada. He asked me if, the next time I was in England, I would be so kind as to call in on the Queen and explain how his people felt – that the 'white man' had not kept to his side of the treaty. I could hardly begin to explain that protocol prevented one from simply 'popping in' to see the Queen at Buckingham Palace. In any case she would have already been fully *au fait* through diplomatic channels of the unresolved land claim questions – already a matter of major public concern in Canada! But I accepted the copy politely.

SO MUCH DESK WORK STILL NEEDED

Back in Chile there was church planting to attend to, a general synod in Santiago to prepare for, and matters of church discipline to cope with. A 'Chileanised' prayer book and a hymn book were being prepared, besides some work on the constitution of the *Iglesia Anglicana* in a form that was compatible with Chilean law. There was the need to prepare canons to guide the church still so much in its infancy. But we lacked a sufficient number of mature indigenous leaders to provide the necessary educated input for these developments – especially in the field of liturgy. If this were to be suitable for a truly Chilean culture, this work would have to be pioneered by Anglican Chileans who had sufficient appreciation of the role of liturgy in worship and some understanding of both the history and current developments within the rich traditions of the Anglican Communion. Without this liturgical dimension it was hard to see how we could justify our continuance as a separate denomination. We had tried to point the way with a *Libro de Oracion Comun y Manual de la Iglesia*

Anglicana whose publication in 1973 we were able to finance through the favourable exchange rate as the value of the escudo kept falling.

Those intensely packed years flew by and we found ourselves once more returning to the UK on leave.

CHILDREN'S FUTURES

Having already started Charlotte at King Edward the Sixth's School, Witley, in Surrey, we had followed this up the following year by sending Debby to the same school. Whilst the two older girls were destined to complete their education in England this raised questions about the two younger ones. The political climate in Chile was by now settled once again. Should we try and keep them in Chile with us, and allow the family to become permanently divided with their education being developed under two different systems, in two different countries so many thousands of miles apart? In which case what would happen if one of them were to start a permanent relationship with a boy, and we were not there for them in their country when they needed us? In Chile girls start *pololeando* when they are only twelve or thirteen. To *pololear* is quite a serious commitment. It means that the parents formally approve of the relationship and this gives it a kind of status. Though not quite an engagement to marry, the young couple concerned usually hope that it will come to that.

We were now facing a whole new scenario with regard to their futures. Where the children were educated could very easily determine where they made their future home. We were committed to the process of gradually easing ourselves off the scene to speed up the Chileanising of the church. If the children settled permanently in Chile and we returned to the UK to work, we would be cut off from them pretty well for good without the finances to fly back and forth.

Charlotte was bravely assuring us that she felt OK about our staying longer in Chile, though we were sensing she really felt otherwise. When we eventually decided to pull out of Chile Charlotte confided that she was really glad to have us home. Teenagers need their parents more desperately than they may care to admit.

HEAT WAVE AT HOME

We arrived in England in the middle of a heat wave. There was plenty of deputation work in the offing. This could be hectic and quite boring in fact. Every church usually had the same Scripture readings and the same old hymns – *From Greenlands Icy Mountains* and *Let The Song Go Round The Earth* – *Hills Of The North Rejoice!* – all especially chosen as most suitable for a missionary Sunday. And we usually preached the same sermons. Finding my way to some of the churches was a problem!

It was nearly as confusing finding the way forward about our own future. Jean Hedderly who, with Vernon, had undertaken the guardianship of the first two girls seemed visibly shaken when we mentioned we were now considering the possibility of putting the other two into the same school – especially since Jean now had an ailing relative making extra demands upon her time and energy. We could see it would be too much for them but we could not just ask anyone to be a guardian if the girls had no previous bond or close relationship with them.

Currently we had accommodation in a cosy attic at a friend's house. This was a very sacrificial and generous gesture on the part of our hosts and without them we could never have managed. But during the holiday times it was quite difficult with four lively young teenage daughters. It was awkward too for entertaining visitors and particularly hard for Mary when I was away deputising with the only car we had, leaving her feeling slightly trapped.

Finally I went to see Hugh Montefiore, then a suffragan bishop in Southwark, to find if the diocese (which originally 'sent' me out) might have a vacant rectory[2] we could rent. This could serve as a base for Mary while I returned overseas.[3] But there was nothing for us in the Southwark diocese, apparently. Then I had a most generous offer from a friend in the USA. This was John Howe, since elected bishop of Central Florida, who was then rector of a large SAMS supporting church near Washington. He said that his church would be sympathetic towards paying all expenses for our children's fares out to Chile every holiday so that we could return to our work there. But we had no peace about that either. How would our national clergy feel in Chile if we were having our children flown out three times a year at such great expense while the Chilean nationals were expected to keep their families on very small salaries? Everyone knew that airfares were costly. And if we could tap such resources for ourselves why could we not get more help for them?

SORTING OUT PRIORITIES

Suddenly I got a fresh perspective on my priorities when reading St Paul's letter to Timothy: 'If anyone does not provide for his relatives, and especially for his immediate family, he has denied the faith and is worse than an unbeliever'.[4] The needs of my own girls at this time of their emotional and educational development were paramount. I have enlarged on these tensions because this kind of domestic crisis creates difficult decisions for those who have particular responsibilities abroad. The people to whom one would normally turn to discuss things were friends of many years but were all naturally prejudiced towards the needs in Chile. Even Donald Coggan, the new Archbishop of Canterbury thought I ought to go back. The choice to stay at home seemed to mean one was letting down the church in Chile and a wonderful missionary team there; letting down SAMS and its dedicated staff and supporters; and more subtly still, letting down the Lord. Then again it would be only a matter of time before a new province of the Southern Cone would materialise. This meant that the office of Primate or Presiding Bishop could sooner or later come to the diocesan bishop in Chile, since this highest office would be rotated on the basis known in industry as '*Muggin's Turn*'. But I would have been like a fish out of water in that role. I had done as much as I could. In the diocese of Chile the principle of spontaneous church planting was already established – many of the new churches being led by laity (who would still need long-term mentoring on the Paul to Timothy model). A relevant but sketchy liturgy was on offer. Also the extension of an adequate sacramental ministry was in prospect through suitable lay-presidency at the Lord's Supper – even if it was to be only a temporary improvisation by which to furnish the local churches with their God-given means of grace. I was beginning to feel we could leave.

FUTURE COMING CLEAR

Still waiting in the UK to be sure of God's way forward for us, we had a kind letter from Canon Harry Sutton (whom we had first met when he came to see us off to Chile in 1959 – just as he was joining SAMS as Home Secretary, before becoming the General Secretary soon after). Harry and his wife had recently returned from a visit to South America. Harry had by then retired from SAMS but took the liberty of writing: 'Olive and I were met by people everywhere, saying how very much they hoped you and Mary might be able to return even if the period was for a very short one. You are not only needed there but wanted, and I am sure this must come as a great encouragement to you . . .'. We were grateful but it compounded that niggling sense of residual guilt about staying back in the UK. There was a final comeback from both SAMS and the diocese. They wanted me to go back for another seven months to tidy things up! But we now had too many unresolved problems of our own demanding urgent attention back in the UK. We needed to find a new parish quickly: its location would dictate where the girls' future schooling would be and we needed to settle where that would be soon. I resigned from the Diocese of Chile, Bolivia and Peru in January 1977 after nearly seventeen years in South America. We started praying earnestly that we would find a parish in the UK which we could move into before for the next school year started in September 1977.

PRAYING FOR A JOB

Most oversees bishops negotiate some kind of transfer to another episcopal office before resigning. This did not seem right for me. The Lord still appeared to be saying what I had heard him say so many times before: 'The way to up is down' and I had underlined that verse in my Bible where John the Baptist said: 'He must increase, but I must decrease',[5] a motto I needed to work at myself. The only objective worthwhile was to exalt Christ and extend his kingdom.

My previous experience of parish work hardly qualified me for Christian leadership in the UK. I had never actually run an ordinary parish here. There was so much to learn. There had been

215

vast cultural changes in the UK. We had left England assuming that the future would carry on like the past. We were experiencing a 'reverse culture shock' on our re-entry to our own country. What was this new anti-authoritarian, multicultured, multifaith, unashamedly morally declining English culture we found? The new morality seemed just like the old immorality. The sexual revolution contributed to an increase in marriage breakdowns and dysfunctional families. Doing what one was told had given way to doing what one felt like doing! A complex gestation was in process for the birth of a new post-modern society almost devoid of all the old values. Britain seemed to be cringeing in shame for its one-time role as an empire builder and was struggling to discover a coherent identity for the future. How had all this happened and what were its implications for a local Church in England?

KEEPING IT UP

Theological developments over here had descended to the hopeless 'Death of God' stuff along with the old chestnuts that denied the virgin birth and the bodily resurrection of Christ. God could no longer be supernatural apparently and therefore he could no longer be God. Then there were the unfamiliar new liturgies, new vestments, new chants, new hymns, and new architecture which alienated the old faithfuls. To what extent had I completely lost touch over here I wondered? There was an increase of violence, racial polarisation, interracial wars, and genocide across the world. Almost everyday there was news of widespread social disorder, strikes, and student uprisings. There was an increase of begging in the streets, sleeping rough or squatting, not to mention the many teenage pregnancies (and later, the AIDS problem).

We had our insoluble tensions in Northern Ireland and agitations from the feminist movement. It was a very different world we were re-entering. But the gospel of the kingdom of God had not changed – only the ways of presenting it.

Secondly I was convinced that the charismatic renewal movement, already started in the UK, could revitalise the Church of England, and the wider church, as we had begun to see it happening so beneficially in Chile. But I knew I still had so much more to learn about its practical application, and I had no idea where I could get more help nor how I would actually be able to further it in the UK. I was looking for a charismatic church that I could visit. I needed to see an established model in the UK for myself.

AN URBAN PRIORITY PARISH PERHAPS?

Also I felt that perhaps we had been prepared, through so much contact with the disadvantaged, for a role in a run-down inner-city parish. We had no money, no furniture, and no ambitions of our own, except to serve the Lord. I think we were both excited about the challenge of an 'urban priority area', but, although we had circulated our availability widely nothing seemed to crop up. I went to see the Bishop of Southwark, Mervyn Stockwood – a notable left-wing diocesan. I had sometimes attended his church when he had been a vicar in Bristol. On the Sunday mornings there he would appear for high mass robed in his full regalia – in the evenings he had a kind of evangelical 'rave-up' with CSSM choruses – inviting such people as the well known evangelist Canon Bryan Green to speak.

I now shared with him our willingness to go to a run-down inner city parish. However after talking things over he came up with a different proposition – hardly a run-down parish though. It was one of the best parishes in the diocese. But it was not going to be available till the New Year. We needed to be well settled before September 1977 at the latest, for the sake of the children. All we could do was to keep praying and knock on doors.

OFFER FROM SAMS

Then Philip King, who had taken over from Harry Sutton as SAMS General Secretary, kindly invited me to become a sort of Co-General Secretary of SAMS with him. This did not quite fit either with what I had imagined I might be doing in the UK but, with the pressure upon me as the breadwinner for the family, and the thought of soon being unemployed, I had to take this offer very seriously. We kept praying that if this was God calling us he would make his will clear. If this offer was right, I thought, our girls would settle back more easily in a church like St Andrew's,

Chorleywood. This had been a good SAMS supporting church which had a reputation for being charismatic – and maybe its way of 'doing church' would be nearer to what the girls had been used to. It was obviously an ideal base for getting around the country, and very near Heathrow airport. It would also be on the M25 when that was finally completed, and that would lead on easily to the M1. So I phoned John Perry, the vicar, whom I had met on a deputation visit there in 1973, and asked him whether he knew of any of his parishioners who might possibly have a house to rent. It was the kind of parish where people went abroad for two or three years in the course of their work or study and might be willing to rent out their homes reasonably cheaply – for a good cause! I explained that we were staying home to work with SAMS on account of the children. John listened carefully on the other end of the phone, and then urged me, rather strangely, I thought, not to make up my mind too quickly. He kindly agreed to make some enquiries about accommodation.

I also had a letter from Dr Jim Packer asking me confidentially to consider applying for a job on the staff at Trinity which was about to be advertised. It involved responsibility for organising the students' pastoral work around the city of Bristol. Though honoured by Jim's kind thought, and urgently needing a job I was sure that with all the administration necessary it was not 'me'. We were then approached about a church quite near King Edward's School in Surrey, which was tempting. But the living was not going to be vacant until the January of the following year. Same problem – we could not wait that long!

SOMEWHERE OF OUR OWN!

Two or three weeks later the phone rang and Mary announced that John Perry was on the line. He surprised me by asking, very confidentially, how I would feel about living in the vicarage of St Andrew's, Chorleywood as the incumbent! He had just accepted an appointment as the new warden of Lee Abbey in Devon, and wanted to put my name forward to the bishop of St Alban's,[6] as his possible successor at St Andrew's. Would we pray about it? And then let him know our thoughts as soon as possible?

In one sense this was rather disappointing. I had been rather looking forward to sitting under John's ministry. He was reputed to be one of the best local church leaders that the Church of England had. We wanted to learn about how he was developing work in a renewing church like St Andrew's. From another point of view it was exciting. This might well be God's will. However, initially Mary was not at all keen. We still had the thought of going to a much poorer type parish. Then, a week or two later we were speaking at Christ Church, Chorleywood, and Peter Sertin the vicar said he thought it would be wonderful if we could go to St Andrew's which was about to become vacant! He left me saying that he was going to write to the bishop about it! I said nothing of the conversation with John Perry. We finally phoned back and told John that we were interested. A week or two later we had a letter from Robert Runcie, the bishop of the diocese, asking if we could meet. We did just that. He asked us about our family and explained that if we came he would like us to be on his diocesan council. I said I would be glad to help in any way I could. I would, of course, have to give myself mainly to the parish and get to know the people there properly to start with. He asked us to see the wardens of St Andrew's: he also discussed the political situation we were leaving behind in Chile. I gave him my views with my usual frankness – which did not seem to faze him at all.

MEETING THE WARDENS

In response to his request we saw Iain Roberts and Michael Riddelsdell, the wardens at St Andrew's. We met with Dick Lyth too – a one-time bishop from Uganda, who had returned to the UK on health grounds. Dick and his wife Nora were on the staff, as were Barry and Mary Kissell (Barry was a New Zealander). There was also an elderly lady worker named Jean Appleton and David Bennett, a full time youth worker, who was about to return to teaching. And also Margaret Knight, a lady training to be a deacon. We loved them all. We felt they wanted us there too. But we waited, and waited, and prayed and prayed. Apparently, we heard from one source, that it was our reputation as 'Fascists' which had worried some on the bishop's council. There were questions about what kind of risk we might be in the diocese? Because of all the problems about settling into a parish before the autumn term, mainly for the sake of the children's education, we were beginning to feel quite desperate about all the waiting. If Chorleywood wasn't right for us we needed to look urgently for another job.

PHONE CALL FROM HEAVEN

One morning after breakfast, with still no letter, we were sitting round the table having our usual devotional time together. I had just prayed aloud: 'Lord, we really thought you meant us to go to Chorleywood. If that's not your will we surrender our wills to yours. We trust you and we believe that if you have closed this door, then its only because you have something better in line for us. May your holy will be done . . .'. We never even had time to say 'Amen' to that prayer before the phone at my elbow started ringing. It was Robert Runcie of St Albans. 'David,' he said, 'I really believe the Holy Spirit is saying to me that you are the man for St Andrew's, Chorleywood. Will you take it?' That had to be God! I had no hesitancy: 'Yes! Thank you,' I replied, 'We will!'

PERSONAL LINK WITH CHORLEYWOOD

Chorleywood had a few claims to fame. It was mentioned in the Domesday book. King John's Farm had witnessed the wedding of the famous aristocratic Quaker William Penn, the founder of Pennsylvania. It also had an occasional mention on the BBC's Radio 4 *Today* programme from John Timpson who lived in Chorleywood and worshipped at St Andrew's. It claimed to have the oldest pillar post box in England – ER VIII.

According to William Hickey in a *Daily Telegraph* column in 1959 it was then considered 'the most fashionable top-drawer town in Britain'. A national survey (1970) had revealed that Chorleywood had an average of two cars per family which was considered remarkable at the time. I don't think that was very true of our end of the village so it probably meant some households possessed three over the other side of the Common – Peter Sertin's parish of Christ Church. Curiously I had also had a family connection with Chorleywood. My godfather, Lex Wilson, my mother's cousin, had lived at Braehead, Berks Hill, for many years, only dying a year or two before our arrival there. I had first visited the parish for deputation work in 1969 and then again in 1974, and had actually been booked to speak at the third annual convention in the marquee on Chorleywood Common on Sunday 15th May 1977. This was four months before I was inducted. It was common knowledge by then that I was going to St Andrew's. My first words at the convention were: 'I am, of course, delighted that God has led us to come to Chorleywood – but I have one little prayer in my heart. It is that I will never forget the needs of the crowds without Jesus and the cry of the cities of Latin America. And that as I walk the streets of Chorleywood, I won't forget the smells, the pains, and the agonies of the poor in South America.' It would be quite wrong to give the impression that all South America is like that. It certainly isn't. There is a large middle class as well as immense areas of natural beauty and appeal there. It's just that where there are smells of open drains, and poverty, they are indicative of a level of deprivation generally unknown in the UK! Having visited nearly every country in South America at one time or another – albeit only briefly in some – I think I have always retained a concern for their needs. The church we were being called to lead was already committed to giving away half its income to mission and work of that nature, and had a proud tradition of caring for the poor – a trait that greatly attracted us there – a kind of guarantee for God's blessing on its future!

St Andrew's had been a daughter church of Christ Church across the Common, and had become a parish in its own right in 1963. John Perry[7] was its first vicar, and with his wife Gay, had completed fifteen very fruitful years there.

HOME FOR THE FAMILY AT LAST

We were allowed to move into the vicarage early in July. We had our own home together at last. We set about finding enough furniture for the vicarage and bought a lot of secondhand items. My 'collation' (instalment as vicar) on 9th September went off well. Even Ken Howell, my former diocesan bishop in Chile, and now a grieving widower, came. Robert Runcie 'collated' me with his domestic chaplain Richard Chartres (now the bishop of London) at his side. Runcie's relaxed and humorous addresses always went down well at St Andrew's. Canon Eric James, a gifted speaker and delightful left winger, came too, I imagined he was there to check out the new 'Fascist' in the diocese!

ST ANDREW'S

Only a couple of fools or desperados would ever follow John and Gay Perry – the ideal vicar and wife. Few could match them. They had imparted to the congregation such love – the greatest gift of the Holy Spirit. St Andrew's really knew how to exercise love. The exciting history of so much that had taken place there (both before we arrived and after) has been written up in some detail by Alex Twells in his book *Standing on His Promises*.[8] St Andrew's had had some very fruitful evangelistic missions – including one led by Canon John Collins, another by Canon David Watson and yet another by Canon Harry Sutton (when he was the General Secretary of SAMS). There had also been significant visits from a number of other leading charismatics – Dennis Bennett, Michael and Jeanne Harper, Edgar Trout, Reg East, Nicky Cruz, Arthur Wallis and Jean Darnell. Just before we arrived the *Reader's Digest* (January 1977) had written up a piece about charismatics, entitled 'Can the Church find room for the Hallelujah Christians?' This reported how St Andrew's, Chorleywood, had raised all the money itself for its new church building etc that had replaced the old corrugated iron mission hall where the congregation had formerly worshipped.

We loved the new church we inherited – it was so accepting. A charismatic church at its best. If, during our nineteen years, there followed still further blessing it was humanly speaking due to the fortunate convergence of the right time, the right place and the right constituency in the leadership team. I spent the first two or three years trying to get to know as many of the congregation as I could, but never knew them as well as John Perry, who would minister the sacrament to each communicant personally by name.

PAINFUL TO LOSE ANYONE

One church couple came to us soon after we arrived to explain that they were *Book of Common Prayer* Anglicans. They had stayed on just long enough to see if there was any possibility I might lead the church back into the good old ways. Once it was clear to them that we obviously were not going to revert they decided to leave. 'No hard feelings!' they said. But in fact it is always painful for an incumbent to lose anybody – for whatever reason. It causes a great deal of heart-searching. We have to ask ourselves how we might have failed such people? But we did not lose many. I think it helped that we managed to keep a regular 1662 Holy Communion service at 8 am going right up to the time we left in 1996.

John Perry had led the church through many changes – new forms of services, new (charismatic) songs, liturgical dance, drama, children's family services, a number of home groups, and a much larger newly built sideways-on church with a kitchen, comfortable lounge, toilets and a little parish office. All quite advanced for a church in those days.

HELPED BY OTHER STAFF MEMBERS
Barry Kissell, a former curate, was still on staff.[9] His special ministry was to organise and direct Faith Sharing teams from the congregation under different lay leaders. These went out evangelising to other places – even overseas – on a regular basis and returned with stories of what they had seen or heard of the Lord's doing during the time of their weekends away. Such feedbacks made the services at St Andrew's very fresh.

The Faith Sharing ministry could have its complications and even embarrassments. The team would usually include one new convert to the faith at least – a feature which added spontaneity and relevance to the overall message being shared. On one occasion, a new convert who was going to speak, with the team, at a church in Kent, decided to 'take courage' at an inn *en route*. He turned up as the first of the team on the vicar's doorstep swaying rather unsteadily and slurring his words – not the first of our embarrassments by any means.

ROBED CHOIR AND PROCESSIONS
St Andrew's still chanted psalms and canticles, and had a large robed choir that processed and recessed in and out of the services to the singing of a hymn. Many had had a renewal experience and received gifts of the Spirit, but there were no manifestations of

this when the church worshipped together. Gifts of the Spirit were still reserved for home groups that liked them. If I had wanted to change the services in any way I really would not have known in what way. I still had so much to learn. It was strange taking over an Anglican church while being still so unfamiliar with the new liturgies being used.

But I was relieved to feel that my travelling days were behind me as I settled back into parish life. Little did I realise what was ahead! Now I was able to spend more time with the family too. My only outside commitment was in the diocese where I helped out quite a lot with confirmations – especially when Robert Runcie went off on a sabbatical the year after I had arrived. Then hardly was Runcie back in office when he left to succeed Donald Coggan as the new Archbishop of Canterbury. John Taylor came to St Albans as bishop. I soon found taking confirmations as a visiting bishop rather unsatisfactory and unfulfilling. Confirmations are an ideal opportunity for diocesan bishops and their staff to get to know their flocks. But I think churches naturally feel a little defrauded with a stand-in bishop officiating who is not actually part of the official diocesan oversight. With the parish work growing and all the added pressures following a powerful visitation of the Holy Spirit upon St Andrew's in 1981, I simply had to limit myself to helping out the diocese only in emergencies.

PASTORAL BURDEN

My particular style of leadership might be characterised as that of an 'external processor'. This has the advantage of letting others know where one is in one's thinking, and also for them to criticise or give advice.

My initial burden was to get to know the people and the different infrastructures and organisations in St Andrew's, and quite simply sense how John and Gay had run the parish so well; and then try and emulate them. I needed to keep evaluating all that was happening and where either I or the church were failing. Also we required some material equipment to keep apace with all that was going on.

Above left: The Rev T.A. Pytches, David's father.

Above right: Irene Pytches, nee Welldon, David's mother.

Left: Bishop J.E.C. Welldon, David's great uncle, whose father and uncle were both clergy and who was himself the eldest of four clergy brothers. This picture dominated the living room of David's childhood.

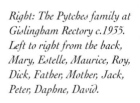

Right: The Pytches family at Gislingham Rectory c.1935. Left to right from the back, Mary, Estelle, Maurice, Roy, Dick, Father, Mother, Jack, Peter, Daphne, David.

Left: The Little Grange, Pytches Road, Woodbridge, Suffolk. This was the family home of David Pytches' forefathers.

Right, centre: Gislingham Rectory, David's first home, with a huge kitchen garden, orchard, stables and two tennis courts! It was approached by a long drive with a pond on one side.

Right, below: Holbrook Rectory looks gloomy, but this large house was light and airy inside, although with eight bedrooms it was hard to keep warm in the winter. It also had a tennis court, billiards room, a badminton hall, kitchen garden, stables and a workshop.

Below: Old Buckenham Hall, Norfolk, where David and his brother Peter went to prep school. Unfortuntely the building has since burned down.

Top: David Pytches, aged 20.

Centre: Mary Trevisick, aged 18.

Below: The marriage of David Pytches and Mary Trevisick, Barnstaple, 1958. The clergy guests included, from left to right, Roger Beckwith, Mac Farmborough, Jack Pytches, Roy Rimmer, Jim Vincent, Peter Pytches, Basil Gough (David's first Rector), Richard Spurrier, Derek Osborne, Michael Farrer and Hector Huxham.

Above, left:
'The Anglicana' in
Valparaíso where the
Pytches' first lived in
1962, with St Paul's,
the old English
chaplaincy church
behind it where they
built up their first
Spanish congregation.

Above, right:
An 'ascensor', the way
people travelled up the
hills in Valparaíso.

Centre: A typical view
of the harbour of
Valparaíso showing the
built-over hills above it.

Below: Santiago,
Chile's capital, where
the David Pytches had
his Diocesan offices.

Above: After David's consecration in St. Paul's, Valparaíso, December 20th, 1970. David and Mary centre left, Bishop Bill Flagg and Bishop Colin Bazley, both just beyond on the left and right and Bishop Ken Howell in the centre.

Left: The family growing up, Becky, Charlotte, Debby and Tasha with David and Mary.

Below, left and right: Mary and David speaking at a renewal conference in Canada.

Top, left: John Wimber, whose generous friendship came to mean so much to the Pytches.

Top, right: A Pytches family gathering outside St. Andrew's, Chorleywood. Mary and David are standing, far right and the four daughters, Becky, Tasha, Charlotte and Debby are kneeling in front of them.

Above: Mary and David on a ministry visit to Hong Kong with Ricky and Louan Feuille and Richard and Prue Bedwell.

Right: On holiday in Vina del Mar, Mary Pytches with their kind and generous friend over many years, Anderly Hardy.

Below: An evening meeting at an early New Wine conference at the Royal Bath and West showground.

Top, left: Inspecting the public toilets in ancient Ephesus.

Top, right:
Enjoying a mud bath in Turkey –
the Pytches' with their friends the Bedwells.

Centre: At the entrance to the cave on the island of Patmos where St. John received his revelations from God.

Below, left: David and Mary visiting the Columbia glacier in the Canadian Rockies.

Below, right: 10 of the grandchildren in the vicarage garden in Chorleywood. To more have arrived since the photo was taken!

Family gatherings:
Top, left: the Cocksworth
family: Matthew, Samuel,
Timothy, Sebastian,
Christopher, Charlotte
and Ashley.

Centre, left: the Wright
family: John, Zachary,
Jordon and Debby.

Below, left: the Barrett
family: Richard, Becky
and Nina.

Below: the Shaw family:
Mike, Philip, Daniel,
Grace, Tasha and Andrew.

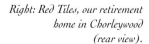

Right: Red Tiles, our retirement
home in Chorleywood
(rear view).

CHANGES?

A new incumbent unconsciously initiates a lot of changes just by his own personality, presence, and style. To push other changes too soon in a church when it still has a lot of momentum (as St Andrew's had), would have been to court disaster. I determined 'to hasten slowly' and like Moses respectfully to be sure to carry 'the bones' of John Perry to the promised land with me.

One thing I had inherited, that was not really 'me', was a weekly meeting of selected elders. I think they had been a real support group for John but I could not see how they quite meshed into the infrastructure of St Andrew's by the time I got there. Some of its members were on the staff, some were on the Standing Committee and some were lay-readers or ex-churchwardens. Since I met three times a week with my staff and once a month with the Standing Committee and again with most of the same people at the monthly Parish Church Council meeting, I decided after a couple of years to reorganise things a bit.

Eldership was all the rage when we got back to the UK. There should be a maximum of delegated leadership in any parish but I never did quite see how elders could ever fit into an Anglican system if it implied an equal sharing of responsibility. The rector/vicar is accountable to the local church through the PCC and also to the bishop. Elders must also be accountable to the incumbent otherwise the set-up is a recipe for disaster. Equal sharing may have survived somehow in some parishes but it would not have worked with me in Chorleywood.

Bishop Dick and Nora Lyth stayed on with us for four years leaving to retire very much loved at the end of 1981. Dick's health never really got better during all his seven years at St Andrew's. But he eventually recovered in his retirement. He carried a heavy load on the pastoral side and was very greatly valued for his patience, gentle wisdom[10] and absolute integrity. He also preached excellent sermons which were much appreciated.

A REAL APOSTLE

Dick's father-in-law, Dr Algernon Stanley Smith, had been a missionary pioneer in Uganda and Rwanda and in 1977, at a great age, retired back to the UK. He came to live with the Lyths in

Chorleywood. Stanley Smith had been an army medical officer during the World War One and was stationed in Rwanda whither he returned to work after the war under the Church Missionary Society (Rwanda Mission). When he eventually died during the time of the Lambeth Conference in 1978 there were eleven bishops present at his funeral – mostly from Uganda, Rwanda and Burundi. Unfortunately the addresses went on for so long that I had eventually to interrupt the Chancellor of Makerere University, so that Dick and the coffin could leave for the crematorium!

On my first pastoral call to Dr Stanley Smith, soon after his arrival in the parish, I found him sitting at his table and was – to use his own words – 'writing a letter to the Church of Rwanda'. It sounded as though he felt he had some kind of apostolic role and I found myself recoiling slightly before this dear man, thinking he must have gone slightly batty in his old age. Visions of an apostle writing his epistles to New Testament churches sprang to mind!

Inwardly I was rejecting the idea of a man presuming to write to a national church in this way, even though he had been one of its founders. Then it dawned on me that I was in fact in the presence of a real live apostle, though such a self-effacing one who would never have called himself that. I have been assured since that he was so greatly loved and respected that any letter from Dr Algernon Stanley Smith would have been read with great attention and prayed over throughout the Churches of Rwanda and Uganda. That holy meeting with Dr Stanley Smith left a lasting impression upon me.

COME OVER AND BISHOP US

Demands on time were mounting with increasing pastoral work. Besides we were being honoured by more and more invitations to speak at outside conferences – laughable really since I am such a mediocre speaker. I had two encouraging trips over to Canada – one for Anglican Renewal Ministries, involving visits to several centres, and one for a church in Toronto celebrating its 150 years. In one really delightful place I was asked if I would allow my name to go forward for election as their bishop. The diocese apparently was desperate for change – similar kind suggestions have been repeated to me elsewhere since. I had no clear sense of this really being God's will and I did not feel I had yet discovered how to manage renewal in an English parish church. Until I had sorted that out it seemed I ought to stay where I was. But I was flattered into signing all the necessary papers before leaving though I insisted that I must consult with Mary first before proceeding further.

Mary was not at all keen on the idea. She reminded me of why I had felt called to settle for parish work in the UK. It was not difficult to phone back and withdraw from the election. I would not probably have got the job anyway. The incident provided just another interesting adrenaline buzz that could have deflected me from my life's true calling. How easy to stumble into what John Bunyan called By-Pass Meadow.

THE MAN FROM BP

We were feeling the need for a full time administrator at St Andrew's. There was a rather high-powered businessman in the church named Alan Tweedie. His father had been a much respected minister for many years in the Congregational Church in Luton. Alan and his wife Eleanor,[11] had been very committed to children's work over many years before they joined St Andrew's. Job-wise Alan had experience in many overseas projects for BP, and was currently involved in the installation of an oil terminal in the Shetland Islands. He would be ideal for us! What cheek to even think of him. Could I really approach such a man? But after prayer I did just that and told him: 'Alan! I need your help! Would you ever consider resigning your job, take the pension they offer, and come and be my administrator for nothing?' He did not appear to bat an eyelid at such a preposterous idea, but quite simply asked me what it would involve? 'Well!' I said, 'That's the problem. I need someone very special because I'm not really sure what the job involves! But if you could come and just hang around I will keep pushing all the work I can from my desk onto yours!' I had never met a local church administrator before and so had not got a clue what one would look like or do, but I thought it might be fairly similar to the work that Chris Simons had done so well for me in Chile as our diocesan administrator there.

Amazingly Alan accepted the challenge and served with me till my retirement fifteen years later, and then continued on with my successor for at least two more years. When he wrote out his job description before my successor arrived it was evident that he had been doing the work of three men! In spite of Mary's rightful concern about the length of the book already, I included the job description in *Leadership for New Life*; it filled over forty pages. Some of the items listed were peculiar to St Andrew's but most were common to any church. It would serve as a checklist for any other leader who might have had as little aptitude for administration as I ever did, but who might be planning to take on an administrator for his church. Many people have told me since that they thought it was the best part of the book! So much for my feelings of self worth over the other part, but Alan proved a wonderful choice for St Andrew's and still serves as secretary for their PCC.

Brian and Gill Skinner came from Chile to join St Andrew's staff in 1987.[12] Brian and his eldest son David were computer buffs and encouraged us to use them more. The church soon provided them for our office secretaries and all the pastoral staff were connected up so we had an updated church diary in each staff home and ready access to the full church directory. We could see who was in which home group and who each leader was. We could also quickly discover such details as who was doing the flowers on a certain Sunday.[13]

David also worked with us part-time, helping to maintain and update all our electrical equipment while administering the church sound system etc. Gill took over the Day Centre for the elderly which had been started by Nora Lyth and both developed and oversaw the two children's Sunday Schools for two of the morning services.

ACTIVATING THE LAITY
In the area of spiritual renewal I was beginning to feel frustrated that we still seemed no further forward in equipping the laity for the work of the ministry at St Andrew's – no nearer than we had been out in Chile at the time of my leaving. Martin Luther, the

sixteenth-century reformer, had brought into focus the doctrine of the priesthood of all believers which re-affirmed the biblical teaching that through Christ each believer has direct access to God the Father, but he did not leave the reformed church with a lot of ideas about what this ministry might involve. I was desperately looking for ideas on how to equip the laity and train them in leadership for home groups and the use of the gifts of the Holy Spirit for a more effective ministry at St Andrew's – and encourage them in both mission, social and community concerns. Too many fine charismatic leaders had left their local churches because apparently they could not make their theories work there; I was still searching for a model charismatic church where they were actually working their charismatic theories out in practice.

Chapter 17

SEARCH FOR A MODEL

*Worship is sometimes difficult to define because it's both an
attitude and an act*
(ANDREW HILL)

*Many Churches miss God's blessing because they major on minor things
and minor on the major things of God*
(ANON)

I prefer the way I do it to the way others don't do it
(APOLOGIES TO D.L. MOODY)

Our old friend Eddie Gibbs from Chile days had settled in
Chorleywood with his family while he worked for the Bible
Society in the UK and was studying externally for a doctorate at
Fuller's Seminary in Pasadena, California. I talked to him about
the kind of church we should be seeking to build in Chorleywood
and he told me of a significant church leader in California, named
John Wimber, a former staff member of Fuller, but by then the
senior pastor of a large growing church. Its membership had
increased from some forty to 2,500 in about three years. Although
I personally do not think we should normally set out to build
churches of that dimension in the UK – too much talent gets lost
between the pews, yet, I had to admit that the dynamic of such
growth were too impressive to be ignored.

WATSON'S MINISTRY WOULD NEVER BE THE SAME AGAIN
The late David Watson – a British leader in renewal – happened
to be a visiting lecturer at Fuller at the time, and Eddie had
suggested to him that he meet up with Wimber on his next visit

there. They met and afterwards David told Eddie that his ministry would never be the same again! David Watson was a leader I particularly respected. He was attempting to put renewal into practice in his own church at St Michael le Belfry, in York. Hearing of his comment I immediately invited John Wimber to visit us at St Andrew's since David was also inviting him back to York. Wimber came to the UK soon after (1981) and we were tremendously impacted by what we learned from him. It was a privilege later to contribute a chapter on Wimber for Canon John Gunstone's book *Meeting John Wimber*[1]and to be asked later to edit another on *John Wimber – his Influence and Legacy*[2] in 1998, after he had died.

Since he became the major human influence in my own ministry over the last twenty years, a period that has brought me the deepest sense of fulfilment as a church leader, I digress to repeat something of his fascinating story here. He was a very open, laid back person, who truly loved the whole church and not just the Vineyard Christian Fellowship. He really disliked the term 'denomination'. I never heard him use it except for legal purposes.

THERE WAS A MAN CALLED JOHN

A *Daily Telegraph* obituary[3] described John Wimber as an evangelist. Very true! In the early years after his conversion, following the example of Gunner Payne, his spiritual mentor, God used him to lead many hundreds to Christ. Evangelism was fundamental to all John's ministry but he became much more than an evangelist. He was growing into an apostle, a prophet, a pastor and a teacher beside. And as these gifts were being added he was used increasingly to inspire the wider church. It was reported that Robert Schuller, renowned pastor of the Crystal Cathedral and world-wide tele-evangelist, once referred to John as 'one of the twelve most influential Christian leaders of the last two decades'. Peter Wagner, co-pioneer with John of the School of Church Growth at Fuller, and prodigious producer of books, has written that 'John was one of those extremely rare people who will be remembered as a moulder of an entire generation'. Jim Packer, revered orthodox theologian and extensive writer, described him as 'one of the outstanding leaders of our time'.[4]

Others have been raised up specifically to impact the ministry in the pulpit but John Wimber had a unique way of activating the man in the pew as well. There were not many Christian leaders who could expect to gather between 2,000–5,000 in most of the major cities across the world while at the same time drawing in a record number of leaders from all the different Christian churches. It is because he had such an unusual influence that I give him so much space here. It should also help to explain where I have been coming from latterly. He re-shaped my thinking significantly and my whole approach to 'ministry' – the anointing through the Holy Spirit, equipping the saints in the gifts of the Spirit, evangelism, church growth, leadership training, church planting and above all the Kingdom of God.

WHEREVER DID HE COME FROM?

John was born, an only child, on 25th February 1934, in Peoria, Illinois, from the American mid-west. His father had left home soon after and he was raised in a one-parent family. 'I had barely emerged from my mother's womb when my father abandoned both mom and me', he wrote. 'This, along with the fact that I had no brothers and sisters, explains why I was so withdrawn as a child spending long hours alone . . .'. Years later, towards the end of his life, he met up with two half-brothers for the first time – his father's offspring from a second marriage. His grandfather (mother's father) was a significant influence during his early boyhood. John used to watch him training horses to trot in a particular style by yoking an experienced horse with a younger one. He became so impressed with this technique, that he used the model later to explain his method for training the laity. There was no religious influence in his early life. He described himself as a fourth-generation pagan: 'I didn't even know God had a book out!' he used to say. 'I do not think I had ever met a Christian – if I did he never blew his cover!'

He could recall the familiar scenes of poverty around his early home; streets well on the way to dereliction. His mother remarried after a few years and moved to California; this State, except for a short break in Las Vegas, was to become John's home for the rest of his life. His stepfather was a good man but never filled the void left by his natural father. Feelings of rejection and abandonment were not helped when he finally met up again with his real father after twenty years. Sadly his hopes that a meaningful father/son relationship might still develop were dashed after that longed-for meeting.

One of John's consoling interests as a lonely teenager was his music – he had a fine tenor voice. He could play a wide range of musical instruments that included the piano, strings and wind, his favourite being the saxophone. He also developed a gift for the teaching, writing, directing, orchestrating and the recording of music.

INTO THE WORLD OF JAZZ

Then, while still a teenager, he became involved in the local jazz clubs playing his first professional gig at the Dixie Castle, Orange County, CA, in 1949, when he was only fifteen. In 1953 he won first prize at the Lighthouse International Jazz Festival. He was soon earning a living providing musical back up for Hollywood films. In 1962 he brought a music group together that called itself 'The Righteous Brothers'. There was nothing religious about the naming – the term was simply a frequent response of appreciation from black audiences. This group got to the top of the charts in the US a couple of times.

John had married Carol in 1955, a non-practising Roman Catholic. She was the eldest child of a local medical practitioner with three sisters and a brother. John and Carol lived in Westminster, CA. By the time they had three children – two boys and a girl – their marriage had deteriorated and they separated. It was 1961 when John moved out to Las Vegas, 250 miles away in Nevada, a neon-lit gambling centre. He went there to look into the possibility of a sixty-day no-fault divorce. While there he shared with a friend in the band the despair he felt over his marriage. The friend encouraged him to go out into the desert and watch the sunrise. 'It's great! A really cool way to "groove in" to a religious experience,' he said, 'You should try it!' John had to confess he had never been particularly interested in watching sunrises, let alone a religious experience, but he decided to give it a go.

Motoring out to the desert very early the next morning he found himself weeping uncontrollably. He felt he was being overwhelmed by Someone or Something without the vaguest idea of who or what it was. Choosing a suitable spot he pulled up in his car and got out. Looking up he pleaded from his breaking heart: 'If there is anyone out there, please help me!' He thought he was alone but, sensing he might have been seen, he suddenly felt embarrassed. Irritated with himself he muttered: 'I am talking to the dark. I am going crazy. I'd better commit myself to the hospital.' Then remembering his mother's advice about having clean underclothes in case of an accident he thought he had better get back first and change – besides there were some drugs he would need to hide also!

'COME AND GET ME'

Once back in the hotel, John was stunned to find a message from Carol asking him to phone her. He was even more amazed, after calling up, to hear her say: 'Come and get me, John. I want to try one more time to make our marriage work.' Only hours before John had been crying out to the heavens and now this – there had to be some connection. 'Hot Dog!' he shouted, looking up to heaven once again, 'You got her to change her mind!' Earlier she had been so determined about divorce that he knew only a force bigger than his wife could have made her change her mind. John believed he had discovered Something greater than himself too though he did not have a clue what or who he might be. Unknown to John at the time was the fact that Carol had also been praying for help to the God of her Catholic childhood. Dropping the phone John drove at top speed to collect her, and the children, and take them back to Las Vegas. He told her how he thought he must now be in touch with the supernatural. Carol suggested it was prayer.

OLD FRIENDS: NEW LIFE

In November 1962, one of John's old friends suddenly turned up in Las Vegas looking for him. This was Dick Heying, who had at one time been a stand-in drummer for their band – 'The Righteous Brothers'. Dick, and his wife Lynn, had very recently become Christians. They wanted to share their good news with John and had travelled quite a distance from LA taking a bottle of gin with them in the car as a gift for him. They were surprised, however, by the severe drop in temperature, so to warm up, the Heyings sampled the bottle for themselves. The journey got colder and the gin got lower. By the time they arrived it was very low but their spirits were certainly high – an intoxicated state that was far from what they had intended. In spite of this John realised that something wonderful had happened to them even though they were hardly able to share their good news coherently. He was intrigued and questioned them closely. Dick left feeling ashamed at the way they had arrived to tell their story and could only pray for another opportunity to share it.

'KING JAMES VIRGINS'

Both John and Carol now found they had a thirst for a deeper knowledge of God. Before he left, Dick told them they should get a Bible. Having searched the usual shops in vain they finally discovered where they could buy them in Las Vegas. John wanted to be sure he got a genuine one. A man in a bar told them to ask for 'King James Virgins!' The girl at the Bible shop smiled and sold them King James Versions which they both began reading avidly in spite of some difficulty understanding the quaint language.

Las Vegas was not good for family life and they returned to Orange County where Carol soon became pregnant with their fourth child. In their search for a suitable spiritual environment, and a school for their children, they went to the Catholic church in the area where Carol had been brought up. John started taking instruction in the Catholic faith and Carol went to confession. They renewed their wedding vows with the church's blessing since their first marriage conducted by a Baptist pastor, picked at random from a telephone guide, was not considered valid by the Catholic priest. They felt themselves to be drawing closer to God, though John began having difficulties with his priest. He found out later that the priest was himself going through some problems of his own at the time.

JOHN'S FIRST TASTE OF CHURCH

Dick Heying, now so much nearer the Wimbers in their new home, began dropping by casually to talk to John. Lynn would be frequently on the phone with Carol. The Heyings wanted to talk about their faith and the Wimbers could not hear enough of it. The Heyings begged them to visit their church. John shared his impressions later at a public meeting. He admitted he might have been exaggerating a little but he was making a point. Men he took to be 'bouncers', with flowers in their lapels, showed the Wimbers to the very front seats and one of them handed John a 'menu' with a big smile and a loud greeting. John studied this paper uncomprehendingly. 'What does it say, Dad?' asked one of the boys. 'Hell, I don't know, son,' replied John, never previously having been confronted by such a thing. He was troubled because there were no ashtrays in the pews and wondered what he would do if he wanted to smoke? Then he was disturbed by the musicians and singers; to John's professional ear they were awful.

Next there was the preacher's voice. It seemed strangely 'throttled'. Dick explained later that they all sounded like that – they were trained to speak that way in seminary! Finally there was an 'altar call'. In spite of his unfamiliarity with religious language and ecclesiastical furnishings John knew an altar when he saw one – he'd been to the cinema and seen the heroine on the altar surrounded by leaping flames of fire waiting to be rescued! As the call was being made John was still looking round for the altar when people came forward and knelt at the rails right in front of him. 'Most of my problems,' John explained later, 'were due to the fact that I did not understand Christian-ese.' When the service finally closed John could not wait to get out.

Dick caught up with him. 'Hey! How did you like it, John?'

John: 'That was weird!'

Dick: 'I was about to ask you to come again tonight?'

John: 'How often do you have to do this?'

Dick: 'We come every time they open the doors. We love it. This is our church!'

SPARE TIME EVANGELIST

Dick had introduced John to Lawrence Gunner Payne, a spare

time evangelist who had experienced a great deal of personal tragedy in life and who was currently having weekly meetings for Bible study with a group of about twenty-five people. The Wimbers were keen to find someone who could answer their questions but John was too embarrassed to show his ignorance of the Bible in front of such a large group.

By the April of 1963 John and Carol had started attending a new, but smaller, group. Gunner Payne arranged for this to meet on Tuesdays. Still not sure he wanted to be there, John declined, pleading work. Being a musician who was out playing into the early hours of every morning, he only had one night off a week and that was on a Monday. Half an hour later Gunner called back saying they had changed the night to Monday! John now had no excuse but he was also bowled over by their readiness to switch their diaries around so unselfishly just for him.

Once there, John felt he was not really interested in discussing Jesus. He wanted to know about God. He felt talk about Jesus was getting off track but Carol insisted she wanted to know who Jesus Christ really was? These weekly meetings frequently went on until well past midnight, and continued for three or four months. Week in and week out the Wimbers hammered Gunner with their questions. They were now studying a modern version of the Bible. John was increasingly struck by Gunner, the way he lived embodied the gospel he preached. John was hungry to know his secret.

SHE KNOWS THE ANSWER

After attending the Bible study group for a few weeks, Carol declared she had found the answer. 'Jesus is the Son of God,' she said. 'Yeah! And Chicago is in Illinois. So what?' John replied still uncomprehending. 'But that changes everything, John,' said Carol. 'It means there is something we need to do about it.' But still she could not fathom out what it was.

They kept up with the Bible studies, sometimes driving there hours early just to be in the area – surely God must live there, they felt. They would call in on Gunner at his welding workshop.

'What do we need to do?' they begged him.

'Nothing yet!' he would say. 'It's too soon. You're not ready yet. Premature births don't produce healthy children. Apples fall when they are ripe.'

It was the relevance of the cross and the need for a living relationship with Jesus that finally got to John. 'I remember that evening (in 1963) as though it were last night. I did not arrive having planned to turn to Christ . . . I had learned a lot about Christ and the cross – I could have passed an elementary exam on the atonement. But I didn't understand that I was a sinner. I thought I was a good guy. Oh, I knew I had messed up here and there, but I didn't realise how serious my condition was!'

Carol had said to Gunner that she thought it was time they did something about the things they had been talking through. Then, aghast, John watched her going down on her knees to the floor weeping. She began telling God how sorry she was for all her sins. John followed her onto the floor crying out to God for forgiveness too. At the same time he says he was thinking, 'I hope this works, because I am making a complete fool of myself here.' Years before John remembered going into Los Angeles to borrow some money off a 'druggy' friend. Waiting in the plaza he spied a man parading between a sandwich placard. It bore the words 'A fool for Christ's sake!' on the one side and 'Whose fool are you?' on the other. John had thought it the most stupid thing he had ever seen in his life. It all came back to him now as he realised what it meant 'The cross is foolishness to those who are perishing'.[5] 'That night at the cross I believed in Jesus,' wrote John. 'I have been a fool for Christ ever since.' Something revolutionary had been going on in John. It was the new birth of a sinner and the creation of a future Christian leader.

PEARL OF GREAT PRICE

Sitting at the feet of Gunner Payne, John first heard the parable of the pearl of great price. Gunner was explaining about the need to be willing to sacrifice everything in life for the kingdom of God. 'The kingdom of heaven is like a merchant looking for fine pearls. When he found one of great value, he went away and sold everything he had and bought it'.[6] This suddenly caught John's attention.

'Hold on!' he said, 'Are you saying that in order to become a

Christian somebody might have to give up everything he has?'

'Well, what do you think it means?' Gunner replied.

'I'm not sure,' said John. 'It sounds like it might mean that. But – well, I know a guy who is a musician who does not know how to do anything except play music. I mean this guy can't even tie up his own shoelaces! Are you saying he might have to give up his music career in order to become a Christian? How else could he make a living?'

'Your friend would have to work that out for himself,' said Gunner, who understood perfectly well who they were talking about. 'But in my opinion, he has to be ready to give up his career because it is a possibility.'

'No way!' John was thinking, shaking his head. He was on the threshold of musical success. His group was getting records in the Top Ten of the pop charts.

'This is crazy, I thought. I'm finally a success. And I am about to make a lot of money. No way am I going to give it all up now,' John said later.

During the next few days John felt miserable, cursing and swearing around the house. So far he had liked all that he had learned from the Bible and was inwardly saying 'Yes! Yes! Yes!' all the way, but now this . . . he had run into a real problem. 'To think I might have to give up everything, even my career, to go on with God,' he grumbled. It was hell. But within three weeks he was on the floor crying out to God repenting. 'I knew I had found the pearl of great price. And I was so glad to have it. I just did not care anymore what God might ask of me in return for it.' Over the next few weeks, by the help of God, he began to liquidate his assets and prayed: 'OK, Lord, you can have my career,' and it was as though two giant hands came out of heaven and prized open his fingers to take it. 'Thank you!' said a voice. He decided to get a regular job.

GOODBYE RIGHTEOUS BROTHERS

To the great chagrin of the 'The Righteous Brothers', John told them of his decision to leave the group. He told me later that he would not necessarily suggest that others following Christ should take the same course of action, but it was something he felt God really wanted from him. The course of his life was beginning to move in a completely new direction though for a while he could not see clearly where it was leading. 'Suddenly', he wrote, 'I was in the real world where alarm clocks go off, where people get up and go to work in broad daylight. I had never done this. In a matter of weeks I was working in a factory, clocking in and learning how to relate to normal people.' One day he was assigned to clean some oil drums and was out at the back of the factory. The work was hot, filthy and smelly – the most menial job he had ever been asked to do. John was down inside one of the drums when he heard a car drive up and a voice he recognised calling out: 'Where's John Wimber's office?' Reluctantly John clambered out of his filthy drum smiling at the idea of an office! He felt embarrassed to meet an old friend from the music business in that state. In his friend's hand was a contract John had signed that was worth a lot of money. He wanted John to relinquish his part of it, John explained. But the man just stood staring at the man before him – an absolute mess with grease all over his hands, clothes, face and hair. He gasped almost in horror, 'Whatever are you doing here, John?'

'I looked at him and then back at myself,' said John, 'and I could see how he must have been seeing me. I did not particularly feel at that moment that I had the pearl of great price and I could think of nothing to say.' After a long silence John stated lamely that this was what God wanted. His friend's eyes narrowed, obviously thinking 'I hope your God never gets his hands on me!' John watched him drive off with the signed contract in his hand and realised that sometimes there is no way of explaining how God calls to those who know nothing of the pearl of great price. His friend would never have understood that God could be simply stripping a man like John of a lofty position in the music world in the process of teaching him simple self denial.

John naturally followed the model of Gunner Payne and started evangelising, which he was able to do very effectively, indeed. He and Carol were soon into personal evangelism in a big way. They sensed the 'presence' of God on their ministry. But John said later, 'We did not realise then that the presence and the power were the same thing.'

John was baptised in the Holy Spirit in 1964. His spiritual nurture and then early ministry was to be in the Quaker Church where they interpreted the sacraments spiritually and did not minister baptism or the Lord's Supper in any physical sense. So he was not, in fact, baptised in water until 1978 after he had left the Quakers.

FULL TIME WORK AHEAD

By 1970 John was leading eleven Bible study groups a week. The next year he was taken onto the staff of the Yorba Linda Friends Church where his brother-in-law, Bob Fulton had been appointed a youth pastor. Eager to increase his understanding of Scripture, John also studied at the Azusa Pacific University, a Pentecostal foundation, where he earned a degree in Biblical Studies. During his time with the 'Friends', John saw the church grow from 200 to 800, becoming the largest of their denomination – so much so that they had to build a new facility. But then it seemed it could grow no bigger. John noticed how family power-blocks had their grip on the church. Growth was actually resisted because these families saw that if the church became any bigger their hold on it would significantly diminish. One good lady even accused John of 'ruining her church'. He knew what she meant. John was also becoming frustrated with himself too. He had been in this church for nearly thirteen years and was conforming to a degree where his conscience felt constrained. 'I was institutionalising myself,' he said, 'and was preaching the party line.' It was increasingly on John's heart to explore ways of making church and its message more relevant to his contemporaries. He could never forget his godless friends in the music world.

In 1971 Peter Wagner, a disciple of Donald Mcgavran, and a former missionary in Bolivia, joined the staff of Fuller Seminary to teach on evangelism and church growth. Wagner founded a new School of Church Growth at Fuller in 1974 and John Wimber signed up for a course there. Peter soon recognised John's gift as an evangelist, his talent for clear analysis and his practical comprehension of the principles of church growth, so he invited John to become a founding director with him. That was the beginning of what has since been re-named the Charles E.

Fuller Institute of Evangelism and Church Growth which today is headed up by my old friend Eddie Gibbs.

John also became a church consultant and was soon involved in travelling extensively across the continent and meeting different church leaders from many different denominations. During his three and half years doing this John reckoned that he had met with some 40,000 pastors coming from twenty-seven different denominations and nine para-church organisations. But the physical stress combined with a sense of spiritual barrenness began to weigh heavily on him.

CHURCH CONSULTANT HAS PARADIGM SHIFT

Experience on the teaching staff at Fuller, and amongst the various denominations, had brought John into stimulating and fruitful contact with some deep thinking and widely read Christians. He had been introduced to George Eldon Ladd's writings on the kingdom of God where he began to see that the good news that Jesus preached was the kingdom of God. He was later to write: 'Power for effective evangelism and discipleship relates directly to our understanding and experiencing the kingdom today'. Many who came on the courses at Fuller were very dedicated and experienced missionaries. Their reports on signs and wonders in the Third World, together with Eldon Ladd's teaching, directed John's thoughts towards the Holy Spirit. He discovered Francis McNutt's book *Healing*. 'I carried the book around for months,' he said, 'reading it at a time when I didn't believe in healing. I'd been trained as a cessationist regarding spiritual gifts with the notion that God didn't do that [heal] today.' He became especially interested in the relationship between healing and church growth overseas. And his world-view was changing also. Hitherto he had seen life out of a rational materialistic Western world-view. He realised that he was undergoing a paradigm shift in his approach to the Bible and theology. He was beginning to understand life supra-rationally. It was at this time he began developing a love for the whole church; and in the process he was encountering more and more evangelical anomalies – such as when he met a beer-drinking Lutheran priest who led a barmaid to Christ in a pub! In John's

book Lutheran priests were not supposed to be able to do that –
let alone a beer-drinker in a pub! He came to love Richard
Baxter's maxim: 'In necessary things unity; in doubtful things
liberty; in all things charity.' As Wimber was learning to love the
whole church he would often remind his friends: 'Your brother is
not your enemy. Your brother is your brother – is your brother!'

QUAKER REJECTS

Although John had left the staff of the Quaker Church his family
had still remained members there. Then his wife Carol, her sister
Penny with her husband Bob Fulton, and nearly forty others, all
became baptised in the Holy Spirit. According to John, Carol had
been particularly hostile to any thing supernatural; especially
concerning divine healing, possibly due to being the child of a
medical doctor. She described the result of her new Holy Spirit
experience as a 'personality meltdown' and soon after she had a
dream from which she awoke speaking in tongues! She went
through some weeks of deep repentance with a lot of weeping,
believing she had grieved the Lord by her previous attitude –
prejudice and resistance to the Holy Spirit. Others were going
through similar experiences. Ironically the Quaker Church, that
traced its roots back to a mighty move of the Holy Spirit at the
time of George Fox (1624–91), was increasingly uneasy about
these things and finally asked them if they would leave. This they
did regretfully and began meeting in a private home to worship
God. Carol, who had always said she would not want John ever
to lead a church again, became convinced that God actually now
wanted John to do so. So she casually let him know that if he ever
felt God calling him back into pastoring she would support him
but John brushed off the idea emphatically! His excuse was that
'churches were much too hard on their pastors'. But clearly God
had other plans.

One winter's night in 1977, when John was flying into Detroit
he was desperately crying out to God, feeling spiritually bankrupt
and physically sick – the latter was an early symptom of the heart
troubles that were to haunt him for the rest of his life. He had
missed the first plane and was flying late and arrived to find it was
snowing hard and there was no one there to meet him. So he

booked into the Metropolitan hotel at the airport. Ill and exhausted, he knelt at his bedside to read his Bible 'for himself'. 'Don't get me wrong,' he said, 'I was reading the Bible all the time preparing one talk after another but I realised it was a long time since I had actually read it "for myself".' He turned to Psalm 61 (a psalm which was to become a favourite and was read at his graveside years later): it ran 'Hear my cry, O God; listen to my prayer. From the ends of the earth I call to you, I call as my heart grows faint; lead me to the rock that is higher than I.' The psalm reflected his desperate condition exactly. Still crying out to God he fell asleep. He awoke later and crawled into bed. During the night he sensed that God was speaking into his heart and he heard the Lord say: 'John, I've seen your ministry. Now I want to show you mine.' He began to weep. 'Lord, that's exactly what I want,' he said. He did not understand how much this would affect his future work, but the experience proved to be a definitive moment in his on-going relationship with God.

GOD WAS 'ON HIS CASE'

John was speaking on the subject of spiritual gifts at a church conference near home soon after and the pastor told him there was a female in the church who had a prophecy for him. John had already noticed the rather plump little lady being referred to, and felt the last thing he wanted was a prophecy from her. But the pastor insisted that she really did hear from God, and he should speak to her, so he reluctantly agreed to meet her. She arrived at the appointed time and commenced weeping. She went on and on and on. After about a half hour of this, and feeling very perplexed and even slightly annoyed John eventually stopped her and said: 'When are you going to give me the prophecy? I thought you had a word from the Lord for me!'

'That's it,' she said, 'God is weeping over you!' And saying that, she was gone.

Later she came to him again with another word: 'God wants to know when you are going to use your authority?'

'What does that mean?' said John.

'I don't know what it means,' she said, 'I just get the messages!'

Wimber felt that for some good reason God was certainly 'on

his case' especially when following this he sensed God speaking to him in nineteen different ways about his future ministry. Peter Wagner casually suggested to him one day that he ought to think about starting a church that modelled what he was now teaching – the connection between evangelism and signs and wonders. As if that was not enough a Lutheran pastor in a church growth seminary in New York came up to him soon after saying he was very embarrassed but he felt that a message God had given him was for John. He had written it down on a folded piece of paper that he gave to John. It read simply: 'Go home!' John was finally getting the message.

JOHN'S NEW FLOCK

This was enough to prepare him to take over the little flock of ejected Quakers – his wife among them. To begin with he could not understand why they spent so much time just singing tender worship songs. Then he began to discern the new thing that God was doing and entered into it with all his heart. He even wrote some songs himself and joined the music group playing his synthesiser, a practice he was to continue for the rest of his life. The group soon developed its own particular values and ethos. Needing the freedom to do just that it became an independent congregation now calling itself the Vineyard Christian Fellowship (VCF).

As the VCF grew numerically the search was kept up for new premises to rent. They settled for a time at the Canyon High School in the Anaheim Hills for their Sunday worship. In spite of an early commitment to plant churches out into other areas, (over eighty were planted out from this original fellowship in the first twenty years), the school premises eventually became too small and they moved again to larger rented accommodation until they finally acquired their own property. The vast complex at La Palma, Anaheim Hills, which became their new home, had been built originally for a company dealing in the production of high-tech aero-equipment. After several internal re-developments, including a worship centre with seating for over 3,000, there were still numerous large halls on site for lecture rooms and classrooms and plenty of office space, storerooms. Besides a large Christian bookshop, there was room also for a separate business department for producing Vineyard Ministries International music tapes and CDs. A number of new musicians and composers were encouraged through the opportunities John gave them from this platform. The interiors of the building were well equipped but decorated very simply; nothing ornate except for a few appropriate banners – a hangover from Wimber's early Quaker disciplining. The only exception was a most beautiful gift to the church by its craftsman – a remarkable life-size sculpture in bronze of Christ washing the disciples' feet. This was placed near the main entrance for all to see on their way to the main sanctuary for worship.

Another huge facility alongside the main building served as a warehouse for storing foodstuffs. They were latterly distributing thousands of dollars' worth of food to the poor on a regular basis, amounting to a million meals a year for the destitute. There was still plenty of floor space in this adjacent building for a Christian school.

From the beginning John sought to be faithful to his commitment to try and discern and to do whatever he sensed God was doing, rather than making his own plans and asking God to bless them.

LIBERATED PREACHER

John had read widely and always listened carefully. He was proud of his large library packed with Bible commentaries and knew where every book should be, systematically numbered and categorised. He had a clear mind for easy analysis and a very retentive memory for facts. This made him a fascinating speaker or conversationalist and, wherever he was, people within earshot would fall silent to listen, giving him their rapt attention. His pulpit (actually a platform) practice was to expound passages of the Scripture with plenty of illustration (often personal). He majored on the central meaning of the Word, constantly stressing the old adage that 'the main thing was the plain thing and the plain thing was the main thing'. John could relate a story brilliantly and could make it very humorous so that his hearers were frequently crying with laughter – a very cathartic experience. As we read in Proverbs 17:22, the King James Version: 'A merry heart doeth good like a medicine'. Once John sensed he had expounded for long enough he would simply break off at that point, to pick up from there the next time. Each talk was recorded.

Over the last twenty years with the Anaheim VCF John worked through thirty-seven books of the Bible, verse by verse. Besides this he preached through many major series on such subjects as the kingdom of God, the cross, worship, prayer, discipleship, holiness, the fruit of the Spirit, deliverance, equipping the saints, the gifts of the Spirit (especially prophecy and healing) giving, leadership, church-planting, temptation, trials and suffering, and the call for mercy ministries to the poor. It was all very orthodox and practical and his balanced laid-back approach was an immediate attraction to numerous Anglican clergy who began to visit him at Anaheim, LA.

'CORPORATE RENEWAL'

In 1980 the Anaheim Vineyard had had a corporate experience of the Holy Spirit. On the evening of Mother's Day, Lonnie Frisbee, one of God's irregulars and an early convert of the 1960s Jesus People, gave a testimony that he followed with an invitation for young people to come forward. He then simply called the Holy Spirit down upon them in the name of Jesus. Some 400 of them fell about crying, groaning and speaking in tongues. Neither John nor the others present had ever experienced anything like it before. Though John sensed it was good, it was so unusual he was concerned lest they could be being deceived in any way; as their pastor he needed to protect his flock. Staying up all night reading through the history of revivals and praying, John finally cried out, 'Lord, if this is you, please tell me?' Within moments the phone rang at John's side. A friend from Denver, Colorado, was on the line. 'John,' he said, 'I'm sorry I am calling so early but I have something very strange to pass on to you. I don't know what it means, but God wants me to tell you, "It's Me, John!"' That was far more a word of encouragement than the caller could ever appreciate. It was precisely what John needed to know. He would never be alarmed by outward manifestations again. 'I'm not saying that that is necessarily God making them do that but I think it's their response to God!' he would observe, if things got lively. Of course there were odd occasions when he thought it was not God and had people who were manifesting too strangely moved off to a quiet room for counsel and prayer.

NEW DIMENSION

Leading up to this 'Pentecost' John had been disappointed about the very limited number of physical healings they were experiencing in the fellowship. A Bible verse impressed John where Jesus had said: 'I tell you the truth, anyone who has faith in me will do what I have been doing.'[7] His new understanding of this verse was another life changing moment. He began to preach sermons on healing. When after some ten months someone was actually healed John could hardly believe it. A member of the VCF had asked John to visit his home and pray for his wife. John went with a sinking heart to find the woman in bed with a heavy fever. Very diffidently he laid his hands on her head and then turned to the husband to explain why people were not often healed. As he talked he realised the husband was not listening but looking past John's shoulder and grinning. Turning round John was astonished to see the woman already up out of bed and looking perfectly healthy.

'What's happened?' asked John.

'I'm well!' she said. 'Would you like to stay for some coffee?' John politely declined and left excitedly.

'I could not believe it,' he said later. 'She was well!' He needed time to think about this alone. Once away in the car he at last allowed himself to get excited. 'We got one!' he yelled at the top of his voice.

This was the beginning of a whole new dimension in John's ministry. On the way home John saw a vision of a huge honeycomb – it was high up in the sky and dripping with honey. All sorts of people were gathered round it, some simply catching it and eating it. Some were taking it away to share with their families and friends. Others were watching on fascinated and yet others standing by scoffing. He felt God was saying to him: 'John, that's my mercy. For some it's a blessing and for others it's not, but there is plenty for everyone. The problem is not with the supply – the problem is with the people.' John became convinced that while not everyone would be healed in this age yet some healings could be expected as signs of the coming kingdom of God.

By the time of his death it was estimated that a million sets of John's teaching tapes on healing and the kingdom of God had been distributed, with probably double that number duplicated and shared around the world. I sent one set to a friend in Chile. He listened to them with another Chilean friend who went off and planted a Vineyard Fellowship, the first of five he planted in Chile. I ought to add here that while John was used by God to refocus the church on its mission to heal he also had a very biblical theology on the place of suffering and the cross.

FAMOUS COURSE

Peter Wagner invited John, to teach a special course at Fuller in the January of 1982, believing that the School of World Mission was in danger of over-concentrating on the behavioural sciences and the technology of church growth. Peter felt that they were in danger of over-looking the sovereign work of the Holy Spirit in the ministry of world missions. The course was called MC510,[8] and it was the first course of this nature to be offered in a major accredited seminary anywhere in the world. They never imagined that the course, which was repeated each year for four years (1982–85), would attract as many theology students as mission students. John lectured on such subjects as the kingdom of God, the biblical records of the miraculous, different world-views, spiritual gifts, contemporary faith-healers and the relationship between modern evangelism today and evangelism in the power of the Holy Spirit with signs and wonders following. Then John would invoke the Holy Spirit on the class and minister as he sensed God leading him. There were some quite amazing signs and wonders following these 'clinics'. Robert Walker, of *Christian Life* magazine, had flown out from Wheaton, Illinois, to attend the first course and write a report on it. Walker was so impressed that, in the event, he dedicated the entire issue to the course.

THE SOLD OUT ISSUE

This sold out faster than any previous edition and orders for reprints were numerous. It quickly became known as 'the sold out issue'. This seminary experiment soon became a centre of public debate across the Christian world. Robert Meyer, Dean of Fuller Seminary School of Theology, was reported as saying to a joint faculty meeting: 'I know of only two seminary courses that have become famous. One was the course on dogmatics taught at Basle by Karl Barth and the other is the MC510 taught by John Wimber at Fuller here.' John was a risk-taker (he would often tell us faith was spelt R I S K). He took huge risks of faith, publicly (not least by making himself personally so vulnerable). This often made him a hostage to fortune but the positive effects were widely recognised. Of course no Christian teacher is ever beyond criticism, and John was soon being sniped at and misquoted maliciously by a certain brand of Christian who no doubt felt they were doing God a service by that kind of behaviour. He was often urged to fight back but he dismissed the temptation, saying: 'I don't think the Lord would have responded that way – it's not our thing'. But apart from criticisms true or false, after MC510 some gifted theologians began to take John seriously.

Wimber was soon being invited to teach on signs and wonders in most continents around the world. He made a return visit to London in 1984 and another visit in 1985 going to London, Sheffield and Brighton and after that a stop-by in Britain probably every year for the rest of his life. He taught and modelled overseas just what he had ministered back at home – a ministry that increased in momentum as year succeeded year. In 1993 John was diagnosed as having cancer and underwent a difficult period of treatment before getting back into his travelling ministry as quickly as possible. His son Chris, who had previously had treatment for skin cancer, came over to England pushing his father in his wheelchair. He seemed to be gradually regaining his fitness and energy once more when he suffered a stroke. He eventually underwent heart by-pass surgery.

ONLY ONE HERO
While recovering from an operation after a fall in his house, John, at the age of sixty-three, died from a massive haemorrhage on 17th November 1997. He was sixty-three. Looking older than his years by this time, he often said that it was not the age of the car that

counted but its mileage! John had faithfully run the race and finally finished his course. Some time before he died he talked publicly of the trauma of living with uncertainty during his bout with inoperable cancer two years previously. 'When all is said and done, dying is the last, worst thing that any of us will face. As Christians, however, we need to recognise that it's also the best thing. Going to heaven is what we signed up for. That's not so bad, is it?' Looking back on his times of illness and difficulties he said: 'I don't know about you, but I haven't done so well with "prosperity" in life, in times when everything's good. But believe me, everything gets focused when I'm in trouble. Do you know that prayer: "Oh God, oh God, oh God . . .?"' His simple, honest, self-effacing ministry had been quite unique in our generation. He had so often described himself (on the platform) as just a fat man trying to get to heaven, but he was, of course, a very talented musician, an apostle, a prophet, an evangelist, a pastor and a teacher who married Pentecostal experience to biblical evangelical teaching.

John was also the eventual founder of a new denomination who led us into new forms of worship; he was a deeply spiritual thinker, a joint author of many books, a model healer, a trainer of leaders and laity alike. He was a most generous friend to many. Who can ever remember being allowed to pay when John was at the restaurant table? He was a wise counsellor of leaders, a relaxed inspirer of youth, a pioneer church planter, a gifted administrator and businessman, a preacher of righteousness. He shared his insights readily for the blessing of the whole church; his focus was ever 'the Blood and the Book' as he often used to remind himself: it had to be the Cross and the Bible. His guide was the Holy Spirit. He listened to God. John would never be anyone's hero. 'There is only one hero,' he said, 'Jesus Christ!'

He left behind his wife Carol, three sons and a daughter and many grandchildren. His eldest son Chris, whose cancer re-appeared, followed his father soon after.

Such is the background for the chapters that follow.

WATSON'S TRIBUTE
In his book *Fear No Evil*,[9] David Watson described John Wimber

as a large, loveable, warm and gentle person, reminding one of a teddybear. He also had an able mind, wide Christian experience, and shrewd spiritual discernment. 'Every now and then in my travels I meet someone whom I feel I can really trust – someone who loves me and accepts me as I am, who is not trying to use or manipulate me, and who is full of godly wisdom. There are not many like this but John Wimber is one.'

This was the man who was to visit us at St Andrew's in 1981 and change the course of so many lives – including mine.

Chapter 18

A PENTECOST TO REMEMBER!

The kingdom of God does not consist in talk but in power
(1 CORINTHIANS 4:20, RSV)

You shall receive power when the Holy Spirit has come upon you
(ACTS 1:8, RSV)

*My speech and my message were not in plausible words of wisdom, but in
demonstration of the Spirit and of power, that
your faith might not rest in the wisdom of men but
in the power of God*
(1 CORINTHIANS 2:4–5, RSV)

THESE STRANGE AMERICANS

I had looked forward to John Wimber's first visit. This man could
well have something significant to offer us. Besides, I told myself,
he'd been a church consultant for Fuller for several years. Never
having met one of those before I felt he was just the kind of person
I needed to talk to – especially one who was a practitioner in
equipping the laity for the work of the ministry with something to
show for it, according to Eddie Gibbs who had met him. And what
was more I had been positively biased towards what came out of
Fuller from my earliest adrenalin rush with the *Revival Hour*
broadcasts that we had listened to more than thirty years before in
Bristol.

Ever since my return to the UK I had been searching for a
model charismatic church. We had a good biblical basis for
renewal, and good teaching about the gifts of the Holy Spirit, but
there was no one in the Anglican Church, that I knew of, who was
actually working it out in his home church base except perhaps for

David Watson in York – but even he had not taken his church as far as John Wimber had done.

GOD WANTS HIS CHURCH BACK

The first talk John gave was entitled 'God wants his church back'. Rather silly I thought! If it isn't God's church whose is it? But then he showed us how different power groups seek to control the church – making it hard to do what God is really wanting us to do. He stressed how vital it was to try to discern what God was doing, and to bless that. He explained how it was really a waste investing time, money and energy in anything else – 'Except the Lord build the house, they labour in vain that build it',[1] and 'Every plant which my heavenly Father has not planted will be rooted up'.[2] He taught us practically how to equip the saints for the work of the ministry.[3]

He also reminded us of God's concern for the sick, the poor, the outcasts, the aliens, the prisoners and the oppressed, and showed us that through simple sacrificial acts of serving and caring anyone could make the kingdom of God good news to others.

A PENTECOSTAL PENTECOST

John Wimber had arrived on the weekend of Pentecost, 1981. I liked the man from the moment I picked him up from our local railway station – large, unassuming with a disarmingly cheerful smile and an easy way of communicating. He said his team would be coming along in the evening. I felt a little confused by what I thought I had heard him say but simply nodded without comment. Perhaps he'd bought a couple of others with him for company!

We had our first meetings on the Friday morning, to which I had invited any clergy from the deanery who might be interested. To my delight a lot of people came – including a number of young folk. John spoke about the kingdom of God. He emphasised that it really was 'good news'. He wanted us to demonstrate it was so, not just by preaching it, but by showing that healing the sick and caring for the poor brought foretastes of the kingdom – a kingdom that would finally come in fullness and glory at Christ's promised visible return. John also cited some statistics about the state of the church today and our need to use all the resources and tools that God had given to his church to do the job. He had an evangelical theology, greatly influenced by the writings of men like Jim Packer, John Stott and Michael Green. This he combined with a Pentecostal experience, influenced by yet more British writers like Michael Harper, David Watson and Tom Smail, and some Catholic charismatics in the USA. As evangelical charismatic Anglicans we shared a lot of common ground with him.

Of course this list by no means constituted the full extent of the theological influence in his life – he was still on the staff of Fuller part-time and was in frequent discussion with theologians there who kept him in touch with biblical thinking on the widest front.

LOW-KEY

His delivery was very low-key.[4] There was a surprising absence of hype. He seemed to have no controlling techniques, manipulation or threats, and whilst stressing the kingdom and God and his righteousness, there was no condemnation. John quite evidently did love the whole church. In all the years I knew him, I never heard him criticise any denomination or leader, though he often playfully mocked some of our practices and never failed to explain what he felt was a truly biblical perspective on orthodox Christian doctrine.

That evening a large team he had brought over from California to model lay ministry for us, rolled up in a spanking new coach from the hotel rooms they had taken in London. Before going into the worship centre of our church they gathered in the lounge – the males all in their new sports jackets with elbows suitably leather patched, supposedly to accommodate to our culture.[5] John wanted to meet with them and give them a last minute briefing – I could not imagine what for. He reminded them casually of a few of their values and practices, and then said: 'I think that in deference to our British hosts you might moderate your ministry a little tonight.' Suddenly he checked himself: 'Wait a minute. I'm sorry. Let me just backtrack there. That was not the Lord; that was me. I was wrong. You must do whatever you sense the Lord telling you to do.' I was both worried (what were they going to do?) and also pleasantly surprised by this. I had never heard a speaker backtrack so humbly and so publicly before – let alone in front of unknown outsiders. He was obviously not out to impress.

HOLY CHAOS

It is difficult to describe that first evening meeting. One had to be there to experience it. Carl Tuttle led us in some worship using simple songs we had never heard before. John seemed to have taken a back seat. One of John's team was addressing us now. The atmosphere was extraordinary. Finally Lonnie Frisbee got up at John's invitation. Lonnie simply asked everyone to stand – and quietly invited the Holy Spirit to come. And Frisbee was obviously expecting something to happen! His invocation sounded both familiar and odd, since we knew we already had the Holy Spirit. We could not truly believe in and confess Jesus Christ without him. But often the Spirit burns low in us through our grieving, quenching and resisting him. As D.L. Moody once put it quite plainly but quaintly: 'I have the Holy Spirit but the problem is I leak!' And often the Holy Spirit wants to anoint, release gifts in us and bring healing. According to the Bible, God 'gives the Spirit without limit'.[6] so there is obviously always more of his Spirit available for us. And the Holy Spirit who came to the church in a most remarkable way at the first Pentecost came again in a most remarkable way that night! Unless one is in the middle of such an outpouring it might seem almost scandalous to describe it by its outward manifestations. Each outpouring may be a little different but the long-term impact for any church or individual is full of surprises, blessings, new vision, new initiatives, fresh energy, motivation, and resources. This visitation turned out to be a church-changing event for us.

HAVE YOU ANY OIL?

Not only were people being touched in many extraordinary ways by the Holy Spirit both regarding personal blessing but also for their future ministries. One of Wimber's leaders, Blaine Cook, called up a number of people (about twenty) to the front of the church that first evening. There was a commonality about those coming to the front – they all had burning hot hands that were tingling or hands that felt very heavy. Blaine suddenly called out:

'Pastor! Have you any oil? I want to anoint these hands for healing.' I was rather slow at first to grasp that he must be addressing me as we are not often addressed as 'pastor' in the Church of England. Not having enough oil on the premises I hurried over to the vicarage. I knew I had a large bottle of olive oil that I had brought back with me from the Holy Land in 1953. This had travelled with us to South America and back; there never having seemed quite the appropriate occasion to open it during our seventeen years out there. 'For such a time as this!' I thought. I found the bottle and took out a pretty cut-glass dish as most suitable for conveying it back to the church. But once the bottle was open I was overcome by a most awful stench. It had gone bad! This was never going to bless anybody. Time was passing!

MARY'S COOKING OIL

I glanced desperately around the kitchen when my eye rested upon Mary's cooking oil sitting bottled in its golden glory by the kitchen cooker. 'Just the thing!' I poured some into the dish – about two thirds full. 'Wait a minute! We are Anglicans!' I thought. A little Anglican 'decency and order' would certainly not be out of place in the circumstances! I selected a nice starched serviette from the dresser drawer and unfolding it, like a wine waiter in the Savoy, I draped it over my left forearm! Then I traipsed back across the car park, and presented the cut-glass dish with the cooking oil to Blaine with a little bow, hoping he would be suitably impressed by our reverential little Anglican rituals! Sadly it all seemed lost on him. He hastily grabbed the long-awaited dish in a very un-churchy way, and moved quickly down the line where each still stood patiently – palms opened and upward. What I saw next was rather startling. He scooped up the oil by the handful and sloshed it onto their hands, declaring loudly: 'Anointed for healing! Anointed for healing in the name of the Lord!' to each in turn. Oil was pouring off his hands, and theirs, dripping onto the carpeted floor. 'Oh dear!' I worried, 'Whatever will the cleaners be saying on Monday about all those nasty splash marks on our new carpet?' But passing from shocked reaction to serious reflection I concluded that perhaps this was much nearer to biblical practice than ours. Pictures of Aaron (in

Psalm 133) flooded my mind. On that occasion the oil had poured down his beard and no doubt soaked into the collar of his robes, and on down to the ground. Rather different to the gingerly way we usually anointed with oil, I reflected! Blaine was soon finished and handed the almost empty dish back to me. 'Twenty people from one church all anointed for healing!' I puzzled, 'Whatever shall I do with them all? We'll never get enough sick people to go round for all this lot!' How wrong I would be proved to be!

WHEREVER WAS WIMBER?

I looked around for John Wimber. 'He has left!' someone said.

'Left! Where has he gone?'

'He said he was going over to the vicarage!' came the answer.

Something's wrong – he must be feeling unwell! 'I'd better go across and see.' If ever I thought I needed him I needed him then!

I slipped back hurriedly to our house only to find John in the lounge – feet up, munching a peanut butter sandwich – and watching TV!

'However could he do that on a momentous night like this? He just sneaks out and leaves me to it!' I thought.

John looked up, smiling. Before I could speak he addressed me. 'Having fun over there?' he drawled casually.

'Fun!' I thought inwardly, then aloud: 'Oh yes! We are having plenty of fun if that's what you call it!' Then calming my pastoral anxieties, I asked him, 'And how are you, John – are you all right?'

'Oh I'm fine,' he smiled, 'But I've done all I can do and I just leave the others to finish off these meetings.'

'You do?' I gasped, and dashed off back again to the church to see how 'the others' were doing it and thinking that this was the most extraordinary church leader I had ever met.

'These laid back Californians certainly have a very different approach!' I mused.

There was a real buzz in the parish next morning, and not all of it was favourable by any means. I doubt if I would have felt well disposed either, had I not actually been present at the meeting myself, and sensed in my own heart that this had to be God! Of course reports, both good and bad, get distorted and exaggerated in their repeating – people recount the truth, the whole truth and a little bit more than the truth!

YEARS OF SUPPRESSED PAIN

Sometimes when God is dealing with people, years of suppressed pain and grief come to the surface as they open to God to be touched by the Holy Spirit. Folk may cry out loudly as they begin to feel the hurts they have been suppressing all their life. They may move quite violently trying to diffuse it. They may not immediately appreciate the processes and effects of emotional healing. One man told me he had never before experienced any feeling between his neck and his knees. But now he felt a whole man at last – certainly he believed it had been a beneficial experience for him. Because of examples like this, I grew weary of those who automatically assumed that any unusual manifestation had to be demonic and wanted to launch into a ministry of deliverance. Every now and again deliverance may be called for but church people are often far too fast and superficial in assessing what God is really doing during such times. We know of many people who have gone off to conferences and returned claiming excitedly that they had had so many demons cast out and now felt so much better but six months later they were back to their original state where they had started. People would not make such a superficial diagnosis had they known the person in question over a longer period of time. Learning in the local pastoral context is so much more profitable than learning to minister from what one has simply picked up in a book or heard passed on by word of mouth.

BUT IT COULD BE THE REAL PROBLEM

Demonisation should never be assumed but neither should the possibility ever be ignored.

I happen to believe that some people's problems are a direct result of demonisation – and they need deliverance. In fact I was a recognised exorcist in the diocese of St Albans and witnessed some remarkable deliverances. But I also discovered that many people, even Christians, were only too ready to blame the devil for their bad behaviour. Deliverance does not help those who are simply hoping to evade responsibility for their own behaviour.

The only way to deal with the flesh – which we all have to do constantly – is to exercise self-control and to mortify it. That way we grow in grace. If there is no clear evidence of a demon no amount of casting out will solve the problems of the flesh.

One case we dealt with where there seemed to be clear evidence was that of a parson's son who, out of extreme anger with his father in his teenage years, sat on a gravestone in the churchyard next door to the rectory, and in a highly rebellious spirit, deliberately invoked the spirit of the deceased person whose remains lay interred beneath his feet. Judging by his story and his extraordinary blasphemous behaviour pattern there was good reason for believing that he could have been demonised – as indeed he turned out to be. But by the grace of God he appeared to be totally delivered in the name of Jesus Christ. The first case in which I ever had any involvement was in Chile. This ended up with the delivered man making a bonfire of his magic books by a lakeside, and professing Christ in baptism by immersion. As an infant his parents had dedicated him to the spirit of some heavenly body. Unlike the parson's son he was an innocent victim of its torments. There seemed enough obvious evidence to deduce, after prayer, that this man needed exorcism also.

There are clearly some conditions where it is very unwise to proceed with deliverance without professional advice from a responsible medic. For example cases of paranoia or schizophrenia. If and when it was ever right to take matters further in such cases then there would need to be some very clear indications, and such ministry needs to be effected under proper authority and preferably with a medical doctor present. The media get very excited when they hear about exorcisms and deliverances. But TV coverage in these situations may not be objective and could be sensationalised. Though frequently bombarded with requests, we rarely allowed TV people to come into the church with their cameras but we did sometimes allow them to interview folk after the services or meetings were over.

EARLY MORNING PRAYER

Following John's visit I announced that we would have an early morning prayer meeting each day at 6 am for a week, to ask God what this 'visitation' had been all about, and how it was meant to be followed up? Especially what we were to do with twenty people anointed for healing. At the end of the week we gathered for a feedback session to determine how to proceed. As a result we decided that in future, every time we preached the kingdom, we could rely on the Holy Spirit to back up the message with signs and wonders. From the next day on we would invite people forward for prayer ministry at the communion rails after the service, and the team could continue with ministry to them following the formal blessing of dismissal. And this we continued to do morning and evening for the rest of my time at St Andrew's – and I believe this continues to this day. People started to come forward for prayer from the very beginning. Members of our team were always there to pray for them. But it was soon clear that we needed to increase their numbers in order to have sufficient for two major services each Sunday (later three) – not to mention the teams going out with Barry Kissell and his different leaders as well.

Latterly we found we really wanted about 250 people on the lists to keep this ministry going and, because Chorleywood sees a lot of movement of personnel, we were constantly training new members to replace those who were moving off to other parts of the UK or overseas. We also kept some space for training teams from other churches as well – the more the merrier!

HE LEFT HIS MINISTRY WITH US

Some one commented after Wimber's visit: 'We have had many visiting preachers who have blessed us and when they have gone they have taken their ministry with them but John Wimber came and left his ministry with us.' John was surprised at the positive impact of his visit. We were delighted to see (and experience) such a powerful lay ministry being modelled for us. This was very significant. In the UK, the charismatic movement, which had affected many Christians profoundly since the 1960s, was turning into a preaching bandwagon. In our individual spirituality, we had benefited greatly from their teaching. Many had been filled with the Holy Spirit and received gifts but now there was a great longing to see how it could be worked out in the life of the local church.

Dr John Webb, my friend from St Ebbe's days, changed the course of his previous career at Harwell to fulfil a vision for training future leaders in modern methods of communication. He was given a position at the London Bible College and moved to Chorleywood. His students were given experience in the use of all kinds of modern media equipment (making videos etc) to enhance the spread of biblical truth for modern times. We had an excellent arrangement whereby we bought some of his expensive equipment for the college, and he paid us back with his time and skills, initially helping us to make some teaching tapes on healing which both Mary and I had prepared. We financed these to start with through a Trust we had set up called Kingdom Power Trust – the tapes sold well and the profits were ploughed back into the Trust.

One video we made became an official documentary that was later used by the BBC without my permission, and seriously distorted in their editing of it. This documentary was in fact requested by a University in Finland and we gladly let them use it since they wanted it for serious research – something which certainly needs to be undertaken objectively. Similar phenomenology occurs so often at revival times when churches are being blessed. The church needs to examine these things and not simply brush them under the carpet, as though they have nothing to do with God. How would today's church have coped with the first Pentecost where the first Christians were accused of being drunk and disorderly! It seems tragic that God is continuously sending new life to his church and the church can't receive it because such strange manifestations which are often the starting point are considered the stumbling block! If they are stumbling blocks they are much greater stumbling blocks to traditional worshippers than they are to outsiders who are usually much less surprised to find God working supernaturally!

EDITING REVIVAL ACCOUNTS

Too often church historians have tidied up accounts of revivals in the name of 'editing'. As a result the average reader knows nothing about the strange behaviour that has often accompanied revivals, though it need not always be exactly the same each time.

For instance sometimes there has been no reported release of tongues etc. But genuine researchers can easily discover the true records of revival phenomena that have usually been reported – even if exaggerated – in the local church press and the current newspaper accounts at the time. There are other clues from the past, as in Isaac Watts' hymn 'The prisoner leaps to loose his chains'[7] which gives a hint incidentally of something physical happening through an encounter of this nature with God, as they found themselves being set free.

One leader, who had prayed fervently for the East African revival in the 1930s, was away when it broke out. At first he refused to recognise that it actually was God at work when he saw what was happening on his return. Like most of us he had his own preconceived ideas of how a revival should look when he met one!

PENTECOST SUNDAY

John Wimber preached at our Communion Service on the Sunday, the final morning of his first visit. It was the day of Pentecost. I wondered later if he had been aware of that before the service. Probably for them every Sunday was Pentecost Sunday, I thought. Perhaps he imagined the set Bible readings for that morning had been especially chosen for his visit! Being a good Anglican I allowed him twenty minutes to preach on the subject of Pentecost. John seemed a little subdued and nervous. I think he found both our liturgy, our time limits and our pulpit rather too constricting – he liked to take plenty of time and take up space to wander across a wide platform. Carol, his wife, said years later that she had never heard him preach so badly as he did that morning. He included references to Montanus and 'glossolalia'. Even if he had been speaking with a familiar accent our people had never heard of that second century Phrygian prophet. Nor would they have known that 'glossolalia' was simply speaking in tongues. After the service we invited folk to come forward for prayer and John Wimber's team came up to pray for them.

One elderly lady, a visitor from Wales, who was staying nearby with her daughter, came and knelt at the rails asking prayer for a problem. A couple of the team were still praying for her when she suddenly said that the sight in her right eye had come back! They were totally amazed since they thought she had said she wanted prayer for arthritis in her right side! What a wonderful thing! A miraculous restoration of sight happening in an Anglican church! I would have thought any Christian of whatever tradition would want to glorify God for that! Another lady who had had to give up her job as she had become paralysed in both hands through arthritis was also marvellously healed that day – and was able to start work again as a secretary and go back to teaching in her local church Sunday school. She used to write to Mary regularly after that to tell us how blessed she had been. It all contributed to a very exciting weekend! Even John Wimber seemed surprised.

We knew of no model churches where people could actually go to see the laity ministering in the gifts of the Holy Spirit. John was more than an answer to my prayer. We observed and experienced the potential for lay-ministry in the power of the Holy Spirit that weekend.

He was back in England soon after when he paid us another brief visit before going off to South Africa in 1982. Again there were powerful responses. He also flew over once again especially to pray for David Watson, by then diagnosed with cancer. Physical healing was not granted and John was heart-broken when David died. But he kept returning, simply teaching what he believed the Lord had been showing them in their local Anaheim fellowship, and usually bringing a team with him to model the ministry he was leaving behind wherever he went. John Wimber related some of his impressions of that visit (and some of mine too!) in his book *Power Evangelism*, published in 1986.

CALIFORNIAN HOSPITALITY

I have already described how, after John had invited us, we decided to go out to visit them. They welcomed us to their home to enjoy their hospitality – the first of many visits made over the next twelve years. John had made enough money through his music business to buy a nice bungalow with a swimming pool – at about half the price of an equivalent English home – but they clearly lived modestly and were certainly very generous as we could personally testify. We were able to attend a 'teach-in' day on that first visit to the Vineyard, and I learned a lot more about the significance for the church of the 'here now' and 'not yet' of the kingdom of God. And how Jesus taught about the kingdom throughout his ministry frequently using parables to drive home the message – and using miracles to demonstrate its power. We learned about the relevance of world-views (we had assumed our way of seeing things to be the norm for everyone); about culture (we had already been struggling with that in our efforts to plant 'Anglican' churches in South America and then again in re-entering Britain), and about paradigm shifts. We were certainly experiencing such shifts ourselves as we suddenly began to see familiar things in so many new ways. We were also learning to listen to God in a new way for revelation about conditions of people God wanted to heal. To use their own graphic expression – we were having 'the doors blown off our minds'!

PLENTY TO TELL
By the time we were flying home at the end of the week we certainly had plenty to tell our friends back in Chorleywood. We were very exhilarated ourselves, but even so, I think we were surprised to find how much the church was excited about our report.

I recounted the case of one man who was troubled by warts on his feet! He was asked to take off his socks and shoes and sure enough they were covered in warts! After prayer the warts simply fell off onto the carpet. In telling the story in St Andrew's I joked that I almost picked one up to bring home in a matchbox to show them but I thought I might not be able to get it through the Customs at Heathrow! Most of my listeners smiled painfully at my feeble attempt at a joke because in any case a wart in a matchbox would have proved nothing, but one of the congregation came up to me afterwards and said sweetly, 'I can't think why you were worried about the Customs officers, David? I'm sure they would not have minded you bringing your matchbox through.'

CUTTING DOWN ON OUTSIDE COMMITMENTS
One of the sad things for me during the last fifteen years of my parish ministry was the sheer lack of time to join up with so many

other delightful groups and leaders across the country, but it was obvious that we simply could never do all that was desired of us. But I did agree to become a member of Michael Harper's SOMA committee (Sharing Of Ministries Abroad). I was honoured to be its chairman and also an international director. But after three or four years it became clear that I could not keep up the pace with so many other things we had growing out of St Andrew's itself, and felt sadly that I must hand it over. It was urgent that we pressed on with our training programmes in St Andrew's for the laity, teaching them how to minister in the power of the Holy Spirit. We had started these in 1982 following our second visit to John Wimber in California, using much of their material. Leaders from other churches were beginning to ask for help.

COME HOLY SPIRIT

Soon after we had started our training days for healing, I suggested to John Wimber that he ought to write a text book that we could use in the healing ministry, teaching people the simple way that he and Blaine had taught us. Leaders could take this book back with them to use for training in their own churches. Surprisingly I could not get any enthusiasm out of him for it. He obviously did not want to do it. 'No!' he said, 'I'm not ready. I might have changed my mind on some things before the next six months are up.' My mouth fell open. I had never before heard a leader talking about the possibility of changing his mind about anything. How refreshing!

'But we really do need something urgently – it seems irresponsible to get all these people inspired and then offer them no real help with follow-up in their own churches,' I countered.

'OK,' he said, 'You write it! You can take what you like out of my notes.'

With this encouragement, I re-read Francis McNutt and other books on healing, and added some practical insights gathered from what we were beginning to learn at St Andrew's; with all this, I put together a simple 'how to do it' book called *Come Holy Spirit*. John Wimber kindly added a brief Foreword. The book was published by Hodders in 1985 and is still on sale today after more than sixteen years, having been reprinted several times and having been translated into Spanish, German, Swedish, Finnish, Chinese and even Arabic. A large team of Koreans who visited St Andrew's for a special conference in 1994 told me that it had been printed on rice paper there and had passed through six reprints! We had given away the rights for this to churches overseas. With such encouragement Mary and I have been writing books ever since but none have had quite such a wide circulation as *Come Holy Spirit*.

Incidentally, one young man reviewed the book in a very disparaging way for a reputable evangelical magazine. I was saddened by his dismissal of it and surprised that the magazine would even publish it. But about four years later I had a letter from the same man saying he was really sorry he had written it, and having had a change of heart and mind and was now actually finding the book useful himself!

Later, John urged me to write a book on leadership. 'I wouldn't know how to begin,' I confessed. He got up for some more coffee and, coming back, pushed a pen and paper towards me.

'Here,' he said, 'Let me give you an outline of the areas you need to cover,' and he reeled off ten chapter headings one after the other. I jotted them down but was still not sure I could develop them. I shared my doubts with him.

'I'll help you,' he insisted. And then with easy analysis he proceeded to a breakdown for each chapter. I thanked him but knew I could never have done it that way – it just was not my style either of writing or of leadership.

Some years later, remembering what John Wimber had said and after reading and observing what other leaders in both churches and industry had said and done, I began to analyse what had been my own approach. This led to my book on the subject called *Leadership for New Life*,[8] which soon involved me in a new round of talks on the subject.

Chapter 19

COME OVER AND HELP US

Come over to Macedonia and help us
(PAUL'S VISION, ACTS 16:9, RSV)

*We cannot build our own future without helping others
to build theirs*
(PRESIDENT BILL CLINTON)

*I have only one skill. I'm a facilitator. I can make other people
believe in themselves. If I believe something is going to
work, my belief seems to rub off*
(TIM SMIT – VISIONARY LEADER FOR THE EDEN PROJECT
IN CORNWALL)

John Wimber had challenged us with the words of Christ: 'Freely you have received, freely give'[1] when he refused to consider any repayment for the airfares of the thirty Vineyard folk that came on that first visit to us in 1981. 'Now give it [the ministry] away!' he told us. Ever since Barry Kissell had been appointed Director of Faith Sharing on the staff of St Andrew's, the church had been accustomed to sending teams out to other churches to teach and encourage. After John Wimber's visit the invitations from other churches increased considerably and teaching on the kingdom of God, worship, healing, and prophecy were now regularly included by Barry in their programmes. I had also initiated my teaching programme for training both our own members and those sent to us by other churches 'to equip the saints for the work of the ministry'. Mary and I also had an increasing number of invitations to visit other churches across the country which we accepted so long as these optional commitments outside the parish did not override our proper obligations within it. But the majority of church people, like ourselves before our meeting with Wimber, have no idea how to begin, how to continue, nor how to conclude such prayer ministry in the power of the Holy Spirit. It was good also to take other layfolk with us to help in this ministry.

GO WEST YOUNG MAN

An early request came from the West Country. A visiting vicar pressed us to come to his parish. He also asked me to impart the gift of revelation[2] to him. 'Help,' I thought, 'I am just scraping the barrel and not really getting enough revelation myself yet to start giving it away – in fact I'm not sure I will ever have enough to give away.' I had not yet read one of the ancient Fathers who had said: 'You can light a thousand candles with one candle and still not diminish the light of that candle.' But the vicar continued to press me. How could he minister in the things of the Spirit without this gift, he asked? So I did something I had never done before and laid hands on him to impart the gift, praying briefly that God would give him revelation.

The day came when we were due in his parish. As we drove up to the vicarage Mary admired the vast house where we would be staying the night but changed her mind about it after experiencing the temperature of a typical vicarage bedroom. The vicar kindly showed us to our room upstairs where we unpacked our things, then we came down, had a cup of tea and moved off almost at once to the church.

SIGN AND WONDERS

I gave my first talk about signs and wonders – one of the ways that Jesus taught his disciples to advance the kingdom of God. I gave some teaching also on how to hear God and prayed that he would give us some revelation about what he wanted us to do. Then I asked the people what they thought God was saying – were there any 'words' about conditions of people that he wanted to have mercy upon? Several people called out 'words' they thought that God was giving them – including one from the vicar himself.

We took them one by one and invited any who thought the 'word' fitted their condition to come forward. Mary and I then prayed for them on the platform. One lady had an internal ulcer, a man had blood pressure problems and a woman wanted a baby but was unable to conceive. We prayed for them all and a few others. It was a good start in one way but the congregation had been unable to see any really beneficial results, though I am sure now that there would have been in time. We've had extraordinary feedback over time and often after many years.

A FEW EXAMPLES

Once, after a radio interview about one of her books on personal growth, the interviewer happened to mention to Mary that her sister had come to St Andrew's some ten years previously with an ovarian cyst the size of a grapefruit. She had prayer for this. She was due to be operated on the next day but the medical check up just before it apparently showed there was now nothing to operate on – Glory to God! It had never come back and she had since had two children. Another man came up to me at the door of St Andrew's one evening. He had been brought to St Andrew's in a wheelchair several years previously. He told me how his healing had begun that night. He now felt called to the mission field and asked for prayer as he was off to Kazakhstan in a couple of weeks time. I was amazed at the work of God in his life. Another man – an Indian student from the London Bible College – received a prophecy from a visiting speaker, that he was going to India to evangelise his fellow countryfolk – thousands of them! I met him two years later at the door of St Andrew's. 'Aren't you the man who was going out to India to evangelise thousands?' I asked. 'Yes,' he said, 'And it's tens of thousands! I've just returned to get married and take my wife back with me to India.'

But nothing like that was happening right there in that West-Country church that night. I was beginning to feel rather desperate. It is hard to look calm when you don't feel it!

LARGE LUMP ON LEFT HAND

Our meeting in the West Country was concluding when a man suddenly came to the front with a large lump on his left hand. He said he'd had it many years, and really would not have bothered to ask for prayer, but he was impressed that the vicar himself had given out such a precise 'word' about it. I began to feel a little bit excited. God was surely going to vindicate our stepping out in faith after all! Smiling, I held up his hand for everyone to see. 'This man has had this lump for thirteen years,' I announced. 'The vicar has had a word of revelation about it and we are going to pray that the Lord will remove it!' I was feeling an increasing boldness in faith.

Holding up the hand before the crowd I began mentally to ruffle through the pages of my New Testament all the while praying silently – indeed desperately. I was mentally searching for some precedent to instruct me how to proceed, but could not recall any ministry by Jesus or his disciples in the New Testament for lumps on the hand! Surely one of those disciples would have met a lump somewhere!

'Help, Lord!' I prayed, 'How should I pray for this one, Lord?'

'You know!' I seemed to hear him saying.

'But Lord, I don't think I do. I can't remember anything in the Bible about lumps on the hand?'

Again I seemed to hear him saying, 'I have told you to speak to a mountain and it would be removed – isn't that enough?'

'Ah, but this is not a mountain, Lord!'

'But it seems to be a mountain to you!'

'Oh yes!' I felt suddenly encouraged.

'Now,' I addressed the congregation, surprised at my own calmness, 'You remember how the Lord said we could speak to a mountain and it would be removed if we had enough faith? Well, now we are going to speak in faith to this lump and tell it to go!'

I held the hand up high so all could watch the action and quietly commanded the lump to go in the name of the Lord. Everyone seemed to be watching intently. And of course I was watching too. Nothing seemed to be happening. Nothing! I thought a little pressure on it might help it go down. Nothing! I turned the hand over to see if anything was coming through on the other side? Nothing!

NOTHING HAPPENING

'Well, that is disappointing,' I said. 'Nothing really appears to have happened this evening but we can only do what we sense the

Lord is telling us to do and leave it at that. And I don't sense he is telling me to do any more.'

We never chided people for lack of faith nor accused them of some secret sin that might hinder the healing, though at the beginning we had made it plain that we all needed to put things right with God. So we just had to leave it all with the Lord and closed the meeting.

Mary and I returned to the vicarage in a despondent mood. No one would ever be inspired to pray for any healings after that public exercise in failure. I was being strongly tempted to give up all ideas of continuing in such a ministry myself, let alone trying to teach others how to set about it. The vicar came back to his house with hardly a comment about the evening at all (thankfully!), but he did ask us if we would pray for his daughter. She was very unwell with lumps in her groin and was booked to see a specialist. 'Lumps!' I groaned inwardly. However could he ask us to pray for another lump? Couldn't he see how useless we were at it? That man really must have faith!

Praying for one more person to be healed of lumps was the very last thing we ever wanted to do again. I was sure now that I had been going down the wrong track entirely. I had learned my lesson. But how could we ever get out of it? Playing for time and pretending not to have heard the vicar properly I changed the subject quickly. I said we were very tired and just needed a cup of tea.

Whilst we were drinking it a phone rang and the vicar went to his study to answer it. Still desperately searching for some way out I said to Mary, 'Quick! Let's get up to bed!' The vicar already knew we were tired.

It was a cold and uneventful night – except that I had a call of nature and had to creep down a spiral staircase about two o'clock in the morning to reach the necessary port of call. Unfortunately my foot slipped at the top on one of those angled steps that taper off at one side, and I arrived down at the next landing rather faster and more noisily than I had intended. Bedroom doors burst open on every side, but when they saw it was just a backsliding bishop vanishing into the bathroom, they discreetly closed them again and crept back to their beds.

BLACKMAILED OVER BREAKFAST!

When we went down to breakfast the next morning, the vicar tactfully avoiding all reference to 'things that go bump in the night'. He was much more concerned about getting us to pray for his daughter before we left. What a man of faith! Her temperature was even higher this morning, he explained. I tried smiling sympathetically as I stifled an inner groan. I could not muster an ounce of faith for that poor girl's healing – besides I was very anxious to avoid risking any possible West of England 'flu bugs. It was hard enough dodging the Chorleywood ones. But there was obviously going to be no breakfast until we had prayed for his daughter so back up the stairs we went, like lambs to the slaughter. As we ascended I started repenting of my rebellious spirit, and managed to get myself into a humbler frame of mind by the time I had reached the first landing. He led us to her bedroom door and took us see to his ailing daughter. She lay pale and sick, amidst her pillows. I surveyed the scene solemnly, praying silently for a further minute or two, and then I rebuked the fever in the name of Jesus, just as Jesus had done with Peter's wife's mother. After another moment or two Mary commanded the lumps in the groin to go in the same way. And that was it. There was absolutely nothing more that seemed appropriate to be done.

We had our breakfast and dashed off back to Chorleywood feeling we had just been through one of those awful nightmares when one is fruitlessly trying to fight off giants through the night with a feather pillow.

THE PHONE CALL

About three weeks later the phone went. Mary answered. It was that vicar again! He wanted to discuss some matter with her. Then he happened to mention his daughter. 'Do you remember how you prayed for . . .?' (How could we ever forget? Yet one does not want to sound too keen for news.)

Mary replied with calculated calm: 'Yes! How is she getting along?'

'Well!' he said, 'The fever was down within half an hour and the lumps had completely disappeared by 5.30 that evening. And so we've cancelled a planned appointment with the specialist.' Wow!

That had to be God!

And that was not all. 'Do you remember the man with the lump on his hand that he had had for thirteen years?' the vicar continued.

'Ye-e-es,' she replied, again not wanting to sound too excited. 'What happened about him?'

'That lump had completely gone by the end of the week, praise God!' he said.

We were dumbfounded. God had done that too! Suddenly we felt we were getting back on track. We sensed a new commitment to teaching others how to pray for the sick and to minister healing in the power of the Holy Spirit of God. Now we could not wait. The fact is that the more one does the more blessing one sees. If we never do it we will never see it!

SOUTH AFRICA

The first year we went to South Africa we visited a most terrible Soweto shanty-town outside Port Elizabeth (Soweto stood for South West Township – the even more infamous Soweto lay outside Johannesburg). The people were seething with anger at the way they felt they had been treated by the whites. Had there not been black clergy to accompany us, we would probably have been lynched. It was a scary but a deeply moving experience to see the conditions they lived in. I felt quite helpless as I silently prayed for them. There seemed so little we could do practically. Their problems were massive. One could never forget them.

Arriving back at the bishop's home he warned us to watch our words as his house was bugged. Apparently every conversation that he had there was recorded – and he had often been called by the police to account for things he had said or things others had confidentially shared with him in his home. He had two sons and both were on the run (one was a newspaper journalist) because of their open opposition to the system. The bishop had invited us to stay for lunch and as a conversational piece for any police snoopers listening I repeated the gist of the story of the man in the West of England with the lump. One of the younger clergy was listening intently to this simple account as we sipped our drinks – waiting to enter the dining room.

Later, still sitting round the bishop's table, just starting on our dessert, the young man suddenly let out a most unseemly yell. We all turned to his direction. 'Look!' he said, 'I had a nasty lump on my hand coming up and I was going to have it operated on. I had a similar operation once before and I was not looking forward to another like that. It was very painful.' But he continued: 'When I heard the story about the lump that was healed, I addressed the one on my hand and told it to go in the name of Jesus! And now look everybody – it is completely gone!' Again God had done it! We saw many wonderful things that God was doing on that visit, and we went to quite a number of churches. I remember praying for one black boy in an Anglican church who began crying out from the floor of the front pew, 'Jesus! Jesus! Jesus! No more! No more!' He was shielding his eyes with his forearms as though the glory of God was overwhelming him.

These stories are included to encourage people to minister to others in prayer. Over the years we have ministered to thousands of people, and there have been many times when no one appeared to be healed. But again we have often seen wonderful healings too. And later reports have also brought to light some of the lovely things that God had done – seemingly as a result of those prayers. Knowing all the positive results at the time would have left us too big-headed – and made us unusable by God. He will never share his glory.

UNUSUAL DEANERY MEETING

Strangely I once had an invitation to speak on this subject at a neighbouring deanery meeting. I took Mary, my daughter Debby and my son-in-law John with me to give me some moral support. On arrival my family thought we had come to a business meeting of undertakers. A handful of women present made the environment a little more sympathetic. As I listened to the notices being given out I recalled a good definition of manners: 'Politeness is knowing how to yawn at deanery meetings with the mouth closed.' Such meetings may well have changed considerably today.

When it came to my turn to speak I shared the basic teaching about the kingdom of God and then talked about how God speaks to us today. Jesus had clearly said: 'My sheep hear my voice'.[3] Having explained about the many ways that God speaks through the Bible and apart from the Bible, but never in contradiction to the Bible, I suggested we try to listen to him. We waited, and then I asked if any one thought God might have spoken.

Debby immediately responded, 'I think there is someone here with a chipped coccyx.' 'My Giddy Aunt! Whatever could that be?' I silently wondered. 'Who on earth would have a chipped coccyx at a deanery meeting? Forget it!'

'Has anyone anything else?' I pleaded hastily, looking round desperately at the 'undertakers' before me. My faith was wilting fast. At last a few bravely shared what they thought they had been shown or heard and I invited those who identified with any of those words to come and form a queue at the front. I approached the first lady.

LADY WITH THE CHIPPED COCCYX

'What do you want Jesus to do for you?' I asked.

'I'm the person with the chipped coccyx!' she replied. Now I had no idea where or what a coccyx was. One really likes to have some idea what one is praying for, but obviously I needed to be careful here – it could prove embarrassing asking her where her coccyx was and how it affected her. It might be better just to pray 'blind' as it were. So I simply explained that, of course, I could not heal anyone, but Jesus could. The revelation given out seemed encouraging and could imply that God wanted to heal her, so I said, 'Let's press on and pray!' As she stood in front of me I invoked the Holy Spirit of God to come upon her. I remembered how the Holy Spirit once came and hovered over ('overshadowed') the Virgin Mary in some mysterious way for the supernatural conception of the Son of God leading on to a natural birth. I sensed the Holy Spirit hovering over this lady as I waited in prayer. She now seemed truly engaged with God so I addressed the coccyx and spoke healing to it in the name of Jesus! Normally, had it been an arm or something I would have suggested checking it out by bending it, but not knowing and not daring to ask I said, simply, 'Well that seems all we are meant to do for the moment. See how things go?' I turned towards the next person in the queue. It was a year and half before I learned that the woman had been completely healed. Glory be to God! But in the car driving home after that deanery meeting I reminded Debby of the lady who had had the chipped coccyx. It seemed most remarkable that anyone had even been present with that condition.

'You were spot on,' I said. 'However did you get that word?'

'Oh!' she said, 'After you had prayed for us to receive some revelation from God I saw something that looked like a coccyx. And then I saw a chip so I said chipped coccyx!' I didn't know if it was a potato chip or a stone chip but she had certainly got it right.

Faith building

In our travels I would illustrate the teaching with a couple of stories telling of what God had done. This proved to be a faith building exercise. Some think this could be a form of manipulation but I don't think I agree. There always has to be faith somewhere along the line – either in the sick person, or the people bringing the sick person, or the person ministering the healing. Many of those who came to Jesus had heard about others who had been healed, and that undoubtedly gave them, or their friends, the faith to believe they could be healed too. Jesus often said to people who were healed 'Your faith has made you well!' It seems that faith is a great conductor for bringing the power of God to the point of need. The amount of faith is not important. Just a tiny fusewire of faith is enough – 'faith as small as a mustard seed', Jesus had said.[4] On the other hand we must never belittle people by suggesting that they are not healed because they do not have enough faith or they are too sinful or unworthy. Faith in itself is a gift of God and we can't manufacture it. But if it can't be taught it can be caught. The Jewish Council threatened the apostles to prevent the good news of Jesus' healing spreading any further.[5] It seems to imply that faith was somehow contagious!

It is important to watch the person whilst praying for them. I remember teaching in Finland once about healing. These teach-ins were held in a beautiful conference centre but at night we returned to our own centrally heated cabins round a lake that was frozen over. It must have been an ideal setting during the warmer seasons. To reach the main meeting and eating places one needed to walk through some bitterly cold snow. The wind was about minus twenty and I felt frozen each time I made that walk. I finally resolved the problem by wearing my pyjamas underneath my trousers. This served me well until one evening session glancing down whilst speaking on the platform I suddenly noticed two inches of pyjamas hanging out over my shoes. The Finns must have imagined the Brits had rather unusual dress sense! We concluded that conference with an open meeting in the Lutheran Cathedral in Helsinki. I can still picture a lady who had just been attending our training course, standing in the centre aisle praying with her arms up in the air and her eyes still tightly closed, and the person she was praying for was spread-eagled out on the floor at her feet. The lady who was praying was totally unaware of what God was doing.

A friend of mine in Jersey was praying for a woman as he stood with closed eyes in front of her. He had his hands gently touching either side of her head when he sensed the head was beginning to feel rather 'mushy'. He pressed a little harder and could soon feel his own hands through the lady's head! At this point he thought he ought to open his eyes and saw the woman he was praying for stretched out on the floor below him whilst in his hands he was still clutching something – her wig! It was quite obvious that she really needed this so he bent down and replaced it quickly. Soon after she suddenly began crying again thinking she had lost her sight! My friend had replaced the wig back to front! I have found one can discern so much by watching people's faces as one prays for them and as the Holy Spirit hovers over them to do surprising creative things. In these situations its always best to pray with one's eyes open.

Spontaneous healing

I was recounting the coccyx story at the beginning of one of our conferences in a place called Temple in Texas. A lady who had been sitting at a reception desk signing up late-comers in the vestibule, was listening over the PA system when she suddenly realised that God had healed her own coccyx problem as she was listening to the story. She had been experiencing great pain but now it was completely gone and she could stand and sit easily. That had to be God! Her unexpected interruption to tell us about it in our meeting enhanced the faith level wonderfully. We had a good time there. It's always been good going to Texas.

Chapter 20

TO LOVE MERCY

When I have got food for the poor they call me a saint. When I ask why the poor have no food they call me a Communist
(Archbishop Helder Camara)

What is the matter with the rich is uselessness
(G.B. Shaw)

Kindness is Christianity with working clothes on
(Anon)

Write your name in the hearts of thousands in kindness, love and mercy
(James Chalmers)

We were visiting San Antonio in the west of Texas. Because over forty couples in our hotel were at the same conference where we were speaking the management gave us the Presidential suite on the top floor for our accommodation. It had many rooms and two bathrooms as well as numerous TV sets. Far too much luxury for us, we didn't need it but we enjoyed it! It was at this conference that we first met the Feuilles. Ricky Feuille is a lawyer and heads a large firm of attorneys in El Paso – a practice that he has built up over many years. For some reason we mentioned that following the conference we planned to take a break in El Paso[1] in Texas, and from there we wanted to visit the inspiring mission work headed up by Fr Ricky Thomas (a Catholic charismatic priest) who was pioneering a mission in a deprived community of some 200,000 Spanish speaking inhabitants at Juarez over the border in Mexico. Ricky Feuille happened to be the chairman of this Mission Trust. Most of the folk among the Juarez outcasts existed without electricity, clean water, proper drainage or sanitation. We knew about the work there from a very popular video made by Fr Bertoluche for the Pope entitled *Viva Cristo Rey*[2] which had been widely circulated round UK charismatic circles. If ever a work demonstrated that the kingdom of God was really good news, this truly compassionate, sacrificial and effective work did so conclusively. The video had also spurred on many other charismatic churches to initiate new projects to help the sick, the poor, the prisoners, the oppressed and the elderly. For Ric Thomas it all started in the autumn of 1972 – after he had read a passage from the Gospels to his small Catholic charismatic prayer group. 'When you give a luncheon or dinner, do not invite your friends, your brothers or relatives, or your rich neighbours; if you do, they may invite you back and so you will be repaid. But when you give a banquet, invite the poor, the crippled, the lame, the blind, and you will be blessed . . . they cannot repay you . . '.[3]

The reading was followed by a time of prayer. Then a simple word of prophecy was given that resulted in a plan to share their Christmas dinner with the poorest folk they knew of in Juarez – the 'trash grabbers' who lived off the garbage dump. Two gangs collected whatever was worth salvaging from that vast mountain of rubbish – one great simmering stench under the scorching sun. These 'wretched of the earth' scraped up a bare existence in their wasteland of cardboard dwellings, crawling around among the garbage during the daylight hours, picking out scraps of food, cans, plastic, cloth, iron, wood (for cooking fuel) and any other cast-offs that might still be wearable or saleable. It was not unknown to discover a stillborn baby tumbling from the latest delivery tip.

These Catholics had never tried anything like this before but they began to seriously discuss how it might be done. They knew it would involve getting the two hostile groups that eked out their meagre livelihood there, to come to some sort of agreement amongst themselves if this was ever to happen. The antagonism between them frequently resulted not only in violent injuries but even deaths. Somehow a truce was actually arranged.

GATE-BUSTERS AT CHRISTMAS

The helpers counted about 150 people from that dump who would welcome such a Christmas lunch if it could really be laid on for them. In their preparation the church made allowances for a few extra. When the day came however, over 300 'guests' turned up, expecting something to eat! It was then that our new friends experienced their first miracle. Knowing there was not nearly enough food for so many, they prayed, and not only did sufficient food materialise to feed everyone, but there was enough over to take food to two orphanages. One thing led to another and a mission was started; they even had doctors and lawyers from across the border lending their professional skills to alleviate the sick and suffering and to counsel the inmates in the local prison.

Several of Ricky Feuille's colleagues in the law firm also went there to help. One was a nominal Catholic, going through 'a dark night of the soul' and searching for a living faith. Ricky Feuille encouraged him to get involved with the work in Juarez thinking it might help him spiritually. While the folk were lining up for food he looked at the full basket of grapes he had been asked to distribute – and then at the endless queue of hopeful people in front of him. That amount of grapes seemed a ridiculous amount to offer to such a vast number and he asked what he should do when all the grapes were gone. 'Just go on giving till the basket is empty' he was told, which was exactly what he did and when he got to the end of the huge queue he wept. He knew that what he had had in his basket had been totally inadequate for all those people yet every one had received the same amount of grapes. This experience revolutionised his life and he became a committed Catholic Christian. He knew it had to be God working a miracle like that!

When in San Antonio, we happened to mention our intention of visiting Fr Ric's work, the Feuilles insisted that we all[4] stay with them in their home in El Paso. They had plenty of room, they said. We tried to put them off because we usually end up exhausted from our conferences and really need the break before going on to the next one – where we are again speaking and praying for so many people all the time. We had found from past experience that well-meaning hosts in private homes often come up with tremendous family problems (theirs or their friends) just when we are dying to get off to bed, and would keep us up praying for them till the early hours. Excusing ourselves from ministering to the family would seem too ungracious to such generous hosts. So our custom was to book a reasonably cheap hotel in which to rest up before flying off to the next conference. But our new friends were most insistent and there seemed no way we could politely put them off.

STAYING WITH OUR NEW FRIENDS

When we eventually got to the Fueilles, they invited all their friends for a meal the first night as agreed, and we prayed for any that needed help. Quite wonderfully one of them (Marylin) was healed of a cancer by the Lord as we prayed. (We will never understand why some are healed and others don't seem to be!) Since then Marylin, and her husband Tom, have flown over many times at their own expense, to help us in the prayer ministry at the New Wine conference in Somerset. They also visit other churches teaching the things that we had shared with them – that we had learned straight from John Wimber! Tom has since become the national director of Faith Alive, a lay movement for sharing the Christian faith among the churches in the USA.

SISTER MARY VIRGINIA

Apart from looking after us in every way, the Feuilles made all the contacts necessary for us to get out to the work in Juarez. A dear nun[5] drove us out there, talking animatedly all the way. Fr Ric had described on video how in their group for daily devotions they would read the Bible. Then, he said, Sister Mary Virginia would give a prophecy. Evidently it was our Jehu-like driver who had given that original word that had started off this great work amongst the poor. We had raced a fair way along the road when we discovered we had brought no passports, which we would need to get into Mexico. Sister seemed to be taking it all very good-humouredly and did not expect any problems. Fortunately she was well known and much respected by the guards at the check-point and no questions were asked.

Driving at speed did not seem to distract Sister Mary Virginia from talking fast. I was trying my hardest to follow her conversation. But my eyes kept darting nervously to the track ahead of us. How we missed some of those gaping potholes on the Mexican side I'll never know!

By her accent she was obviously a North American and I asked her if her parents approved of her working down in Mexico.

'Oh yeah,' she said, 'They pray for me every day.'

'How great to have such support,' I said, 'Where do they live?'

'Oh! They've both been dead a long time now,' she replied.

This was definitely going to be a very new kind of experience for us in more ways than one, I thought! Whilst we do not pray for the dead nor communicate with the dead, it was just possible to deduce from the silence in Scripture that the dead in Christ might be interceding for us, though I'd find it difficult to preach it from the pulpit. Admittedly, according to the Bible, Moses, Elijah and Samuel among others all appeared to men after their death but I would not be happy about our initiating any communication with the deceased even if the deceased might be used by God to communicate with us. Necrology is forbidden in the Bible.

MASS AT 6 AM

Finally we reached *La Mesa del Senor* (The Lord's table), and unloaded the supplies she'd collected to feed a few hundred more families. We were there just in time for the open air mass at 6 am. When they sang they were accompanied by guitar playing and many of the Spanish worship songs were ones we already knew from the Pentecostals in our Chile days, so we joined in heartily. Then came a cry *'Viva Cristo el Rey'*, and we all responded enthusiastically by repeating it. After the mass we visited round the site as the men were being formed into teams – some making concrete blocks, and others using blocks already made to build simple little homes for their neighbours – far superior to their cardboard shacks! Fr Ric Thomas had given them the leadership and direction they needed for this. Everyone seemed to be enjoying working together. I was impressed with Ric who, though lacking any Franciscan attire, exhibited the Franciscan spirit. He appeared extraordinarily shoddy in his ragged coat, pants and boots. I asked the Feuilles why some of their friends could not get him some decent clothes. They told us that they constantly bought him new clothes and boots but a couple of days later he looked just as scruffy again.

'What happened to that lovely jacket we bought you, Fr Ric?'

'Oh! I met this poor guy who was so cold and had no jacket so I gave it to him! His need was greater than mine.' His Christlike dedication to the poor drew us to him. We just loved him. Fr Ric seemed very surprised to learn that we had heard so much about his work in the UK – and that we had read the book about his work *Viva Christol Rey* by the French Catholic theologian and priest, René Laurentín, and also seen the video by that title that had inspired so many churches to get more involved in social action.

I was asked to pray for the sick in some of those grotty cardboard hovels and to anoint them with oil. In each shack, baking under the Mexican sun, we found tiny listless babies. I looked at one lying on a kind of wooden ledge for a bed. Hosts of black flies, crawling over the poor child's eyes, nose and mouth were clustered as thickly on the baby's face as on the dog's dirt just outside the doorway. This was far worse than any shanty-towns I'd ever visited in Chile. I thought, 'How totally inured we are most of the time to the poverty and suffering across our global village!' Fr Ric Thomas' work among the living destitute in Mexico equalled Mother Teresa's merciful work among the dying beggars in Calcutta.

We get so used to seeing poverty in the media that it was a refreshing challenge to meet these humble Christians quietly getting on with a ministry so near and dear to the heart of God.

LIBERIA TO LONDON

I had always believed that outpourings of the Holy Spirit must be directed among other things into works of mercy – something so close to the heart of Jesus. Soon after I had arrived I asked a former warden at St Andrew's if he would gather together a group of businessmen to start a Christian Businessmen's Initiatives Group. These men were soon researching the whole area to see what needed to be done and got involved in several projects for the community. But there were very few really poor people about in our area – not even on the council estate behind the church.

Later, one of our young people, Paul Cowan, went out to Africa for his gap year to pray about his future. He returned from the forests of Liberia believing the Lord was leading him back to London, not to university as his parents no doubt had hoped, but to help any of society's runaways and throwaways that he found there. His first move was to go and sleep rough among the homeless in a cardboard box in central London – sitting where they sat.[6] Experience on those London streets day and night was both an eyeopener, a heart-breaker and even a life threatener (some thought he might be a police plant and wanted to cut his throat). He was almost overcome with emotion when he reported back to the church how that, after three weeks of it, he could stand it no longer. The weather was cold, the conditions were hard but the mistrust of the very people that he most wanted to help was devastating. However, he was soon back and became deeply involved with a project for helping society's drop outs. He was faithfully involved in this work for nearly a decade before he went on to train for the ordained ministry of the Church of England. The effect of his example on St Andrew's was salutary. People began to look for new and practical ways of helping others anywhere with greater needs than their own.

In a money raising venture for Paul's work, it was decided that some St Andrew's folk would sleep rough for the night and bring in some extra cash by getting financial backers for this venture. My friends seemed keen to volunteer me for this experiment so with two friends I spent a night under the railway on Chorleywood Common. Some parishioners took it upon themselves to trail out at all hours of the night to see that I was undergoing the discomfort properly! I was reminded of my times of sleeping out in trenches on manoeuvres during National Service training in the Army many years before.

One lady who was at St Andrew's at that time later moved to Watford, and soon became concerned about the drop outs there on the streets. Before long she was a leading pioneer in the vision for the Watford New Hope Trust. With good people around her and the backing of her new church in Watford this has developed into a major charity. The different New Hope shelters and projects in Watford are supported by nearly all the churches in the area and have greatly impressed the town council by their vision and commitment in catering so effectively for such practical needs.

QUICK FIX

One Sunday I had a desperate phone call from a Christian organisation asking me to help them find a suitable person to head a project for setting up a refugee camp in the Sudan. A team of volunteers was all ready to go but their leader had dropped out at the last minute. Could we help? They wanted to know immediately if I could think of anyone, and then, if that person could decide by the next morning and be prepared to leave within the week? Quite a tall order! 'Give me an hour to think about it and I'll get back to you,' I said, beginning to pray fervently. When they mentioned the Sudan my mind went to Brian Halton, a regular church member at St Andrew's, who had once served as a senior police officer in East Africa. He had been back in the UK for a while by then and had some kind of consultancy work that gave him a certain amount of flexibility so I phoned him, and told him what was wanted. He was, naturally, slightly taken aback at the urgency of the request but said he would think and pray about it. I then dropped the bombshell and asked him to give me his answer by 7.30 am the next day. The following morning he phoned early to say he would do it for six months. The agency was most grateful. Brian's wife Avril, who headed up an advanced adult education establishment in the area, was able to go out and join him for a few weeks. He did a splendid job and I felt very proud of him.

ANOTHER MISSION TO THE POOR

I was leading a training day in Tonbridge for the prayer ministry teams at our New Wine conference when I met up with a couple there who had been attending New Wine for eleven years and had just come for a refresher course. They told me a story backed up by a cutting from the local press about their work. In 1989, they had been to one of our packed evening Communion services at St Andrew's Church, Chorleywood. Apparently this couple, Mike and Angela Prentice, whom I recognised vaguely but could not place, were visiting us from St John's Church, Redhill. They now reminded me of something I had completely forgotten: I had moved down the line of those kneeling at the rails distributing the bread at the sacrament, and had suddenly returned to lay hands on them and to bless the 'special' ministry that God was giving to them! I do not often do that kind of thing and as far as I can recollect I had no idea whether they had a 'special' ministry; I just felt led to take the risk and to say it.

To date they had been married thirty-nine years and had fostered 130 children besides bringing up four of their own, one of them being severely handicapped. Thanks to a windfall tax rebate they were able to visit Kenya for a holiday, where Michael had once served in the Army. On the ferry to Mombasa they were greeted by hordes of homeless little children begging. It broke their hearts. They met a Baptist minister from the village of Shona nearby, and asked him if there was anything they could do to help. He said quite simply that he wanted to build a school and run it for these children. So my friends set up their 'Shona Project' at Redhill in 1993 (it was later given charitable status in England) and began collecting money for it, which they then forwarded to their minister friend in Kenya. More and more money seemed to be needed. The school was initially for 150 children. At last my friends went back to Kenya to see how things were going. They had no idea what to expect: they did not even know if the pastor had been able to start building the school yet! But they were delighted to find it up and functioning already. They felt so privileged to have been able to help. The local churches and schools in Redhill had been involved with them in the project. The 'Trust' was soon receiving between £2,000–3,000 pounds a year. In 1998, there was another word of encouragement at New Wine from the platform for 'Someone named Michael who is going on a mission.' They were just about to make a return visit (having been back eight times to see how the work was getting along) but this time Mike was having second thoughts about whether it was really God's will for them to go again. They had always re-visited the work believing that they were being sent by God, and this 'word' was the encouragement they needed.

Not only do the local school children in Redhill bless the Kenyan children by their commitment to the project, but after a recent Ofsted visit the inspectors reported they were most impressed with the English children's social concern and their knowing so much about Africa itself! It was exciting to meet and pray for Michael and Angela and to hear their story. The work of the Spirit certainly includes missions of mercy.

STREET FAYRES AND FÉTES

We also had an expanding ministry locally helping to recreate 'community' and getting some social projects off the ground. Jeannie Morgan and her husband once bought and ran an open club in a bus for non-churched young people, in conjunction with Mike Pilavachi, our youth worker. Then Jeannie opened a coffee shop in our village centre. Later she went on to organise a Street Fayre in the shopping area at Christmas time. Once this was established she handed it over to the shopkeepers themselves to continue – something they still do to this day. Jeannie then set about organising a huge village fete in which she involved just about every organisation and club in the village. It was great fun but too big a headache to repeat again too soon. St Andrew's PCC invested some £2,000 in this but did not disclose its close commitment to avoid appearing patronising. It was a great social venture for helping to build up the community.

Some of the folk in the church with nursing experience, worked hard in the homes of various parishioners caring for the terminally ill. One of their number, Margaret Slatford, had a vision for a nursing home for them. Again the church gave it good support. Most of the trustees were St Andrew's people. They acquired a very large house and converted it – even installing a lift. But eventually the running costs proved enormous and it was too difficult to maintain. The place was sold to Mencap at a very reasonable price to repay the many private loans. The effort and sacrifice was not wasted since it was now redirected into helping another section of disadvantaged people, even if this was not what had been originally envisaged.

One of the joys of coming to St Andrew's was that under my predecessor the church had made a commitment to give away 50%

of their offerings to work beyond their own needs. God truly blessed this commitment. I was in California in the early 1990s, attending one of John Wimber's conferences and staying once more at the Wimbers' home, when halfway through the week a man came to me rather apologetically and said he thought he was meant to pass on a message to me. He believed the Lord had told him to give it to an Anglican minister, and the only Anglican he knew was me.

'OK,' I said, 'Tell me what it is.' In his dream the Lord had told him to instruct an Anglican minister to teach his congregation to tithe – and if he did this, his church would be doubly blessed! This immediately alerted me as I had never actually taught people to think of giving away a tenth of their income to the Lord's work. I never wanted to seem to be putting people under law about giving in any way. But when I got back to the UK I explained what I had been told and began to teach the people about tithing at a morning and evening service once a year – sheep are only meant to be shorn once a year! The Jews had been taught to measure their giving in the Old Testament by donating a tenth of their income. I reminded them of Malachi's challenge: 'Bring the full tithes into the storehouse . . . and thereby put me to the test, says the Lord of hosts, if I will not open the windows of heaven for you and pour down for you an overflowing blessing'.[7] Without pressing it I left it to each member to pray about it. Not only did our weekly offerings go up but so did the covenants – I never knew who gave what but at the end of each year we all saw the increase in the accounts. The treasurer told me when I was leaving that the income of the church had increased on average 13.5% for every year (of the nineteen) we had been at St Andrew's. That was good, but it was not the main thing.

RUSH FOR A LAND ROVER
A family from St Andrew's was returning to Niger. They were involved with translating the Scriptures – something I strongly supported, having realised how difficult it would have been for us in Chile had we not had the Bible already available in Spanish when we went there. Our missionary friends had not told us earlier of their prayers for a long bodied Land Rover to get their

equipment back across the desert, but now they faced having to return without one. Because of the urgency there seemed no time to lose. I launched a spontaneous appeal by-passing the usual consultations with the Standing Committee – something I would normally have wanted to do. There were just three weeks to go – the vehicle would cost £16,000 (at that time). At first our treasurer thought I was out of my mind to be so rash. 'We are in the middle of an economic slump – don't you realise?' He was the company secretary of a shipping firm and they were having to sell off vessels for whatever they could get! Things were bad in the world of commerce; he clearly wanted me to know.

But the money just flowed in. We had it all in less than a week and our missionaries were able to return to the field with a new Land Rover. I tell the story because what surprised me was the way people thanked me for giving them the opportunity to be involved in such an exciting and worthwhile challenge. They had really enjoyed giving – just as the Bible teaches we should. Getting that Land Rover was good news and gave the church a real buzz! God did not seem to let the slump be a hindrance at all! Our treasurer was gracious enough to rejoice with us when the money began to come in and to say afterwards that he could see that this had all been in the will of God.

Chapter 21

GETTING OUT AND ABOUT

He [Jesus] sent them out to preach the kingdom of God
and to heal the sick
(LUKE 9:2)

If you never do it you never see it
(JOHN WIMBER)

One of the early invitations we had from abroad was from Paris. I had yet to appreciate the real value of taking others with us (as Wimber had done when he first came to us). We gave our usual teaching and then, wanting to bless what God was doing, we prayed for revelation concerning any conditions that he wanted to have mercy on. I felt there was a lady present who had a sight problem in her left eye. I could sense a little cloud before my own left eye, so I knew the problem was a 'seeing' one, and not some kind of infection. I included this when we shared the 'words' we believed that God had given us. As soon as I mentioned the sight problem in the left eye a French lady stood up. 'That's me!' she said. 'I'm that person.' I confess my heart sank a little. I didn't mind praying for headaches or bad necks, but eyes seem so intricate and delicate. But when one starts walking on water one just has to go on taking the next step!

There was nothing for it but to invite her to come forward. I asked her how long she had had the problem? 'I was born with it,' she said. 'Panic stations!' I could hear myself thinking. And then another thought quickly followed: 'It's congenital. She must be meant to have it!' But there was no going back on it now. She said that she had never been able to focus clearly on anything through that left eye. I explained that, of course, I could not heal anyone, and any healing now had to be the Lord's doing. I reminded her that our God was the God of the impossible and that nothing was too hard for him. I urged her to sort things out with God silently first, making sure that there was nothing that might block her relationship with him, or that nothing might hinder the ministry of the Holy Spirit in her life. And I did the same myself. I then explained that I was going to invite the Holy Spirit to come upon her and wait – that was what I then proceeded to do, conscious of all eyes being on us.

During the waiting I prayed one of my 'under-the-breath' arrow prayers usually along the lines of 'Lord, it has to be you! I know you alone can do these things. Please heal this eye! I promise I will give you all the glory, Lord!' When I don't know how to keep on praying, but more prayer is obviously needed, I often start praying in tongues under my breath – a gift that some find very odd, but being a gift of the Spirit it is in no way to be despised.

A STRANGE THOUGHT

As I stood waiting on God it suddenly flashed across my mind that I was meant to put some spittle on this lady's eye just as Jesus had done. 'Oh no!' I thought, 'Help, Lord! You are not calling me into a spitting ministry, are you? However am I meant to do that?' I had never seen it done.[1] But there was biblical precedent for it[2] so I could not just ignore the thought completely. 'Do I just spit on the ground as Jesus did and make some mud, apply it to the eye and give the command to go and wash it off?' I wondered? 'Or should I spit straight at her eye and risk missing it – and possibly catching someone else in the process?' Tricky!

'Well!' I thought, 'I'd better check it out with her first. She probably won't like the idea and certainly won't want me spitting in her eye right in front of all these other people. Her response should settle the matter once and for all!'

So I explained to her in hushed tones what I felt I should do, and asked her how she felt about it? 'That's perfectly OK,' she said, 'Feel free!' Oh dear! I was getting deeper and deeper into this thing and there seemed no way out. 'Help!' I called out inwardly.

I still had no idea as to how to proceed and prayed desperately for wisdom. Thinking, 'all things decently and in order', I decided the most sensible thing was just to open the palm of my left hand behind my back and turning spit into it quickly. I then rubbed my thumb into the spittle, trying to look nonchalant, and explained to her what I was about to do. I asked her to close her left eyelid partially while I applied the spittle to it, praying as I did it in the name of the Father, the Son and the Holy Spirit. Then I drew my thumb across her eye three times – not that I felt God telling me to do that but it seemed a good Anglican kind of thing to do! I followed this by addressing the eye directly, as Jesus once addressed an ear, and I said: 'Left eye, let the light of Jesus shine in you and be healed in his name!' The lady remained standing there with her left eye still nearly closed. What was I meant to do now? I wondered.

I CAN SEE

Not wanting to push this thing any further I was tempted to move on to the next person in the queue. I'd made a big enough fool of myself already for one day. But no! I felt I had to do something more so I looked at her and said, 'Now open the eye!' and then asked, 'How is it?' 'I can see!' she said, very matter of factly. I reeled a bit and said, 'You can't really, can you?' 'Yes,' she said, 'I can!' When I had recovered I suggested she closed the good eye and double checked – which she did. 'Yes! I can focus much more clearly with it!' she insisted. 'Are you sure it's really OK?' I said. 'You're not saying that just to please me, are you?' 'No!' she said, 'I can really see as well with my left eye as I can with the right.' So I looked up and told the people: 'She says she can see! – Jesus did that! Glory be to God!' I have only felt the freedom to use spittle like that a half dozen times in my life – and again on one of those occasions the result had been an immediate restoration of sight though, once more, I did not grasp that this could really be true at the time. The man surprised me by coming later to St Andrew's to tell me personally all about it. There is such a mystery to the whole area of divine healing, but if one never gets involved one will never see it. Those who are blessed by these healings bless so many others also with their testimonies, so long as they do not exaggerate them or make others feel guilty if they themselves don't get healed because of lack of faith.

CATHEDRAL VISITS

I never set out to minister in cathedrals but I suppose by now I have probably spoken on healing in over twenty of them, and in quite a number of theological seminaries, both in the UK and in other parts of the world. I should say, in passing, that in only a few have I ever been invited back again! I can easily imagine why. I was booked to go to one cathedral and learned later that there were strong objections from the bishop about my proposed visit. He had conveyed his feelings to the dean. This was rather difficult for the dean, as he had already agreed to my coming with the renewal group in the diocese that had invited me. After all, the cathedral is supposed to be home to the whole diocese and to all the traditions of the church! But the dean wrote to the renewal group and informed it that the bishop did not want me. The group replied that, since they had already invited me with the dean's original approval, and I had agreed to come, the dean would have to write to me himself giving me the bad news – and the reasons. No letter ever arrived and I went. To my surprise and delight, the bishop himself greeted me in the vestry beforehand and was frightfully civil. He even stayed to hear me speak – just about the worst talk ever, as it happened. So much for pride!

PROTOCOL

To save me a lot of paper work, for many years I used to get the inviting party to request the necessary approval for my visit from the diocese first, before they did any advertising. Once I was invited by the minister of another denomination to speak at a major conference they were holding about eight months ahead. I asked him to clear it with the bishop and to get his blessing first. The bishop referred it to the local clergy in the relevant deanery. They finally sent their agreement about two weeks before my advertised visit. I was very embarrassed by their delaying tactics. It was hard to expect ministers from other denominations to understand the finer points of our ecclesiastical protocol. None of the members of the deanery turned up at the conference.

We have had some interesting experiences with bishops whose responses are very varied. At one conference the bishop was the first up to be prayed for. In another a bishop sat silently at the back through every session. At the end I mentioned to him that I hoped nothing I said would have put him off having charismatic clergy in his diocese. 'Would to God that I had just one!' he responded – and two years later he had organised a conference for us in his own diocese. Another, an archbishop, came to a conference we held near his home! I was very encouraged by a diocesan bishop who came because of the changes for good in two of his clergy who had attended a conference the previous year that we had had in the vicinity. So he thought that he should check us out for himself. He also seemed appreciative of prayer for himself.

RITUAL IN WORSHIP

Of course the extemporary nature of the ministry I was teaching could jar quite seriously with the traditional rituals of a cathedral. Not that I object to ritual. Any form of worship soon creates its own rituals, whether we recognise them or not – even for Pentecostalists. Pentecostal pastors in Chile frequently interrupted a service to bid their congregation cry out: *'Tres Glorias a Dios'*.[3] To say the least it served to keep everyone awake! If we have liturgies we might as well have good ones (even if we don't use all parts of it or use it all the time) and traditional ones have the advantage of having been tested by time. Cathedrals have them *par excellence*. Ritual and liturgy maintain a healthy focus on the transcendence of God. A selective and exclusive emphasis of the divine immanence and intimacy can so easily create an imbalance even amounting to heresy in our spontaneous worship. It's a great loss when the sense of the transcendence, the majesty and the mystery is lost or overlooked; when the wholesome dimensions of biblical content, discipline and order become too conspicuous by their absence.

But ritual and liturgy can also become horribly mechanical and deadening, smothering and inhibiting for spontaneous worship. Liturgy needs to be readily available but also needs to be a resource to use creatively and sensitively, never rigidly or legalistically.

But what if the preacher wants to do something unusual – to conduct some ministry time from the pulpit? What if he feels the need to invoke the Holy Spirit, not as a formality but out of a spontaneous prompting to give the Spirit of God space to do some special sovereign work? The late Martyn Lloyd-Jones, a great Free Church preacher, once commented rather dryly: 'Fancy upsetting the clock-like mechanical perfection of a great service with an outpouring of the Holy Spirit! The thing is unthinkable!' Not only unthinkable but abhorrent for many. There is little traditional precedent for coping with an unusual prompting of the Holy Spirit!

On one occasion I felt we needed to move straight into ministry following my talk in a cathedral. That's what most of the people had come for; it was a special mid-week service. I suggested from the pulpit to the diocesan bishop present that it would be nice if he dismissed the congregation at that point so that people who wanted to leave could do so, and the others desiring further prayer could feel free to move forward to the communion rails at a side chapel. But the dear bishop was concerned that the choir must sing their special item as per order sheet. Actually I had cleared it all before and was told by the precentor that I could drop their programme at any time. So the bishop announced that the choir should sing their item first and then he would pronounce his blessing and dismiss the congregation. A formal recessional hymn then followed. How else could they leave with a congregation still present, he was doubtless wondering! For the bishop the idea of the choir just getting up and ambling out was unthinkable! Such are the traditional processes of the C of E! But finally the choir was gone and we could proceed with ministry to people. It was a minor detail but it illustrates the difficulty.

SUPPRESSED SHOCK

In one cathedral, a man had come forward after we had invoked the Holy Spirit and by his violent heavings he was obviously struggling with some kind of inner emotional tension. Kneeling at the communion rails he was pulling at them so hard that I feared he might wrench out the whole rail. I gradually unloosed his grip and with the help of someone else held him down on the floor, while asking him what was happening? He said he felt strangely sick. I enquired whether he had ever had this particular feeling before and he said 'yes'. He said it was just once after a road accident. 'And what happened then?' I asked. 'Nothing,' he said. 'I just got back in the car and forgot all about it.' I prayed as I was talking to him and felt that the Lord was surfacing some suppressed shock that might well have caused something seriously detrimental to his physical health in the future, if it had not surfaced then. But this might well have been just guesswork. I never heard from him again so don't know how he got on.

IMPOTENT MAN

One weeknight near Pentecost Sunday, we were invited to minister in a cathedral, and the power of God came down. The noisy response took us all by surprise as chairs were crashing over backwards in a most uncathedral-like manner. I was embarrassed. Our team was soon fully occupied praying for people on the stone-slab floor. I remained at the front so that I could oversee this ministry. But a spontaneous queue began to form by people still on their feet wanting prayer. A young girl nearby suddenly rose up from the floor looking radiant. 'Oh!' she said, 'I always dreaded something like that happening to me but that was such an unexpected blessing!' 'Well!' I said, 'These anointings are given for a purpose so you had better help me to pray for this man here at the head of the queue.' She willingly obliged, and stood beside me as I asked the man what he wanted prayer for. He explained that he and his wife had been married seven years and they badly wanted a baby. He had had tests that revealed the problem was his. We prayed for him and asked the Holy Spirit to come to him in healing power. Meanwhile I was silently praying my usual desperate prayers to God. 'Lord, it will have to be your doing. I know I can't do anything. You do it please, Lord!'

More waiting! I looked over his shoulder at the crowds of people still wanting someone to pray for them. 'How long do I wait, Lord?' I asked. 'These others all want help too!' As I prayed the thought came to me: 'Ask him what's happening. You can't go wrong with that!' So I asked the man: 'What's happening?'

He looked straight back at me and said, 'Tingling!'

'Oh good!' I thought. 'Something is happening.' And I continued to bless whatever it was that God was doing and waited. Again I saw all the people standing patiently behind him waiting for prayer.

'Lord, what should I do now? How do I know when you have finished, Lord?' As I continued praying, I thought I should ask him again what was going on?

'What's happening now?' I whispered.

'Tingling!' he repeated.

'Where?' I asked.

'I can't tell you!' he said, glancing uneasily towards the young girl beside me.

'Praise the Lord!' I responded, 'God bless you and go in peace!'

We moved on to pray for the next and the next and the next as the rest of our team were doing. And I forgot all about the impotent man. It only came back to mind some eighteen months later when someone told me they had been at a baptism where the father had shared how he and his wife had waited all these years for their baby. He explained that the doctors had diagnosed the problem as being his, and how he had been to the cathedral for that renewal meeting the previous year, and been healed. This baby was certainly the proof of it! Glory be to God!

THE RELUCTANT HEALER!

We were at a renewal conference in Scotland. Again there was the local diocesan bishop present. The meeting room was not all that large and the place was packed so that the chairs were arranged right up to the small platform. There were probably sixty to eighty people present. After giving some teaching on the kingdom of God, which Paul said was not a matter of mere talk but of power (see 1 Corinthians 2:4), I invited the people to stand and the Holy Spirit to come. I waited and waited. I looked around the room. I could not invite people to come forward to be prayed for as there was no room between the front row and the platform that I was standing on. I could not ask them to come out into the aisles as there was only a small passageway down the centre of the meeting place. Uncertain of what to do next I prayed. Suddenly the thought came into my head again: 'Ask them what is happening.' So I did just that. Immediately a lady right under my nose at the front said: 'I can hear thudding in my ear!' I was encouraged. Faith was rising within me that God was about to do something for her. She happened to be deaf in her right ear. Not only was it obvious from a hearing aid she wore, but also I had been sitting beside her earlier when we were drinking tea and she had not laughed at any of my jokes! The faith level was so high that I thought I should invite someone else to be involved, and asked the man just across the aisle if he would stand up.

'I want you to pray for this lady,' I explained.

He looked at me appealingly: 'Please,' he said, 'Couldn't you use someone else? I have come here to learn.'

'I know,' I said, 'Everyone here has – and you are going to be learning now!'

I sensed God telling me that he was to put his finger in the lady's ear and speak healing to it. So I prayed that the Holy Spirit would 'fall on' her ear and then turned to the man and told him to stretch out his hand and do as I felt God was telling me to do.

'Would you put your finger in her right ear?' I said.

He looked quite aghast. 'Please,' he said, 'I can't do that. I don't go around poking my finger in some strange lady's ear!'

'Oh! I see.' I turned to the lady. 'Do you mind if this gentleman puts his finger in your ear?'

'That's quite all right!' she said.

'OK then', I replied, 'would you kindly remove your hearing aid?'

She readily complied and I turned to address the man before me: 'Please would you put your finger in her ear now.'

He did this with a somewhat limp finger while casting his eyes helplessly up to the ceiling as though he completely disowned it. 'No!' I said, 'You need to mean business. Insert your finger gently but firmly in the lady's ear and speak to it.'

Again, he gave that appealing look. 'Speak to it?' he queried. 'I have never spoken to an ear in my life. What do you mean?'

'Well!' I said, 'That's what Jesus did. He spoke to an ear and said "Ephphatha" meaning "Be opened!" So just speak to that ear in the name of Jesus and command it to open!'[4]

The man then did as I had asked, speaking to the woman's ear in the name of Jesus followed by the words: 'Be healed!', I waited for a moment or two more.

Then I said: 'Well, let's see how things are going,' and turning to the woman I asked her: 'How is your ear now?'

She replied, 'I can hear!' I have to say that I was surprised even though I felt God had given me sufficient faith to proceed vicariously through this other man.

'Wait a minute!' I said, 'You can hear through the good ear. Would you block the good ear with your left hand this time?'

She did just that. I spoke to her again and she assured all present that the hearing in her left ear had come back. That was a miracle! It was done in the name of Jesus through the power of the Holy Spirit for the Glory of God. He did it!

WHICH ONE IS IT?

We have had many invitations to Scandinavia. I can hardly remember the names of so many of those beautiful places or lovely people. One visit to Ostersund in Sweden still stands out in my memory. We were praying in an anteroom before a meeting. It was one of those occasions when the presence of the Lord was so strong that my interpreter fell to the floor under the power of the Holy Spirit almost immediately we prayed. This was rather awkward to say the least! With no interpreter we might have to cancel the meeting? Eventually he sat up but was so weak that we actually had to carry him into the meeting and dump him on a chair in the front row. Finally when it came to the talk he staggered to the front like a drunk and started interpreting for me. We had not been going two minutes when he was down on the floor again.

I appealed for another interpreter. This time a Bible college principal came forward. Before he started I suggested humorously that perhaps we should have another interpreter lined up just in case! I have no explanation for all this except that the power of the Lord was overwhelming that day and dozens of people were on the floor. There was real concern when a whole queue of people who had lined up for prayer suddenly toppled backwards on top of each other like dominoes. The lady at the end of the line went over too. She had had a major problem with her leg and seemed in real pain. I consulted with a doctor present who examined her – and told me he really did not think she was seriously hurt by the fall, just frightened. However, unbeknown to me, a nurse spoke to her a little later and feeling there really was something wrong she called the ambulance. Within 10 minutes, or so, some men arrived with a stretcher and stood gaping in the doorway. Eventually they were spotted by the nurse who approached them – 'Which one is it who needs our help?' they asked. There were bodies lying all over the place. It must have been a very perplexing sight if they were unused to such things! A team went to visit the old lady in hospital with a big bunch of flowers. Thankfully she was soon up and about and the next morning was back again at the meeting. She did not want to miss anything apparently! The doctor had been right – she had just been a bit frightened which was quite understandable, especially if it was the first time that she has seen God moving in such a powerful way.

KNEE IN AGONY

On another occasion we prayed for a man with a bad knee who did not appear to experience anything beneficial from the prayer, but fell to the floor, where we left him relaxing. However, to our horror the next person we prayed for fell straight down on top of him, right onto his bad knee. He sat up abruptly and nursed his knee in agony for a minute or two. I was quite worried. Suddenly he gasped: 'My God, the pain has all gone!' He stood up declaring he was healed, and I believed him. Mystery and glory! God did it again! And he does, again and again. It certainly gives people something to talk about to their friends and opens up hearts for the gospel. The kingdom of God is good news in so many ways!

We sometimes had to cast out demons. Of course we have authority from the Lord for a deliverance ministry in the name of Christ and we have seen some wonderful cases where people have been set free, but we always wanted to be sure it was a demon and that we didn't slime people by implying that their problem was demonic when it was not. The signs were usually pretty obvious – such as the son of a clergyman who sat on a tombstone and invoked the spirit of the dead from the church graveyard beneath him. We once had a case of a man being delivered of several demons and vomited when each one came out. His wife held a bucket ready and tipped the contents down the loo following his fits of vomiting. Finally he entered a state of peace and asked for his false teeth back. He had apparently vomited these out in the course of his being prayed for. Too late – they had already been flushed away by his wife. He left us liberated of both demons and dentures, very grateful for the former if not the latter. He has been abroad serving God faithfully on the mission field for many years since then.

Chapter 22

BLESSING WHAT GOD WAS DOING

More persons, on the whole, are humbugged by believing too little
than by believing too much
(PHINEAS T. BARNUM)

He is no fool who gives what he cannot keep to gain
what he cannot lose
(JIM ELLIOT – MISSIONARY MARTYR IN ECUADOR)

If you were arrested for being a Christian would there
be enough evidence to convict you?
(PRESIDENT JIMMY CARTER)

In 1985 Michael Harper, a prime mover in the UK renewal movement had asked me if we would be willing to host a SOMA[1] conference at St Andrew's? We were involved in a major internal re-building programme that included the whole sanctuary area of the church. Though it was rather an inconvenient time for such a residential conference, we felt it would be a privilege to be so involved and many members of our congregation gladly offered their homes for hospitality. A very interesting crowd from the UK and overseas turned up. We had some excellent international speakers and had times of ministry when our guests came forward so humbly and so hungrily to the communion rails for prayer. It was simply amazing to see how readily and easily our people moved amongst those leaders to pray for them. They had no idea who was who. In fact a number of future bishops, and a couple of archbishops were there too. Michael Harper was marvellous in keeping in touch with so many leaders across the world.

MAR THOMA BISHOP

One leader from the Mar Thoma Church in South India was Bishop Timotheos who created quite a stir in Chorleywood walking about in his pink cassock and turban-like headdress. He was lodging with Barry Kissell in a bedroom vacated by Barry's teenage daughter. Occasionally his hosts had to enter this room (to collect some clothes that their daughter needed) and would find the bishop there sitting cross legged in prayer or meditating over the Bible. Timotheos came up to me after one session and in his clipped, high-pitched voice, said: 'I want that!'

'What is "that" exactly?' I asked.

'That!' he murmured, pointing to someone falling on the floor by the communion rails under the power of the Holy Spirit.

'Why "that"?' I asked.

'Well, I need to take it back with me to my diocese in South India,' he explained.

I looked at him and felt very touched by the wonderful humility about him. He obviously wanted me to pray for him on the spot, but I did not feel it right just then. And I wanted to avoid giving any impression that I was a kind of Kathryn Kuhlman superstar person. In the first place we know we can never be superstars for God; in the second place people must see clearly that it is not us but God who does the healing or the miracles or who imparts whatever blessings he wills. In the third place we must constantly remind ourselves that God will not share his glory with anyone. We liked the way Wimber tried to keep himself out of the picture in such ministry. We had a number of experienced laity up at the rails praying very effectively for people. So I encouraged the bishop to go forward whenever an invitation was given, usually following a teaching session, but I never actually saw him again at the conference. There are so many situations like this and one rarely discovers what happens. But in this case it was different.

THE SURPRISES OF GOD

Soon after I was at another renewal conference[2] and met Timotheos there again – this time he was shaking quite visibly. He seemed pleased to see me. He told me how he had gone forward at Chorleywood but when they prayed for him the only thing he felt was an almost imperceptible tingle going down from the centre of his forehead and into his innermost being. Nothing more! He admitted that he had been disappointed.

Afterwards he was picked up from Chorleywood by Tom Abraham, a fellow South Indian, and a member of the Mar Thoma Church. Abraham and his wife Anna lived in Bishop's Stortford and Timotheos was staying with them between the conference in Chorleywood and the other one at Swanwick near Derby.

I did not know Mr Abraham, though apparently he often came to St Andrew's after that visit of Bishop Timotheos to their home, but some twelve years later I met Tom Abraham's son, Stan, for the first time. He told me of the remarkable work his parents had been involved in. He sent me a little tract written by his father. I include the gist of it in this account because it is closely linked with Bishop Timotheos and demonstrates how far-reaching and wonderfully unpredictable is the work of the Holy Spirit.

Their story started with his collecting the late Bishop Timotheos from the Chorleywood conference and taking him to their home in Bishop's Stortford. 'He stayed with us for the next four days',[3] he wrote, 'my wife Annamma and my children June and Stan were so delighted to have the bishop's presence in our home.' After the evening meal the bishop told them all about the conference at St Andrew's and led them in a time of worship and prayer before retiring to his bed. At about 2.30 am, the household was woken up by a most unusual rushing noise coming from the bishop's room. It sounded like 'the blowing of a violent wind' – akin to something experienced by the disciples in the upper room on the day of Pentecost. Tom's wife shook her husband to awaken him and asked what the noise could be. The children started calling from the adjoining rooms, 'Dad, what is happening?' Tom went up to the bishop's bedroom door and called out, asking if everything was OK? No answer! Suddenly, everything in the bishop's room went quiet. Tom returned to bed very puzzled.

BLOWING OF THE WIND
Then after a few minutes they heard the same noises again. Once more Tom called from outside the door asking the bishop if he

wanted anything? No answer! All quiet again. Yet a third time the sound began to shake the house. This time, Tom got up, and opened the door of the bishop's room and peered in. He saw the bishop kneeling in the middle of the floor totally absorbed in prayer. His hands were outstretched and lifted up. But he was also shaking all over. Tom felt loathe to intrude into such a holy moment and said no more. 'The bishop is praying,' he explained to his wife and they went back to sleep.

ANOINTED AND FILLED WITH THE HOLY SPIRIT

At 6.30 in the morning Tom's wife knocked at the bishop's door to take him a cup of tea. He explained to her what had happened during the night. Wave after wave of the Holy Spirit's power came upon him and filled him over and over again. Later on, at breakfast, he told them the full story.

There was just one little detail Tom does not mention in his account which Timotheos told me when I met him at Swanwick. It concerned the way the Lord had awakened him in the night and told him to get out of bed and pray. 'All right Lord!' he said, 'I'll give you ten minutes!' He then recounted how that from 2.30 am onwards the Holy Spirit had come upon him in such power that it made his body shake violently though he was otherwise unable to move – totally immersed in the presence and glory of God. 'The experience was so beautiful,' he told me. And ever since, whenever he started to read the Bible, worship or pray – or even hear the mention of the name of Jesus he found he would start shaking again. He held out his shaking hands towards me now. The thing is he asked: 'What am I going to do with all this power?' 'Well!' I said, 'I thought you told me you needed it for your diocese. I think you are meant to take it back there.' And he did just that.

Tom and his wife noticed a strange 'presence' about him. The Holy Spirit visited him in the same way during the next two nights at the same time – 2.30 am. Just before his time came to leave he asked Tom's daughter for a piece of paper and wrote the Abrahams' address, followed by a memorable comment about his visit:

'In the upper room where I stayed here I was greatly blessed by the Holy Spirit in a special way for the first time. On September 20th morning 2.30 to 6.00 am I experienced with great convulsion in every part of my body. The same experience repeated in the following nights at the same time Sept 21 and 22nd and 23 Sept 1985. MAY THE LORD'S NAME BE PRAISED!

Signed *B Timotheos* – 23 Sept 85

Easow Mar Timotheos, Episcopa,

Hermon Aramana, Adur, Kerala, South India.

TOM'S OWN STORY

Tom Abraham's own story illustrates the effect and extent of some of these extraordinary visitations. Although we have witnessed so many such anointings no-one at the time could ever guess their full effect over the longer term. We remained almost totally unaware as to how God processed the varied experiences of so many people in so many different lives, and in this case, as with others, we would probably never have known anything about Tom's experiences had I not spoken to Tom's son.

'Although I had had a Christian upbringing,' Tom wrote, 'I never knew God personally. I went to church regularly, had family prayer at home, went to Sunday School – and later became a Sunday School teacher. I prayed when I had problems but I found God remote. I never had the assurance that he ever heard my prayers. Coming to the UK, I was attracted by the western lifestyle. I began to indulge in worldly pleasures and became separated from God. I lost whatever faith I had and became an atheist. I pursued my career and qualified as a Chartered Management Accountant. I had a job with an oil company that enabled me to jet set around the world and indulge in all kinds of pleasures and drinking. Soon my lifestyle caught up with me. At the age of forty-one I was confined to hospital with a heart attack. There at the Intensive Care Unit where I lay, God showed me my past sinful life as on a screen. I asked for his forgiveness. He healed me and gave me a second lease of life.

'I changed my lifestyle and I soon found that I was slowly recovering my faith in God. I began to pray, read the Bible and go to church. But the guilt of my past life, the addictions I had, and the fear of man haunted me. I desperately wanted to be set free. I knew the hand of God was with me in saving my life, in spite of what I was. He kept on knocking at the door of my heart but I was reluctant to let him in. Finally, at the age of fifty, I opened my heart to him when the Bishop Mar Timotheos laid hands on me in our house.

'The next day, my wife and I had a life changing experience. The bishop had asked us to arrange for a prayer meeting in our home. I invited a few families who came in the evening. The bishop challenged us and asked whether Jesus was our Lord. His words "Jesus Christ is Lord" were as something new to me and they penetrated my soul like a sharp sword. Later on, when the bishop laid his shaking hands on my head and prayed for me, I felt a warmth coming over. I was convicted in my spirit and something happened within me. This was my conversion experience. My wife's heart was also stirred from that very morning onwards and experienced an inner change.' Their children had been converted two years before through a youth camp and had been praying for their parents. 'At a youth meeting organised at the Indian YMCA two days later, the bishop spoke again and prayed for those gathered. Many were touched by the Holy Spirit's presence and gave their lives to Jesus.'

'After the bishop's departure', wrote Tom, 'we sat in the upper room praying and meditating. Our children would bring the guitar and we sang and worshipped the Lord to our hearts' satisfaction. Then we would read the portions from *Every Day with Jesus*, look up the Bible texts, and meditate on them. We had such hunger and thirst to know God more. Then, all of us would pray that he would pour out his Spirit upon us. For six months, we met like this every day without fail. We also began to visit other Churches where there was evidence of life. We joined with other believers for fellowship and prayer. Simultaneously, we began to witness to others of what Jesus had done in our lives.

'In April of the following year, I was sent out to Las Vegas, USA for a business conference by the Corporation I worked for. This was a five day Information Systems and Technology conference which was attended by some 5,000 delegates. I was booked into the MGM Grand Hotel. The highlight was to be a ball on the last night. For that I put on my best suit and bow tie. At about 7.00 pm I went to the hotel grand ball room, passing many casino gambling stations on my way. There was music, food of various kinds, drinks, glamour and glitter and a great excitement in the air. I took a gin and tonic and started talking to a few colleagues – representatives from my Corporation . . . Usually, I enjoyed the party atmosphere very much and would stay on till the late hours. However, on this day, I was not relishing the food, the drink nor anything that was going on there. Suddenly I heard an inner voice asking me to go back to my room. This sounded very strange – but the voice repeated itself a second and a third time. By now I realised the Lord was speaking. I put my drink down, told my friends that I had to go to my room and left.

'Back in my room, I sensed a particular urge to read the Bible and pray. I took the Gideon's Bible from the hotel locker and read it, asking the Lord to reveal his heart to me. Then for no particular reason, I put on my pyjamas and went to bed. It was still only about 8.00 pm (my usual bedtime is 11.00 pm). My thoughts were focused on Jesus the Glorified One – and soon I fell asleep. By about 2.30 am someone was tapping on my shoulder and telling me to "wake up". The tapping and the voice "wake up" came a second time. No one was physically present in my room. I realised it must be the Lord speaking to me again so I responded, "What shall I do, Lord?" He said, "Open the Bible." I asked, "What shall I read, Lord?" He said, "Open the Bible." I reached out for the Bible and opened it at the second half of Psalm 50 and Psalm 51. By now, I was kneeling down and reading the Bible resting my elbows on the bed. Psalm 50 verse 22 particularly spoke to me. "Consider this, you who forget God, or I will tear you to pieces with none to rescue". Then I read Psalm 51 (the psalm of repentance) which King David wrote. The Lord wanted me to repent of all my sins like David. This was why he was showing me these two psalms.

'I read these psalms once and tears began to roll on my cheeks. I read them a second time. "Have mercy on me, O God, according to your unfailing love; according to your great compassion blot out my transgressions . . . ". By now I was bathing in my own tears. I asked the Lord for forgiveness. Immediately, the love of the Lord began to flow into me, pure, heavenly love. I began to shake all over. It was a beautiful experience . . . bathing in "liquid love", if there is such a thing. Then the Lord began to speak: "Son, all your sins are forgiven. I am calling you. So many are called but few are chosen. Go, in my name and preach the good news to all creation – over hills and mountains, over radio, television and everywhere" – the Holy Spirit bathing me in ecstatic emotions of love and peace all the while. Tears of joy and repentance came over in wave after wave till 6.00 am. You can call this experience baptism of the Spirit, filling or anointing, or whatever name you want to ascribe to it, but it left me with a new power and total exhilaration.

'The next day, I didn't want to know anything about the conference although I attended the rest of the sessions. In the afternoon, I caught the plane back to the UK. Nothing unusual happened on the plane. Back in my home, the Holy Spirit visited me at 2.30 am till 6.00 am for the next three days. He would come in with power as if I was plugged into electricity, kindling feelings of love, awe and reverence within me. His glory and warmth would begin to flow over me and he would speak the most wonderful things about Jesus, his death and resurrection, and about the kingdom of God. My wife was a witness to all these things lying in the same bed. Even now, the Holy Spirit visits unannounced on many days and reveals his heart of compassion and love urging me to pray and to intercede for the lost and to go in his name. Sometimes, when this experience happens, I get very tired but he revives me every time. Glory be to his Holy Presence!

'Some five months after the above experience, I was reading in my bed the book *Prison to Praise* by Merlyn Carruthers in which he describes how he began to speak in tongues. I simply closed the book and asked, "Lord, why am I not speaking in tongues?" The next moment, this new language was pouring out of my lips, praising God. I don't know what language I speak, whether it is an earthly or heavenly language. All I know is that every time I pray in tongues, I find the presence of God within me invoking feelings of love and praise for him. Also . . . whenever I can't find words to pray, I can start to pray in this new language. I simply concentrate my mind on the person or the situation for which I am praying or interceding and the Holy Spirit begins to pray within me. And I have the assurance within me that he has heard my prayer. I am able to stay immersed in his presence without being distracted by things around me. This is one of the gifts the Lord wants to give to everyone who asks. As Paul says[4] "anyone who speaks in a tongue does not speak to men but to God". And later he says, "I thank God that I speak in tongues more than all of you".

In the same tract, Anna Abraham, his wife, shares a similar story. Quite wonderful!

This couple, Tom and Anna Abraham have been revisiting India regularly now for the past twelve years, preaching, circulating Scriptures, tracts, books, tapes and videos and helping the poor, the widows, the homeless, the sick and the outcasts under the auspices of St Thomas' Mission.[5] And that much-loved saint, Bishop Timotheos, completed another ten years as a faithful leader of his diocese in South India until his death. His ministry made a tremendous impact on the church. Those who minister in the power of the Holy Spirit will often have no idea how far reaching for good the effect of such ministry may be. I have no idea who prayed for Timotheos at that SOMA conference, and probably whoever did would have no idea of the truly wonderful results of their prayer either.

Chapter 23

A CHURCH BUILT ON PROPHECY

*Scholars can interpret the past. It takes prophets to
interpret the present*
(A.W. TOZER)

*Surely the Lord God does nothing, without revealing his secret to his
servants the prophets*
(AMOS 3:7, RSV)

A priest is never happier than when he has a prophet to stone!
(DEAN W.R. INGE[1])

*He who receives a prophet because he is a prophet shall receive
a prophet's reward*
(WORDS OF JESUS, MATTHEW 10:41, RSV)

It was Saturday 6th May 1989. We had just flown into Kansas
City after leading three conferences arranged for us by the
Episcopal Renewal Ministries at centres across the USA. Our
small team consisted of Richard and Prue Bedwell, my wife Mary
and myself. It was late. It was hot. We were very tired. Mike
Bickle, the leader of the Kansas City Fellowship, had promised
there would be someone to meet us at the airport but as yet our
luggage had not appeared and we were not expecting to meet him
until we had got through the Customs check point.

I spent those waiting moments reflecting on how we had come
to be there of all places. 'This is crazy!' I thought. 'What we need
is a complete rest after those hectic conferences – not to start
meeting a whole lot more people!' My mind flitted back to 7th
November 1988, when our old friend John Wimber had come for

an overnight stay in our home following his visit to Edinburgh. John had asked us if we could also host a fellow speaker who was travelling with him. He introduced us when they arrived.

'Hi, David,' he drawled, 'Meet my friend Mike Bickle from Kansas City. I think you'll find he has an interesting story to share.'

LISTENING TO OUR VISITOR

Never a truer word! What Mike had to say blew my mind. He related an extraordinary tale about his experiences with some prophets whom he had first met in St Louis. He had originally treated them with very great suspicion, but in the course of double-checking he had finally come round to accepting many of their revelations as clearly from God. It was through these prophetic words that he had been led to Kansas City.

His story so intrigued me that I wrote it up in a little book called *Some Said It Thundered*.[2] I chose the title from the words in John's Gospel[3] where it records God speaking very audibly to the public about his Son Jesus and the people simply dismissing it as thunder! Like *Come Holy Spirit* the book got into the top ten of the *Church of England Newspaper*'s sales chart for several weeks.

A memorable example of this ministry was an occasion (not mentioned in my book) when I heard Paul Cain getting up to speak at a conference for about 3,000 people in California circa 1991. He pointed to a lady near the front, calling her by name and inviting her to stand. He then asked her, 'Do I know you?' And she replied, 'No!'

'Did I get your name right?'

'Yes,' she said. Then he pointed to the man on her right and called him by his Christian name. He asked the same questions adding, 'Are you married to each other?' The couple said they were.

Paul then addressed himself to the wife: 'Elizabeth,[4] I have this word for you. It's all over – it's all over? I see Jesus holding a little boy safe in his arms – I feel that must mean something significant for you. But it's all over! The Lord has everything in hand.' The couple just collapsed into their chairs sobbing while Paul carried on delivering prophecies to others. No one knew what those words were all about but clearly they were very meaningful to the couple concerned. A friend of ours went to find them afterwards and discovered that they were missionaries on leave from the Far East. Apparently, while out there, the husband, a very hard worker, had decided to go hunting on his day off. His wife insisted that he take their two boys with him. 'You are their father,' she said, 'and they need time to be with you. You really should take them!' It was a fair point, he conceded reluctantly, and took them.

During the day the elder boy shot his younger brother dead – it was a tragic accident. The father and elder brother returned home, weeping, with the body. Both the boy and the father blamed themselves for the tragedy. But the mother, on hearing the news, took all the blame upon herself. Was it not her fault for urging her husband against his will to take the boys hunting with him? They were all saying, 'If only . . . !' After a long compassionate leave in the US, the father and son had both worked through their initial grief and were ready to return. But the wife remained inconsolable. She had tried counselling but to no apparent avail. No one can work through another's grief for him or her. Each of us has to do it at our own pace. The husband had unfinished work to do on the mission field but could see no way of getting on with it. Someone suggested they go to this conference where Paul Cain was speaking and she reluctantly agreed. But when they got there she felt she could not even get out of the car. The husband implored her: 'Elizabeth, please! It's all over! It's all over!', the exact phrase which Paul Cain had used when he picked them out of the crowd – and adding the comforting words which obviously meant her younger son was safely cared for in the Lord's presence. They were both overwhelmed and very encouraged by Paul's words to them.

THE PROPHETS COME TO LONDON

Soon articles in Britain were beginning to appear concerning these prophets in Kansas City – and John Wimber was planning to bring some of them over to the UK. This confirmed my belief that the public would appreciate some background material about them. Hence I cobbled together *Some Said It Thundered*. Obviously the Kansas City Fellowship were on a learning curve but I did not seek to hide anything that I had seen or heard happening there. There are always dangers of some types of prophetic persons trying to set themselves up as some sort of authority figures for propagating new unbiblical teaching or seeking to enhance their own image in some way, or using their gift to control others improperly etc. But Mike Bickle seemed to be successfully handling all the usual kind of problems to do with prophecy. I included some of Mike's tips in my book. I sought to tell the stories of two prophets taken from tape recorded talks given by them at Kansas City. I was surprised to find how fiercely this book was criticised in the UK.

SAD STORY

Later, another matter sadly came to light. This was that Bob Jones, one of the prophets, was believed to have behaved improperly with a mother and daughter. He was immediately disciplined for it appropriately after the prophet admitted what he had done and repented of it. But without countenancing such behaviour in any way this did not make him a false prophet. King David also brought disgrace on the Lord's name by his adultery with Bathsheba and the ensuing 'murder' of her husband. Though he was seriously disciplined by God for it this did not make David a false prophet either. We are still edified as we meditate on David's psalms today, both in our churches and in our private devotions.

AT THE CROSSROADS

What had convinced me that God was definitely in this somewhere was the practical outworking of some of these prophecies in building up the church. One of them was about the crowded premises they used as their worship centre in Kansas City. In a vision Paul Cain had seen an intersection of two main roads and green grass on a site nearby that God had reserved for Bickle's rapidly expanding church. They searched the city high and low to find such a place, but in vain. Their growing congregation was being urgently pressed for more space but they still could not locate a suitable place – let alone anywhere like the one described by Paul Cain. Meanwhile Mike Bickle had a visit from a couple of Kansas City venture capitalists who were Christians. They had a business that had not been doing well and felt the Lord wanted them to offer the place to a Christian congregation. In their praying they were led to think of Mike and his church. Mike initially felt rather negative about their kind offer as he still believed the Lord had already indicated that he had a place especially chosen for them. Their new church was going to be on green grass near a main road intersection!

But the businessmen were pressing them. Sensing it would be ungracious to spurn their generous offer outright Mike reluctantly agreed to go and see the place with them. Arriving at some main crossroads they turned into a very large sports complex. The first thing that struck him about the spacious centre was the flooring. He could hardly believe his eyes. The whole area was covered wall to wall with artificial green grass – not surprising seeing it was originally built for athletics! Outside were the crossroads; inside was the green grass! This was quite obviously the place that God had reserved for them. By the time we arrived they had a regular attendance of about 1,500 at each of their Sunday services in this sports complex which they had by then renamed the Grandview Worship Center. They had also branched out into five other fellowships across Kansas City.[5]

I had found the story of their church intriguing from my first contact with Mike and suggested we might call in on them the next time we were in the States. Mike welcomed the idea and even offered us hospitality. So here we were at last.

THE FIRST SURPRISE

While still trying to spot our luggage on the airport conveyor belt we were suddenly hailed by Mike himself accompanied by two others whom we had never met before. Mike introduced us to the first man who was soon taking charge of our baggage. Then he introduced us to the other man in the party, a medium-sized, gentle, greyhaired man aged between fifty-five and sixty. 'David,' he said, 'I'd like you to meet Paul Cain.' After shaking hands Mike took me aside and explained *sotto voce* that this man was one of the prophets – though he never wanted to be addressed as such, preferring rather, like all the others at Mike's church to be thought of as a prophetic person.

We had the usual long haul from the airport to our destination. I was seated beside Paul in the minibus. Very relaxed, he had a good sense of humour and not surprisingly enjoyed puns and riddles as one might expect of a prophetic person.[6] Paul, like us, was also tired from his travels. We stopped before we reached our final destination to drop him off at his motel.

There being no need to make polite conversation to the now empty seat beside me, I found myself reflecting on prophets in the Christian church down the ages. In fact, I had been doing quite a lot of reading about them before leaving the UK. It would be true to say that I was definitely intrigued but still disposed to be suspicious. My religious upbringing had conditioned me that way. We had never personally met a 'prophet' and certainly did not want to be 'conned' by a false one?

PROPHETS OF THE PAST

History, I reflected, had not been very kind to the prophets. Anyone who has claim to be speaking a word from God, down from Old Testament days to the time of Montanus (c AD 170) and on to the present. Admittedly we only know about most of them through their critics.[7] All sorts of weird accusations had been laid to their charge across the ages – some cynically invented and others sinfully exaggerated. Nevertheless some of the charges, sadly, were only too true.

England has had her fill of strange prophets also. Those from the time of Oliver Cromwell (1599–1658) were especially remembered. That was supposed to be the age of the Spirit when any believer could receive a word from the Lord and speak it out! George Fox and his Quakers were a fast growing movement in the seventeenth century that thrived on prophecy. People trembled before Fox's piercing gaze and his powerful prognostications.

Many freelance prophets (some known popularly as the 'Ranters') appeared. Cromwell even appointed some of these as chaplains to the Army. On at least half a dozen occasions between 1647 and 1654 the Council meetings of the Protector himself were even interrupted by prophets, apparently without objection. However, while some of those prophets and prophetesses may have been genuine, there were others who were obviously not.

Certainly there was a lot of prophecy in the Bible and the promise of more prophets being sent[8] and teaching about the gift of prophecy for today is there too. Leaders needed to learn how people might become anointed for it, when it might be appropriate to utter a prophecy, how prophetic words should be given, and how they should be received and tested. All the church lacked was teaching about it; the gift could soon be revived as we welcomed the Holy Spirit to minister to us once more in this way – and that is exactly what has happened. No man did more than John Wimber to make the wider church aware of the gift of prophecy, and, like Mike Bickle, he taught us from his own hard experience how to use it constructively. It was John Wimber who had brought these Kansas City prophets over to the UK.

AN ANGEL ON THE ROOF

Soon after this, Mary and I were having a pub lunch with a missionary on leave – Elspeth Cole. She had had a dream/vision which she shared with us of an angel on the roof of St Andrew's Church. The angel had removed a number of tiles and was busy shovelling something from a sack into the building beneath as the congregation worshipped the Lord. In her dream Elspeth had peered through the hole in the roof and saw something like gold dust tumbling into the church. She asked the angel what it was? He replied that he was distributing gifts to the worshippers inside.

More intrigued than ever, Elspeth then began to study what was going on inside the building more closely. 'If that is the case,' she said, 'Why are the gifts just piling up in heaps in the aisles and the sanctuary?' The angel replied simply: 'Because God's people are not picking them up!'

God spoke to me clearly through Elspeth's dream. We had not given sufficient practical teaching about the gifts of the Spirit to the church, nor was it plain to people when it would be appropriate to give out a prophecy or use any of the other gifts in a church service. So we began teaching and allowed a limited time for prophecy and tongues to be exercised appropriately in our times of worship together in church.

Out of my visit to Kansas City I wrote a book called *Prophecy in the Local Church.*[9] The first part covered what we had been trying to learn about prophecy at St Andrew's and its practical outworkings. I hoped other churches wanting to get started might have found it helpful. The second half covered some of the history of prophecy in the wider church, highlighting the mistrust or dislike of it down the ages by the establishment. I also wrote of the misuse of prophecy by some of the prophets themselves that had brought the gift into disrepute – especially when they indulged in fixing dates and so on, which was usually a futile thing to do, especially concerning the promised Second Coming of Jesus Christ, bearing in mind Jesus' words just prior to his Ascension: 'It is not for you to know times or seasons which the Father has fixed by his own authority.[10]

Chapter 24

NEW WINE AND SOUL SURVIVOR

I being in the way, the Lord led me . . .
(ABRAHAM'S SERVANT – GENESIS 24:27B, KJV)

The Lord has helped us up to this point
(1 SAMUEL 7:12, NCV)

Honour the Lord with your substance . . . and your vats
will be bursting with wine
(PROVERBS 3:9,10, RSV)

John Wimber's visit to us in 1981 made such an impact on so many people that it seemed right to follow it up with regular Saturday night celebrations at St Andrew's to which anyone was welcome. These proved to be so popular that after a while we had nowhere to seat all the people. Eventually, we closed them down, and arranged for different centres in the south of England to host them.

After Wimber's conference at the Central Hall, Westminster, in 1984, organised by Duncan (when the building was packed out day after day), Mary and I received a kind note from John Mumford. John at that time was still a curate to Teddy Saunders at St Michael's, Chester Square. He asked us if we would be willing to come up to London and meet a number of younger clergy and their spouses who wanted to know more. We were not sure if we could help but it was a privilege to be invited, and to meet these couples there, some of whom have been close friends of ours ever since. John and Eleanor Mumford eventually pioneered the first Vineyard Fellowship in Britain and John is now the overseer of the whole movement in Britain. John and Ann Coles, who had just moved to St Barnabas, Woodside Park,

North Finchley, were also regulars at these rather select meetings, and were to become key people in the future development of New Wine. Another person there was Bruce Collins, still a curate in London, but soon to become rector of Christ Church, Roxeth, Harrow, and eventually a widely roving apostle and prophet for New Wine both at home and overseas.

Back at St Andrew's we were soon holding one-day conferences for leaders, which became very popular. These were held on a Wednesday or a Thursday from 10 am to 3.30 pm. By the time I was finishing at St Andrew's (1996) we were holding three one-day conferences in the spring and three more in the autumn. Neither Barry Kissell nor I spoke very much at these though I was always there to chair them. My aim was to get speakers from other churches in this country or from overseas who might have something relevant to contribute about renewal. I found we could easily cover return air-flights for overseas speakers from the love offerings given at the church door on these occasions. Hodder & Stoughton reproduced selected talks from one of those early days in a book called *What is the New Age?* We soon became accustomed to seeing a full church for these leaders meetings, with many members of our own congregation turning up to help us with the hosting – getting the rooms ready, setting up and manning the PA system, welcoming arrivals, handing out programmes and printed notices, assisting with the bookstalls, providing drinks, soups and eats. Our ministry team also got into action praying for the visiting leaders after each session. Our people loved it. Those were very encouraging times and many who attended became regular supporters of later New Wine projects. Often numbers attending these conferences overflowed from the church building to the church hall, and across to the back of the lounge. All this created an extraordinary buzz about the place.

FORMING A NEW TRUST
In the mid-1980s we set up the Kingdom Power Trust with a gift of £3,000 from John Wimber to help us in promoting the work of the Holy Spirit in church renewal, church planting, church growth and church leadership. This was generously supported by other churches. We also used the KPT to provide us with a house

for David Parker and his family whom we had brought over to Chorleywood from Kansas City to help with the renewal. David Parker exercised a most timely and inspiring teaching ministry across Britain and Europe for a couple of years before he returned to the USA to lead the Lancaster Vineyard in California.

Barry Kissell and I felt it would be good to get the leaders away for three or four days mid week, and booked the whole of the Swanwick Conference Centre in Derbyshire for a residential gathering in 1987. The Centre was soon full. We did all the teaching ourselves and we repeated this at another full residential conference at Swanwick the following year. During this time it became apparent that many clergy were longing to get something started in their own churches but their people did not know what they were talking about. We needed somewhere to gather leaders with their people into their own 'village' camps on one big showground. But wherever could we go?

NEW WINE IS BORN
Up to this point we never sat down and dreamed up a massive showground conference. With my total inability to organise anything, and also lack of time to do such a thing, the very idea was a joke. But New Wine was so obviously the next step from Swanwick. It was the most practical way to bring the greatest number of church families together – the leaders and their layfolk – for a week's residential gathering (camping and caravanning) to worship, to be inspired, to be taught and to have the opportunity to be prayed for individually if they so wished. The conference would be planned for all ages with lots of different workshops – eventually over forty-four in a week A showground offered the best facilities for camping and caravans and we were able to take the week previously used for a Christian Family Holiday Week (CFHW) at the Royal Bath and West Showground in Shepton Mallet. The CFHW folk generously gave us a lot of help on how to get started but they must have wondered how this motley crew from one local church would ever cope. Margaret Maynard, who had been my church office secretary, took over the planning for this with the help of willing volunteers, using her home as a working base that first year.

We gave the conference the name of New Wine '89[1] – a good biblical description for new life in the Spirit. We were delighted to have some 2,500 'punters'[2] at that first conference in 1989 and were able to repay the eight church councils who had each helped us by advancing £1,000 – the extra money needed to hire such well known grounds, the marquees and all the equipment for sound etc. Besides what we had made from the Swanwick conferences we could also fall back on some of the £3,000 'seed' money from John Wimber, which we had used to open the Kingdom Power Trust. This all helped us to get the whole project started up though it was soon necessary to form New Wine into a separate charity for tax purposes. We could never have managed without the wonderful support of St Andrew's who provided about 400 volunteers to help us staff the first ones and Margaret Knight, on our staff who with her husband George, organised the many healing and prayer ministry teams.

Actually we never intended keeping New Wine going long-term. As we prayed, we were always ready for God to close it down and point us in a new direction at any time.[3] The second year we bought a secondhand caravan, which we used as an office, parking it in the vicarage drive! After those first two hectic years, Margaret Maynard handed over the management to Joyce Wills, another member of the St Andrew's congregation, who had been involved in business for some years with her husband, and had very recently completed a degree in business management. She had just the gifts we needed to take things forward.

It was tremendous fun hosting these conferences with Barry Kissell for the first few years, and later with John Coles, to whom, after ten years of leading New Wine, I eventually handed over the leadership. At the same time Joyce handed over the management of the actual New Wine conferences at Shepton Mallet to Mark Melluish (originally brought up in St Andrew's and married to Lindsey, a St Andrew's girl) by then the vicar of a flourishing congregation in St Paul's Church, Ealing. We eventually moved our offices to Ealing at Mark's invitation. New Wine has been a very demanding venture but very worthwhile. There has been a lot of fun and a great deal of blessing and the usual challenging crises.

CRISES OF ALL SORTS

One year, the drains simply could not cope with the crowd and we had sewage leaking out from under the manhole covers and flowing across the road. Another time we didn't have enough loos. Then another year there was not enough hot water in the showers.

One year a number of teenagers, who had been dragged to the conference by Christian parents hoping it would do them some good, smashed up several tiers of seating in an open air stadium, which we had to replace. Fortunately we were insured. (Actually some of the youth, reluctantly peering inside one of the marquees full of young people, were amazed to see so many obviously happily involved. This led from time to time to their conversions or re-commitments!) There was a misunderstanding with the local vineyard growers who felt they should have had invitations to any conferences about wine – this meant clarifying that it was a family Christian conference for renewal! There were also complaints from neighbouring farmers about the decibel measurements of the beating drums. Parents complained, too, about the speed of cars driving round the Showground, and eventually, we had to forbid vehicles on the camp sites once the conference was started. One year we nearly got drowned out with a storm. One soaked couple actually went home but once there decided it was a lot more fun at New Wine and came back!

THE UPSIDE

That was the downside. It was the upside which made it all so worthwhile. There were so many testimonies of blessing. People were regularly being healed – even if not always immediately. One bricklayer had been out of work for months with agonising pain in his wrists. He discovered his wrists were clearly healed when he tried moving them about the next morning after prayer the previous night and found the movement free and painless. People were healed of whiplash, skiing problems, muscle problems, gynaecological problems, lumps on the breast, cysts on the ovaries, marriage problems – and lots of couples who could not conceive were prayed for and came back the next year with babies! There were people with hearing problems, seeing problems, sleeping problems, skin problems. I remember a man coming up just before the conference finished. We were exhausted but he simply begged us to pray for his twelve-year-old son at home who was covered with eczema. The next year he told me his son had been healed that very same day and had been kept completely clear the whole year through. Hundreds received fresh fillings of the Holy Spirit, fresh anointings, new callings and giftings. For all these blessings we gave (and still give) all the glory to God. Not everyone was healed; we never told people they were healed or told them to give up their medicines or stop seeing their doctor. If they were really well, the doctor would confirm it – usually. I did meet an architect once who had MS and felt certain he had been healed as a result of being prayed for. He saw his doctor who insisted he could not be healed. 'No one is ever healed of MS,' he said. So the architect asked if he still had any symptoms. The doctor examined him again thoroughly and admitted that he certainly did not seem to. 'Oh, well,' said the architect, 'I don't mind having MS if I have none of the symptoms!'

Supporting network

As a result of a number of prophecies a supporting network for New Wine via e-mail has gradually sprung up across the country. This has such potential for linking up leaders in different areas that an office has been set up to manage it under John Knight at St Barnabas, Woodside Park. Also, with extra help in leading St Barnabas, the vicar John Coles is now released more fully to encourage these network groups by visiting them personally and with teams. John Coles and Bruce Collins, ably supported by many others, have together also built up a very fruitful ministry in the UK through the running of small residential retreats for church leaders (the vision for these retreats was first given to the Rev Teddy and Margaret Saunders).

Meanwhile, separate New Wine regional and national conferences were springing up under different names across the UK and overseas. For three years now a small conference for some thirty regional leaders of the New Wine network has been meeting at the High Leigh Conference Centre. Over many years, Mary, with help from Pru and Richard Bedwell, has been running weekend retreats for some twenty to thirty layfolk four or five times a year.

Recently, New Wine has also restarted the leaders' residential conferences at Swanwick. They appear to meet a continuing need in the church. There are also well attended regional day conferences for ladies, for leaders in worship and training days for ministry in the gifts of the Holy Spirit.

ENTER PILAVACHI

Chris Lane, one of the staff, invited a young Greek Cypriot named Michael Pilavachi, then worshipping with us at St Andrew's, to join our youth leadership team. Few would have known how enterprising Michael had been for the Lord in a previous church. But he had left it feeling very wounded and needing time to heal.[4]

Michael Pilavachi, now well known as a gifted speaker across the world, had a remarkable talent with youth and when Chris left to plant a Vineyard – fired up to break new ground for the kingdom of God in St Albans – Michael took over the youth work at St Andrew's. He proved a great help to a large number of youth, including a youngster named Matt Redman, who has since become well known for his songs and music.

After Mike had eventually handed over the youth work in St Andrew's we kept him on staff in another role. Part of it was responsibility for arranging musicians to help lead the Sunday worship and Mike began to use young people, like Matt Redman, to do this. Mike came to see me in the summer of 1993 and said there were a number of young people he had nurtured who did not really fit into St Andrew's any more. I was rather hurt, thinking we were trying so hard to have something for everybody in the church, but he explained that he thought they really needed a challenge and that he should start a youth club in Watford and call it something like 'The Dreggs'! This didn't sound very 'Anglican' to me but Michael seemed very excited and asked me what I thought. I could not resist teasing him for a moment and told him that it sounded a pretty crazy idea! I watched his face drop! 'But it could just be God,' I added, quickly, 'So you had better have a go!' Michael's face relaxed into one of relief. Subsequent developments have proved that Mike was right – it really was God. Whilst still supporting him financially from St Andrew's, we released him to lead this strange new venture. Some twelve young people met with Mike to pray, worship together and plan how they might reach some of the many unchurched young people in Watford.

By the following January they started a drop-in club which they duly called 'The Dreggs'. This moved to various centres around Watford, according to the toleration level of different hoteliers. A few months later Mike started a monthly evening service on Sundays, in a school.

That work amongst youth later became a church for young people, picking up some enthusiastic older members along the way – the latter attending on the clear understanding that the worship was for a post modern generation! This church has since been called the Soul Survivor Fellowship and now meets in a large warehouse.

We also drew on KPT to help with Michael Pilavachi's accommodation. Later KPT helped towards the purchase of a warehouse for the local Soul Survivor Fellowship Church in Watford and later contributed quite considerably towards the purchase of Joshua House there. This can house some twenty-five young people who come for the various residential courses at the Soul Survivor Centre. (Soul Survivor, needing more facilities, are now buying a second warehouse alongside the first.)

YET ANOTHER TRUST!

Mike Pilavachi and Matt Redman led the youth section at New Wine. In 1993, Soul Survivor geared up for a special conference for young people led by Mike – which was carried for the first few years on the back of New Wine. This quickly took off.

The national and international side of Soul Survivor under Michael Pilavachi's leadership, which has grown up in parallel with the Watford Fellowship, operates through a separate trust now, under the chairmanship of Graham Cray, the Bishop of Maidstone. Between the local church and the mission, they have set up separate training courses for young people. These youngsters have gone out all over the UK (and the world) as missionaries, leaders in youth work, leaders in music for worship, and pioneers in social work. They have already provided a youth worker for another local Anglican church in Watford itself as well as for other UK churches. The local Soul Survivor Fellowship has also supplied help at the Watford New Hope Trust besides pioneering a new Pregnancy Crisis Centre in Watford.

A young man who, for some years, led one of those training courses at Soul Survivor, has been recommended by the Church of England Selection Board for training as a full time Anglican minister and is now finishing his time at Ridley Hall, Cambridge.

There are certainly aspects of the Soul Survivor set-up that I might constructively criticise, and I do. But on the other hand they are gathering a great crowd of committed young men and women for the worship and service of God – something that many other churches, for various reasons, find hard to achieve. The bishop has since seen fit to licence an ordained associate to assist Mike Pilavachi with this Watford congregation. The new chaplain and his wife (Bob and Ruth Yule) were originally converted and called to ordination while they were worshippers at St Andrew's, Chorleywood. They gave up a flourishing parish in Nottingham to come down and help with this pastoral oversight at Watford.

MESSAGE 2000

An extraordinary experiment recently grew out of a vision given to Andy Hawthorne, an energetic evangelist among the youth in Manchester, who had founded the World Wide Message Tribe. In the summer of 1999 Mike Pilavachi was given a matching vision. The idea was to mobilise a number of young people who attended the large annual Soul Survivor conferences at the Royal Bath and West Showground and get them up to Manchester in the year 2000 where central rallies, youth activities and creative social projects would be organised for helping the communities in Urban Priority Areas. Through 'servant' evangelism they would also persuade some of the local unchurched youth to attend the giant evening rallies in the centre. In spite of many labour pains in bringing this to birth, it proved a most effective and worthwhile experiment. I had to be at our New Wine conference during that time and could not be in two places at once! My own minor commitment was simply that of a trustee of Soul Survivor with my house on the line (like that of the other trustees) as costs expanded to well over a £1,000,000 – all eventually covered by generous donations.

This project's usefulness was highlighted by William Hague MP, then the leader of HM Opposition, who made very positive reference to this imaginative venture in his address to the Charities Aid Foundation. He stressed that faith-based groups created great potential. Charities should see them as valuable local assets and resources for vision, sacrifice and energy in the recreation of their communities, adding: 'A project's religious character is often the reason for the success of that project. When we make faith-based communities dilute their religious ethos to apply for grants, we endanger these energetic projects.'

The Soul Survivor *Message 2000* project is a good example of religious conviction moving people to social action. 11,000 young people spent ten days at *Message 2000*; a Christian event that has changed many lives in and around Manchester for good. Each afternoon they had gone out in teams of twenty-five to serve the various communities. Some staffed play schemes for children, many helped old people practically, digging, weeding and exterior and interior decorating; lending a hand to local residents in their homes, gardens and communities; cutting the grass in play areas.

The superintendent of the Greater Manchester Police Force noted that, for the first time in his experience there had been no reported crime in the deprived areas visited by *Message 2000* volunteers during the time they worked there. He wished they could have stayed in the area permanently! A book about this inspiring project, which must have been about the largest Christian venture of its kind ever in the UK, has been published under the title of *The Urban Adventure*.[5]

Among other things, the local Soul Survivor Fellowship in Watford has continued to organise visits to a deprived housing estate locally with teams they called the 'Noise'. They generally plan to clean up a depressed area, cut grass and hedges and build up contacts – much as they did in Manchester. Similar experiments were repeated one weekend in 2001 by some 250 youth groups across the country, who had networked with Soul Survivor and caught their vision for doing a comparable kind of thing in their own town or city. Even in Chorleywood the local youth groups found there was room for cleaning up to be done in the community! The Three Rivers council supplied all the equipment needed for that weekend and the young people provided the workforce. The local MP even came over to encourage the combined Chorleywood church groups in what they were doing.

Soul Survivor and its former 'parent' New Wine have proved a great encouragement to many churches and both are examples of the way God has led through his Holy Spirit step by step.

Soul Survivor plans to combine with a number of London churches and repeat what happened at Manchester in 2004 – but dividing up into different regions around the capital to involve as many churches as possible to reach as many young people as possible.

Chapter 25

IS THIS REVIVAL?

The word 'revival' has been used over the centuries to describe anything
from a church trebling in size in a year to the conversions of a million
people across a nation
(DR PATRICK DIXON)

I would describe what is happening to us now as a time of refreshment
for the church
(PREBENDARY SANDY MILLAR, COMMENTING IN 1994 ON A REMARKABLE
MOVEMENT OF GOD AT AND OUT OF
HOLY TRINITY, BROMPTON)

We all have our own ideas as to what revival is. Some envisage a
kind of Wesleyan revival that spreads widely across the nation
and deeply into the working classes. Others recall local revivals in
a town or a particular church. Whatever the form it takes I would
welcome and want to foster any such new life in Christ whether it
be personal, local or national. I remember what that local revival
in Lowestoft in 1921 had meant to my father. We need to keep
praying for that spark of the Holy Spirit, prepare for it and move
with it whenever it comes. We had experienced it personally and
in some of our churches in Latin America, and again in 1981 after
John Wimber's visit and following, but however should or could
we keep that fire burning?

I once met a man who had seen God, the Holy Spirit, working
in a wonderful way in the UK. He was interested in going out to
Latin America and I could not help querying whether it was right
for him to leave when he had had such a remarkable ministry in
this country. I suggested he might do better to stay and get a
similar model church started in another UK parish! He looked at
me blankly and said he had no assurance that he could. I knew

what he meant. It is such a sovereign work of God – but God honours the weakness and humility that I saw in that man.

Preaching at St Andrew's on the subject of revival one Sunday night in February 1994, I referred back to an awakening at Hamilton, near Toronto, Canada, in 1857 under Walter and Pheobe Palmer. Reports of this sparked off a powerful movement of God in a large daily prayer meeting in New York, which spread across to Boston, Chicago, and then Washington in 1858. I happened to remark, incidentally, that something significant was happening very near Toronto again which would need to be watched. I did not realise immediately how prophetic those words were. Even as I spoke I felt a nudge from the Lord telling me that I had better be ready to get over there to see for myself as soon as possible. I told Mary but she did not seem too interested just then. It took a couple of months before I could get there. I went with Peter Wilson, a greatly respected member of St Andrew's.

EMBARRASSING PUBLICITY

We met a lot of leaders at Toronto who, like myself, had found it helpful to get away from their people, just to take the time to be open to the Holy Spirit of Jesus Christ in a relaxed environment where there was no expectation being put upon them. I soon found myself being powerfully affected. God's Spirit was manifestly moving people around me when I was suddenly struck and let out a roar. I had no real idea of what exactly was happening to me – except I gradually sensed a whole new level of anointing and authority. I was not too alarmed about the noise I had made because I had previously noted from John's Gospel, chapter 11, that even Jesus groaned in the spirit – the Greek there is *embrimaomai* which could be translated: 'He snorted like a horse'.

Good church people would be quite horrified to think that Jesus ever snorted like a horse – 'deeply moved' sounds so much more respectable and nicer. Without wanting to sound messianic I could certainly say I felt 'deeply moved in the Spirit' at that point and I was delighted and excited by it. But I had no intention of recounting this very personal experience back in the UK. Some who heard me might think that they ought to 'snort' or 'roar' or something as a kind of proof that they had experienced God in a significant way, and that if they didn't do these things they could not really believe they had been touched by the Holy Spirit – a totally erroneous assumption of course. But quite probably some would respond inappropriately in that way. Such mistaken ideas need gently correcting and directing.

SUNDAY TELEGRAPH REVIEW

Of course I told Mary when I arrived home (who by now could not wait to get out to Toronto). She also felt that it would be better for me not to talk about the details of my personal experience to anyone – and I didn't. But a news reporter from the *Sunday Telegraph* who had visited Toronto to cover this revival identified me by name in his full page article, as an Anglican bishop who had 'had been down on the floor roaring like a lion'. Oh dear! Reading it like that in cold blood was highly embarrassing to say the least. But then the Lord had already told me not to be concerned about reputation! It was no good worrying about it now. We just had to get on with trying to follow where we sensed the Holy Spirit was leading us.

The day I arrived back I called the parish office and asked them to phone the home group leaders: 'Tell them I want to meet any of their groups who can come and to report back about our visit to Toronto,' I said. Arriving at the church that night I was absolutely flabbergasted to find the place already packed. And we had an amazing time with God moving powerfully among us. In the months that followed, there were many wonderful testimonies from people affected in extraordinary ways by the ministry emanating from Toronto. It affected churches such as Holy Trinity, Brompton, St Thomas' Crooks, Sheffield, St Barnabas, Woodside Park and our own St Andrew's in Chorleywood and many other churches besides.

ENTER ELEANOR MUMFORD

I had no sooner returned from Toronto than the *Church of England Newspaper* reported a remarkable meeting. On 29th May, Eleanor Mumford, who had just come back from Toronto, had given a very inspiring talk at Holy Trinity Church, Brompton, London. God moved manifestly, both immediately following that Sunday talk and for many days and months to come. The news spread fast. Curiously a little time previously Bob Jones, when still at Kansas City, had prophesied a coming revival with news of it spreading round the world via taped recordings – and that's exactly what began to happen with Eleanor's tape. Eleanor was the wife of John Mumford, the Anglican clergyman who had once invited Mary and I to meet with some younger clergy couples regularly at St Michael's, Chester Square. Because we knew them, we were very interested in Eleanor's visit to Holy Trinity, Brompton.

Some who had heard her there came to St Andrew's for one of our regular leaders' gatherings for the wider church. Some of the visitors from round about had also been to us following my own report back from Toronto. There were between 300–400 present in St Andrew's that day. The subject was Charismatic Renewal and Social Action.[1] It was an important theme that we needed to address, but there were many there who wanted to know more about 'Toronto'. After the two morning sessions. I tactfully suggested to our speaker that recent happenings in Holy Trinity, Brompton, had been reported on the front page of the *Church of England Newspaper* and I felt from feed-back received during lunch that it was important not to let it pass without some comment at this meeting. He graciously agreed to this unexpected change of direction in our programme.

STRANGE MOVEMENTS

Not having come particularly prepared to address so many church leaders, I simply read out some of the *CEN* front page report, commenting ad lib as I went along. I began to notice the Holy Spirit moving strangely on people all over the place. I had still not specifically prayed for any particular visitation on ourselves. At this stage I was just updating the leaders on what was happening at Toronto (where I said I had been so recently blessed myself) and now what seemed to be happening at HTB. In order to check out what the Holy Spirit appeared to be doing among us I invited some of those under these extraordinary anointings to come up to the front. Some were shaking; some seemed to be jumping up and down as though on pogo sticks; some were running on the spot; some were laughing. I called one or two of them up to the platform and asked them to tell us what they thought was happening? Since we were filming the meeting, we still had the cameras running so we had a remarkable record of that time. Although we do not usually film this sort of thing I thought a spontaneous video like this could be useful for future serious discussion on such phenomenon. It was soon in great demand under the title *Is This Revival?* – serving as a small complement to the major work of Dr David Lewis, a social anthropologist, who had published an analysis of the healing ministry initiated among us by John Wimber: *Healing: Fiction, Fantasy or Fact?*[2]

A later video from Toronto called *Go Inside The Toronto Blessing* contributed to the same end, as did a further positive sociological study on the beneficial effects of the Toronto Blessing by a North American Christian sociologist Dr Margaret Poloma.

RECURRING PHENOMENA

Similar phenomena, with a few variations, seem to have recurred at almost all times of spiritual revival – but then strange things also happened to many people in the Bible. I am thinking of a particular manifestation in the case of a prophet like Daniel when he crawled about on his hands and knees after a revelation from God, and in a general way when people were thought to be drunk at Pentecost. But again and again in history these visitations and the accompanying phenomenology have taken the church by surprise. There is an accumulation – a corpus of received wisdom in so many areas of church life – but strangely there is so little readily available to help us in our understanding of what might really be going on beneath the surface in these moves of the Holy Spirit – both their immediate impact and their long-term benefits, apart from a study by Herbert Thurston SJ[3] dealing with strange phenomena among some individuals in the Catholic traditions of the church.

The accounts of those being interviewed that afternoon were certainly captivating, even amusing, to say the least. Then the Spirit of God began to move more and more extensively across St Andrew's. I soon spotted some of our Lutheran friends – clergy from Bergen, with us on a ten-day retreat, who were by now spread-eagled corpse-like on the floor. People were collapsing everywhere. It was quite extraordinary. A couple of mothers had to leave early to pick up their children from school in London. I watched them crawling out of the church, out of the main door – still on their hands and knees. They crossed the car park to their cars where, once inside, they told me later, they had managed to 'sober' up. Such remarkable behaviour would most certainly have been commented on under 'normal' circumstances, but no one else seemed surprised that day!

CATCHING THE FIRE

We began to experience regularly what was happening in Toronto and HTB, as did many other churches across the UK and the world. We were not about to turn St Andrew's into a revival centre, but we were compelled to start a regular Thursday night 'Catch the Fire' meeting following our first night back from Toronto. These became the source of great blessing to many people. After that first 'Catch the Fire', Noonie Kissell had a dream of a huge queue of people leading from the St Andrew's church door, across the car park and right down the drive into the road below. The next week, when I came out of the vicarage for the meeting there was this enormous queue stretching from the church door, right across the car park and down to the road below, just as she had seen it in her vision! This was a new phase of quite extraordinary times and there were some extraordinary stories resulting from it. We had one lady who was the head teacher of a very well run and popular secondary school. She, and some of her staff also, worshipped at St Andrew's. I often saw her on the floor at the front of the church on Thursday nights following that outpouring and she would usually be groaning quite loudly!

This never worried me because I found that one could easily quieten things without quenching the Spirit. I would bend down and say to whoever it was, 'I can see that God is blessing you and I want to bless whatever God is doing for you so don't move. Just lay there and keep receiving. But you may not be aware that you are making rather a lot of noise and it is actually disturbing one or two people. It is also making it difficult to pray for the others around you.' I invariably found that they immediately quietened down having been blissfully unaware of the amount of noise they were making, and they were certainly not out of control.

But back to our head teacher! Jane came to me after one of those evening meetings saying: 'That's it! I am resigning my job, selling my house and car and going off to the CMS training college in Birmingham to prepare for a future ministry in Pakistan for the Lord!'

'How nice and how come?' I quizzed her.

'Well!' she said, 'In my student days I felt called to Pakistan but somehow I got off course. I could never see how I was ever going to obey that early call with all my increasing responsibilities. But now the Lord has re-commissioned me to go and train school teachers out there.' She moved off to the Church Missionary Society college to prepare for her new work in Pakistan where she went the next year to serve her first three years. Before fully completing her second term she was recalled by the CMS, because of possible reactions against UK Christian leaders, while the war continued against Muslim terrorists in Afghanistan.

I often think how I would probably have responded had Jane come to me to talk about going off to the mission field at her stage in life. I would probably have tried to dissuade her on the grounds that she was doing a wonderful job where she was, and that she was one of the most respected head teachers in our area, and should not even dream of packing it in to go abroad. I would have sympathised with her over the heavy responsibilities of her job and apologised for not doing enough to support her and asked her how we could support her better. But God had his plan and she had heard his voice. She felt totally fulfilled and happy in that new role on the mission field. There is no more fulfilling place to be than in the centre of what one believes to be the will of God.

Once started, we continued these 'Catch the Fire' meetings every Thursday night – crowded events that continued until I retired in July 1996. They helped to encourage folk from other churches – people who wanted to remain in their own places of worship on Sundays. We had a continuous stream of interesting speakers at those meetings to share how their lives had been impacted by the Holy Spirit. The meetings usually included some biblical teaching touching some area of renewal.

MORE AND MORE SURPRISES

One clergyman (and his wife) who spoke at that Thursday night gathering had come from a central church background in Liverpool to an ecumenical church in Bedfordshire where once a month the music was led by a charismatic group. When a friend heard he was going to this church he asked him how he would cope with the charismatics there and in reply he asked: 'What are they?' The clergyman's wife, still an unbeliever at that time, never went with her husband to this church. After a while one of the charismatic music group invited this clergyman to accompany him to what was then the Airport Vineyard in Toronto. He generously offered to pay for both his return airfare and a week's hotel accommodation there, with the only request that if he accepted he would go to a couple of meetings at the Airport Vineyard. He accepted, though his wife warned him not to come home *changed* in anyway. He attended the meetings on the first two evenings but did not think much of them. He spent half the second one on the floor not quite understanding what was happening to him. Arriving home at the airport, his wife met him and her first comment was 'Something's happened to you!' Though he flatly denied it she was so cross she would not talk to him for several days. Finally she asked him to pray for her. This amazed him since she had never asked him to do anything like that before. She wanted him to pray for her in the church. He thought of taking her up to the communion rails at the front. But she walked round the church first and when she came to the exact spot where his charismatic benefactor used to stand to lead the music – something, of course, that she was completely unaware of – she suggested he prayed for her there. He did this but she seemed disappointed. Worse still she felt very weak and unwell – in fact for days after she had to crawl around the house on her hands and knees unable to attend to her normal household duties. One day still crawling she noticed a book on the bottom shelf of her husband's bookcase called *Born Again* by Chuck Colson.[4] She pulled it out and started reading it. The miracle happened. She became born again and has since become a dynamic helper in her husband's church. One never ceases to be amazed by the ways of God!

DISILLUSIONED MISSIONARY

On one occasion, I met a lady who had invited her missionary brother from East Africa to come over to the revival in Toronto at her expense when she discovered that he was becoming disillusioned with his missionary work there. He came for two weeks and was prayed for many times but went home even more disillusioned. He felt he had asked and not received and had in fact experienced nothing. A few weeks after his return he was approached by someone feeling unwell. 'You have been to Toronto,' she said, 'Would you please lay hands on me and pray?' Put that way he felt he could not refuse and as soon as he prayed, the lady went straight down Toronto-style on the floor. An observer standing by stepped forward and begged him to do the same for her. She went down on the floor too. Another then asked for prayer and the same thing happened. That was God! Soon the news began to spread and it became a turning point in his ministry.

I gladly share these stories because they have always amazed and inspired me – truly 'Thine [O Lord] is the kingdom, and the power, and the glory'.[5]

Seeing so many of those men and women in all their faults, frailties and frustrations, just weeping before the Lord as the Spirit of God came on them, was a most moving and unforgettable experience. Watching the outworking in different lives following these anointings was even more wonderful to observe.

INCREASING INVITATIONS OUT

Ever since John Wimber's first visit in 1981 and even more frequently after the starting of New Wine, and then following our fresh experiences at Toronto, Mary and I have received an increasing number of invitations from both home and abroad. This caused some major heart-searchings: 'Who were we to go?' and 'Could we spare the time?' Such were the questions we asked ourselves. But we could never forget how we had so valued visits of encouragement from others over the years.

Our diaries reveal the extent of the visits – indeed right across the world. On each overseas trip we usually went to about three different places, spending about three days running a conference in each area. In this way the total travelling costs could be shared between the different centres. In the hundreds of flights we made, we always turned left for the cheapest seats when we entered the plane – except for two occasions when for some reason we were given better accommodation by the airline. The memories, all fascinating for us, are too repetitious to record here.

Our objective was 'to equip the saints for the work of the ministry' so that they might also be encouraged, envisioned and empowered to go out to others both at home and overseas. And so they did in many churches.

In our talks we simply shared what we were actually teaching and trying to do at home. That was what the church leaders who invited us had asked for. Churches are crying out for practical training and that was our speciality. They can get plenty of the theory from books. Most Christians believe in healing – its biblical – (that's the A part) and they see the good effects from prayer for healing, (that's the D part), but how does one get from A to D? What about parts B and C? People often don't know who to pray for, how to go on, and when to stop – especially if the person does not appear to be healed. It was the same with prophecy or any other gifts – and leadership and church planting – getting from A to D.

THE PLACE OF FRIENDSHIP

We were taught at college that clergy should not have close friends in the parish. Obviously this should never be allowed to distort the leader's judgement, and friendship must never seem to be exclusive – but close friendships within the parish can be a bonus. Brian and Gill Skinner were long-term friends. Peter Maskrey, a churchwarden at St Andrew's, who later joined the staff, has helped us enormously as a loyal trustee for New Wine and Soul Survivor International, with endless work, wisdom and encouragement. Alan Tweedie, our full-time unpaid administrator, already mentioned, became a great friend to us. So did Richard and Prue Bedwell. Richard's family business in Slough had been taken over and we were able to use his administrative and practical gifts on the staff. He was a great completer/finisher. They moved to Chorleywood from their lovely home in nearby

Gerrards Cross. Richard was soon heading up the counselling ministry in St Andrew's. He volunteered to take on the administration for all our overseas engagements, arranged the programmes, the transport and the flights, and usually he and Prue would accompany Mary and myself – to model up front the way we 'do' healing, to help in praying for people, and to oversee any programme adjustments, book sales, accommodation and internal travel arrangements. They were very generous, patient and understanding. Richard checked out any new area and knew all the best places to visit for sightseeing or shopping. Due to the hectic pace, there were times when I was not quite sure where I was.

We were once visiting the West of England – a different town each night. I started a meeting by saying how good it was to be in Exeter and there were roars of laughter! I was startled to learn we were in Taunton!

Richard would say: 'Pick you up tomorrow morning at 7 am! Pack your case, bring your notes and don't forget your passport!' Once we arrived at the airport early one morning for a flight to New Zealand and Richard asked me for my US visa that was in my old passport. I had not brought it with me.

'I thought we were going to New Zealand?' I said, puzzled.

'Yes we are,' he replied.

'Well, don't we go east via Singapore?'

'No! We are going west via Los Angeles!'

Oh well! No panic! Life is full of surprises! We found we could get some kind of 'pink slip' at the airport in place of a visa. Not such a disaster after all!

Richard has now 'managed' us for twenty years. Prue, being a great friend of Mary's, has also worked with her in regular conferences on inner healing. They have also shared the leadership (with Mary) of small weekend retreats. Until recently these were held in a nunnery at Windsor.

Mary often gets exciting invitations from abroad with a thoughtful PS: 'Do bring your husband if he would like to come for the ride!' But when she gets her separate invitations I usually accept others which do not involve her so that we can minimise our times apart. Richard often comes with me to oversee things and helps by giving talks in my programme; Prue goes with Mary and assists her, likewise. We have so enjoyed the teamwork.

TIME OUT OF THE PARISH

When we first left Chile I imagined that this would be the end of our travelling days overseas. Since I don't particularly like flying I was not really sorry about that. Earning only a vicar's salary it seemed unlikely I would ever travel extensively again. But now we suddenly began travelling overseas once more. With Richard on the spot to manage these trips we experienced the minimum distraction from parish responsibilities. In describing something of the ministry we embarked upon and the places we visited outside the parish it may give the impression that we were away too much, but over the next fifteen years until retirement, we rarely had more than eight Sundays away during any one year. We were entitled to eight weeks' holiday a year and took out six of those Sundays for ministry trips away – and just occasionally one extra – and then two Sundays for holidays. These breaks for ministry abroad were like a holiday for us really, often including a week in California with the Wimbers. I made a few shorter trips away inside the week. Several times I flew in early on a Sunday morning from Ireland or Europe etc. On those Sundays I would be present morning and evening in St Andrew's to lead but rarely to preach. With so much time taken up with 'mission overseas', I resented the idea of more time away for holidays, but Mary rightly insisted that we must have a clear two weeks per year of real relaxation (which for her meant guaranteed sunshine). Anderly Hardy (Mary's great and most generous friend) has often paid for us to revisit Chile in style and go to resorts we could never have afforded as missionaries there. One year she even invited us to accompany her on a luxury yacht, visiting the different Gallapagos Islands. We also went to Quito, Ecuador, and have visited Argentina and the Norwegian fjords on another luxury liner. On different occasions, we have visited Turkish and Greek mainland resorts, and Greek islands with Richard and Prue. We have travelled to the Holy Land four times, and have seen many places visited by St Paul and St John – including Patmos, where I was most profoundly impacted. The thought that St John the

Divine might actually have had his revelations in the traditional cave where he is remembered, moved me to light a candle there to mark that unforgettable visit.

TV FILMING AT NEW WINE

We had our usual New Wine conferences in Somerset again following Toronto and a female reporter asked to come and do a TV news item on the 'Toronto Blessing'. To protect the privacy of individuals, we forbade any intrusive filming in the meetings but eager to take whatever pictures they could, they lost no time filming people coming out from the conference centre. The trouble is, in my experience, the media's main objective is to create a visual image guaranteed to provoke a strong reaction of some kind. Consequently, footage may be edited in a way that totally misrepresents what has actually taken place.

Without asking my permission, selected cuttings from our video *Is This Revival?* were spliced in with a lot of strange goings-on from meetings we would have had nothing to do with. There were shots from other places of practices that would never have been countenanced either at St Andrew's, New Wine, or at Toronto – pictures showing gross manipulation such as people being pushed over (something we are totally against), and people being hyped up and shouted at. These were the kind of abuses we abhorred and sought meticulously to avoid while trying not to quench the Holy Spirit in any way. This final mishmash was played over on TV at least five or six times on one day as a news item and later in a separate, highly publicised, TV programme. We took the media to task for false representation and failure to pay royalties etc. They eventually paid up and we put the money into our Kingdom Power Trust – but there was no way to repair the damage done.

TALKING OF THE MEDIA

One of the interesting results of having a certain kind of notoriety, was that we made contact with some quite surprising characters, both in the media and in the church, who came incognito for counsel and prayer. We continued receiving pressing requests from the media wanting to come with their TV cameras, which in general we turned down but we did allow one other televised morning service that went out direct to the public without editing. It seemed to go well but having TV cameras present completely changed the ethos of our worship and robbed the service of some of the spontaneity we had come to value so highly. We often did interviews for Radio 4, the *Sunday* programme, but that had come to be so depressing that it was hard to muster the enthusiasm necessary to make time for such interviews – even if the BBC did pay for the taxi ride to and fro. I once had a fascinating – and quite extensive – recorded interview with the late Brian Redhead of the *Today* programme. He was collecting material for a book he was writing but unfortunately he died before its completion. Not all my feelings about the media are critical but I do feel they attempt to coerce people into saying things they never intended, rather than seeking truth.

Mike Wooldridge, who later became the official BBC reporter for India, visited us in Chorleywood for an interview which went out on their World Service. We did a number of interviews for TV, radio and the press overseas. Also some of our videos have been used in the religious programmes on Sky Television.

Once, in Bath, Ohio, Richard told me that there was a reporter present who had problems with all that was happening at our conference as she saw how people were being touched by the Holy Spirit. But Richard also said I would have to keep any interview very short because we needed to get off to the airport almost immediately. I talked to her briefly telling her I had a plane to catch but tried to answer one or two of her questions as she stood before us, pen poised and notebook in hand. Then I felt I ought to just say a prayer for her before leaving. She agreed. The next second I was amazed to see this rather cynical young woman laid out on the floor. I had to leave her there with friends.

THE CHURCH HESITANT

Ysenda Maxtone Graham came once and claimed later that I laid my hand on her head and spoke to her in a tongue after the evening service. I remember praying for her because she was so concerned about what was happening to our traditional churches in rural areas where they had no clergy – and I found it hard to encourage her about the future of some of those churches, with the way things were currently going. I would probably have prayed for her in tongues under my breath, as I put my hand on her head, but it would have been done almost imperceptibly. I often prayed for people in tongues when I was unsure of what the Lord wanted me to pray for. I have never spoken directly to someone else in an unknown tongue in my life. It was intriguing to read her comment about our meeting in her book *The Church Hesitant*.[6] It ran: 'It sounded African and holy. He did it in a spirit of selfless prayerfulness and I didn't ask him "What did that mean?" because it would have broken the benign spell which the Holy Spirit had cast!' I took this rather peculiar observation to be well meant. Another religious affairs reporter, however, writing for a respectable daily newspaper, showed up at an evening service. Finding nothing exceptional to write about, he invented the story of a genuine disabled person being prayed for after the service, at the front of the church. He said evil spirits were being cast out of him. A deliberate misrepresentation of what was happening. Although there is a place for a deliverance ministry, our prayer teams were very careful, for good pastoral reasons, never to assume that someone's problem was demonic. It might even be possible for someone to be disabled through demonisation but that is the last assumption anyone on our team would have made. And if they had finally come to that conclusion they would have referred it to one of the staff to deal with at an appropriate time later on. It was just one more case of the media's apparent willingness to invent any story to make sensational copy.

TAKING RISKS

But in general I was prepared to take the risk of talking to reporters rather than seeming to have something to hide – which was certainly not the case. I would far rather be vulnerable and open to God in every way that I could be, than to be clever and closed and miss it. I would never have exchanged the ministry God has enabled me to be part of during the past twenty years. Ever since meeting John Wimber I have been endeavouring to discern whatever I sensed God was really doing and to bless it. This has involved trying to listen to what he was saying ('my sheep hear my voice'[7] and discerning what God was doing (the Son only does 'what he sees the Father doing'[8]). We began to discover that the fruits of this were radical and far-reaching. Ecclesiastes 11:1 tells us to cast our bread upon the waters and we will find it after many days – how true! The blessings, often not known about till years later, and sometimes never reported back, appear quite extraordinary and most encouraging and one recognises that it just has to be the work of God.

Chapter 26

SURPRISED BY THE WORK OF GOD

Prayer's power is in the One who hears it, not the
one who prays it
(ANON)

I want to learn to move God to move men by prayer alone
(HUDSON TAYLOR)

God is only a prayer away
(ANON)

We could never have sat down and planned the kind of developments that we observed coming out of St Andrew's. Quite early
on in my time there, I was under pressure from some of our high
powered business folk to produce a five-year plan. I fought shy of
it, since from my experience in South America, one could never
predict which way the wind of the Spirit might blow tomorrow –
let alone five years on.

As a church we only had one real committee – the Standing
Committee which I usually chaired. This dealt mainly with
finance; watching our income and how we were spending, or over-
spending, any money budgeted. The ministry God gave us, with
the growing number of people in the church, just kept unfolding
before our eyes in a most remarkable way as we tried to 'walk in
the Spirit'[1] – trying to tune in to what the Lord was saying. This
sounds very superspiritual. But for us, it meant that in the process
of reading the Bible, prayer and weighing up prophecy, with
plenty of commonsense and sharing in the staff team, 'walking in
the Spirit' was often just like any other walk; taking the next
obvious step in a spirit of prayer. We would try to keep moving in
that direction until we sensed the Spirit lifting off, leading

elsewhere or adding to the vision.

King David bears out how vital this is in the service of God when he wrote 'Except the Lord build the house, they labour in vain that build it'.[2] That was why he himself never built the Temple in Jerusalem but left it to Solomon. God gave him the vision for it though God withheld permission for him to build. King David's greater son, Jesus, endorsed this principle when he prophesied: 'Every plant which my heavenly Father has not planted will be rooted up'.[3]

It was a very fulfilling exercise trying to bless what one senses God wants to bless. It meant that we scrutinised the way the church spent its money. We found we had been supporting many things that were actually 'dead horses' – the Spirit had already lifted off them years ago. Obviously flogging a dead horse is a complete waste of one's time, talents and energy.

It would be quite wrong to pretend that we were always listening as we should have been, that we always heard what he was saying exactly, and that hearing him we always obeyed and took the appropriate steps. It is so easy to block one's ears to God. But when we thought we were hearing him we checked it out with other people we trusted and respected, and if the response was positive, we tried to work out the practical implications and to obey – on the good grounds that if we truly loved him we should keep his commandments.

AN ORDINARY PRAYER MEETING

There are no gimmicks for growing churches – there are only the basics laid down by the New Testament. Christian Schwarz, in his book Natural Church Development,[4] summarises research from over 4.2 million replies to questions sent to members of growing churches of all traditions across the world – and concludes that churches grow when they have processed quality development in eight major areas – one being prayer.

Our friend Mike Bickle resigned his pastorate in Kansas City after seventeen years to give himself to prayer, which he rightly regards as the most vital way of keeping a relationship going with God. He has formed a people of prayer that intercedes twenty-four hours a day. Folk attend this from all over the city. We never aspired to anything like that. I am sure God will bless Kansas City in most wonderful ways as a result, though I think Mike's enthusiastic emphasis could put quite a burden of guilt on the ordinary church member. It is certainly not a practical model for everyone, but awareness of what he, and others like him, are doing, may spur us all to pray more – which can only be good. One reason, I believe, why St Andrew's was able to keep growing, was due to the daily, 7 am, prayer meetings we held there for our last twelve years.

We had this time in the church lounge every morning, spending the first ten minutes silently reading a passage from the Bible, and, afterwards, sharing thoughts about it for five minutes. Then, we just waited on God in prayer for the next half hour. During this time some sat, some lay out on the carpeted floor, some walked around or simply stood. Some knelt, some wept, and some never opened their mouths. Some prayed quietly in tongues, some prayed using a traditional prayer and some prayed an extempore prayer. We had thanksgiving, praise, intercession, confession and repentance – whatever seemed right. We hoped at some point we were touching the merciful heart of God. Promptly at 7.45 we ended by reciting the Lord's Prayer. During those years of early morning praying together, we read the whole Bible through three times. We announced publicly every Sunday that all were welcome but there was never any pressure on others to attend. We knew that the early morning was a particularly inconvenient time for some and we did not want anybody to feel guilty for not being able to make it at such an hour – especially those that had family responsibilities (and we put a high value on the family). But we suggested that some folk might like to make their own arrangements to pray with others (maybe only weekly or monthly) in much smaller groups at mutually convenient times; if that seemed right for them.

Some folk tried to attend our church prayer meeting every day, holding up my arms like Aaron and Hur who had supported Moses on the mountain, for a victory in battle over the marauding Amalekites.[5] Some people came to us once a week and some even more sporadically. Sometimes there might be thirty plus there and sometimes as few as seven or eight – but we just kept going. I truly believe that so much of the blessings in and out of the church at that time grew out of that daily prayer time together and the concomitant prayer meetings provoked by its example. I found these meetings helped me too in my own spiritual life – especially when the pressures were heavy. Week-night meetings often did not finish till 10.30 (occasionally 11 pm) by the time we had locked up. I needed something like this open commitment to force me out of bed in the morning when one could so easily make the excuse for a lie in. But I had a day off on Tuesdays.

Most people would leave straightaway after the prayer time though some stayed around for a few minutes to chat which I enjoyed. George Knight, who invariably came, would usually share his latest joke with me at the door which was why I later dedicated my first joke book, *Burying the Bishop*,[6] to him. This was followed with another booklet called *Out of the Mouths of Babes*[7] and then *Four Funerals and a Wedding*.[8]

REGULAR STAFF MEETINGS

We had staff meetings three times a week – about twelve of us gathering for this. We met from 10 to 1pm on Mondays, followed by lunch together with spouses. We always checked through the sick list together for prayer and took brief reports back at these times, ensuring that any necessary advance planning was proceeding apace; that the building and grounds were in good order and that requests for outside help were being properly considered. There were so many aspects of church life to keep a watchful eye on but we all loved the buzz. Then I would meet briefly with the staff again for half an hour on Wednesdays and Fridays so that we could all touch base with each other and touch base on everything that was going on. These meetings were vital for relating with each other, and ensuring that all in the church and parish were being cared for. The fellowship with those men and women was challenging, rewarding and fun.

To our delight the church still kept filling up. These services were just a sea of worshippers in a packed building, spreading out across the upper hall, vestibule, patio room and to the back of the lounge – every seat filled often with still others standing (even in the kitchen) nearly every Sunday. Those exciting liturgical[9] celebrations included spans of guitar-led worship, and a time for the spontaneous manifestations of the gifts of the Spirit (keeping these reasonably brief and low-key). Those services Sunday after Sunday remain permanently etched in my mind. People seemed so eager to get into the church early – and there were endless queues lining up for the Lord's Supper followed by the prayer ministry for any and everyone who stayed behind for it. This had to be experienced to be believed – talk about a tingle factor! I could well understand that verse where Paul says the unbeliever coming in 'will fall down and worship God, exclaiming "God is really among you!"'.[10]

I remember one man, who was divorced and homeless, falling under the power of God and rising up to become a committed Christian. The man has remained a faithful member of St Andrew's over many years now, and has even been as far as India more than once with a ministry team, praying for others there in the Lord's name.

It surprised me that when the wider church was being faced with acute numerical haemorrhaging, few in the diocese enquired how this might all be happening in St Andrew's. They simply did not seem to want to know. Perhaps they thought they did know but did not want to hear the answer – not wanting new life on those terms!

Talking to a young lady who had started attending regularly I enquired out of pastoral concern about where she was in her spiritual pilgrimage? Was she a seeker or a Christian?

'Christian,' she said.

'How long have you been a Christian?' I asked.

'Six weeks,' she replied, very definitely.

'But you have only been coming here just about six weeks. Tell me how this happened?'

'Well,' she said, 'The first Sunday I came here there was a prophetic word given out and it struck right home to my heart – I repented and gave my life to Christ.'

'Thank you Lord!' I responded inwardly.

What I did not tell her was that I remembered that prophetic word when it had been given out. It was almost a verse of Scripture and I had not been very sure whether it had been a prophecy at all or just a blessed word.

BLESSED WITH MUSIC DIRECTORS

Jacqui Webb, who had been directing the music for some years at St Andrew's, was asked to become a member of the Archbishops' Commission on Church Music.[11] She rose to the challenge and her contribution was incorporated in the Commission's published report.[12] We had some great directors of music at St Andrew's. One of them was still a teenager who showed a lot of promise when he started with us – none other than Matt Redman. Matt has since produced a large number of his own CDs besides writing a delightful book: *The Unquenchable Worshipper*.[13]

All liturgy and words for songs, and even, latterly, the Bible readings, were on the overhead at St Andrew's and picked up on the internal TV camera for the monitors arranged through the building, so that people had no need for any books – though many brought their own Bibles.

Our good friend Peter Maskrey, a greatly valued church-warden and later staff member, gave a lot of time and expertise – together with his team – to setting up an adequate sound system. Brian Skinner and his son David helped to get the church staff and offices computerised. Such expenses rightly caused some members of the PCC to have occasional reserves over the costs involved. But we found that the better organised we were at home the more we could help others elsewhere to resource their work too.

EXTRAORDINARY – SO ORDINARY

An article in a Norwegian church paper delighted me. 'The extraordinary thing about St Andrew's is that it is so ordinary', it said, ' – no great architecture, no great liturgical processions, no great choir or organist, no great preacher'. Anything good that was happening just had to be God. All we had to do was to try to keep hearing him and to give away what he was giving to us. Visitors from churches where a St Andrew's team had been would regularly report back on some of the blessings resulting from their ministry. It helped everyone to see that the gospel was certainly relevant for today. In order to keep these reports brief and brisk we directed the interviews, interrupting with questions, while keeping a firm hold on the microphone. Congregations don't usually want more than one sermon in a service!

RETREATS

Also in the mid 1980s the Rev Teddy and Margaret Saunders[14]
came to live in the parish. They had bought a house not far from
St Andrew's. Teddy, who had known David Watson well, was in
retirement in Oxford where he was co-writing David's biography.
They began to sense that God wanted them to develop a kind of
retreat for church leaders based rather on what Canon David
Watson had done at York. When they talked the idea over with
John Wimber he suggested they approached us and we were
delighted to encourage them to start. It was very timely. We were
receiving frequent requests from clergy who wanted to come to
Chorleywood for a few days and see what was happening. Our
problem had been how we could help them profitably when we
could properly spare only a couple of hours maximum with any
one of them. What could they do with the rest of their time to
make their stay with us really useful? Teddy's idea was to accept
up to twelve couples to stay in the parish as paying 'bed and
breakfast' guests, whilst the Saunders would organise a daily
programme for them based at the 'Hensol' – their home. Hence
the name of 'Hensol Retreats'. Each retreat originally lasted ten
days. They held four or five of these each year. In this way all the
church staff could share some prime time with our visitors –
leading a couple of sessions and joining them for one or two meals.
It worked very well – especially with the extra help of John Coles
and Bruce Collins, two neighbouring clergy who led their own
thriving churches and made their own considerable contributions.
David Parker and Ann Watson were also a great help in the
earlier stages. The Saunders had an excellent team of co-workers
from the parish laid on. Margaret, a gifted organiser, kept in touch
pastorally with all those who attended (some 600 came during the
time they were running it). She sent them books and tapes of
things she thought they might be interested to hear about and
drew their attention to meetings and conferences she thought they
'ought' to attend. Many clergy have shared since just how much
this care has meant to them – a real turning point for some. I
recently attended the funeral of a man who, with his wife, hosted
a number of these visitors. One of the mourners was a Lutheran
minister from Finland[15] who came all that way for the funeral. He

claimed the retreat he attended ten years previously in the home of my now deceased friend, had completely revolutionised his life and ministry. Those retreats were a brilliant idea and such a profitable venture for a retired married couple, with so much wisdom and pastoral experience still to give in the service of their fellow clergy. The latter, in turn, highly valued that extra refreshing and encouragement. Mary and I felt it a great privilege to be so closely involved with the Saunders in such a worthwhile ministry.

Chapter 27

I LEAP OVER THE WALL

. . . and by my God I can leap over a wall
(PSALM 18:29B RSV)

See, I am doing a new thing! Now it springs up; do you not perceive it?
(ISAIAH 43:19, NIV)

*Getting out of a rut is the highest mountain most
of us ever have to climb*
– (ANON)

*. . . I have been to the mountain top . . . I've looked over and seen the
Promised Land. I may not get there with you, but I want you to know
tonight that we, as a people, will get to the Promised Land. So I am
happy tonight . . . I'm not fearing man – 'Mine eyes have seen the glory
of the coming of the Lord'*
(CONCLUSION TO MARTIN LUTHER KING'S LAST SPEECH BEFORE HIS
ASSASSINATION IN MEMPHIS)

We need able politicians . . . but sometimes prophetic action is called for
(ELIZABETH CANHAM)[1]

I could not resist taking my title for this chapter from a fascinating
book written about sixty years ago by a former middle-aged nun.
She shocked the church when she walked out of her closed
religious order after so many years inside – a rare thing to do in
those days. I cannot claim to have physically leapt over many
walls myself but I seem to have been crossing barriers of some sort
for most of my lifetime.

I suppose it was inevitable that sooner or later after our arrival
at St Andrew's we would get into church planting again. Firstly

the building was becoming packed out and there was no room to expand; secondly Bishop Brian Skinner, like myself, had previously been involved with church planting in Chile. Thirdly there was the wholesome influence of John Wimber. Finally, statistics for membership in the wider church were declining rapidly and we felt we obviously wanted to do our bit and help put this right – especially in reaching to hold the younger generation.

In the providence of God, there is a life cycle of death and resurrection operating in the natural world (evident in the seasons) and this operates also in the church. Some congregations are decimated by external forces, others fall into heresy and apostatise, slowly self-destruct or die, while a few re-invent themselves and survive. History demonstrates how local churches and particular denominations have died out. What has happened to the Quakers, the Congregationalists, the Methodists and the Plymouth Brethren? What is happening in so much of the Church of England as we know it today?

FUNERAL OF A CHURCH

I heard once of the funeral of a 'church' in New York! This had formerly been a flourishing congregation that had planted out at least three healthy daughter churches. But the aged mother church became tired. After ample consultation, the old pastor wisely divided out the residue of his congregation among his daughter churches and then he closed the place down with a funeral celebration of thanksgiving. But the life still went on – in different modes and lifestyles in the daughter churches and elsewhere.

Church is basically family – God's family. Parents have children. Children grow up and have their children. Grandparents die. The next generation may not want to meet in the same buildings, wear the same clothes, use the same furniture, speak and pray in the same way, read the same religious books, enjoy the same amusements or sing the same songs as their parents. We don't find that strange – it's natural and normal.

It is only when the church of Jesus Christ (but not necessarily all the different denominations) embraces and adapts to the new life God is giving that it can survive,[2] though it may have to assume some diverse shapes and forms in the process.

Indeed it more than survives – it grows. There have been more Christians existing in the world during this last ten years than the sum total of all the Christians added together during the previous 1,990 years: in spite of some massive persecutions. Much of this new life came (originally) out of the traditional churches, though it did not continue in so many of the traditional parent churches.

OLD WINESKINS CAN'T COPE WITH NEW WINE!

When God blesses the church with the new wine of the Holy Spirit, even today the old wineskin usually wants it to conform – or get out. This has happened again and again in the history of the church. Following the eighteenth-century Wesleyan revival, the new wine was largely lost to the C of E – when John Wesley's followers were reluctantly forced to start a new Methodist denomination. Most of the new wine from the revivals in Wales, California etc in the first decade of the last century was obstructed in traditional church circles and channelled into new Pentecostal movements. Much of the new wine from the Charismatic revival of the 1960s flowed into the House Church Movement. Much, but thankfully by no means all, of the Wimber new wine revival of the 1980s was eventually filtered off into the Vineyard Christian Fellowships – Wimber was reluctant in agreeing to VCFs in the UK, but eventually yielded to those younger Anglican clergy who were pleading to take it forward. They had not the heart to fight ecclesiastical battles over the *adiaphora* (non-essentials or literally *things indifferent*[3]) of the traditional church at so many levels – battles they knew they could not win.

In so many of these revival movements of the Spirit, the Anglican Church seems, as a whole, to have lost out again and again. This is catching up on us today and is clearly reflected in our slow numerical decline which has now reached a point of crisis.

PROGRESS AND 'THE UNREASONABLE MAN'

When it comes to the need to save souls, the missionary in me becomes passionately unreasonable about the church's seeming inability to make the necessary adjustments which would allow spontaneous things to happen in these times of renewal. The work of the Holy Spirit is contagious.[4] This needs to be understood, encouraged and harnessed. But although the ship is wind-driven it needs to be wisely steered.

Perhaps its just arrogance but I take some consolation from G.B. Shaw who wrote: 'The reasonable man adapts himself to the world. The unreasonable man persists in trying to adapt the world to himself – therefore all progress depends upon the unreasonable man!' God is not always rational. At times he is supra-rational. He is not against our using our brains but wants us to understand that his thinking and his ways are so much higher than ours.[5] Often, the only way to progress a vision is by taking the unreasonable course of prophetic action as Elizabeth Canham did – in her case[6] trying to be a living model of what she believed was right – to become a woman priest – and in our case trying to create a living model of what we believed was right, to plant churches beyond our parish boundary.

Lacking the ability, diplomacy, subtlety or the patience to negotiate with the traditional church for the successful acceptance of any visions of mine, I have always relied on other prophets to articulate clearly, what I express so inadequately, to reach circles that that I could never reach effectively.

A Pastoral Letter circulated to all the bishops at Lambeth in 1988 could not have said it better: 'In many parts of the world, Anglicans have emphasised the pastoral model of ministry at the expense of mission. We believe the Holy Spirit is now leading us to become a movement of Mission . . . the emergence of basic communities and house groups requires us to review our traditional structures in parishes and dioceses'.[7]

But did anyone really pay any attention to these things? Apparently not then.[8] That was the reason why in the end one was driven to prophetic action – going ahead and doing it. And clearly today there is evidence of fresh thinking and radical action by more and more bishops.

CHALLENGES OF LIFE IN A LOCAL CHURCH

With St Andrew's so full we felt like a pregnant woman wanting to give birth. Regular members were complaining that they had to arrive half an hour early to obtain a seat in the main building of their own church!

Our first two church plants had been within our parish boundaries but we still kept filling up. Wherever could we go? The most sensible thing was to inspire some of the congregation to start new churches back in their own localities with a suitable leader. These plants of course would be beyond our parish boundaries. Some suggested, with regard to our worshippers coming from outside the parish, that we were duty bound to send them back to their local churches. But they had come to us in the first place because they no longer felt they fitted into their local churches for a variety of reasons – some of the same reasons that so many give today for travelling long distances to attend their nearest cathedral. And one simply can't tell other people where to go. People choose for themselves where they and their families want to go to church. Sheep will go where they like the grass.

But they can be inspired to go back to their home environment with a vision for starting something they believe could be relevant for today. That is the most natural thing to do even though it may risk upsetting the powers-that-be of the traditional church. Having tried it, we know – but it has been worth it.

NATURAL DEVELOPMENT

At St Andrew's Church growth just came about as a natural development from within a loving congregation committed to the gospel of Jesus Christ, where the discipline of the church was to prayer, to the regular reading, preaching and obedience to God's Word, to the frequent sharing in the sacrament together, and the constant ministry in the power of the Holy Spirit; there was both the pioneering and the support of evangelistic mission and mercy ministries so near to the heart of God, and an attitude of trying to listen to what the Spirit might be saying to the church today.

With this kind of ministry, the congregation just seemed to flourish – 'all by itself'.[9] It may not happen in the same way for others. There are no clone churches or clone leaders. But that was how it worked for us. We were, of course, in a very favoured area. There was certainly no special effort on our part to grow. We just thanked God for it and kept asking him how we should co-operate.

Of course, any model for church planting is worth our study but even more importantly is the need for motivation. Where can we find that? This, I'm sure, can only come from the anointing of the Holy Spirit. There is no stereotype for how this may occur but it needs to be prayed for and sought after. It may happen in many ways to many people at different times but there has to be an openness to some such experience. There can be no birth without a conception. Church planting comes naturally when it is conceived of the Holy Spirit through such anointings and then born of a local church.

INTERESTING EXPERIMENTS

Because the diocese seemed a bit edgy about St Andrew's, with its name for being charismatic, our first experiment had been to export a dozen of our folk to a neighbouring church to help out there. But over half of them came back in less than a year because the local vicar only wanted people to fill seats in pews. He offered them no opportunity to minister, which they were used to doing in St Andrew's. He had little concept of the priesthood of all believers. In his view the real ministry of the church was limited to his priesthood. It was obviously unprofitable to continue suggesting to our people that they go off and support incumbents who had no practical vision for breaking new ground in new ways.

Our next thought was to offer to take over one of the neighbouring churches that seemed almost empty. We made it plain that we would be willing to take over any other local parish church round about. Help from our staff during interregna among one or two of these diminishing congregations seemed to have been much appreciated.

We liked the way Holy Trinity Church, Brompton, had planted out one church after another from their own congregation. We would have gladly followed suit. But church politics (which I understand only too well) frustrated such practical initiatives however sensible the vision may have seemed to us.

WARY OF CHARISMATICS

Bishops in general are wary of charismatic churches (sometimes with good reasons) and they fear for the future of a diocese flooded with charismatic church plants. But common sense tells us that people are people and within a couple of decades, those new plants that have survived will be reflecting many different church types. They will range from broadly evangelical churches to rigid fundamentalists, from evangelical charismatics and liberal charismatics, from outright liberals to Anglo-Catholics – while others will be Baptist, Vineyard, Pentecostal, Assemblies Of God, Independent House Churches etc. Some by then may even be meeting under extreme persecution in caves, catacombs, secret forest glades, prisons or concentration camps. As in any family there can be strong reactions to the parent churches which first birthed them. Like children, some may recoil from their traditional upbringing in quite a pronounced manner.[10] Reactions from particular ways of 'doing church' or interpreting the faith are commonplace, being sparked off from various motives and then usually justified on the grounds of Scriptural principle or cultural preference, even though initially they have probably developed out of personality differences.

THRUST OUT TO PLANT

The filling up of St Andrew's meant that we were being forced to plant out into other places – whenever there were suitable people to lead the plant, and wherever there was the available accommodation to do it. We had already done this twice within our own parish boundaries, but then we planted two more into Watford, one into Rickmansworth and another into Amersham. The Rickmansworth experiment never really took off. Each plant raised its own little furore from within the host parish. Parish boundaries,[11] which once served the church well, tend to operate today like a contraceptive, and block the new life that our God is ever willing to give by his Spirit.

We could have planted out many more churches if only we had pushed through the parish boundaries sooner! Local congregations need to be ready to foster such spontaneous expansion and start training local leaders for this ministry well before their church becomes full, so that when that happens they can do the natural thing and plant out again. Obviously they will want to keep the bishop and the other churches as fully in the picture as possible, even though diocesan authorities may not always be co-operative.

AND OTHER WAYS

There are a number of other ways new plants may spring up. Shirley Webber, our one-time music director, was appointed to a new secular job in 1993. When she later married the couple settled in North Wales. They soon found Christians in their area who no longer attended places of worship on Sundays. (There are supposed to have been over a million people in Britain who have just stopped church-going over the last decade or so.) The most natural thing for Shirley and her husband to do was to invite these neighbours to gather in their home to worship the Lord. Soon they needed a bigger meeting place. What else should they have done? It was just common sense on their part. They perceived the new thing[12] that God wanted and went for it in a very practical way.

These were not our only members contributing to church growth. I recently counted five or six layfolk from St Andrew's who had gone out to plant Vineyard Churches – one of them led by my son-in-law who has a regular gathering now of some six hundred or more meeting in the local city football club in Nottingham. (After four years they started looking for another building and they may have now found a site to buy and build on.)

Another couple moved north, and found a home with the Assemblies Of God where they are now leaders. I like to think that the Lord may have been preparing them for this ministry when they were still with us, since they were both in one of our original church plants in Chorleywood.

St Andrew's continued producing ordinands for the Church of England ministry. A healthy stream had begun before, and continued both during and following our time at St Andrew's, to go out and serve in the ordained ranks of the Church of England.

NEEDING EACH OTHER

Jesus said new wineskins were necessary for new wine. The situation has not changed. New wine fizz usually wrecks old wineskins and then both the old and the new wine are lost. Having said that, Jesus never denigrated the old wine. Indeed, he conceded that those who were used to the old wine would still prefer it. No sensible person rejects anything simply because it is old. Certainly not! When parents die they bequeath what they leave to bless their children and this is usually greatly appreciated. Our traditional church has many beautiful antique riches – the witness of its martyrs, the carefully thought-through creeds, the beauty of its prayers, sacraments, hymns, liturgies, the Christian year and the finely tuned lectionaries. It would be a sacrilege to reject them all simply because they were associated with the old. The parent church will need to patiently hold such an inheritance on offer for whenever it might be appreciated in the future. Being the product of so many generations of Anglican clergy,[13] I delight in my Christian heritage. But, like the progenitors of any family, the wise old parent church will not insist that its new church plants take on board all the top-heavy, often unwieldy old wineskin family ecclesiology into the next generation when it probably considers it inappropriate for a post modern generation church.

At the same time the new wine in the new wineskin cannot usually continue long-term without some healthy link with the old. The old needs the new and the new needs the old! If only a way could be found to let the new wine form a new wineskin with the old wineskin still owning it – instead of ousting it!

Whilst the church plants coming out of Anglican churches do not want all the old diocesan structures they would value some kind of relationship with the bishop. This could easily happen through a specially appointed caretaker assistant with a brief from the bishop to keep in with unofficial new plants. Maybe we could take a hint from the Catholic Church and its religious orders.

HOW THE CATHOLICS CATERED FOR NEW WINE

The Catholic Church has been farsighted and surprisingly flexible when at different times in the past, she discerned a new movement of the Spirit. Separate Religious Orders were created – Dominicans, Augustinians, or Franciscans etc that were made directly accountable to Rome. The Pope gave them freedom from the diocesan structures while they retained a link with the Papacy through their Fathers Superior. They were in no way subject to the local diocesan bishop. The Pope obviously would have wished them to work as harmoniously as possible alongside the diocese though historically it did not always work out that way.

HOW THE LUTHERANS COPED

Following the 1850s revival and the creation of so much new wine, the Lutheran Church in Denmark, Norway and Sweden allowed the establishment of *'folken kirken'* – peoples' churches, where the congregation chose their leaders who were then licensed by the bishop. They found their own premises and paid their own pastors. They had freedom over the use of dress and liturgy. The object was somehow to keep the new wine (new believers from the revival) within the Lutheran Church. Some fifteen of these still exist in Denmark today and we have just returned from a conference in Sweden for some of these 'free' Lutheran pastors and their people there. We know personally of a similar church in Stavanger, southern Norway.

ANGLICANS AND NEW WINE IN THE PAST

At home we know how many churches in the past have grown up out of missionary congregations coming together in different parts of the parish. Then later their area in the original parish was carved off and made into a separate parish under a vicar appointed by the rector[14] and licensed by the bishop. This was an effective model that served the C of E usefully for centuries.

A classic example of Anglicans creating new life out of an irregular church planting model abroad comes from the evangelical Church Missionary Society (founded in 1799). This voluntary Anglican society even used Lutheran/Moravian clergy in planting some of their early churches in India. To begin with the new congregations sat very loosely within the traditional Anglican structures. But their incomplete model served to secure new footholds for the work of the worldwide Anglican Church that we boast of today. To get to this stage of development, their Christian missionary expression had to find a fresh mode for organising itself. Initially they had to step out of their ecclesiastical boat in faith and learn to 'walk on water'. They had no exact precedent for Anglican missionary expansion overseas. (It was a similar pattern later for us in Latin America.)

They operated in the beginning on minimal funding, with no parish structure, no dioceses, and a very limited unlicensed lay and ordained ministry – and no bishops. Crown appointed bishops from England began to appear in India after 1813[15] but these usually lived hundreds of miles away from missionary work, to oversee the expatriate congregations. The first bishops were rarely sympathetic to missionaries who might disturb the natives by proselytising them and thereby prejudice the commercial prospects of the English businessmen in the chaplaincy congregations. He who pays the piper calls the tune: the missionary societies paid the salaries and moved their missionaries where they wanted. There were other areas of tension where the patronage of the Missionary Society and the powers of the State-appointed bishops clashed, but in time they began to work together. Out of this vortex many new disciples of Christ were added to the church, many new churches were planted, and many new dioceses were eventually created to cater for this enthusiastic expression of new life.

ANGLICANS AND NEW WINE TODAY

Dr George Carey, the Archbishop of Canterbury, drew attention to our first efforts at cross-boundary planting in his address at a conference at Holy Trinity Church, Brompton (1991) organised by Bob and Mary Gardner Hopkins, who have worked for years to encourage church planting. The archbishop said that he welcomed church planting beyond parish boundaries so long as it was done with the consent of the neighbouring clergy. Of course such common agreement would be ideal – but we know from our own experience, and from similar experiments by others across the country, that such consent is invariably denied to potential planting churches.

NOT IN MY BACKYARD

A typical example was that of a church plant in Cheltenham. The Rev. Dr Nigel Scotland[16] ran a large Anglican-friendly fellowship there. This had grown out of the overflow from another parish church in Cheltenham that was bursting at the seams. Finding it impossible to locate suitable premises in their own parish they eventually spilled over into a neighbouring school – and into a parish where the church of a different Anglican tradition was reaching a very limited number of people. This church strongly objected to these church planting squatters in their backyard. There being no other suitable premises available, the new plant had to settle there – though feeling most unwelcome. And from then on the diocese appeared to take no further interest in this large congregation. Happily now, after nearly ten years the diocese is about to reconsider the situation and may be something positive will emerge this time. But I believe the decision on this has to come from the bishop. The average Anglican incumbent still seems to think that every Anglican in his parish must come under his control, and if s/he does not like something s/he just won't allow it to happen in their parish. But if the bishop could or would create some kind of simple alternative parallel structure to cope with the new plants, the incumbents eventually get used to such a sensible idea.

BREAKING NEW GROUND

In 1994 the Church of England produced its report 'Breaking New Ground' (BNG) as a reaction to the irregular practice of our parish church.[17] The official report which set out to consider the feasibility of church planting beyond one's parish boundaries, seemed to counter our spontaneous unilateral church planting model by stressing the need for 'long term diocesan and deanery planning if plants are not to be the enthusiasm of the moment, here today and gone tomorrow'.

If the best way forward for church planting is really through such long-term diocesan and deanery planning, why is the church not doing more to sponsor it now when church growth of any kind is vital? Actually I believe the method proposed in BNG is too unwieldy and too unrealistic to be truly viable. The first thing our nearly bankrupt dioceses would have to consider would be the costs involved in maintaining a new leader for such a new work, besides the needs for housing, transport, and some kind of building in which to gather a congregation. Even the thought of this would be a definite deterrent factor for any diocese strapped for cash, as most are! And no one really knows whether any pioneer plant planned in that way will take proper root and flourish. If it fails, then such diocesan experiments would prove too great a financial loss.

We have to ask what other resource a diocese might perhaps have to exploit for the purpose of church planting? The answer is any thriving church could do it and at no financial cost to the diocese.

PRECEDENTS FOR CHANGE

Many bishops operate on precedents. Brian Skinner and I felt it might help if we produced a little book called *New Wineskins*,[18] giving a number of historical precedents illustrating some radical changes in traditional churches. The book spelt out examples of where the traditional church had adapted its ecclesiastical structures to cope with the new life God was giving it. We believed there was now an urgent need for some creative thinking about our ecclesiology in the UK. We hoped some examples from the past might serve to encourage further thought about the possibilities.

To keep the ball rolling on the subject of church planting, we put out our first and last Kingdom Power Trust publication in 1995 – 'last' because we did not have sufficient marketing facilities to get our money back. The book was called *Recovering the Ground*.[19] We had a good range of contributors and our general editor was the Rev. Dr Nigel Scotland.

We felt something had to be done to help all these spontaneous church plants coming into being until a way could be found for them to be welcomed back once more to the Anglican fold. We felt the Church of England could ill afford to lose them in the first place. For that reason we founded the Fellowship of Independent Anglican Churches (FIAC) to provide a loose knit network and create a holding body to give some simple oversight in matters of doctrinal orthodoxy, help with mediating in the event of difficulties within congregations over their leaders, and to offer suggestions when a new leader might need to be appointed.

I was interested later to discover that Dr John Rodgers,[20] the Dean of Trinity Episcopal Seminary in Pittsburg, had created something similar in North America. He called it 'The Association of Anglican Congregations in Mission'. We claimed that the FIAC was 'Anglican friendly' which it really was. Most of the new fellowships would have liked to have remained within the Anglican Communion. But the 'Anglican friendly' claim came in for some especially hostile criticism.

LOONY LEFT!

All the fuss following the creation of FIAC triggered off interesting letters to the press – both church and secular. One in *The Daily Telegraph*[21] was from a retired canon we had never met. He likened us to the militant tendency (nicknamed the 'Loony Left') of the Labour Party that had recently been a considerable irritant through their local councils in London and Liverpool. He discerned in us four similar characteristics:

1. The absolute personal conviction that we must be right.
2. Certainty that we represented the 'soul' of the larger body and that those officially in charge are 'betraying' it.
3. Willingness to ride roughshod over the procedural niceties in order to forward our own beliefs.
4. An unconsciousness of doing anything against the rules.

As a pleasant afterthought, he added that no doubt Bishop Pytches and Bishop Skinner 'are nicer people than some of the militant leaders', but then, less kindly, he wrote that just as the Church of England was unable to contain the Methodist Movement under Wesley, so we would function more happily out of it than in. The problem, he thought, was best tackled sooner than later!

Doubtless he would have become even more confirmed in his view once he learned of my involvement in the Singaporean consecrations.

ANOTHER THREAT TO 'TERRITORIALITY'

I was invited to Singapore in the spring of 2000. My hotel had a beautiful view across the bay and overlooked St Andrew's Cathedral. We gathered there to consecrate Dean John Rodgers[22] and Charles H. Murphy III[23] – both widely respected evangelical clergy in the USA. They were being made suffragan bishops, one officially representing the province of South East Asia and the other, the province of the Anglican Church in Rwanda. Archbishop Moses Tay of Singapore (since retired) and Archbishop Emmanuel Kolini both presided at the service, along with three other bishops and myself. We all laid hands on these two godly men. Through the involvement of these two arch-bishops regnant it was hoped they could be formally recognised within the Anglican Communion. Their mandate was to head up the Anglican Mission in America (AmiA). This 'province' in America could continue to hold together many of those orthodox clergy within the Anglican Communion who were in despair about the recent radical changes (doctrinal and ethical) and desperately concerned about the rapid numerical decline[24] of the Episcopal Church of the USA. There is ample room and need for mission in North America today. As *Newsweek* magazine reported: 'Countries that were once considered Christian homelands (such as the USA) have become the mission territories of the new millennium'.[25]

OVERLAPPING JURISDICTIONS!

These consecrations (and four more since) have been condemned by the hierarchy of the Anglican Communion as 'irregular and irresponsible'! Since then, the 'Forward in Faith' movement in the USA (opposed to the ordination of women) have decided to elect their own bishop who will also be consecrated by a sympathetic overseas archbishop.

Incidentally, for my minor role, I was later forbidden by two bishops in Canada from teaching in their diocese, and warned by another from South Africa that it would damage renewal if I attended our New Wine conferences there.

But if some accommodation towards this new missionary province could ever be made in the USA, it might yet keep a large number of very unsettled clergy and churches within the Anglican Communion. Admittedly any such compromise would constitute an over-lapping of episcopacy – something the Anglican Communion mysteriously maintains is out of order, though there is, in fact, plenty of precedent for overlapping episcopal oversight. At one time, while I was in Latin America, when the missionary

Church in Brazil was under the jurisdiction of *La Igreja Episcopal,*[26] the English chaplaincies in Río de Janeiro and Sau Paulo, in Brazil, opted to remain under the jurisdiction of the English Anglican bishop down in Argentina. While the English chaplaincies in Europe still came under the Anglican bishop of Fulham, an Episcopal bishop was overseeing the USA military chaplaincies based in Europe too. In New Zealand, Australia and North America there are dioceses for native peoples that overlap in an irregular way with the territories of some of the regular dioceses. Even within our own Church of England, the principle of one bishop and one diocese with boundaries is distorted with the appointments of suffragan and assistant bishops. And recently, under the primacy of George Carey, we have recognised provincial episcopal visitors and consecrated them as 'flying' bishops to care for a number of traditional clergy who have had conscientious objections over the ordination of women. There is plenty of precedent for the overlap of episcopal authority which has long been part of our tradition in spite of the 1988 Lambeth Conference attempting to establish a norm of one bishop with territorial jurisdiction over one diocese. There were exceptions in the past and there can be exceptions in the future. It would seem a necessary expedient for the *bene esse* of the Episcopal Church of the USA to be inclusive about AmiA – just as Catholic popes have sensibly appointed heads of religious communities to be directly answerable to them, to operate within dioceses but independently of the diocesan bishops, in order to keep the new life available for the church in its God-given mission.

THE ANCIENT ABBEY/MINSTER MODEL

Wherever there is a full church with vision, energy, commitment and willingness to make great sacrifices, there will be the potential within it to finance and promote a new church plant. The faith was largely pioneered in Britain by the Celts who developed the abbey/minster model. Something similar is discernible today in what is actually happening out of Holy Trinity Church, Brompton, where an enlightened Bishop of London has encouraged their potential for new church planting in dying parishes. This no doubt explains why London apparently has been the only diocese in the land to record numerical church growth recently (45,000 members in 1990 to 64,000 members today).

The Anglican Communion currently registers far more members overseas than at home. Should some of our new models of 'doing church' abroad coupled with a few old paradigms, encourage our bishops regarding the Church of England for the new millennium? I think they could, and should!

Chapter 28

ARROGANT, ALTRUISTIC OR SIMPLY ASININE?

Man is born unto trouble as surely as sparks fly upward
(JOB 5:7)

A man who makes trouble for others is also making trouble for himself
(CHINUA ACHEBE – NIGERIAN POET)

With lateral thinking one is always trying to generate alternatives, to restructure patterns
(EDWARD DE BONO)

On reflection, I think I detect one recurring trait in my own ministry – perhaps a significant one – that of ruffling other people's feathers. Was this arrogance, altruism, idiocy or all of them put together? If true then may be it was inherited. My great uncle upset the Viceroy of India on a matter of principle and lost his job. But for that breach, according to his contemporaries, Welldon might easily have become an Archbishop of Canterbury.

AT THE EDGE

Canon Michael Saward (recently retired from St Paul's Cathedral) is an old acquaintance, a strong evangelical and a truly establishment man. He wrote a fascinating autobiography in which as an aside he referred to me as 'a charismatic bishop on the Anglican fringes'. His perception was, of course, so right. The fringe has always seemed the place with the most freedom to pioneer some of the changes needed for the church's growth and survival. Incidentally looking at the set-up of a diocese from the outside today it is apparent that many dioceses still think of

373

themselves erroneously as a church *per se*. But a diocese is simply a super-structure with the bishop as a pontiff (bridge) spanning the local churches. A diocese would be a meaningless entity without local churches – like a general's HQ without troops. The problem is that few of the leaders of growing local churches, the real movers and shakers we so urgently need, have time over for deanery and diocesan synods and their endless committees. But those who sit on them are the ones who usually get promoted for their commitment to the structures, and eventually come to dictate to those with growing churches. Sounds arrogant to say it, but in these days of crisis such deadly realities need to be spelt out. Many of our 'higher' clergy have little or no real experience of leading dynamic churches. Where they have had such experience, before being made bishops, then the pressures of their office soon drain their ministries dry. 'If we are not careful we can find that enormous energies are expended in maintaining our institutions. We have a massive inheritance of buildings, assemblies and committees . . . which can have greedy appetites for time and effort', wrote Archbishop George Carey.[1] Few of these good people who have been moving to the centre and up have been very able to make any significant difference to the crippling diocesan structures they inherited once they have found themselves sitting in the top seats. And some have clearly sacrificed too much of their cutting edge in the process of getting there. Many will be retiring over the next few years leaving their dioceses in a bankrupt state. Other good people have moved to the *edge* and *out* in despair. We must do everything to help those godly and gifted leaders to stay in or to stay close. They are too valuable to lose.

Although during all my working life I have stayed within the established church out of a sense of love and loyalty, nevertheless most of my ministry has been exercised at the edge – especially if considered geographically. Canon Harry Sutton used to talk of Chile as one of 'the uttermost parts of the earth – any further and you drop off!' Thomas Merton, I believe, once wrote of 'the edge where the future is both endangered and engendered' – I liked that! And Archbishop Robert Runcie asserted that 'The centre of the church's life lies on its circumference'. The circumference covers a lot more ground than the centre! So I was by no means original in thinking that the 'edge' was a strategic if risky place from which to exercise my ministry! And perhaps it could be the 'cutting edge' too! For that reason I have opted to stay there in spite of some strong temptations to move. About twenty years ago a big church in the United States asked us to consider becoming their rector with a salary of $90,000 a year and excellent accommodation including a furnished flat for visitors and a pension commensurable to my salary on the year that I retired. I turned to Mary and said jokingly: 'Surely this must constitute a "call" '? I knew she would be thinking as I was.

FERVOUR THAT THROWS DISCRETION TO THE WIND
Bishop Welldon once wrote: 'In all the Christian Church ... truth has ascended from the lower regions to the higher. It has sprung up in some humble cell or distant valley; it has been despised and eschewed, and even persecuted; it has fought its way to credit and honour; and only at last, after many days, has it received the stamp of official consecration.'[2]

Perhaps another trait acquired from Welldon was something which Richard Holle, the hermit of Hampole, taught his neighbouring Cistercian nuns to pray for: 'a fervour that throws discretion to the wind'. In a recent letter to *The Daily Telegraph* Earl Russell observed that 'the glue between the Church of England and English society is respectability'. Nothing so disturbs those who pride themselves on their respectability as enthusiasm that 'throws discretion to the wind'. The Establishment is always very wary of it in religion. Prime Minister Disraeli once queried Queen Victoria's desire to appoint Bishop A.C. Tait as Archbishop of Canterbury. 'There is in his idiosyncrasy a strange fund of enthusiasm, a quality which never ought to be possessed by an Archbishop or a Prime Minister', he cautioned. Yet it is noteworthy that the great movers and shakers of society like John Wesley, George Whitefield, Dwight L. Moody, Charles Spurgeon and Billy Graham – very real heroes of mine, who have motivated my life and clarified my calling – have all been ridiculed both by the church and secular society for their enthusiasm.

They have been a potential threat as they challenged other world-views and threatened accepted standards of respectability.

Without wanting to put myself in their class I am thankful that I have been able to share some of their zeal. I have felt that fire burning in my guts from the beginning to the end of my ministry.

In spite of my life-long commitment to the Church of England I often seem to have been a thorn in the flesh to the establishment. I recall a few instances. A lot of people were apparently embarrassed in 1973 by my defence of the military intervention in Chile. This drew fire from the international press at the time and certainly left me feeling very isolated from the wider church – especially when my direct boss, Archbishop Michael Ramsey expressed a very different view on the matter. But it would have been difficult to live with myself had I not said what I did at the time. Of course, with the wisdom of hindsight one can always think of ways one might have expressed oneself differently and perhaps avoided much painful criticism and hostility. Naturally one always has to examine one's motives. Did one have some kind of messianic or martyr complex knowing what the inevitable cost would be?

FRUSTRATIONS OF A CHURCH PLANTER

A consistent aspiration for me has been a commitment to initiate, foster and bless the new life God gives his church. I first recognised how absolutely vital this was when trying to church plant from scratch in Chile. New church plants need a great deal of long-term nurture and oversight; not all of them flourish immediately, and some fade away. While order in any church is essential, there must be some understanding about what that order ought to be. Should it be something fixed like the law of the Medes and Persians or flexible like the authority of a father at home with a growing family? New wineskins inevitably have to be different from old wineskins. We can't expect the new life to survive in an inflexible old order. But when it comes we can patiently encourage and guide it into an order that is relevant for its own new life – and even be a blessing to the remaining old life as well. This new life is too vital to lose. Order is man-made. Life is God given. The church can't generate this life by itself. But the church must nurture the new life when God gives it. This is why we can never dismiss or despise renewal. The new life may sometimes come from a messy birth but given time it will assume many of its parents' characteristics if the parent doesn't first reject it. Rearing a new wineskin church may not always make for an easy time but rearing a natural family has always had its problems too.

REGIONAL BISHOPS

As already mentioned we once had a bishop over us, a delightful and godly man, with whom I found myself at odds for some years. This may have been because of some awkward idiosycrasy of mine but also because of his difficulty in making decisions. I was not alone in wanting decisions but no doubt there were others who saw his hesitancy quite differently, and saw me as a pain in the neck.

If a process of indigenisation (something on which we needed decisions) was out of the question then we had to reconsider how our role in Chile as Anglicans should be defined. There remained other major questions also which we hardly knew how to articulate. We had envisaged the Anglican Church in Chile as a *via media* between an effective grassroots movement of Pentecostalism working among the masses, and the powerful Roman Catholic Church well integrated into the political structures and the families of the social elite. Of course the RCs also had another strata in the *callampas* (shanty-towns) – the poor with their synthesis of superstition and folk Catholicism. We had always felt that the Anglicans could offer a middle way between something evangelical and something traditional. This might serve to catch some of the upwardly mobile of the more educated Pente-costalists, or some of the many alienated Catholics suffering from disillusionment about their church. But the major problem with this vision, which I had never fully comprehended until we started to work in Chile, was that there is an inherent English ethos about Anglicanism that had blurred our cultural perceptions. And how compatible would such an Anglican Church be, imposed on the Chilean culture, in maintaining the vital dynamic necessary for spontaneous expansion? Our traditional church hardly copes with this even in the UK! Planting new churches in Chile also involved our putting a great deal of stress on the values of a church as a denomination rather than the gospel of Jesus Christ as the way of salvation and the kingdom of God and his righteousness as the way of life.

COULD A CHILEAN BISHOP BE REALLY ANGLICAN?

Again, could we realistically expect to see such an Anglican Church run by Chileans? How assured would the Chilean leadership ever be in the theology, liturgy and ecclesiology of the Church of England, if it was all imposed on them from the English, like us, with our cultural blinkers? So much of our own English church life had developed spontaneously from particular church crises and more slowly and pragmatically through the evolving cultures of English church history. Episcopacy overseas, without our cultural traditions and restraint could quickly become dictatorial, or, worse still, tyrannical. Obviously leadership by a foreigner was inappropriate if it continued for too long.

We, as a mission, had had a major focus on the poor but should we now be putting more energy into developing a Chilean middle class church to draw on for a unique kind of future leadership who would appreciate our more liturgical setting for worship? These were all considerations that affected how we should be leading the church in Chile into the future. These were the unresolved questions that we wrestled with continuously amongst ourselves, and where needed, our bishop to help us in forming some creative policies.

THE FIELD ADVISORY COUNCIL

We had a Field Advisory Council[3] set up to look after the care and placing of missionaries on the field. It also became a forum for sharing some of these longer term concerns. As a first step, assuming we were still intending to develop an Anglican Church in Chile, there was obviously a need for a different model for bishops. Our thinking on this was soon put together in a document compiled by Douglas Milmine and Eddie Gibbs. They were both living in Santiago at the time and produced this study called 'Regional Episcopacy'.[4] It spelt out a practical process for dividing a huge diocese geographically into much more manageable areas under 'front line', 'hands-on' pioneer bishops –

who were to be paid no more than other missionary clergy. Since finance was a controlling factor in so many ways, these 'regional' bishops would be unencumbered with the normal diocesan structures or the trappings of a diocesan office. But they were to have delegated authority from their diocesan bishop to make the necessary decisions for their regions – leading in counsel with their field teams. We encouraged our bishop to take copies of this 'study' to the Lambeth Conference (1968) where it was shared more widely amongst his peers. It aroused the interest of the then Anglican Executive Officer, Bishop Ralph Dean, and several dioceses around the world took some of it on board soon after. It was believed to have had direct impact on the dioceses of London in England, and Sydney in Australia – to mention just two that began to delegate much more authority to area bishops. In Chile it led to Colin Bazley eventually being consecrated a bishop for the Cautin region in the middle south of Chile in 1969 and myself for the region of Valparaíso in the middle north the following year. These consecrations were meant to point towards the not too distant appointment of national bishops as our replacements so it was obvious that our role in Chile should be reasonably short lived.

LAY PRESIDENCY

Soon after these consecrations we seriously mooted the matter of lay presidency for the sacrament of Holy Communion. This was something which had bugged me ever since I had been asked to consider that call to the Argentinian Chaco in 1957 to minister the sacrament to churches among three Indian tribes there. Surely, from the start, our new churches should be receiving this sacrament regularly from their own elders in the church! In trying to do things properly the proposal initiated from Chile was taken up, via the diocese to the Southern Cone Council of Bishops. From there it eventually reached the Anglican Consultative Council under the Archbishop of Canterbury, where it got thrown out. Later it was again picked up and debated by the General Synod of the Church of England and went on to the House of Bishops who dismissed the idea as untimely. Later it was taken up by the Sydney diocese in 1999 and although passed by a good majority, their own Archbishop Goodhew refused to give it the final seal of approval. Had he done so it would then have established a precedent for the whole of the Anglican Communion. Sydney has a new archbishop now and I don't think we have heard the last of lay presidency in the Anglican Church. From within the embryonic structures of the early church itself there is precedent for embracing such a practice. A travelling 'prophet' was permitted to preside at the Eucharist according to the first century Didache and later we find a 'confessor' (one who kept the faith under torture and threat of martyrdom) could also celebrate at the Lord's Table according to The Apostolic Tradition (third century AD). Today it is openly accepted that prisoners of war, lacking an ordained chaplain, could celebrate the sacrament among themselves. Another current model is that of the Catholic Church in the rural shanty-towns of Latin America where the poor have apparently been mobilised for ministry and mission in their own context; and where, according to one Catholic commentator, a lay community leader may preside at the Lord's Supper.[5]

LAY MINISTRY OF THE SACRAMENT NECESSARY
When we later started to plant daughter churches we had no 'ordained' leaders to put in charge of our new congregations that were outside the parish. I had to suggest to the lay leaders that since they were able to pastor regular congregations of fifty or more adults that they would have to celebrate the sacrament of the Lord's Supper with them. Christ had instituted this sacrament as a means of grace that all God's children need. I explained that what I was suggesting was officially 'out of order' in normal Anglican circles but not in their exceptional circumstances. With officers on the field of battle, the senior surviving officer was able to commission new officers from the ranks if the need arose, these newly created officers serving in this way until the war was over, when they would revert to their war substantive rank; this model seemed the best way forward for our new church plants in these exceptional circumstances – there being no 'ordained' person available to preside at holy communion for them. And these exceptional circumstances would pertain until the Church of

England could find a place for the new wineskins within a more flexible order. This could happen under a sympathetic diocesan bishop, and incidentally this is why I have always believed in the ideal of episcopacy if only for pragmatic reasons. A sensible bishop could come to some arrangement about good order, such that either he would ordain the church plant leader already *in situ* (as indeed has been done) or the church plant could choose an 'ordained' person mutually acceptable to both the bishop and themselves. They could then be licensed to take over the running of the new church plant. Incidentally I never allowed laity to preside in St Andrew's where I had been appointed by the bishop under oath to preserve Anglican order. But in our church plants the situation was different – and the diocese was as yet unready to propose a radical approach in this area. To soften the radical nature of this step we called the celebrations 'agapes' rather than holy communion.

QUOTA CAPPING

In the latter part of the 1980s, the time came when we eventually had to cap our quota to the diocese. Although I was personally asked for my opinion I left the discussions about this to our financial experts who frequently appealed against the unfairness in expecting our members to contribute 2.5 times per capita more than any other church members in the diocese. This unjust system was voted in by a large majority at the diocesan synod. Obviously from the other churches' points of view the more we paid the less would be asked of them. There was no way of changing the system democratically and we were granted no leeway by the diocese. So our PCC decided to continue paying a generous amount to fully cover the total upkeep of our own clergy (training, housing and pension contributions etc), and a further donation towards the costs of running the diocese. This unilateral action caused a lot of ill-feeling. The official diocesan year book with information on all the parishes continued to publish the quota demanded and the actual sum rendered by each church which might be regarded as an act of shaming! We were accused of running a congregational church and opting out of the Church of England! Rather unfair when we were still giving more generously than any other church in the diocese and running at no cost to them at all, unlike the majority of Anglican churches and producing some of the highest numbers of baptisms, confirmations, communicants and ordinands.

But what made things worse was the growing realisation that the costs for the maintenance of our episcopal oversight were rising significantly. Diocesan staffing and structures continue to grow while church attendance and the number of parish clergy generally declines. Michael Moynagh sums it up as 'Tadpole Christianity – all head and no body'.[6] The cost of resourcing all our bishops would be equivalent to putting 600 clergy in front line ministry today! What is more, it will take a while for the laity to forget how the Church Commissioners (which includes all the diocesan bishops) recently lost some £800 million of their church's money in bad investments, money originally intended to supplement the stipends of parish clergy.

Having said this we always honoured our bishop and prayed for him and gave him a warm welcome when he visited. Bishops have many headaches just trying to maintain the status quo and we wanted to mollify such pain as far as is possible in a good Christian spirit.

FINANCIAL COMMITMENTS OF GROWING CHURCHES
Our church members trusted their PCC because they knew their offerings would go towards the objectives they were supporting, whether this was a social project in a needy area which had particularly moved them, the salary needed for a full-time secretary, an extra youth worker, or the support of a missionary. These are the realities in a local church that must be faced honestly by any diocese without trying to bully them for more money when they are already giving very generously. We had a big staff at St Andrew's. Few clergy and bishops seem to have much idea about how demanding in time, energy and money it can be to run a large growing church. I had inherited a congregation that was already giving away 50% of its annual income to evangelism, missionary work overseas, and needy inner city churches staffed by personnel who had gone out from St Andrew's or with whom we had built up a relationship through

our Faith Sharing visits. We continued paying our full quota for years until the demands became totally unreasonable. We could not risk killing a goose that laid such golden eggs.

The question of St Andrew's non-compliance was recently raised again in the deanery and one man from another parish rose to its defence saying he had known St Andrew's since before it became a parish in 1963. It had since built and furnished its own church, its vicarage and housing for three other members of staff, besides three extensions on the church building and its original premises, now an extra church hall and it fully paid for all its staff. It still contributed generously towards its high quota without costing the diocese a penny.

Holiday Week

Ever since I had been at St Andrew's, we had been very proud of our annual Holiday Week for children on Chorleywood Common. But by 1988 I felt that we could no longer go on running it. This was a tricky move because it had been operating for some twenty-three years, the original vision of John Perry. From the beginning, St Andrew's had overseen the planning of this week in a huge marquee and St Andrew's had always provided the organiser. Barry Kissell, with his great gift for communicating to children, usually gave the lead at the morning gatherings during the week. After that, each day, the children were divided up into groups and went off for teaching and other activities with their leaders. The whole thing was a great success story and children were soon coming in from miles around. It was a united venture supported by all the churches. Over 1,000 children collected each day on Chorleywood Common during that week. But it became increasingly difficult to find an overseer to organise such a major event. And it was even harder to find leaders with sufficient experience to take responsibility for the smaller groups. In the end we were relying on a number of extremely young volunteers. But latterly there were warnings of stranger-danger – men, unknown in the community, had been spotted wandering about on the common and approaching the children. Fortunately we had no tragedies but I felt we could no longer carry the responsibility. I put it to our PCC that, although this Holiday Week had become the pride of all the local churches, we would be acting irresponsibly if we could not provide better oversight. The PCC agreed. There was a very strong reaction when we said we could not go on supporting it – indeed a minor explosion from the other churches in the community – and when we started New Wine the following year it was mooted that that was the real reason for its closure, but such is the price of leadership.

RUFFLING MORE FEATHERS

Every now and again, after I have spoken at some lively young church plant, I get a letter or phone call of disapproval from a bishop's chaplain. The complaint is that I have ministered to an orthodox body of Christian believers which for some reason is out of favour with the local vicar or the bishop of the diocese. Our policy has always been, where practical, one of bending over backwards to keep any of these enthusiastic, orthodox and godly fellowships as warmly disposed towards the traditional church as possible. All too often the new wineskin congregations get written off. Permission to preach in them is withheld from visiting Anglican ministers. Officialdom tries to forget them, ignore them or perhaps sits back to criticise them as they pass through their natural growing pains. Some of the faults for division may have originated from people in the new plant but we cannot help them by our ostracisation. Many of their members do in fact have a great respect for so much that they have learned in the church they came out of, and very often these new wineskins are built up around ex-Anglican/Methodist/Baptist leaders.

When the gospel seed is planted in a community there is enough DNA within it to reproduce a congregation with all the potential for a church with its own leadership. The call today in our prevailing post modern generation is for a renewed confidence in the gospel of the kingdom to enable us to envisage the exciting possibility of new kinds of church for the future and to grow these new churches without presuming the exact form they should always take in the process. The best way is to allow the new wineskins to develop under the resourceful eye of the parent body. Then the parent church leader and the new wineskin leader should foster a climate of mutual relationship which could be profitable for both. From time to time the new leader's authority is going to be challenged and that's when the counsel and support of the sponsoring church leadership will count for a great deal. The parent body can try to impose as much of its tradition as it can get away with but must be very sensitive not to insist or smother the new life. There can only be a limited standard approach – and this must be offered in the context of a caring, understanding, and patient relationship.

WONDERFUL EXCEPTIONS

Of course there are wonderful episcopal examples of bishops who have taken bold risks. Sometimes things have gone wrong. One was the tragedy of the Nine O'Clock Service in Sheffield where the bishop took a risk, but as we have learned since, the signs of trouble brewing were not picked up in time by those he appointed to oversee it. I speak with some understanding as I had a hardworking and highly committed daughter involved. Although the leadership there failed tragically yet their vision for the post modern generation inspired many other initiatives in other places. By saying this I am not implying that all the new life is limited to young people. My friend Martin Down was a Norfolk vicar running two rural parishes. Renewal broke out in one of his churches. It was mooted that they might need to remove the pews. When he saw how much this was going to upset the village community he decided to continue ministering to the traditional residue in the traditional way but to start up a third church elsewhere in a local social centre. He now had three congregations – two traditional ones, with twenty worshippers in one and about forty in the other. Quite good really for those tiny Norfolk villages! But, on a recent count there were over 130 in the new church plant. This soon acquired some land to build its own centre – in spite of considerable opposition. The two traditional churches eventually gave Martin a vote of no confidence. He did not have to leave. He did not want to leave. He had the parson's freehold. He is an orthodox, wise and gentle leader, able and caring, and wonderfully supported by his wife. But the two traditional churches did not want to share him and considered that he could not give them sufficient time and energy for pastoring their two small churches properly while running this new plant also. His wise bishop released him, provided a house for him, and licensed him to go ahead with the newest congregation. He, in return, gave up his 'freehold', and his original two parish churches were then linked with two other churches under a new vicar. I was at the Norwich Showground where Martin and his team had organised an annual conference called 'Living Waters'[7] with over 2,500 attendees present in the year 2000 – including many clergy. Martin's example in church planting and spiritual leadership over a wide area in Norfolk provides inspiration and encouragement for the wider church and a number of its clergy.

No one really likes doing it, but sometimes someone has to take the risk of ruffling a few feathers. But I would like to think maybe there's a more positive side to this; we are called to 'hold fast the confession of our hope without wavering . . . and let us consider how to stir up one another to love and good works'[8] – even if we sometimes slip up in the process of stirring up.

IN CONCLUSION

Man goes to his eternal home
(ECCLESIASTES 12:5)

O that there were such an heart in them, that they would fear me, and keep all my commandments always, that it might be well with them, and with their children for ever!
(DEUTERONOMY 5:29, KJV)

It was Einstein who made the real trouble. He announced in 1905 that there was no such thing as absolute rest. After that there never was
(STEPHEN LEACOCK)

Asked about when he might retire the ageing, Lord Chief Justice Denning replied that he had been credited with every virtue except that of resignation
(TV INTERVIEW)

How blessed it is to do nothing and to rest after it
(PERSIAN PROVERB)

In peace let me resign my breath and thy salvation see My sins deserve eternal death but Jesus died for me
(ANON)

The time leading up to our departure was hectic. I could not attend any of the courses thoughtfully laid on by the diocese to help us prepare for retirement. Admittedly I became a little dubious when my one-time colleague Dick Lyth returned from one session. Apparently an elderly doctor was billed to speak to these all-male clerics on the brink of their retirement. He had rushed into the lecture room belatedly, smoothed out his crumpled notes and after apologies and some reshuffling of the pages, proceeded to deliver his rambling address! When, an hour later, the old doctor finished, and for the first time scanned his audience for questions, he suddenly became very agitated. Not surprising since he had just addressed the gathering on the hazards of the menopause for women! Dick Lyth did his best to assure the nervous doctor that he had found his address most helpful – and persuaded him that everyone else present would have found great value in it also! Dick always was the personification of grace and tact.

WHERE WOULD WE LIVE?

I hardly ever stopped to think how it would feel when it came to stepping out of harness. Bishop Hensley Henson from Durham, who put himself out to grass at Hadleigh on the Essex/Suffolk borders, succeeded in making it sound a miserable affair. I think a lot of people do indeed find it very hard. Others just seem to have sat down and died – or cried – like Alexander the Great weeping that he had no more worlds to conquer. When the time came I wondered how, as a retired clergyman, I would manage – especially financially. What kind of a house could we possibly afford? And where would we live? With a loan from the Church Commissioners, and generous help from Sir John and Lady Paulson (my brother-in-law and sister), we managed to buy a bungalow in the neighbouring parish of Christ Church, Chorleywood – an ideal home and a most convenient place to retire. Mary and I pray together daily and in our prayers we thank God for his goodness in giving us this delightful little house – since enhanced by an extra two rooms and a bathroom in the attic. We both have the luxury of our own study with our own books and word processors. The place has a landscaped garden at the back that we look out onto as we eat our meals together. The garden may prove just a little too much in the long-term – but when that time comes we plan to put up a fence and turn half of it into a nature reserve!

CONSIDERED BAD FORM

Some consider it bad form to retire too near one's last parish. The old vicar might upset the new one by criticising any changes he may make! Well, if he wanted to do that he could do it on the telephone, even if he had retired to the other side of the country. Most of us retire with the well-being of the church family we are leaving at heart, and we want to encourage every gift our successors may bring to the parish. There was no desire to interfere from our proximity – any more than Archbishop Runcie's retirement back to St Albans made him want to interfere in the running of his old diocese. In our case we needed to be near the New Wine and the Soul Survivor offices – half of which at that time were still in Chorleywood and in Watford. I hope we have not inhibited our successor at St Andrew's. We have not interfered, leaving him absolutely free to press on in the radical new ways that he has thought right for the church.

In retirement one does need to live reasonably close to one's support systems – the medical and dental centre, reliable electricians, plumbers, gardeners, window cleaners, garage and car mechanics etc who have all become trusted helpers over the years. There is also the need to be near friends and family if possible. Our youngest daughter Tasha still lives in Chorleywood. The other daughters are all further afield. We have twelve grand-children, and feel very blessed.

Since retirement, when at home, we have worshipped with the Soul Survivor Fellowship in Watford led by Mike Pilavachi – in Anglican terms a layman. The congregation are a completely unchurchy breed and usually this vibrant post modern generation (with a sprinkling of older folk) pack out the warehouse that serves as their worship centre. The vicar of the local parish, Chris Cotty, has acted as the chaplain and ministered the sacraments there on a regular basis using a minimal liturgical framework. The suffragan bishop has visited to take confirmations and we have had several weddings there too.

VIRTUOUS WIFE WHO EXCELS
Ashley Cooper[1] was reading about the virtuous woman in the book of Proverbs[2] and wrote in the margin of his Bible: 'Would to God I could find such a wife!' Some years later he added – 'Praise the Lord, I have!' I too have been blessed by the best wife I could possibly have found – faithful, courageous, caring and her own

person; not long after we first met, we had an ardent discussion over the subject of infant baptism, and we have probably discussed every other issue ardently ever since. I am constantly delighted to discover, as surely most married couples do, that even after so many years together, my appreciation of her still grows. Our love sprang out of a friendship that has proved both endearing and enduring. Anne Landers hit the nail on the head when she said: 'Love is friendship that has caught fire'. It is, but fires don't keep burning at the same intensity for long otherwise all would be consumed. W.E. Sangster once wrote a marvellous dedication to his wife. It ran: 'To Margaret, my wife, with whom it is as easy to stay in love as it was to fall in love'. I was tempted to borrow it. In our experience true love keeps evolving, from near blind attraction into a deeper, richer, more realistic commitment of loyalty, common interests, mutual caring concern, companionship and devotion – where Mary, I'm sure, has done a lot more work than I have to make it succeed. I think most older couples would resonate with such words. But partly inspired by Sangster I dedicated my first book *Come Holy Spirit* with the words: 'To my wife Mary, whose questing spirit for the things of God has continually challenged me and inspired me since we first met thirty years ago'.[3]

Mary has been a tremendous wife and mother in the home, and a wonderful helpmeet on the mission field and in the parish – and a speaker much sought after across the world, especially in the areas of spiritual growth and maturity. She is also the writer of many books – just finishing her twelfth. This makes me very proud of her. The downside is that when she is scratching her head for illustrations in her talks and books, it's my shortcomings, foibles and worse, that seem to come most readily to her mind! Admittedly it does what she hoped and holds the attention of her audiences.

FOUR DAUGHTERS
We have enjoyed very happy relationships with each of our four daughters. The eldest, Charlotte, is a trained teacher of the deaf and an interpreter for Spanish speakers. Her husband, Canon Christopher Coxworth is now the Principal of Ridley Hall,

Cambridge, besides writing a number of books and doing liturgical work for the wider church. They have done so well together and we are very proud of them with their family of five sons – Timothy, Ashley, Samuel, Sebastian and Matthew.

Our second daughter, Debby, is married to John Wright, who grew up in St Andrew's. He has since grown into an outstanding church leader. He and Debby went to New Zealand on a Faith Sharing mission with Barry Kissell and he stopped off with Debby on the way home to work as an intern on John Wimber's staff in California. When they returned to the UK for further biblical studies they worked with John Mumford for seven years in starting up the South West London Vineyard Fellowship. John and Debby later moved up to Nottingham, with a van, a ladder and a paint brush – to earn a living interior decorating and to plant a Vineyard Christian Fellowship there. They were joined by three other couples from the SWL Vineyard Fellowship and they now meet in the Nottingham football club, and after less than four years they have such a large congregation that they need new premises. They have two boys – Zachary and Jordan.

Becky, our third daughter, was a gifted evangelist with a great talent for friendship. She caught Chris Brain's vision for reaching out to night-clubbers in Sheffield. This led to her joining the now infamous Nine O'Clock Service there. After ten years of dedicated work with the NOS, it broke up, leaving Becky and her husband Robert totally disillusioned.

The personal result for Becky was not only a breakdown of trust in the church but the break-up of her marriage. She is now settled again, still in Sheffield, with Richard Barrett. They have a baby girl called Nina.

The NOS was not a total disaster, however, as its pioneering of alternative worship for our post modern generation has inspired many other churches since to do the same. Soul Survivor in Watford is a case in point, where our youngest daughter Tasha (Natasha Clare) and her husband (Mike Shaw a successful financial consultant) worship regularly with their family. Mike committed his life to Christ the weekend of John Wimber's first visit. Their children are Philip, Andrew, Grace and Daniel. They now live in the same road as ourselves.

Mary and I pray daily for each of our grandchildren by name as most Christian grandparents would do. I can never forget just how much I owe to God for my own parents' prayers. A six-year-old grandchild of mine once told me with great sadness about the loss of his grandad, his father's father – his first close encounter with death! When I arrived at his house he suddenly blurted out: 'Grandpa! Grandad's dead,' and looking greatly concerned, he went on: 'And Grandpa, you'll be the next!' 'Well, yes,' I said and added, 'It could well be that I will be the next, and that's why I always keep my hand in the hand of Jesus. He has done everything for us so that we can live with him for ever.'

BLESSED BY FRIENDS TOO

We have been most fortunate. So many invitations for both of us to speak at conferences in so many interesting places overseas (three times in six months to Sweden already in this last year) have continued since retirement. We have kept up our regular annual holidays in Turkey, Greece and its many islands greatly enhanced by the presence of our consistently loyal friends Richard and Prue Bedwell. Through the extraordinarily generous help from another friend Anderly Hardy in Chile (whose late husband was the first to help us on our arrival at Valparaíso in 1959 and often since) we have been enabled to make many enjoyable return visits to Chile and Argentine, a luxury trip to the Norwegian fjords and another to Ecuador and the Galapagos Islands – blessings totally undeserved, unexpected and greatly appreciated.

NO RESTING ON OUR LAURELS

Entering his fifties, a well known spiritual director, Henre Nouwen, was faced with this simple question: 'Did becoming older bring me closer to Jesus?' And he continued, 'After twenty-five years of ministry, I found myself praying poorly, isolated from other people, and very much preoccupied with burning issues. Something inside was telling me that my success was putting my own soul in danger. I woke up one day with the realization that I was living in a very dark place and the term "burn out" was just a psychological translation for spiritual death'. I read those words as a humbling challenge!

There's a passage in Dickens' *Pickwick Papers* where Sam Weller leads his hard-worked nag back to his yard at the end of a long day's work. A friend offers to take the animal out of the wagon's shafts. Weller hastily protests, warning him that if he did that the beast would just lie down and die. It was being in the shafts that kept his horse alive! I soon found something similar was happening to me and was surprised and shocked to find, on my retirement, just how much of my own Christian discipline had been bound up with my work. Being unharnessed, it's only too easy to get undisciplined over things like prayer and meditation on the Word of God.

Over the years, we have witnessed many good things that God has done. But we must never fall prey to reliance on past experience or resting on our laurels – that would be flirting with disaster. We cannot relax in any comfortable world of accomplished dreams or imagine we have fulfilled our life's work. We know, only too well, that when we have done all we are still unprofitable servants. Who is not humbled by Christ's words about the hungry, the thirsty, the stranger, the naked, the sick and the prisoner, and who can forget all those wasted opportunities when one could and should have done more? We have no excuses. We can only trust in the grace of God to forgive.

As the years pass I am frequently challenged by the words of St Paul, who, after all his incredible achievements, could still write: 'Not that I have already obtained this or am already perfect; but I press on to make it my own, because Christ Jesus has made me his own . . . one thing I do, forgetting what lies behind and straining forward to what lies ahead, I press on toward the goal for the prize of the upward call of God in Christ Jesus'.[4]

LAST INSTALMENT MISSING

'An autobiography is an obituary in serial form with the last instalment still missing'.[5] We never know if we have nearly finished the race or whether there are miles of years still to go.

Since amusing anecdotes are an irresistible passion, I must conclude with just two – first, the comment of a teenage girl: 'When I die I want to go peacefully in my sleep like my grandfather. Not screaming – like the rest of the passengers in his car!' I hope my passing will not endanger others but if I am still conscious when the time comes, I want to prepare for my going with that simple 'Jesus Prayer' I often use to fill my in between moments – 'Lord Jesus Christ, Son of God, have mercy on me, a sinner!'

I have always loved the eighteenth-century story of John Newton, one-time slave-trader and then himself a slave, who lived such a long and saintly life after his amazing conversion to Christ. In his blinding old age he remarked to a friend: 'I am like a person going on a journey in a stage coach, who expects its arrival every hour, and is frequently looking out of the window for it.' And when that stage coach finally calls for me I want to go like St Paul – knowing nothing 'save Jesus Christ and him crucified'[6] and, like him, to depart, fully believing that 'for me to live is Christ, and to die is gain.'[7] What more wonderful way could there be to go?

'Some day you will read in the papers that Moody is dead.' D.L. Moody once said. 'Don't you believe a word of it. At that moment I shall be more alive than I am now . . . That which is born of the flesh may die. That which is born of the spirit shall live for ever.'[8] I could not express my own belief more clearly than that.

When I was a child I laughed and wept –
Time crept!
When as a youth I dreamed and talked –
Time walked!
When I became a full grown man –
Time ran!
Then, as with the years I older grew —
Time flew!
Soon I shall travel on –
Time gone!
(ANON)

NOTES

PREFACE:
1. Quoted by Michael Parkinson at Harry Secombe's memorial service in Westminster Abbey 26th October 2001.
2. Alex Twells *Standing on the Promises – A History of St Andrew's Church* (Wimbledon, Clifford Frost Ltd, 1998).
3. Max Depree *The Art of Leadership* (New York, Dell Publishing, 1989).

CHAPTER 1 – INTO THE FRYING PAN
1. Revelation 1:17.

CHAPTER 2 – EARLY DAYS
1. 1 Samuel 17.
2. 1 Samuel 17:45b,46a,47b, RSV.
3. This is taken from published research by my nephew Richard Pytches about father's side of the family.
4. I visited this imposing building in the 1980s. It was by then owned by a millionaire businessman.
5. Alfred Lord Tennyson 'Home thoughts, from the Sea'.
6. Order for the Burial of the Dead, *Book of Common Prayer*, 1962. Attributed to the Celtic Saint Columbanus.
7. James 4:14, KJV.
8. Hebrews 9:27, KJV.
9. Cf Stanley Griffin's *A Forgotten Revival* (Day One Publications).
10. There were two Abbot's Halls in Suffolk. One was in Pettaugh, the other in Stowmarket. The latter, which once belonged to a Pytches forebear, is now an Agricultural Museum.
11. For many years father had to pay a third of this as a pension to his predecessor who gave up 'the living' for retirement. That was normal practice in those days. These were the days before stipends and pensions were standardised: one of the few good results of the centralised management of the Church of England.
12. Mary D. Duncan, 1814–40.
13. Job 1:5c.
14. 1 Samuel 3:4.
15. Genesis 37:2.
16. Peter accumulated numerous degrees, including a doctorate. He became a prebund of St Paul's, London.
17. Jack died while serving as the Rector of Palgrave, Suffolk. His widow, Thora, later married Wilfred Stott the one-time missionary to China one of the parsons round about us who had helped me greatly.

CHAPTER 3 – EDUCATION
1. Since burned down and relocated, then relocated again to Brettenham Park, Suffolk under Donald Sewell, younger son of the current head in my day. I was a contemporary of Donald's at OBH.
2. 1 John 3:3.
3. Now renamed 'Crossways'.
4. His youngest son Stephen, then about six, later became Regius Professor of Divinity

at Cambridge and then Bishop of Ely.
5. Genesis 6:4, KJV.
6. 'Furlough' was the term they used for this.

CHAPTER 4 – ONWARD CHRISTIAN SOLDIER
1. Ezekiel 11:16, KJV.
2. Luke 15:7, RSV.

CHAPTER 5 – TESTING MY VOCATION
1. Twenty years later (1972), after some difficult negotiations and strong pressure from the centre of the Anglican Church, Tyndale was united with Clifton Theological College and Dalton House, to create Trinity College, Bristol.
2. Matthew 10:32,33 KJV.

CHAPTER 6 – I TURNED MY COLLAR ROUND
1. This was known as a title.
2. Named after Ebba, a sixth-century saint who supposedly sought to cleanse her soul more thoroughly by spending nights up to her neck in the icy waters of the Isis river on its way along to the Thames.
3. A one-time nurse.
4. Cranmer's masterly English style, still preserved in the 1662 Prayer Book, ensured his greatness as a liturgiologist.
5. Between them they led one of the longest and most fruitful revivals in our church history – 1730s onward.
6. Resigning from there in 1843.
7. Later also ordained in the C of E.
8. The latter was reputed to have conducted ordinations wearing crimson gloves!
9. This expression was first coined by Charles Spurgeon.
10. Years later his professionally trained wife became our Music Director at St Andrew's, Chorleywood, and John became one of our organists there too.
11. Psalm 27:8, KJV.
12. Oxford Inter Colleges Christian Union.
13. Owned by Britain and France at that time.
14. Fully supported by the French.
15. Alfred Lord Tennyson, *Locksley Hall.*
16. I could not help feeling a little smug when fifteen years later I invited the BCMS (by then Crossways) to help us by supplying missionaries for Peru. This was the northernmost part of the immense diocese in South America that I had taken over from Ken Howell. They graciously rose to the challenge and sent personnel.
17. Psalm, 2:8 KJV.
18. He had the chair there for the study of Christianity in the Non-Christian World.
19. *The Occasional Bulletin of Missionary Research* – April 1979.
20. A former Principal of Clifton Theological College.
21. Up from £300 to £750 pa.
22. *The Unfinished History of St Patrick's*, 1982, p14.

CHAPTER 7 – RELUCTANT MISSIONARIES
1. *The Story of John G. Paton* (London, Hodder and Stoughton, 1899). This book, which I still have, had been strongly recommended to me by that phrenetic reader of biography, Peter Dawes, long before he became the Bishop of Derby.

2. Elizabeth Elliot (London, Hodder and Stoughton, 1957).
3. 2nd January 1956.
4. Wallington, under Vernon Hedderly's leadership, raised extensive funds for the repair work to our hospital and school in Chol Chol, following the terrible earthquake of 20th May 1960.
5. Matthew 10:39.
6. John 12:24.
7. Matthew 10:37, KJV.
8. Matthew 19:29.
9. Literally the 'Land of Fire'. Passing sailors had so named it after the sight of so many fires along the coast where the Indians, the Onas and Alacalufes, were cooking their fish suppers in the open air.
10. The *Spectator*, 26th May 1884.

CHAPTER 8 – THOSE WHO PAVED THE WAY
1. 20th May 1960.
2. Tidal wave – often the result of an earthquake with its epicentre out at sea.
3. The obituaries were not worth the paper they were printed on, according to my friends at home.
4. 1 Thessalonians 3:1.

CHAPTER 9 – VALPARAÍSO – HERE WE COME!
1. Valparaíso could boast of fifteen of these *ascensores*. Our hill (Cerro Concepcion) was reached by the oldest one, built in 1883.
2. 22,000 feet above sea level.
3. Luke 2:29a,30, KJV.

CHAPTER 10 – SPONTANEOUS CHURCH
1. Romans 16:5.
2. See verse 3.
3. The Humming Birds.
4. Probably reflecting a deeper issue of authority between missionary societies and bishops. The former tended to control so much manpower and strategy within a diocese by their ongoing (almost) lay patronage. Cf. Hans Cnattingius, *Bishops and Societies* (London, SPCK, 1952) p186.
5. Lord Louis Mountbatten also came on one occasion and HRH Prince Philip on another during our time in Valparaíso, but for them we laid on a special service in English.
6. Doug Milmine was later to become Bishop of Paraguay and Eddie Gibbs Professor of the School of Church Growth, California.

CHAPTER 11 – RETURNING
1. Luke 11:11–13.
2. Psalm 30:5.
3. Luke 11:9.
4. 1 Corinthians 13:4–6.
5. London, Hodders, 1998.
6. And many other missionaries since.
7. Since their chaplain had his own house.

Chapter 12 – Chile's Marxist President

1. Prague, Orbis Press Agency, 1979.
2. London, Collins, 1984. Cf. chapter on Chile pp 123–152.
3. The election was close-run. Allende's left-wing Popular United Party had 36.3% of the votes. Allesandri's Conservative National Party had 34.98% of the votes and Tomic's Christian Democrats had 27.84%.
4. 'Fatherland and Freedom'.
5. International Telephone and Telegraph.
6. Cf. Regis Debray, *Conversations with Allende/Socialism in Chile* (New Left Review Editons, 1971). These frank conversations are significant and revealing. Allende trusted Debray, a French journalist and left-wing sympathiser, who had just visited the revolutionary Che Guevara's freshly disinterred remains in Bolivia. The late Che Guevara had been a personal friend of Allende since Cuba days; op. cit. p 119.
7. Ibid 120.
8. Long before his presidency he had been one of the founders of Chile's National Health Service.
9. Popular Unity.
10. Allende's own party which was itself faction ridden.
11. Literally *Movimiento Izquierdista Revolucionario*.
12. Naval intelligence later led to the uncovering of a plot to promote rebellion among the Naval ratings on board the cruiser *Latorre*, stationed off Valparaíso, which involved the murder of officers in their bunks, the bombardment of on-shore installations by the ships the rebels had hoped to capture. Some 300 sailors (mostly ordinary ratings under the age of twenty-five) were arrested and interrogated. This triggered off a violent demonstration by the MIR-istas in Valparaíso who erected barricades against the Naval garrison – cf. Robert Moss, *Chile's Marxist Experiment* (Newton Abbot, David & Charles, 1973) p 200.
13. Mainly over drink.
14. Its high standard of discipline stood in marked contrast to the others.
15. According to the Weimar rate.
16. Popular basket.
17. For Chile this meant mostly the owners themselves.
18. I have inserted this heading – it was not in the original text.
19. Published in *El Mecurio* on 2nd September 1973 – just nine days before the coup.

Chapter 13 – Civil War

1. Sheila Cassidy, *Audacity to Believe* (London, Collins, 1977) p 161.
2. Fidel Castro had overthrown the Batista regime in 1958 and summarily shot all its leaders. Many more killings followed Castro's rise to power (supposedly 50,000 victims – far in excess of anything that ever happened in Chile) as did torture in Fidel Castro's one-party State – but the British have made little protest on those continued violations of human rights either then or since.
3. I had been given an introduction to the Editor by the Bishop of Manchester.
4. 28th November 2000.
5. Article 5 of the Universal Declaration of Human Rights.
6. How much cognisance did the Allies take of the Fourth Hague Convention of 1907 which forbade the bombing of civilians – an edict which seemed to be overlooked when both Kosovo and Afghanistan were bombed causing many civilian losses far more recently?
7. 1976.

8. Sheila Cassidy, *Audacity to Believe* (London, Collins, 1977) pp 157,158.
9. Broadcast on Radio 4 *World News* programme, 21st November 2000.
10. Sheila Cassidy, *Audacity to Believe* (London, Collins, 1977).
11. A nephew of the deposed President Salvador Allende.
12. Probably confusing him with a former 'red' dean of Canterbury.
13. Cf *Chile: An Accusation and a Warning* (Prague, 1979) p 102.

CHAPTER 14 – IN THE HOT SEAT

1. Years later I told this story at a conference in Victoria, Vancouver Island, and a man stood up in the crowd and said 'I was one of those new converts being baptised!'
2. Community of very cheaply built home-made houses.
3. I used to say the place looked like a grotto inside but grotty outside but the pun didn't work in Spanish.
4. Francis McNutt OP, *Healing* (Ave Maria Press, 1974). The story of three Indians. pp 327–331.
5. Successor to Michael Hemans.
6. Who was it that did that?

CHAPTER 15 – CONDEMNATION

1. Philip Larkin put it this way in *Annus Mirabilis*, 1974.
2. Between 1946–64.
3. These were the bishops gathered for the 1968 Lambeth Conference.
4. Romans 13:4.
5. *Aesop's Fables*.
6. 28th August 1974.
7. Original quote of Dean Inge about himself.
8. Including meeting the British community and visiting St Paul's School.
9. Horace.
10. Owen Chadwick, *Michael Ramsey* (Oxford, Clarendon Press, 1990) p 230.

CHAPTER 16 – OUT OF ONE HOT SEAT, INTO ANOTHER

1. By the late Colin Fawcett QC, and quoted with his widow's permission.
2. Sometimes when two parishes were merged the diocese would have a vacant rectory or vicarage.
3. I was thinking possibly of coming home for the children's school holidays and combining this with some deputation work.
4. 1 Timothy 5:8.
5. John 3:30, RSV.
6. He was the patron and had the right of appointing John Perry's replacement.
7. John Perry moved on to become the Warden of Lee Abbey in Devon, later the suffragan Bishop of Southampton and then the Bishop of Chelmsford.
8. Ibid.
9. He served there for nearly thirty years in total – staying on after I had left.
10. He had once been a British Government commissioner in East Africa.
11. Currently my secretary.
12. Brian had been the regional bishop of Valparaíso, Chile, following Bishop Dick Lyth. The unique staffing at St Andrew's saw at least two bishops helping to run the same local church over a long period of time.
13. Such information is often quickly accessible for couples planning their church wedding.

Chapter 17 – Search for a Model
1. Crowborough, Monarch, 1996.
2. Guildford, Eagle, 1998.
3. 25th November 1997.
4. Carol Wimber and Other Church Leaders: edited by David Pytches, *John Wimber, His Influence and Legacy* (Guildford, Eagle, 1988) p10.
5. 1 Corinthians 1:18, NRSV.
6. MATTHEW 13:45–46.
7. John 14:12.
8. So named I think after the lecture room on campus.
9. London, Hodder and Stoughton, 1984.

Chapter 18 – A Pentecost to Remember
1. Psalm 127:1, KJV.
2. Matthew 15:13, RSV.
3. Ephesians 4:12.
4. 'Laid back' was the Californian term for it.
5. Much in vogue in the UK at the time.
6. John 3:34.
7. Isaac Watts (1674–1748), 'Jesus Shall Reign', No 272 (verse 4) *Methodist Hymn Book*, 1933.
8. London, Hodder & Stoughton, 1998.

Chapter 19 – Come Over and Help Us
1. Matthew 10:8.
2. Words of knowledge, cf. 1 Corinthians 12:8.
3. John 10:27, RSV.
4. Matthew 17:20.
5. Acts 4:17.

Chapter 20 – To love mercy
1. Trans: The Pass over the Rio Grande into Mexico.
2. Trans: 'Long Live Christ the King'.
3. Luke 14:12–14.
4. Mary, myself, Richard and Prue Bedwell.
5. Mary Virginia – a St Vincent de Paul sister.
6. Ezekiel 3:15.
7. Malachi 3:10, RSV.

Chapter 21 – Getting Out and About
1. One of my highly respected evangelical friends told me later when I told him about it, that he hoped I would never do anything like it again.
2. Three cases are mentioned in the Gospels where Jesus had apparently used spittle for healing.
3. Calling out 'Glory be to God' three times.
4. I had never had the faith to ask someone to say 'You are healed!' – I usually say 'Be healed in the name of Jesus' when I sense the person is truly engaged with God's Holy Spirit.

Chapter 22 – Blessing What God was Doing

1. 'Sharing Of Ministries Abroad' Trust.
2. ARM – Anglican Renewal Ministries.
3. From 19th–23rd September 1985.
4. cf 1 Corinthians 14 verses 2 and 18.
5. A charitable mission they themselves have founded.

CHAPTER 23 – A CHURCH BUILT ON PROPHECY

1. *Christian Mysticism – Bampton Lectures* (London, Methuen & Co, 1899).
2. London, Hodder and Stoughton, 1990.
3. John 12:28–29. Some knew they had heard God speak and believed him. Some would have attributed the sound to natural phenomenon and dismissed it. Yet others would have accepted that the voice was certainly extraordinary but would not have believed that it came from God.
4. I don't remember the real names of this couple, only Paul Cain's words to them. So, for the purposes of this book, I am calling the wife Elizabeth.
5. With another 1,500 membership between them – David Parker, who later joined us at St Andrew's, leading one of them.
6. See Numbers 12:8 and Jeremiah 1:11.
7. Cf Eusebius, *The History of the Church* (Penguin Classic Series, 1965) pp 150 et al.
8. Matthew 23:34, 1 Corinthians 12:28 and Ephesians 4:11.
9. London, Hodder and Stoughton, 1993.
10. Acts 1:8, RSV.

CHAPTER 24 – NEW WINE AND SOUL SURVIVOR

1. The idea for the name New Wine '89 originated with the Rev Bob Maynard, Margaret Maynard's late husband.
2. By the end of March there were already more than 17,000 booked for the two August 2002 New Wine conferences, now under new leadership.
3. Later we began to pray that the Lord would give us eighteen months' notice if he wanted us to close it down as we were renting an office and employing a growing number of staff to organise it.
4. Michael had been deeply influenced through John Wimber and greatly appreciated Wimber's teaching and model of ministry. Also, the high priority he gave to spending quality time bringing adoration to the Lord in worship.
5. Compiled by Joyce Wills, a fellow Soul Survivor trustee, and published by Kingsway, 2001.

CHAPTER 25 – IS THIS REVIVAL?

1. Two things I have always tried to link in with renewal is the great importance of Bible study and of works of mercy.
2. London, Hodder and Stoughton, 1989.
3. Herbert Thurston SJ, *The Physical Phenomena of Mysticism* (London, Burns Oates, 1952).
4. Chuck Colson had been one of President Nixon's 'cabinet' and more or less carried the can for his colleagues by being sent to prison for the Watergate Scandal. In the time awaiting trial he had found Christ and being a lawyer, was able to help other prisoners during his time in gaol – a service which inspired him to found an international ministry for prisoners on his release, a ministry which still continues today.
5. Matthew 6:13, KJV.
6. *The Church Hesitant – A Portrait of the Church of England Today* (London, Hodder and Stoughton, 1993).

7. John 10:27, RSV.
8. JOHN 5:19, RSV.

CHAPTER 26 – SURPRISED BY THE WORK OF GOD

1. Galatians 5:25, KJV.
2. Psalm 127:1, KJV.
3. Matthew 15:13, RSV.
4. Christian A. Schwarz, *Natural Church Development* (USA edition: Church Smart Resources, 1996).
5. Exodus 17.
6. Guildford, Eagle Publishing, 1999.
7. Guildford, Eagle Publishing, 1999.
8. Guildford, Eagle Publishing, 1999.
9. I never despised liturgy and guarded it jealously, but I may have despaired at the way some people use it.
10. 1 Corinthians 14:25.
11. This was a request from Archbishop Robert Runcie that someone came from St Andrew's.
12. 'In Tune with Heaven', 1992.
13. Eastbourne, Kingsway Books, 2001.
14. Before his retirement Teddy had been the rector of St Michael's, Chester Square and during that time had been closely associated with the Carol Owen musical *Come Together* featuring Pat Boone and modelling personal involvement in worship as opposed to passive attendance at church and the exercise of ministry one to another.
15. A lot of other people on the retreats came from overseas. One bishop sent sixteen of his clergy over from Norway.

CHAPTER 27 – I LEAP OVER THE WALL

1. Elizabeth Canham, *Pilgrim to Priesthood* (London, SPCK, 1983). Whilst studying at the London Bible College, Elizabeth worshipped at St Andrew's under my predecessor. She was the first English woman to be ordained a priest (5th December 1981) but went to the USA for this, as ordination for women was then still considered out of order in the Church of England.
2. cf. Matthew 16:18 – Christ assured the church that 'the gates of Hades [or hell]' will not overcome against it [the church]', and Revelation 19:7, where the end time mystical Marriage of the Lamb with his bride (the church) is clearly prophesied. The church will surely overcome.
3. Anglicans, at the time of the Reformation, regarded matters of church government as secondary issues. Cf Paul Avis, *Anglicanism and the Christian Church* (Edinburgh, T&T Clark, 1989).
4. Acts 4:17.
5. Isaiah 55:9.
6. Cf. last quote at beginning of the chapter.
7. Lambeth Conference Pastoral Letter, 7:23 – 1988.
8. Well wait just a minute! I have just received a remarkable document from the Diocese of London for a 21st-century resurrection. It talks of its commitment to experimenting in new ways of being church in addition to the parish system – for example youth churches, community based churches, cell churches and network churches. It seems like a dream coming true.
9. Mark 4:28.

10. Cardinal J.H. Newman reacted from an evangelical background; the Roman Catholic Mons Ronnie Knox was the son of a Protestant evangelical bishop; the liberal Dean Herbert Ryle was the son of the evangelical Bishop J.C. Ryle. On the other hand, we had a number of Anglo-Catholics, Roman Catholics and Free Church folk coming to us.

11. Initially intended by Augustine of Canterbury from Rome (AD 597–603/4) to be imposed on the native Celtic church. It was seventy years later before Theodore of Tarsus, Archbishop of Canterbury (AD 669–690) set the system up. Writing from Lindisfarne, Ray Simpson comments – 'The mission sent from Rome in 597, which reflected the "civil service" model of the Roman Empire, worked in harmony with the Celtic mission at times, but gradually the regulations of the Roman Church were enforced, the clergy became dignitaries, the Church grew less biblical, less charismatic, less close to the soil and the poor. Much that was good and necessary was brought in but comfort, pomp and uniformity assumed too large a place'. Ray Simpson, *Exploring Celtic Spirituality* (London, Hodder and Stoughton, 1995).

12. Isaiah 43:19.

13. At least seven generations – though the succession often switched across to the maternal side.

14. The rector of the original parish (or his successor) usually retained the rights of patronage in the appointment of any new vicar.

15. 1869 in Latin America.

16. University of Gloucestershire.

17. According to a personal conversation with Bishop Pat Harris, who was the chairman of the commission working on the report.

18. Guildford, Eagle Publishing, 1991.

19. Kingdom Power Trust, 1995.

20. Later to be one of two assistant bishops consecrated in Singapore for ministry in the USA.

21. 10th February 1991.

22. I had first met John Rodgers when he was on the staff of an Episcopal seminary in Virginia lecturing on Martin Luther and the Reformation. He later became the dean of the recently founded Trinity Episcopal Seminary in Sewickly, Pittsburg. I was invited to teach there on a couple of occasions. Later, he even invited me to head up the Missions department there.

23. Chuck had actually visited St Andrew's some years before.

24. Losing a million in twenty years.

25. April 2001.

26. The Episcopal Church of the USA.

CHAPTER 28 – ARROGANT, ALTRUISTIC OF SIMPLY ASININE

1. Weekend *Daily Telegraph* – 9th March 1997.

2. J.E.C. Welldon DD, *Revelation and the Holy Spirit* (Macmillan & Co Ltd, 1902).

3. This was a missionary board of which I was a member. It was chaired by the Missionary Superintendent Archdeacon Douglas Milmine.

4. 1968.

5. Cf Leonardo Boff, *Ecclesiogenesis* (London, Collins, 1984).

6. *Changing World, Changing Church* (Crowborough, Monarch Books, 2001).

7. We were proud to loan some funds from New Wine to help this to get started.

8. Hebrews 10:23,24, RSV.

IN CONCLUSION

1. Later Lord Shaftesbury.

2. Proverbs 31:10,20.
3. It is now forty-seven years ago – the last forty-four of them married to her – and I would still write the same today.
4. Philippians 3:12–14, RSV.
5. Quote from Quentin Crisp, *The Naked Civil Servant*, 1968.
6. 1 Corinthians 2:2, KJV.
7. Philippians 1:21, KJV.
8. J.C. Pollock, *Moody Without Sankey* (London, Hodder & Stoughton, 1963) p270.

INDEX

Finding the Key to Personal Integrity

Mary Pytches

The dictionary describes 'integrity' as moral soundness, uprightness, probity. Many people today would say that integrity seems to be in short supply in a world where society often subscribes to the philosophy of the end justifying the means and that 'white lies' and being 'economical with the truth' is acceptable as long as nobody gets hurt.

Mary writes with great perception that all of us will always find a battle in achieving truth and integrity. As she says 'to say I have reached the place of total integrity myself would be untrue, but as I doubt that I will this side of heaven, I didn't feel I could wait until I had arrived to write this book!'

Mary Pytches and her husband David spent seventeen years in Chile as missionaries. From there they went to St Andrew's, Chorleywood, where she developed her interest in pastoral counselling. She is the author of a number of books including *Yesterday's Child; A Child No More; Dying to Change* and *Rising Above the Storms of Life*.